Transforming t

Other books by Keith Robbins

Munich 1938
Sir Edward Grey
The Abolition of War: The 'Peace' Movement in Britain 1914–1919
John Bright
The Eclipse of a Great Power: Modern Britain 1870–1992
The First World War
Nineteenth-Century Britain: Integration and Diversity
Appeasement
(ed.) The Blackwell Biographical Dictionary of British Political Life in the
Twentieth Century
(ed.) Protestant Evangelicalism: Britain, Ireland, Germany and America
c.1750–c.1950
Churchill
History, Religion and Identity in Modern Britain
Politicians, Diplomacy and War in Modern British History
Bibliography of British History 1914–89
Great Britain: Identities, Institutions and the Idea of Britishness
The World since 1945: A Concise History
(ed.) The British Isles 1901–1951
Britain and Europe 1789–2005
England, Ireland, Scotland, Wales: The Christian Church 1900–2000
Pride of Place: A Modern History of Bristol Grammar School
(ed.)Religion and Diplomacy: Religion and British Foreign Policy 1815 to
1941 (with John Fisher)
(ed.) The Dynamics of Religious Reform in Northern Europe 1780–1920:
Political and Legal Perspectives

Transforming the World

GLOBAL POLITICAL HISTORY SINCE WORLD WAR II

Keith Robbins

palgrave
macmillan

First published 2013 by
PALGRAVE MACMILLAN

Palgrave Macmillan in the UK is an imprint of Macmillan Publishers Limited, registered in England, company number 785998, of Houndmills, Basingstoke, Hampshire RG21 6XS.

Palgrave Macmillan in the US is a division of St Martin's Press LLC, 175 Fifth Avenue, New York, NY 10010.

Palgrave Macmillan is the global academic imprint of the above companies and has companies and representatives throughout the world.

Palgrave® and Macmillan® are registered trademarks in the United States, the United Kingdom, Europe and other countries

ISBN: 978-0-333-77199-0   hardback
ISBN: 978-0-333-77200-3   paperback

This book is printed on paper suitable for recycling and made from fully managed and sustained forest sources. Logging, pulping and manufacturing processes are expected to conform to the environmental regulations of the country of origin.

A catalogue record for this book is available from the British Library.

A catalog record for this book is available from the Library of Congress.

10 9 8 7 6 5 4 3 2 1

22 21 20 19 18 17 16 15 14 13

Printed and bound in Great Britain by MPG Books Group Ltd, Bodmin

To

Edgar, Gabriel, Harry, Heather, Hugh, Jack, Joseph,
Luc, Molly and Tom

Contents

Detailed Contents

Acknowledgements

Any work of synthesis rests heavily on the writing of others more expert in particular fields than this author. That could only be properly acknowledged in a bibliography and reference notes of excessive weight. The short guide to further reading at the close of each part of the book hints at the wealth of material open to the student of global history. It opens up that wider range of material on which this author has drawn with gratitude.

Successive editors at Palgrave Macmillan, Kate Haines and Jenna Steventon, have helped to shape this book through the many phases of its evolution, to its great benefit. W.M. Spellman and John Fisher, from their respective sides of the Atlantic, also helpfully offered critical comment. Responsibility for the final form, of course, rests with the author.

Janet has lived alongside 'history writing' for half a century. So much is owed to her love and forbearance. The dedication is to our grandchildren in the hope that this book may in due course help them and other children of the twenty-first century come to understand the world they have inherited.

Maps

Select Chronology:
Key Moments in Politics and
International Relations
1937–2012

1937 War between China and Japan begins: Japanese troops occupy Tientsin and Beijing: Nanjing.

1938 Japanese troops control most of China, except Szechwan, but urban-based: Chiang Kai-shek establishes himself in Chungking.

1939 Germany invades Czechoslovakia: Italy invades Albania: Nazi–Soviet Pact: Germany (and USSR) invade Poland and partition: Britain and France declare war on Germany: USA declares neutrality in European War: USSR occupies Latvia, Lithuania and Estonia and invades Finland.

1940 Finland capitulates to USSR: Germany invades Denmark and Norway, then Low Countries and France: Italy declares war: France signs armistice: Battle of Britain: Tripartite Pact between Germany, Italy and Japan which Hungary, Romania and Slovakia later join: British–Italian battles in North/North-East Africa.

1941 US Lend-Lease Act aids Allies: Germany invades Yugoslavia and Greece: Japan and USSR sign Non-Aggression Pact: Germany invades USSR: British–Soviet Treaty of Mutual Assistance: Roosevelt and Churchill sign 'Atlantic Charter': Britain and USSR occupy Iran: Japan attacks Pearl Harbor, the Philippines, Hong Kong, Malaya and Burma: Germany and Italy declare war on USA: German offensive halted north of Moscow.

1942 Rangoon, Singapore fall to Japan: British Mission offers India independence post-war – Gandhi launches 'Quit India' movement: Battle of Midway – US success in Pacific War: German–Italian defeat to British Eighth Army in North Africa: British–US forces land in French North Africa: Soviet counter-attack at Stalingrad.

1943   Roosevelt and Churchill at Casablanca proclaim 'unconditional surrender' as Allied goal: German surrender at Stalingrad: Axis forces surrender in North Africa: Allies invade Sicily, Deposition of Mussolini and Italian surrender: Allies at Quebec Conference set up South-East Asia Command: Germany, taking over defence of Italy, rescues Mussolini: Italy declares war on Germany: Greater East Asia Conference held in Tokyo: Allied Conferences held in Cairo and Tehran.

1944   Allied Normandy landings: liberation of Rome: Japanese invasion of India thrown back: Liberation of Paris, then Brussels: German offensive in the Ardennes.

1945   US forces land on the Philippines: Yalta conference of Allied leaders: Deaths of Roosevelt, Mussolini and Hitler: Soviet forces enter Vienna and then Prague: UN structure drafted: German surrender: Liberation of Auschwitz: British reconquest of Burma: Potsdam Conference: USA drops atomic bombs on Hiroshima and Nagasaki: USSR declares war on Japan: Fighting between Nationalists and Communists in China begins – mediation by US General Marshall fails: Netherlands refuses Indonesian independence: Japanese surrender: France rejects Vietnamese independence, claimed by Ho Chi Minh: Foundation of Arab League: Nuremberg War Crimes Tribunal begins: Pan-African Congress, Manchester.

1946   Churchill's 'Iron Curtain' speech: civil war in China (and continuing): Philippines and Transjordan (as Jordan) independent: anti-French war in Indo-China (and continuing): New York to be permanent UN home.

1947   Marshall (USA) proposes his 'Plan': Dutch–Nationalist struggle in Indonesia: British leave divided Indian subcontinent – India and Pakistan: Cominform established: Greek civil war precipitates 'Truman Doctrine': General Agreement on Tariffs and Trade (GATT) signed.

1948   Gandhi assassinated: Tito regime in Yugoslavia condemned by Soviet bloc: Marshall Plan for European reconstruction begins: Communist takeover in Czechoslovakia: Britain leaves Palestine, Israel proclaims independence, Arab armies invade: Independence of Burma and Ceylon: Malaya 'State of Emergency': Berlin blockade: National Party, victorious in elections, develops apartheid: Truman elected US president: Organization of American States (OAS) formed.

1949   Soviet A-bomb: Federal German and German Democratic Republics (FDR, GDR) formed: Indonesia independent: People's Republic of China (PRC) declared (Nationalists withdraw to Taiwan): NATO (North Atlantic Treaty) signed: Council for Mutual Economic Assistance (COMECON) formed.

1950   Korean War, UN (US-led) intervention: Chinese troops join the war: US occupation of Japan ends: China occupies Tibet: Britain recognizes Communist China: Soviet–Chinese 30-year pact.

1951   Libyan independence: Mossadegh Prime Minister of Iran: Japanese peace treaty signed.

1952   Egyptian monarchy overthrown: Mau Mau rebellion in Kenya: Eisenhower elected US President: Britain tests A-bomb: US hydrogen-bomb: European Coal and Steel Community (ECSC): Britain proposes a Central African Federation: Greece and Turkey join NATO.

1953   Stalin dies: Central African Federation begins: Kenyatta imprisoned (Kenya): Korean armistice: Mossadegh overthrown in Iran: Soviet H-bomb test: East Berlin rising: Khrushchev Soviet Communist Party General Secretary: Eisenhower's 'Atoms for Peace' speech.

1954   Dien Bien Phu siege (Vietnam) leads to French capitulation: Geneva Conference on Indo-China – two Vietnams, Cambodia and Laos independent: US–Japan defence agreement: USA guarantees security of Taiwan: War begins in Algeria: Manila Pact – South-East Asia Treaty Organization (SEATO) formed: US Supreme Court rules segregated education unconstitutional: McCarthy hearings in USA: Perón of Argentina overthrown.

1955   Federal Germany joins NATO: Warsaw Pact formed: East–West summit in Geneva: State Treaty ends occupation of Austria: Baghdad Pact – Central Treaty Organization: Cyprus emergency.

1956   Sudan, Tunisia and Morocco independent: Khrushchev's 'secret' speech: Suez Crisis: Pakistan becomes Islamic republic: Revolution in Hungary: Polish crisis: Castro launches Cuban revolution: Cominform dissolved.

1957   Gold Coast independent as Ghana (Nkrumah Prime Minister): Malaya independent: Rome Treaty establishes European Economic Community (EEC): Eisenhower 'Doctrine'.

1958   Federation of the West Indies (dissolved 1961): United Arab Republic of Egypt and Syria (Syria withdraws 1961); 'Great Leap Forward' (China): Iraqi monarchy overthrown: Crisis of French state (and empire) – Fifth Republic under de Gaulle: another crisis over Berlin: US troops intervene in Lebanon.

1959   Castro sets up new Cuban regime: European Free Trade Association (EFTA) formed: Cyprus independent: Tibetan uprising suppressed: Guided Democracy in Indonesia.

1960   Congolese crisis begins: Macmillan in Africa: Sharpeville Massacre (South Africa): French A-bomb: US embargoes and Soviet aid (Cuba): Sino-

Soviet strains: National Liberation Front organized in South Vietnam: New US–Japan Security Treaty: Collapse of Paris Summit: Nigeria independent: Overthrow of Synghman Rhee in South Korea: Kennedy elected US President.

1961 Congolese crisis continues – Death of Hammarskj^ld: UN condemns apartheid: South Africa withdraws from the Commonwealth of Nations: Sino-Soviet split becomes public: Berlin Wall: Tanganyika independent: Failed 'Bay of Pigs' invasion (Cuba).

1962 Algeria, Uganda, Rwanda and Burundi independent: Chinese–Indian Himalayan border hostilities: Second Vatican Council begins in Rome: Cuban missile crisis.

1963 Katangan separatism defeated and Congo crisis moderates: Kenya independent: Trial of Mandela (South Africa): Malaya expanded to become Malaysia: Kennedy assassinated – Lyndon Johnson succeeds: Central African Federation dissolved: Ngo Dinh Diem of South Vietnam assassinated: Organization of African Unity (OAU) formed: Attempted British entry into the EEC fails: Test-Ban Treaty (USA, UK, USSR).

1964 Malawi and Zambia independent: China A-bomb: Mobutu takes power in Congo: Nehru dies: Khrushchev removed, replaced by Brezhnev and Kosygin: Gulf of Tonkin Resolution: military coup in Brazil: Palestinian Liberation Organization (PLO) formed.

1965 Singapore, Guyana independent: Watts race riots (USA): USA intervenes in Dominican Republic: Rhodesian Unilateral Declaration of Independence (UDI): US intervention in Vietnam increases: Indonesian massacre: Indo-Pakistani war: Ben Bella (Algeria) deposed.

1966 Cultural Revolution in China: Coup and counter-coup in Nigeria: Indira Gandhi Prime Minister of India: Suharto takes power in Indonesia: Nkrumah overthrown in Ghana: French forces withdrawn from NATO command: Assassination of Verwoerd, Prime Minister of South Africa.

1967 Nigerian civil war: Six-Day Middle East War: European Community (emerges from institutional mergers): Britain leaves Aden: Race riots and anti-Vietnam War demonstrations (USA): Che Guevara killed: Shanghai People's Commune: Association of Southeast Asian Nations (ASEAN) formed: Greek military coup.

1968 'Prague Spring' and Warsaw Pact invasion in Czechoslovakia: Assassination of Martin Luther King: Tet offensive in South Vietnam: British announcement of military withdrawal from east of Suez: Demonstrations/ strikes in Paris and elsewhere in Europe: Nixon elected US president.

1969 De Gaulle resigns French presidency: Ho Chi Minh dies: River

Ussuri battle (Soviet–Chinese): Arafat head of PLO: Gaddafi takes power in Libya.

1970 Nigerian civil war ends: Nasser dies, Sadat succeeds: Brandt's *Ostpolitik*: USA and South Vietnam invade Cambodia: Kent State killings (USA): Allende President of Chile: PLO expelled from Jordan: Unrest in Poland.

1971 Amin takes power in Uganda: China (PR) takes place of Taiwan at UN: Pakistan civil war – independence of Bangladesh: East–West Treaty on access to West Berlin: Formation of United Arab Emirates (UAE): Soviet–Egyptian Friendship Treaty.

1972 Nixon, and later Tanaka, visit China: 'Bloody Sunday' in Northern Ireland: Strategic Arms Limitation Treaty (SALT) (USA–USSR): Watergate burglary (USA): Sadat expels Soviet advisers from Egypt.

1973 Britain, Denmark and Ireland join European Community (EC): 'Yom Kippur' war (Middle East): Egypt and Libya proclaim unification: Arab oil embargo and energy crisis for industrial world: US involvement in Indo-China ends: Afghan monarchy overthrown: Pinochet overthrows Allende regime in Chile.

1974 Nixon resigns US presidency, succeeded by Ford: Military coup in Portugal: Guinea-Bissau independent: Indian nuclear tests: Turkish invasion and de facto partition of Cyprus: Haile Selassie deposed (Ethiopia): Prevention of Terrorism Act (Britain): Greek military ousted.

1975 Vietnam reunited under Hanoi: Khmer Rouge control in Cambodia: Lebanese civil war: Helsinki Accords on Security and Cooperation in Europe: Indonesian occupation of East Timor: Indian 'State of Emergency': Papua New Guinea, Angola and Mozambique independent: Franco dies.

1976 Mao Zedong and Zhou Enlai die; 'Gang of Four' arrested: Military coup in Argentina: Strikes in Poland: Sadat abrogates 1971 treaty with USSR: Transkei 'Bantustan' in South Africa: Carter elected US President.

1977 Sadat visits Israel: Begin visits Egypt: Fighting in Horn of Africa: Zia ul-Haq takes power in Pakistan: Indian 'State of Emergency' lifted – Congress electorally defeated: 'Charter 77' (Czechoslovakia): SEATO dissolved: Coronation of Emperor Bokassa (Central Africa).

1978 Ascendancy of Deng Xiaoping: Wojtyła elected as Pope John Paul II: South Lebanon battleground: Coup in Afghanistan: Camp David Accords and possible Middle East peace: Vietnam invades Cambodia: Moro killed (Italy): Kenyatta dies.

1979 Khmer Rouge regime overthrown: USSR invades Afghanistan: China–USA establish diplomatic relations: Shah flees and Iran declared Islamic Republic: Israeli–Egyptian peace treaty: Saddam Hussein Iraqi president: Sandinista revolution in Nicaragua: Fall of Amin in Uganda after Tanzanian invasion: Gandhi re-elected Indian prime minister: Thatcher British Prime Minister: Bhutto executed in Pakistan: Chinese incursion into Vietnam.

1980 Gdansk Accords/'Solidarity' formed (Poland): Rhodesia independent as Zimbabwe: Reagan elected US President: Gang of Four trial (China): Referendum to separate Quebec from Canada fails.

1981 Martial Law (Poland): Sadat assassinated, Mubarak succeeds (Egypt): Greece joins EC: Indonesian war in East Timor: Mitterrand President of France: Galtieri President of Argentina: Mahathir Prime Minister of Malaysia.

1982 Falkland Islands/Malvinas conflict: Israel invades Lebanon: Israel completes evacuation of Sinai: Brezhnev dies: Spain joins NATO: Kohl Chancellor of Federal Germany.

1983 Reagan announces 'Star Wars' programme: Alfonsín restores democracy (Argentina): US invasion of Grenada reverses earlier coup: PLO relocates to Tunisia.

1984 Brunei independent: British miners' strike: Britain–China agree procedure to return Hong Kong to China in 1997: Punjab disturbances – assassination of Gandhi: Reagan re-elected US President: Tamil–Sinhalese clashes in Sri Lanka.

1985 Ascendancy of Gorbachev – perestroika and glasnost: South African troops withdraw from Angola: USA imposes sanctions on Nicaragua: Anglo-Irish Agreement on Northern Ireland: Coups in Nigeria, Sudan and Uganda.

1986 State of Emergency (South Africa): Reagan–Gorbachev Reykjavik summit: Portugal and Spain join EC: Iran–Contra scandal: Duvalier (Haiti) overthrown: Marcos flees Philippines: Chernobyl nuclear disaster.

1987 Palestinian intifada against Israeli occupation: Delhi imposes direct rule on the Punjab: Treaty eliminating intermediate-range missiles (USA–USSR): Sino-Soviet border talks: Single European Act: Arias Plan for peace in Central America: Coups in Fiji: Ben Ali President of Tunisia.

1988 Ceasefire ends Iran–Iraq war: USSR withdraws from Afghanistan: George Bush elected US President: Zia ul-Haq dies: Unrest in Burma: Ethiopia–Somali peace agreement: Polish strikes: Mitterrand re-elected President of France: Unrest in the Caucasus: Arafat speaks at UN.

1989   Long-time dictatorship of Stroessner (Paraguay) ends: Tianenmen Square demonstrations, Beijing: Martial Law in Tibet: de Klerk State President of South Africa: Return to democracy in Chile: Collapse of Communism in Eastern Europe: Bush and Gorbachev declare end of Cold War: Ayatollah Khomeini dies: Menem President of Argentina.

1990   Iraq invades Kuwait: Baltic republics of USSR declare independence; civil war in Liberia: Yugoslavia in crisis: Mandela released (South Africa): Namibia independent: Yeltsin President of Russian Federation: German reunification: Thatcher resigns: Rwanda massacres: Lee Kuan Yew steps down in Singapore.

1991   Disintegration of Yugoslavia: Gulf War expels Iraqi forces from Kuwait: Warsaw Pact annulled: Demise of the USSR – Gorbachev resigns: Repeal of apartheid legislation: Assassination of Rajiv Gandhi: Mengistu (Ethiopia) overthrown.

1992   Bosnia–Herzegovina crisis – UN peacekeeping force: US troops in Somalia: civil war in El Salvador ends: Los Angeles riots: civil war in Mozambique ends: Milošević re-elected President of Serbia: Clinton elected US President.

1993   Czechoslovakia splits into Czech Republic and Slovakia: Maastricht Treaty on closer European union, agreed in 1991, comes into effect: Cambodian monarchy restored: Houphouet-Boigny dies.

1994   North American Free Trade Association (NAFTA) (USA, Canada, Mexico): Mandela President of South Africa: South Africa rejoins Commonwealth of Nations: Civil War and Genocide in Rwanda: Russian forces invade breakaway Chechnya: US forces restore President Aristide (Haiti): Bosnian civil war continues: Israel–Jordan peace treaty: Mexican financial crisis: Lukashenko President of Belarus: Kim Il-Sung (North Korea) dies, Kim Jong-Il succeeds.

1995   Drayton Accords settle status of former Yugoslavia after further hostilities: NATO peacekeeping force in Bosnia: Israel/PLO agreement on West Bank change: Assassination of Rabin, Prime Minister of Israel: World Trade Organization (WTO) inaugurated: Austria, Finland and Sweden join European Union (EU): Chirac elected President of France: Sheikh Hamad ousts his father as Emir of Qatar.

1996   Netanyahu Prime Minister of Israel: Benazir Bhutto dismissed as Prime Minister of Pakistan: Taliban seize power in Afghanistan.

1997   Russia–Chechnya agreement: Deng Xiaoping dies – Jian Zemin succeeds: Hong Kong returns to China: Overthrow of Mobutu Sese Seko (Zaire) – Laurent Kabila takes control: Banda dies.

1998   Defeat of Kohl – Schröder succeeds (Germany): Suharto resigns: Pol Pot dies: Chavez President of Venezuela: G5 becomes G8.

1999   Bouteflika civilian President of Algeria – internal fighting moderates: Hussein of Jordan dies, Abdullah succeeds: Hassan II of Morocco dies, Mohammad II succeeds: Musharraf takes control in Pakistan: Mandela retires, Mbeki succeeds as President of South Africa: G8 becomes G20.

2000   George W. Bush elected US President: Putin President of Russia: Eritrean–Ethiopian 'peace' agreement: Another coup in Fiji: Second Palestinian intifada: Switzerland joins UN: Bashar Assad succeeds father as President of Syria.

2001   Al-Quaeda terrorist attack on New York – US action against Taliban in Afghanistan: Taliban ousted: Kabila President of Congo: Berlusconi Prime Minister of Italy: Koizumi Prime Minister of Japan: Switzerland declines EU membership.

2002   da Silva president of Brazil: Chirac re-elected: Erdogan Prime Minister of Turkey: East Timor independent.

2003   US-led invasion of Iraq: Kirchner President of Argentina: Hu Jintao President, Wen Jiabo Prime Minister (China): Mahathir steps down (Malaysia).

2004   Karzai elected President of Afghanistan: Cyprus (but not North) joins EU – UN federal proposal fails: Aristide ousted (Haiti): Hungary, Latvia, Estonia, Lithuania, Poland, Slovakia, Slovenia, Malta, Czech Republic join EU: Manmohan Singh Prime Minister of India: Arafat dies: Barroso (Portugal) President of the European Commission: Putin, Mbeki, George W. Bush re-elected.

2005   Ahmadinejad President of Iran: Morales first indigenous President of Bolivia: Merkel Chancellor of Germany: Prodi Prime Minister of Italy: Abdullah succeeds (Saudi Arabia).

2006   Palestine effectively divided in two.

2007   Christina Kirchner President of Argentina: Sarkozy elected President of France: Benazir Bhutto (Pakistan) assassinated: Milošević dies: Bulgaria, Romania join EU: Erdogan re-elected (Turkey).

2008   Obama elected US President: Raúl Castro President of Cuba: Berlusconi again Prime Minister of Italy: Kosovo declares itself independent: Musharraf resigns Pakistan presidency, Zardari succeeds: Medvedev, President, Putin, Prime Minister (Russia): global financial crisis, with its differing regional impacts, begins – and continues.

2009   Karzai, Ahmadinejad, Merkel, Netanyahu re-elected to office: Zuma President of South Africa: Sri Lankan internal war ends: Darfur conflict (Sudan): 'Power-sharing' in Zimbabwe.

2010   Nepalese monarchy abolished.

2011   Regime change in Libya (Gaddafi) in Tunisia (Ben Ali), Mubarak (Egypt), Saleh (Yemen).

2012   Putin again President of Russia: South Sudan independent: Kim Jong-Il dies.

Preface: Grasping Global History

Historians have written what they thought was 'Global History' for centuries. Individuals in different places and at different times have tried to give it coherence, but not very successfully. Its historiography has a history of its own, as different terms and approaches have been absorbed or discarded. 'Universal history' or 'world history' has sometimes been preferred, each word with its own nuance. More recently, other terms have found some favour: 'shared history', 'transnational history' and 'connected history' among them. Whichever is preferred, however, there is an inescapable problem: what to put in and what to leave out. Decades ago, the American pioneer 'world historian', William H. McNeill, said it was a matter for debate and disagreement. Little has changed.

Over recent decades, academic journals (*The Journal of World History* (US) and, more recently *The Journal of Global History* (UK) being among them) have wrestled not only with particular aspects but with the very field itself. Those historians who have pushed the subject forward have often been impatient with attempts at definition. Establishing firm new boundaries, they have thought, would only box them in again. An 'Encyclopedia of the World', with multiple entries, has its uses, but it is not 'Global History'. Whether attempted over a long or short stretch of time, therefore, books appear in many shapes and guises. Histories of the contemporary world have sometimes tried to provide 'the salient facts', the things every student everywhere 'needs to know', as year follows year. They outline 'what happened'. Since a great deal has happened, such 'outlines', even lengthy ones, cannot probe deeply. They must move on. Their authors know that specialists will not fail to point out their superficiality and inadequacy in particulars, but argue that some sense of the 'big picture' is vital. They have therefore ignored advice to 'leave world history well alone'. This present volume, as theirs could not, builds the post-9/11 era into the history of earlier 'post-war' decades.

No single individual can write a history which repeats on a world scale the kind of detail which might be appropriate if the focus was solely on one country or even continent. Mastery of a myriad of languages would be only one of the prerequisites of any such enterprise. This present volume has drawn on many books, but their authors, almost exclusively, have written in English, That brings its own limitations. The self-understanding of different parts of the world is reflected in the untranslatable terminology employed in different languages. It has sometimes seemed, therefore, that only composite volumes, with individuals addressing specific topics, offer the only way out. Yet, whatever the editorial aspirations, authors in such enterprises focus on different things. If, as the great British historian Lord Acton (d.1902) argued, universal history is more than the sum of the history of particular countries, collaborative history, engaging particular specialists, deals in compartments and therefore cannot present such a summation.

An individual author, however, writes 'Global History' within a particular historical/national tradition and can never entirely shake it off. Some countries have stronger 'world-historical' traditions than others. They, and their historians, have sometimes seen themselves 'in the van' of world development. Such historiography takes its own civilization as normative. Every other part of the world is judged against its values and achievements. 'The story of western civilization', some say, is now 'the story of mankind', since its influence has been so pervasive. Others profoundly disagree. Historians, philosophers, economists, sociologists, theologians and other thinkers have often been drawn to 'world history', seeking to establish its underlying pattern and 'direction of travel'. For a time, for example, Arnold J. Toynbee's twelve-volume *A Study of History* had its worldwide admirers. Humdrum human detail might disappear in pursuing the grand sweep of 'world history' and identifying an 'inner dynamic'. Reacting against the sweeps of 'world megahistory', some have written 'world microhistory', that is to say, a history written on limited topics but viewed globally. Global historians, therefore, are aware of the pitfalls before them in absorbing elements of both perspectives in trying to meet a manifest public need for an accessible but reflective interpretation. There is, however, no need to be paralysed by the nature of the task. There are no self-evident and secure organizing categories in any field of historical enquiry.

It is against this background of many options, therefore, that this work makes its case. It tries to build bridges across the difficulties; note contending methodologies but not be slave to any. It is neither concise nor comprehensive. It tackles some matters in a detail which a short history would not touch. It neglects other topics which a comprehensive account could not ignore. It seeks to situate the reader in different places and, in the process, to present situations as they would have been perceived from different geographical points of view. Even so, though emphatically not conceived as a 'British view of the world', it is the work of a historian born, bred and living in Britain, more intimately knowledgeable, thorough his own previous writing and experience, with British history than with any other. That writing on British history, however, has particularly emphasized the interpenetrating history of four nations. It also reflects a central conviction that it is better for a global historian to accept his anchorage as an interpreter of a particular nation rather than to purport to be a freewheeling 'cosmopolitan'.

It is not sufficient, however, merely to twirl a globe stationed alongside a personal computer or consult an atlas. Maps do not reveal underlying social realities. They have to be constructed. Somebody has to determine what features are important and pertinent. Each individual or society, likewise, is caught up in a constant process of identity formation and dissolution. This author does not claim to know all the world at first hand. However, for one purpose or another, he has visited almost every country in a Europe taken to stretch from Ireland to the Russian Federation. He has held short visiting appointments in universities in Australia, Canada and Algeria. He has lectured in the USA and China. He has visited Malta but not Malaysia, Brunei but not Brazil, the Gulf but not Guatemala, Singapore but not South Africa and Hong Kong but not Honduras: in short, a partial but not an insignificant picture.

It is not only location that matters. Generation also has a bearing. It happens that this author came into the world in an English city on the day German troops invaded Norway in April 1940. It follows, therefore, that the span of this book is the span of his lifetime. It renders him vulnerable to the distortions of memory. Different generations frame the world differently in their minds. Each individual's 'global perspective', in short, has its distinctive character. Gender, age, location, social and economic status, occupation, travel, ideology, education, religion – all play their interlocking part in 'making sense' of a world imagined by pictures, and structured by maps.

Location, generation and half a century's academic experience as writer and editor fuse to give the book its flavour and emphases. There has been the long experience of working with authors in editing the many volumes in the series *Profiles in Power* (Pearson Education). It happens that authors have offered interpretations of the careers of figures who appear in this book – Churchill, Roosevelt, Adenauer, Nehru, Stalin, Mao Zedong. In these and other instances, the personal pervades this book to a perhaps unusual extent. It is not the intention, in so doing, to press a view that 'great figures' do indeed, on their own, shape the world. The purpose, rather, is to see the world as they saw it through travel, contact, language and experience. All the names in these pages, whether dictators or democrats, were 'representative' figures of their times. They represented 'nations' and 'states', and sometimes 'nation-states'. This is not a 'global history' that floats sublimely above such constructs. It accepts that their internal coherence and external rivalries continue to be a vital ingredient in the world-story. It is a perspective, too, which reflects substantial editorial interaction with authors who have contributed to two further series, *Inventing the Nation* (now Bloomsbury Academic) and *Britain and Europe* (Hodder Arnold). The former, whether in relation to China or Germany, emphasize the dynamic character of 'nation'. The latter, covering the Romans to the present day, likewise emphasizes the fluctuating nature of relationships. Should it be entitled *Britain in Europe?* Editing the *Wiley–Blackwell History of the Contemporary World*, with a structure which is basically continental, traces comparable issues globally. Finally, a further series, *Turning Points* (Pearson Education), has served to bring home, through particular volumes – for example on German reunification or the ending of apartheid – that 'events' upset prognoses and happen in ways contrary to prevailing expectations. Global history is not a matter simply of detecting patterns or describing trends.

No historian who has been privileged, over decades, to engage with colleagues in these many books as editor can escape their influence. They have made it the kind of book it is. No doubt it is substantially and unapologetically a political history. Sadly that means that it is not an economic history, a religious history, a demographic history, a cultural history, an environmental history or any other 'special' kind of history, though aspects of all do flit in and out of these pages on occasion. Nevertheless, it seeks to be rather broader than some definitions of political history. It aspires to be a *relational* political history – if such a species can be added to the names jostling for position in the world of global history.

The world has its inherently puzzling mixture of harmony and conflict, unity and diversity, order and disorder. Its 'essence', if it has one, fluctuates with time. 'Past history', over the short or long term, both for individuals and communities, hangs over present 'real worlds'. Relentless pursuit of 'modernity', even though what 'modernity' is cannot be universally defined, rubs everywhere against tenacious retention of codes, customs and conventions deemed timeless. Charismatic figures fleetingly 'capture the moment' and seem 'representative' of their time and place – only for the moment to pass and their reputations fade. Institutions once thought exemplary turn out to be flawed and failing.

States parade flags and symbols which suggest solidity and continuity, but their individual foundations can quickly crumble. It is convenient, but little more than that, to suppose that all states are somehow the same. They differ widely in size and population, and in a multiplicity of other aspects. Some see themselves as having existed for centuries in a recognizable form. Others have had no previous existence in their current mode. Governments vary enormously in their capacity to govern. They also vary significantly in the degree to which a theoretical 'sovereignty', however defined, in fact gives them a capacity – if so minded – to resist cultural, economic or military pressures which are exerted from outside their borders. Some, too, in certain matters, may be less concerned than others to safeguard their 'sovereignty'. In any case, a world of 'sovereign states' may simply be one in which vicious regimes continue unrestrained. But who is to do the restraining and how is it to be done? Is there an 'international community' to be spoken for and if so, who should speak for it?

Moreover, while to grasp the world as 'a world of states' is at one level necessary, it is at another level distorting. The 'world' does function officially through the formal mechanisms of diplomacy. Treaties covering a host of matters are negotiated and concluded. Ministerial visits proliferate, their presence, beneficial or otherwise, made possible by an ease and speed of travel inconceivable to their predecessors in 1945. Who goes where, when and for how long, reveals the global status of both visitor and visited. The architecture of such patterns is under constant scrutiny. Important signals about 'how the world works' are conveyed for public benefit. Yet the world is more than the sum of the relationships, distant or intimate, frequent or occasional, which states have with each other.

'A world of nations', even more a 'world of individuals', is rather different from a 'world of states', but a 'nation' is no more self-evident as an entity than a 'state'. Some nations, however defined, have long believed that states should be formed by nations. Some nations, or at least groups of people with particular linguistic or cultural affiliations, have been content to create or at least live within states which are 'multinational'. The tension between these contrary conceptions has been evident universally. It has contributed to, if it has not caused, the apparently perpetual crisis of 'nation and state' to be found in certain parts of the world. It is hardly surprising, therefore, that the political map in the early twenty-first century is already radically different, in terms of 'nations' and 'states', from what it was when the world returned to 'peace' and 'a new beginning' in 1945. The path to be followed by a particular state or nation could scarcely anywhere have been easily projected forward from 1945 into its twenty-first-century condition.

What can be said, however, is that 'empires' as they had formerly existed were not acceptable in the post-1945 world. It was to be against 'the spirit of the age' that 'colonies' established by some states by conquest, coercion or whatever other means should not survive. They constituted a form of oppression and exploitation exerted by one state over its subjected peoples, however much, in certain aspects, there might have been accruing benefits. The 'Age of Imperialism' was to come to an end. Whether they liked the prospect or not, whether they were determined still to resist or at least delay the 'handover of power' or not, this transition looked highly likely Conspicuously, at whatever precise points it came, it would end the 'empires' of the European Powers – in effect Britain, France and Portugal – established with different structures at different dates in Asia and Africa. Protracted or not, it would end that projection of European power and influence which, in varying durations, had shaped the formal structures of the world and, more difficult to define, had imposed, or conveyed, assumptions of superiority. The revolt against 'imperialism', therefore, might go deeper, in terms of world dynamics, than the simple removal of alien occupying powers.

'World space' is occupied by a host of agencies, organizations and quasi representative bodies which operate not infrequently on a consciously 'transnational' basis. 'Relationships', too, is a difficult word. A multiplicity of 'transactions', both profound and trivial, constantly occur but they may or may not transmit 'messages'. Political systems, and the 'world views' which they encapsulate, have their moment and then are gone. The analysis of what constitutes power, whether 'hard' or 'soft', is never complete. Inter-state alliances, for a time, have an air of permanence, but then lose their coherence and rationale. Centres of power and influence – the two not necessarily being the same – shift, sometimes dramatically, sometimes imperceptibly. National economies flourish and flounder, and with them the theories which explain their performance, at least retrospectively. Climate change ignores the patrolled boundaries of states and their individual capacities to control their own 'destinies'. 'World-views' often have their original anchorage in particular places but they float free across the globe, sometimes in the process, taking on differing colouring. The 'story line' may be one, globally, of ever-widening economic prosperity, increased health and longevity, and peace and freedom. It may also be one of resource exhaustion, environmental catastrophe, gross inequality in life expectancy and demographic disaster. It all depends ...

The matters referred to above, for shorthand described as 'the rise and fall of nations and empires', have formed a staple element in global historiography for many centuries. That continues to be the case. These processes could sometimes be linked to the rise and fall of particular kinds of politico-economic system. All the time, however, it could be assumed that there was some kind of 'equilibrium' or 'balance' at work, even if, in particular contexts, the causes and processes of change were hard to pin down. Power and status did unquestionably move from place to place. One 'Great Power', with its adjuncts and satellites, gave way to another.

This present volume, therefore, highlights certain substantive elements in this mixture. It cannot tell 'the whole story'. Its structure, however, affirms the discrete individuality of particular places, people and parties. It observes 'clashes of civilization' as bitter as any in 'the barbaric past', but also cultural congruence and symbiosis. Each street, each village, each city, each country, each continent goes its own way and creates its 'world-view'. Yet, to greater or lesser degree, in one form or another, 'the outside world' seeps into indigenous cultures and social structures. Often, even in the act of resisting alien hegemony, something of the enemy's ways are absorbed. A process of osmosis adapts and transforms in unpredictable ways. That is the history of the modern world.

Further reading

Bentley, Jerry H., *The Oxford Handbook to World History* (Oxford University Press: Oxford, 2011).

Gilbert, Martin, *Challenge to Civilization: A History of the Twentieth Century III: 1952–1999* (HarperCollins, London, 1999).

Hopkins, A.G., ed. *Global History: Interactions between the Universal and the Global* (Palgrave Macmillan, Basingstoke, 2006).

Iriye, Akira and Saunier, Pierre-Yves, *The Palgrave Dictionary of Transnational History from the Mid-Nineteenth Century to the Present* (Palgrave Macmillan, Basingstoke, 2009).

Kramer, Lloyd and Maza, Sarah, eds., *A Companion to Western Historical Thought* (Blackwell, Oxford, 2002).

Reynolds, David, *One World Divisible: A Global History since 1945* (Allen Lane, London, 2000).

Part 1
TOWARDS 1945:
ENDING WORLD WAR,
BUILDING PEACE

This part of the book sets the context in which the 'new world order' of 1945 emerged. It does not, however, provide a narrative history of the Second World War. Its focus, rather, is on the year 1943, when the war which had begun in Europe in 1939 began to favour the Allies (the USA, Britain, the Soviet Union and their partners) in their battle against the Axis powers (Germany, Italy and their partners). War in Asia, as will shortly be explained, was another matter. The Anglo-American landings in Morocco and Algeria in November 1942 had been followed by the German–Italian surrender in Tunisia in May 1943. The invasion of Sicily followed in July and paved the way for the Italian declaration of war on Germany in October. On the Eastern Front, German forces surrendered in Stalingrad in February 1943 after months of heavy fighting. Further Soviet successes followed into the summer and autumn. Would an Anglo-American invasion of occupied France in that year, rather than in 1944, have ended the war earlier? The question of such an invasion naturally loomed large in inter-Allied exchanges, as in subsequent historical debate. In all major wars, 'events' take control. The world as it had existed in 1939 had disappeared, and was unlikely to return when hostilities ended, not least in Asia. Although US forces in the Pacific made headway, the defeat of Japan in South-East Asia was likely to be an arduous affair. In November 1943 a 'Greater East Asia' conference assembled in Tokyo, supposedly to consolidate a new order. In the ebb and flow of battle, states constantly adjusted their views of themselves and of their Allies. Different wars beginning at different dates and in different places had somehow rolled into one. The first chapter sketches how this had come about.

The year 1943 was therefore a significant one for diplomatic summits: bilat-eral and trilateral. Peacemaking in 1919 had embraced, in the League of Nations, a new vision of world order. Hopes, however, had then soon turned sour. Building a 'world' that worked relatively harmoniously was not likely to be any more simple a task in 1945. 'Summits' took place in Casablanca (Morocco), Cairo (Egypt) and Tehran (Iran). There, in various combinations, Winston Churchill, Franklin D. Roosevelt, Chiang Kai-shek and Josef Stalin, representing Britain, the USA, China and the Soviet Union, respectively, assembled to consider both short- and long-term issues. Assuming the defeat of the Axis powers, these were the men who would determine the future structure of the world. They represented 'the Great Powers'. So it might seem. Yet, the second chapter, while interpreting their personal and state perspectives, also focuses on where they met and the 'other' emerging worlds existing outside the conference room.

1
Struggles for Mastery

In early May 1945, in ceremonies in the French city of Rheims, and then in Berlin, German forces surrendered. Churchill declared 8 May VE (Victory in Europe) Day. It was a day of celebration in a continent of widespread devastation. It was difficult to recall what 'old Europe' had been like when, in September 1939, a small number of large Western and Central European states had gone to war with each other. The ripples and repercussions from the German invasion of Poland that month had spread far and wide. It happened twenty years after what had been the bloodiest war in European history. The war that was now finishing exceeded it in bloodiness. The notion that Europeans would never fight another major war with each other had been shown to be false. Their renewed conflict, however, drew in peoples, subordinate peoples, from across the world whose direct knowledge of Europe was hazy. They had had no option but to fight. The reach of Europe was still worldwide and the war became 'their' war, though an inherently ambiguous one. The world map of 1939 showed British, French, Dutch and Italian 'possessions' in Africa, Asia and 'the Middle East' the product of conquests made over centuries or decades. 'Empires' were an 'established fact'. They expressed power, European power. The world map of 1945 might superficially appear to be returning to 'normal'. The reality was very different. Ruined urban landscapes and fields without crops suggested that 'recovery' would be a long process. The British king, George VI, broadcasting on Christmas Day 1945, acknowledged that young people had only known the world as one of strife and fear. It was time to make it one of 'joyous adventure'.

Each year of the war had presented a different picture of predominance as its tide ebbed and flowed. At six-monthly intervals through the war a British publisher produced J.F. Horrabin's *Atlas-History of the Second Great War*. Battles in faraway places with strange-sounding names, to British ears, were mapped. It was not only a matter of battles. Readers were given a map of the Alaska Highway – running from Edmonton (Alberta) to Fairbanks in Alaska – built at the average rate of eight miles a day over six months. Each map, implicitly or explicitly, had a political message. British readers could note, with some astonishment, that British forces were entering Antananarivo, capital of Madagascar, in September 1943, battling Vichy French forces. American readers were similarly surprised to find that US forces were entering New Guinea. It was difficult, in these circumstances, to relate the apparent certainties of the 1939

Map 1 The
world in 1945

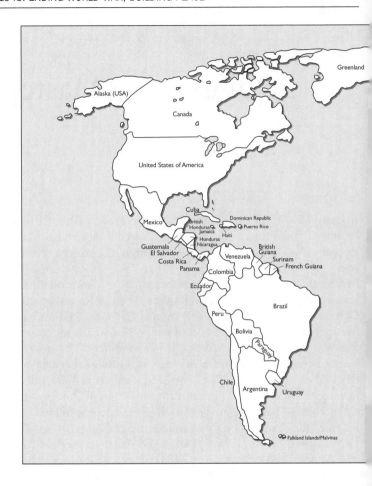

world to the new present. There were, of course, other ways of looking at the world. German maps showed a New Order in Europe, Japanese showed a new one in East Asia. American readers were guided to parts of the world where no American forces had ever before appeared – in North Africa, for example. From many perspectives, the sense of a world 'all mixed up' to an unparalleled degree was evident. The 'Second Great War' was shaking many foundations even as they appeared still to be secure. 'Planning for the future', which went on at many levels, official and unofficial, rested on the frail foundations of an unstable present.

'Power', in these circumstances, might be shorthand for some combination of military might, population resource, technical and administrative capacity or cultural hegemony. It might find its justification in a 'civilizing mission' in which rapacity was balanced by 'improvement'. For several decades, however, there had been abundant signs that 'empires' were in trouble. The empires (and emperors) of the European continent had disappeared by 1919. The British king, however, was Emperor of India, though his survival, in this capacity, might now become precarious. Before 1939 Europe supposedly consisted of a set of

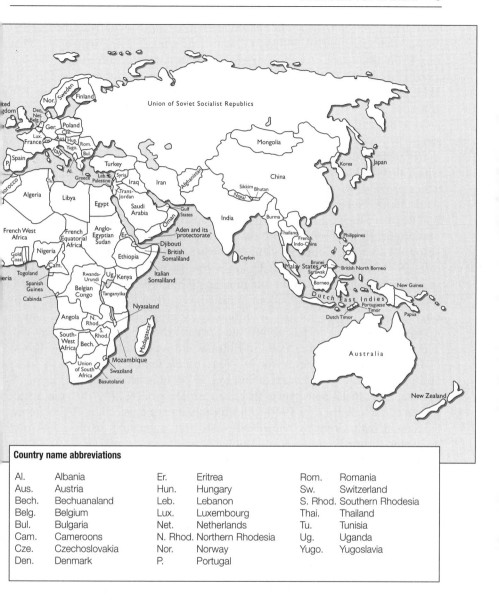

Country name abbreviations

Al.	Albania	Er.	Eritrea	Rom.	Romania
Aus.	Austria	Hun.	Hungary	Sw.	Switzerland
Bech.	Bechuanaland	Leb.	Lebanon	S. Rhod.	Southern Rhodesia
Belg.	Belgium	Lux.	Luxembourg	Thai.	Thailand
Bul.	Bulgaria	Net.	Netherlands	Tu.	Tunisia
Cam.	Cameroons	N. Rhod.	Northern Rhodesia	Ug.	Uganda
Cze.	Czechoslovakia	Nor.	Norway	Yugo.	Yugoslavia
Den.	Denmark	P.	Portugal		

'nation-states', old and new. This principle of 'national self-determination', to put it mildly, had contained many 'loose ends' in contexts of ethnic complexity. The principle was not necessarily the basis on which the world should be organized.

Mastery in Europe

The struggle between the 'Allies' and the 'Axis', largely in Europe, looked straightforward enough, but the reality was more complicated. The 'Allies' of

1943 had not been together in 1939. Different circumstances had subsequently created their partnership. Different circumstances might drive them apart. That they should not easily agree on strategic priorities was not surprising. The way a war ends sets the scene for relationships in an unknown future. The UK, the USA and the Soviet Union all had particular aspirations and anxieties. The emotions and experiences of war threw up fresh suspicions. The overwhelming need to defeat the enemy restrained their corrosive effect, but not necessarily for long.

In September 1939, Germany and the Soviet Union had signed a pact in which they had agreed not to fight each other. It contained a secret protocol which provided for the partition of Poland and gave Moscow a free hand in the Baltic States, Finland and Bessarabia. Following the 1917 Bolshevik Revolution, the 'Russian Empire' had been replaced by a 'Soviet Union', purportedly a partnership of socialist republics. New states emerged in the Baltic – Finland, Estonia, Latvia and Lithuania – but otherwise, after initial wobbles in the southeast, the territory of this Soviet Union was substantially co-extensive with that of the expanded 'Russia' of the late nineteenth century. Moscow was in control. Outsiders continued to talk about 'Russia' even when they were aware, albeit often vaguely, of the country's continuing heterogeneity. Americans, almost invariably, had come to talk about 'the Soviets', though the British rarely did. The Soviet Union was thus both 'in Europe' and yet outside it. 'Placing' Russia had long been a conundrum for its Western neighbours, but European states and peoples were little better themselves at defining what 'Europe' entailed. *Pravda,* the official newspaper, stated on 31 December 1940 that the Soviet Union could look back on 1940 with a feeling of deep satisfaction. An economic agreement with Germany, signed ten days later, apparently marked a further great step forward.

The British could also look back on 1940 with deep satisfaction. History, it was said, would record that it was their finest hour. They had suffered incredible disasters, sustained unparalleled betrayals and run stupendous risks, but they had carried on. So wrote Arthur Mee, a popular British author. Their stand against the odds entitled them, in their collective mood, to a place in determining the future of the world. Such a stance, however, could not disguise the perils of their country's isolated if still imperial circumstances. When Germany invaded the USSR in June 1941, however, the position changed dramatically. Thereafter, pledging mutual assistance as Allies, the common enemy for the UK and the Soviet Union was Nationalist Socialist Germany (and its European allies and conquered or acquiescing satellites). The troubled British–Soviet past was skated over. It could be recalled that, with the exception of the Crimean War, Britain and Russia had been allies in Europe's modern great wars.

The 'Axis Powers' in reality came to mean Germany, such was its ever more evident predominance over its partner, Italy (which had declared war on France and Britain in June 1940). Since 1940, too, after its conquests in Western and Northern Europe, Germany had non-Soviet 'Europe' more or less at its disposal. It could coerce or control directly or indirectly. France had been divided into two, with a French state, established at Vichy, responsible for French overseas territories. All of this could be packaged as a 'New Order' in

Europe and, as such, was not without appeal to some non-Germans who were willing, for whatever reason, to 'collaborate'. It looked from outside like a new German Empire, one now driven by a 'National Socialism', which would create its 'New Europe'. At one level, therefore, as it evolved after 1941, the war in its European aspect repeated that struggle for supremacy evident in the first Great War.

Mastery in East Asia

Victory in Europe had been followed by four months of hard fighting in which Allied forces engaged Japan. The Soviet Union, which had not been at war with Japan, joined the conflict on 8 August 1945. The USA dropped atomic bombs on Hiroshima and Nagasaki on 6 and 9 August. Japan surrendered on 2 September. The war as a world struggle therefore came to an end. But was that the right way to put it? Was it a single war or two wars only loosely linked? Beginning with the Japanese drive into Manchuria in 1931, through conflict in Shanghai in 1932 and then into an undeclared war beginning in July 1937, Japan and China had been engaged in a protracted struggle for 'East Asia'. Britain had vast territorial and economic interests in East Asia and the Pacific but its politicians and diplomats confronted a reality they found humiliating: they did not have the strength to fight Japan. It became ever more apparent that their role in determining the future of East Asia would be limited. The surprise Japanese attack on the US naval base of Pearl Harbor in Hawaii in December 1941 took conflict in East Asia to a new dimension. The British ambassador in Washington suspected that American political circles still made a distinction between war with Japan and war with Germany, but that would not last long. Maybe he was too optimistic.

The USA, joined by Britain, declared war on Japan. The 'European War' was no longer confined to Europe (and North Africa) and the 'East Asian War' was no longer confined to East Asia. Victory in one theatre would certainly have a bearing on the other, but which conflict was 'central'? Populations across the world thought primarily of different enemies. To ask the question was to ponder what 'world' the war was primarily about. It was Japan, not Germany, which had brought the USA into the war, though Germany and Italy did then declare war on the USA. Perceptions of the relative significance of the different zones of the war necessarily suggested different operational imperatives, and could not fail, on occasion, to be divisive. Terminology, too, was indicative. Was the non-European war the 'Pacific War', 'The Far East War' or 'The Greater East Asia War'? Each description carried geopolitical implications. Japanese policy, if it was skilfully executed, might be conceived in some South-East Asian quarters not as 'aggression' but as 'liberation': a 'Co-Prosperity sphere'. The European colonial presence would be permanently banished. But was the imposition of alien rule any more palatable for being 'Asian'? It was a question to be asked in 'British' Burma or the 'Dutch' East Indies. Both in Europe and Asia, conquest could be met, internally, by 'resistance' but, until a late stage, this was little more than futile gesture. Neither 'collaboration' nor 'resistance', however, are easily defined, either in terms of motive or activity. Just as the antecedents of this

'Second World War' cannot be fixed firmly in one single location, so 'planning' for the world that was to follow could only operate at various interlocking but distinct levels. The sands were shifting. In Washington, in January 1942, the USA, UK, USSR, China and 22 other Allies had pledged themselves not to make separate peace treaties with the enemy. The signatories henceforth called themselves 'the United Nations' (a section of American opinion did not quite like the word 'Allies').

One thing, however, was certain. The winner, or winners, would take all. It turned out to be the Allies. There is no intention here to speculate counterfactually on what 'the world' would have looked like if they had been defeated. The prospect of what fate might have awaited them if they were to fail kept the Allies more or less together. The victory they would pursue would not be a compromise or patched-up peace. Germany or Japan could not be 'left out' forever, but the victors would determine the time and circumstances. These 'policemen' would plan the world.

Mastery in the Middle East

Two thousand miles from end to end, wrote a British writer, Philip Guedalla, in late 1943, the Desert War was over. Exuberantly, he claimed that the Mediterranean danced in the winter sunshine. The war that had swung back and forth across North Africa was a war of the Europeans: British, Americans, Germans, Italians and others. The states of the region, with their varying degrees of quasi-independence, had not themselves been prime actors. In the struggle by foreigners to secure or acquire 'the Middle East', the Allies had come out on top. Mastery in the Middle East, however, was an elusive notion. Guedalla's 'Middle East', one extending over two thousand Mediterranean miles, was controversial. There could be no definition universally agreed. It was its 'overlapping' character which made 'the Middle East' fascinating, intractable and unpredictable. Three of the world's major religions – Christianity, Islam and Judaism – had emerged there and, in differing proportions, remained communally present. A wider identity was always contestable. Religion as harmony and religion as conflict was always in evidence. What happened in the Middle East resonated widely among Christians, Jews and Muslims in the world beyond and again gave it its special flavour.

That a 'world war' was being superimposed on its complex structure complicated matters further. Somewhat precariously, the British maintained their significant 'guardianship'. Outsiders in distant places could not leave the region alone. There was oil. More generally, the Middle East was a 'world site' as no other. 'Outsiders', as much in the present as the past, felt that they properly had a stake in its future. Jerusalem 'belonged' to the Christian, Islamic and Jewish 'worlds', all themselves diverse and polycentric, not only because of the more obvious cleavages (between Protestant, Catholic and Orthodox Christians or between Shi'ite and Sunni Muslims) but because of the cultural environments in which faiths had been practised. Churches existed across the world in very different relationships with states. The 'Christian world' did not now have, and generally did not now hanker after, a political expression.

The concept of the 'Muslim world', however, suggested a different scenario. In the course of their evolution, Christianity and Islam had come to have significantly different understandings of 'religion' and 'society' and how the two intersected. Local juxtaposition in the Middle East therefore pointed to deeper issues of cultural, religious and political identification, worldwide ones. Such alignments were not irrelevant to the war that was being fought. How the states of the world might be re-ordered in world conferences was one thing. How societies and communities actually related to each other might be another. An emphasis on *ummah*, a common Islamic domain, sat uneasily alongside the existence of diverse states and nations. There were Muslims in many states, but not many Muslim states. What had happened on the demise of the Ottoman Empire in 1919 might or might not be indicative. Then Kemal Ataturk, who had died in 1938, had created a 'Turkey' as a secular republic with a conception of the separation of 'mosque' and 'state' which owed much to France. Turkey kept out of this new war. On the other hand, in the Kingdom of Saudi Arabia, named as such in 1932, Ibn Saud, protector of the holy cities of Mecca and Medina, had a very different conception of the kind of state in which Muslims should live. The other new post-Ottoman states moulded by France and Britain under 'mandates' from the new League of Nations – Lebanon, Syria, Iraq and Transjordan – had different arrangements. The 'Arab Middle East' was therefore a complicated mosaic. The British Foreign Secretary had spoken in May 1941 of supporting any scheme of Arab unity which commanded general approval. There was the rub. No such scheme existed. Nor was it clear that the voice of a British foreign secretary would continue to matter so much.

The 'Palestine question', during the war, loomed ever larger. Under its League of Nations 'mandate', a British High Commissioner had been administering the territory. In 1917, Arthur Balfour, the British Foreign Secretary, had declared in favour of a 'national home' for Jews in the territory. This would, after all, be a 'homecoming' for such Jews from the worldwide diaspora as wished to 'return': 'next year in Jerusalem'. Jews would stimulate development. They might constitute, or be believed to constitute, an 'alien wedge', clients of outside powers. There was optimism and cynicism. As time went on, the British administration found it increasingly difficult to reconcile Jews and Arabs (Muslim and Christian). In 1936 Arabs broke out in active revolt. Jews had come to number about a third of Palestine's population. A Report which recommended partition, a solution rejected by both Arabs and Jews, was shelved. It seemed to entail, too, much forcible transfer of populations. The territory entered the war with a British White Paper declaring that it was no part of British policy 'that Palestine should become a Jewish state'. It was evident, however, that some Zionists would use violence for just such an end. Arab leaders took some comfort from the British statement, but could not make out what the British proposed. That is scarcely surprising. The British did not quite know.

This Middle East, generously defined and facing in many directions, was where the great men of the war met. Getting around the world in wartime for the Allied leaders was not straightforward. Travel was uncomfortable, even dangerous. Churchill's family, on more than one occasion, feared that his flights would bring on coronary thrombosis. It was also evident, however, that key decisions could in reality only be reached by the men 'at the top'. Their personal predilections, prejudices and styles all mattered. Decision-making in wartime has only a democratic veneer. There was no substitute for summit conferences. Thus, in August 1942, flying from Cairo, with a break in Tehran, Churchill visited Stalin in Moscow for four days. The German–Soviet front was the scene of desperate fighting both then and in the months that followed. The fate of Stalingrad became symbolic. Churchill had argued in Moscow that the American and British landings in North Africa which were being prepared and which took place in November 1942 offered the only immediately practicable way forward. The future of other parts of the world was also now the subject of consultation, and not only by governments. In December 1942, for example, also in Quebec, another conference reflected on 'War and Peace in the Pacific'. Unofficial 'experts' attended from Australia, Canada, China, 'Fighting France', India, the Netherlands–Netherlands East Indies, New Zealand, Philippines, the UK and the USA. The possible 'regional' shape of things to come was set out. Quebec, however, did not perhaps naturally suggest itself as the location for a Pacific conference. It was an indication of the way in which old patterns of alignment and relationship were being jumbled up.

Likewise, back in 1939, Casablanca, on Morocco's Atlantic coast, would not have seemed a likely place for a conference between an American president and a British prime minister. In the wake of the North African landings, however, Churchill and Roosevelt came there to confer in January 1943 about the future direction of their war. They decided upon 'Unconditional Surrender'. Taking time off, the two men found the glow of the sunset on the snow-capped Atlas Mountains the loveliest spot in the world. Churchill knew the country well. Out of office before the war, he had gone there to paint and to write. The Anglo-American world, apparently harmonious, however, was merely 'parking' in Morocco for convenience. It was an 'Anglo-Saxon' intrusion.

Roosevelt and Churchill kept in constant touch. They met again in Washington in May 1943 and agreed, though not easily, on the Allies' next steps: the invasion of Sicily, Italy and Northern Europe. This was the Anglo-American world in operation. The lesser allies of London and Washington would play their allocated parts. In Quebec, in August 1943, Churchill and Roosevelt agreed that the defeat of Germany should take precedence over the defeat of Japan. It should be the aim to invade France by May 1944. Britain and the USA liked 'summits' on their own in the security of North America. Canada was a congenial and collegial partner.

The Morocco of this January meeting was 'normally' controlled by France, but the times were not normal. In the wake of its defeat in May 1940 there was no single France. Who 'spoke for' France and who controlled the French colonial empire was contentious. The 'Anglo-Saxons' themselves were not of the same mind on how to deal with a bitterly divided France. Charles de Gaulle, confident that he spoke for 'Fighting France', was determined not to be left out. In halting English – on a par with Churchill's French – he struggled to maintain French sovereignty over areas belonging to France in 1939 (suspicious of what the 'Anglo-Saxons' might have in mind). Vichy French forces had resisted when

British and American forces landed in North Africa. Free French forces had been excluded from the operation.

It had been but forty years earlier, in the context of cementing their 1904 *entente*, that Britain and France had agreed that Morocco should be 'French' (neighbouring Algeria, where there was substantial European settlement, had been 'attached' to metropolitan France since 1848). The territory had been partitioned between France and Spain in 1912. European control over the forces of Abd-el-Krim (b.1882), a Berber leader of considerable skill, had only been consolidated in 1926 by a large better-equipped French–Spanish army under the French Marshal, Philippe Pétain. It was from Spanish Morocco that Francisco Franco, the man who now ruled Spain (and kept his country out of the war), had launched his ultimately successful bid for power. It was that very same Pétain who was now Head of State in Vichy France.

Every Moroccan in 1943 could see that 'France' was in disarray. Young Moroccans, in the 1930s, had been proposing a 'reform' programme – and perhaps articulating for the first time a 'national' sentiment. They had then been given short shrift in Paris. The political context, however, was now clearly changing. Filmgoers in Britain and the USA, courtesy of Humphrey Bogart and Ingrid Bergman, learnt how complicated political alignments in Casablanca were.

Every Algerian could likewise see that 'France' was in disarray. In June 1943, de Gaulle arrived in Algiers to set up a 'Committee of National Liberation'. The national liberation concerned, however, was that of France. There was no 'Algerian nation'. Ferhat Abbas, university graduate and French army veteran, nine years younger than de Gaulle, had hitherto been an advocate of the complete integration of Algeria into a pluralist France. In 1936 he had declared that 'the Algerian nation' did not exist. In 1943, however, publishing a 'Manifesto of the Algerian people', he announced that it was sufficient simply to be an Algerian Muslim. The inner life of North Africa was on the move. The Anglo-Americans, however, had other perspectives. 'Worlds' clearly operated at different levels.

2
Policemen Meeting

Egypt and its visitors: November 1943

In October 1943, in Moscow, Allied foreign ministers decided, amongst other matters, to establish the European Advisory Council, a forum in which the USA, the Soviet Union and the UK could consult on the future of Europe. No other continent was deemed to require an 'Advisory Council'. A conference communiqué emerged on behalf of 'the Big Four' (though China, 'the Fourth', had not played a part in drafting it). It was agreed that the 'Big Three' should meet in Iran in late November 1943. The locations of these meetings, and who was present, revealed the way the world's wind was blowing. Roosevelt did not come to London. Stalin did not come to 'the West'. The next 'away' location for Roosevelt and Churchill was Cairo in November 1943.

The world 'communicated' through the Suez Canal. After its construction in 1868, it had been the gateway to a 'West' arrogant, or at least self-confident, in its embodiment of 'modernity'. It had also been the gateway to an 'East' in which 'the West', in its various guises, had installed itself. There was a sense in which the region was 'pivotal', and not simply because of its oil, significant though that increasingly was. Terminology necessarily reflected perspective. Whether Egypt was 'the Near East',' the Middle/Mid-east' or 'almost West' depended on where one was sitting. It might be 'North Africa'. Its physical and spiritual location was obscure and mobile. Somewhere here 'civilizations' encountered each other, but there was no precise junction. The past offered many boundary points and revealed fluctuating patterns of conquest, 'East' over 'West' and vice versa. The import of the past was ambiguous. It was a region which did not fully 'belong' anywhere. Its fate, to put it grandly, was to be at a perpetual point of intersection.

The British imprint, following the bombardment of Alexandria in 1882, had been firm if supposedly temporary. As in the Maghreb, however, worlds were in flux. A 'new' Egypt was emerging but its shifting internal politics did not directly impinge on the visiting statesmen as they were driven to their conference centre in a Cairo suburb. The pyramids were nearby. History was at hand, but they had a war to win and a 'world' to create. There could be no wider sense in which, at this juncture, Egypt could act as arbiter or broker. In 1943, the young King Farouk needed no reminder that the British ambassador, in his imposing residence, was a rather special kind of ambassador. He had armoured cars. British troops had remained in the country after independence and did not seem disposed to leave. The Egyptian army was not a significant force, but it was modernizing. A 25-year-old army officer, Gamal Abdul Nasser, then unknown to the world, a diligent reader of biographies of Napoleon, Bismarck and Ataturk, felt his country's humiliation deeply. One day, he avowed, the army would restore its honour and cleanse its dignity in blood. The British had feared that Cairo might have fallen to German/Italian forces. Young Nasser wanted all Europeans out.

Cairo was no mean city, its population having doubled over the previous quarter of a century. Perhaps it would be more accurate to speak of it being two cities, 'old' and 'new', as expressed in its buildings and layout. European communities (French, Italian, Greeks and of course British) gave the city a certain duality. In its past, in stages, its rulers had detached themselves from Ottoman control – but into what kind of future? There were so many strands, at different levels of society. Arabic was the official language but the sense in which Egyptians were simply 'Arabs' was not straightforward. Maybe the 'real' Egypt had been conquered by Arabs. Cairo hosted great centres of Islamic scholarship but also on the skyline were Coptic and other Christian cathedrals. It might be, or might be made to be, a great 'European' city. Egyptians, or at least a certain elite, might want to see themselves as Europeans. These were issues which exercised Egyptian politicians. They knew well, however, as the cars of the world's 'big chiefs' drove to their Cairo suburb in 1943, that Egypt's future was not yet theirs to decide. Despite the evident subordination, their time might be coming.

However, it was not because Cairo, in a certain sense, was a hub of the world that Allied leaders assembled. It was rather because it was a convenient stopover en route for Tehran. They had not come to confer with the Egyptian government, one that had been independent, though under the watchful British eyes, for almost two decades. Roosevelt and Churchill were by now accustomed to meeting each other, though the latter was aware that he seemed to be less listened to. The Cairo meeting confirmed this sense. What brought a new significance to conferencing was the fact that Chiang Kai-shek (Jiang Jieshi) was flying from his then capital of Chungking ((Chongqing) to join them. He might feel particularly 'out of place' in an Arab environment. He was the first to arrive.

Chinese debut: Chiang Kai-shek

A Chinese presence in Egypt was symbolically significant at various levels. The visitor himself took it as recognition that China was indeed one of the Great Powers preparing to shape the world. In January 1943 the British and the Americans had agreed to relinquish their extra-territorial rights in China. Chiang wanted the assurance that Japan would be required to surrender unconditionally. The other chiefs went along with the trappings of China's new status. That is not to say that they believed it. China, in reality, was their supplicant. The USA had poured aid into China after Pearl Harbor. Chiang's Chief of Staff in Chongqing, the US General, Stilwell, saw America as the midwife of a future East Asia. There would be no role for Europeans.

Chiang, 'the Generalissimo', relished this appearance on 'the world stage'. He brought another cultural/political dimension. The facts at the time appeared simple. China was at war with Japan and indeed, arguably could be said to have been so, in a fashion, since the Japanese incursion into Manchuria in 1931 and its rechristening as Manchukuo (Japan had annexed Korea in 1910). Much of China 'proper' was under Japanese control by the late 1930s, though that control was more over urban than rural areas. Chiang's own career illustrated some of the complexity in the Chinese–Japanese relationship and indeed of China itself. In the last years of the Manchu dynasty he had been sent to a Japanese military staff college to complete his training. Other Chinese went to Japan for other purposes. Japan symbolized 'modernity' and held many attractions. Over the fifteen years that followed Chiang's return to China in 1911, the year the Manchu dynasty was overthrown, Japan could claim to be a world power. Its Western neighbour was ripe for 'tutelage'.

Sun Yat-sen (Sun Zhongshan), a man who had spent a lot of his life outside China – he had indeed been born in Honolulu - became its president in 1923 and reinvigorated the Kuomintang (Revolutionary Nationalist Party) along the lines of the Soviet Communist Party. It worked relatively co-operatively with the Communists until his death in 1925. Chiang Kai-shek had served as commander-in-chief of the army. Breaking with the Communists, he established himself as head of the 'national' government in 1928. He had been photographed earlier in the decade standing upright, with shoulders square, and facing the viewer directly. This was a 'modern' and Western-influenced posture. But what was image and what was reality? Sun Yat-sen had been declared president in Canton (Guangzhou). Chiang made Nanjing his capital. Both facts revealed that this 'national' government only had an effective power base in southern China. There were competitors active elsewhere. Beijing was beyond his control. Add in the Japanese invasion and Communist activity, and it appeared difficult to say, from outside, what 'China' amounted to. Quite apart from the issues of territorial control, there was a deeper question. What was the Chinese nation? 'Chinese', as spoken in different parts of the huge country, could be very different. There were issues connected with the script. The Chinese word for nation had been borrowed, significantly, from Japanese. Han Chinese certainly predominated, but there were other ethnic minorities.

Chiang set about making Nanjing into a 'modern city' (some boulevards and government buildings were like 'modern' ones erected, a couple of decades earlier, in Cairo). In commercial terms, it is arguable that the Chinese government was making itself accepted as an equal partner in the world as never before. But was this all façade? An impressive Sun Yat-sen mausoleum outside the city enshrined the 'national' idea. In 1934 Chiang launched a 'New Life Movement' which promoted Confucian virtues and attempted the blending of old values with a 'new nationalism'. On his second marriage, to one of the formidable Soon sisters, he became a kind of Methodist. Madame Chiang had been educated in Methodist colleges in the USA. She had been a frequent visitor to the country. Speaking excellent English (with the accent of Georgia), she came, in the war, to address the Congress in Washington, the first Chinese and the second woman to do so. The US president appreciated hearing from her lips the congenial message that the Lord helped those who helped themselves. Euro-American Christian missions, both Protestant and Catholic, had made some impact – it was Madame Chiang's father who had become a Methodist – but Chinese converts knew very well the handicap of their faith's Western origins. They had to 'indigenize' to flourish. Communists, with another 'Western' import, seemed to have more radical solutions to Chinese poverty to offer.

By 1943, all that efflorescence of 'modernity' expressed in the National Government, partial in reach though it was, had come to an end. The Japanese had captured Nanjing in late 1937 – 'the Rape of Nanjing' had been brutal. Chiang had been forced to remove his administration to the hilly city of Chongqing in the south-western province of Szechuan (Sichuan). It was not then 'a modern city'. There was good reason to suppose that Chiang was bent on stockpiling resources not so much to fight the Japanese as to prepare for a post-war battle with the Communists.

Imperial emissary? Churchill

Churchill knew the way to Cairo well. He was the most well-travelled of the world's statesmen, but he had never been to China, nor to British Hong Kong, now occupied by the Japanese. He wanted that island to remain British rather than revert to China at the end of the war. Egypt, however, was almost familiar territory to the prime minister. Lord Cromer, the British Agent, had briefed him in Cairo in 1899 and introduced him to the Khedive, as the ruler was known. It was, Churchill wrote, like one schoolboy being brought to see another schoolboy in the presence of the headmaster. In 1902 he travelled up the Nile to see the new Aswan dam. As Colonial Secretary, he had arrived in Cairo in 1921 to preside over a mammoth conference to sort out the Middle East as economically as possible while still ensuring a dominant British influence. The British Imperial Conference of that year had declared that the Empire could survive anything else, 'but not the loss of its main artery'. The circumscribed Egyptian independence of 1922 was therefore Churchill's doing. He had protested vigorously against the Labour government's decision in 1929 to with-draw British troops from Cairo to the Canal Zone. He had believed it folly for a British government 'to cast away her rights, her interests and her strength'. In Cairo, in 1943, therefore he was equally determined to preserve British inter-ests, though uncomfortably aware of ebbing strength. He had not become the King's First Minister, he declared, to preside over the liquidation of the British Empire. Yet it was in Cairo that another shift in his assiduously cultivated rela-tions with the American President occurred. He found that Roosevelt did not need lessons on how to engage with the Soviets.

In 1921, riding a camel in Egypt, Churchill had ignominiously fallen off. This could have been interpreted as an omen. However, in 1943, on a good day, it was still possible to believe that 'the British Empire' was a central aspect of the world as then constructed. The British Prime Minister, however, could not speak directly for the British Empire, even if he was in one sense its embodi-ment. He loved Canada, visiting it six times, though he never visited Australia or New Zealand (perhaps sensing, after his part in the Gallipoli campaign in the

Great War, that his welcome would not have been too warm). 'Parity of status' between the UK, Australia, Canada (and a still separate Newfoundland), New Zealand and South Africa had been agreed in 1926. These were the 'Dominions' of settlement from the 'mother country'. This 'family' married 'Britishness' and strengthening nationalism in uncertain balance. Settlement, of course, had been made possible by conquest. It was in South Africa that the ethnic disparity between government and indigenous people was most obvious. The 'family' also contained, in the Afrikaners of South Africa and the French speakers of Quebec, other communities with different European pasts.

Even so, with the exception of the Irish Free State, still grudgingly within the Empire, the family was at war, if with varying degrees of enthusiasm and consequence. To give but one example, the casualty list of the British Eighth Army fighting in the battles of El Alamein in late 1942 featured a large number of Australians. A failed raid on Dieppe that August had produced heavy Canadians casualties. In February 1944 there were heavy Maori losses amongst the New Zealanders killed in the assault on Monte Cassino in Italy. The Dominions, in thus fighting for 'the common good', were doing so 'out of area'. However, as Japanese forces conquered South-east Asia, Australia, in particular, could see very clearly the possibility of invasion. The fall of Singapore revealed the limits of British power in the region. Unsurprisingly, in these circumstances, the presence of Australian troops in North Africa became contentious. Australia, its Prime Minister said, had to look to its own interests. Canada had no alternative but to operate within a 'North Atlantic Triangle', sometimes as a valued 'go-between', sometimes as a neglected third party. White South Africans were fighting on 'their' continent, but still a long way from home. In combination, therefore, the self-governing 'British world' was a significant global presence, though difficult to define as dominion nationalism waxed.

Government in London was still directly responsible for that 'colonial world' which still painted such a large area of the world's map as 'British'. Each territory, from Jamaica to Kenya, had its own particular ethnicities and cultural heritages. The very existence of empire had significantly altered their character – for example, in the Indian presence in Fiji or Guyana. Such was its diversity that to speak of a single 'imperial policy' is impossible. It was 'managed' through a range of structures and relationships. It had not required major military forces to sustain it. All colonies had been required to 'play their part' in the global struggle. Troops from the British West Indies or East Africa found themselves fighting far from home 'for Britain'. India, too, had gone to war because Britain had so decreed. In 1942, however, Gandhi launched a 'Quit India' campaign. Before the war, pressure had been mounting on the British. Indians had been drawn more into government at a certain level but independence had not been on offer. Nor was it now. Indian forces served in North Africa and, of course, in the defence of India itself against Japanese invasion. Inescapably, what they were fighting for was still 'British India'. The British would not quit at this juncture but offered the prospect of substantive talks on independence when the war was over.

The position of India in 1943 was odd. It was a great country but it had no place at the world's 'top table'. It was not an 'Asian Power' as China, in the person of Chiang Kai-shek, seemed to be, and Japan certainly was. Pre-war, Churchill's opposition to greater Indian self-government was well known. Decades earlier, as a young soldier in India, he had been proud that such a vast country should be administered by Englishmen, and by how much was done by so few. On India's North-West Frontier, an embattled 'civilization' faced 'militant Mohammedanism'. In the middle of the war Churchill continued to feel that Britain had made 'India'. Its future was problematic. It was ethnically, linguistically, culturally and religiously more diverse than China. 'Balkanization', some thought, was inescapable if, in the end, British rule was unsustainable. 'India' was perhaps more akin to 'Europe'. There were some 'model', and some less than model, maharajahs who would want to govern their own states. There was already evidence that a single successor state might not even arrive, let alone survive. The Indian National Congress, and the Muslim League, had competing aspirations for the political future. There were contrasting views on how 'unchanging India' and 'the modern world' blended. It was an encounter experienced culturally in the lives of men who occupied the headlines. The paradox is that it was English speakers, a small elite, whose voices were most prominent in fashioning India. Prison was a good place to write on the subject and the British made books available for the purpose.

One of these writers, perhaps the voice of the India that was to come, was Jawaharlal Nehru (b.1889). The son of a prosperous barrister, he had been educated in England. He went to Harrow (where, earlier, Churchill had been educated) before proceeding to Trinity College, Cambridge. He was 'an English gentleman' but he now looked for 'fundamental change of regime, politically, economically, socially'. Indian national freedom, he supposed, should come 'within the framework of an international co-operative socialist world federation'. Such a 'framework' was the commonplace of British left-wing vocabulary. Nehru's senior was Mohandas Karamchand Gandhi, 'Mahatma', a man whom he revered but who brought (to Nehru's 'Western' self) too much religion into his vision of India's future. In 1888 the 18-year-old Gandhi had himself come to London. He called it then 'the very centre of civilization'. For seventeen years, his world was then that of an Indian in South Africa. Returning home, the India he wanted was not a transplanted imitation of the West, capitalist or socialist. Whether he was tugging India backwards or leading it forwards depended on the meanings people attached to these terms. Whether he was a politician, a saint or, in Churchill's own words, 'a half-naked fakir', or all of these things, was a puzzle. Maybe his non-violent message might be one for the whole world, not just for India? He had disciples in many continents. In Cairo, Gamal Nasser, then an obscure teenager, was studying Gandhi's message.

But there were many different voices in the contemporary subcontinent. Mohammad Ali Jinnah (b.1876), orchestrating Muslim fears, though himself a somewhat secular figure, was blunt. Muslims, he declared, who were in a minority, shared nothing with Hindus. To yoke together the two nations (as he described them) would destroy the fabric of any future state. Sikhs, or even Christians, for their part, might observe that India was more than just these two 'nations'. Gandhi, Nehru and Jinnah all thought they could engineer the end of 'British India' by pressure which stopped short of insurrection. Another

Cambridge graduate, however, the Bengali, Subhas Chandra Bose, had early come to believe that the British would only leave if forced out by violence. Escaping from captivity in Calcutta (now Kolkata) in 1941, he found himself, via Moscow and Berlin, boarding a Japanese submarine off Madagascar bound for Japanese-occupied Singapore. It was there that he set up his Free India government. An Indian National Army, made up of Indian soldiers captured by the Japanese would, it was hoped, march on Delhi. It never did. The (British) Indian Army remained substantially loyal to the British Raj. Agendas for what would replace British rule, however, were clearly being drawn. Peace would bring negotiation but not necessarily a peaceful solution. Whatever the manner of transition, however, it would shake, if not shatter, the 'British world'. India, it is true, had been administered, in London, from the India Office and not the Colonial Office. Imperially, it was *sui generis*. Yet it could not but be a signal of a wider 'decolonization' elsewhere.

There were, therefore, manifold ways in which 'the British Empire' flowed through the mind and memory of a British Prime Minister visiting Cairo in 1943 and thinking about the future of the world: India, South Africa, Sudan, Canada were all there. Churchill, however, represented 'Europe', though with all the ambiguity of an Englishman. London, at this time, was hosting, and treating with some circumspection, exiled governments from the occupied continent. They would make their views known, but they would not be decisive. It was by no means certain, when they 'went back', that their authority would be intact. It would be Great Powers, not small countries, who would decide the future of 'Europe'. Whether France, in such a context, was 'great' or 'small' was unclear. In exile, with a certain idea of France, Charles de Gaulle would not easily be elbowed aside by 'Anglo-Saxons', though the British and the Americans were frequently at loggerheads on how to handle him. The 'liberation of France' had multiple meanings. Subject to whatever a revived France might extract by its obduracy, the fate of the continent would probably be decided from 'outside'.

Churchill felt the ebbing and flowing of tides. He did not want Britain to be diminished. He did not welcome voices who thought it inevitable. He thought that there was no other European state, not even France, quite like 'global Britain'. Yet the special characteristics, as he perceived them, did not make Britain non-European. Civilization, the European civilization he had youthfully upheld on the North-West Frontier of India, was good for the world. European states had jeopardized that civilization's hegemony by their behaviour in 1914. Britain, of course, had been party to that war, but as respondent rather than instigator. A solution to the European problem might be some kind of United States of Europe. Churchill was one of the few British politicians to express interest in the idea before the war. He suspected that Americans might not like it, and indeed might make it impossible. Britain would certainly not stand in the way, but equally not be likely to participate. Such observations simply took their place among the plethora of diverse but equally 'unrealistic' plans emanating from various quarters. Whether they could be resuscitated, and in what context, remained to be seen. They might be better than the reconstitution of the nation-states of 1939. The British stance, one way or the other, could be central.

British prime ministers had long been accustomed to thinking of British interests and resources in a global context. It went with the job. A trip to some distant part of the Empire had been often taken when they were political apprentices. The British royal family, likewise, had increasingly been despatched abroad on official visits 'to show the flag'. Presidents of the USA, however, had as yet been more bashful in presenting themselves abroad.

Going global: Roosevelt

Not that there was anything particularly bashful about Franklin D. Roosevelt. He had a family name which was as resonant in the USA as Churchill's was in Britain. Another Roosevelt, his cousin Teddy, had been president in 1901 and had been re-elected in 1904. Teddy had helped organize the 'Rough Riders' who had become national heroes during the Spanish war. In 1904 he asserted his country's right to act as 'an international police force'. The Monroe Doctrine, promulgated in 1823 when Latin America might have been threatened by European powers, stated, amongst other things, that the US would regard any fresh colonization by a European power of any independent state in the Western hemisphere as a hostile act. By Roosevelt's corollary, the USA gave itself the right, in the states covered by the Doctrine, to intervene if they failed to maintain domestic order or honour financial undertakings. It led to military intervention in the internal affairs of a number of South American countries. Thirty years later, however, Teddy's cousin did not wish to wield such a 'big stick'. His 'Good Neighbour' policy accepted that no state had the right to intervene in the internal or external affairs of another. Even so, there was still a mindset which assumed that 'the Americas' was a world over which, in its own estimation, the USA stood guard.

The Roosevelts were not recent incomers to the USA. They were 'thoroughly American', with an ancestry extending back to Dutch New Amsterdam (New York). Franklin was conspicuously wealthy and patrician. A cigarette smoker himself, he felt no obligation to fawn before the cigar-smoking grandson of an English duke. Harvard-educated, he felt no yearning, as some Americans did, for the culture of old Europe. He did not cringe. America was sufficient unto itself. He had visited Paris in a junior capacity during the 1919 peacemaking but felt no need, then or later, to explore Europe further. Besides, the experience there of Woodrow Wilson hardly encouraged American presidents to appear abroad in person. The encounter between a Presbyterian Princeton Professor and the wily dealers of old Europe on that occasion perhaps revealed the chasm between the idealistic optimism of the New World, with its airy talk of 'open covenants', 'national self-determination' and 'League of Nations', and the cynical pragmatism of the Old, with its wheeling and dealing. Arguably, in 1918, it had been latter-day American intervention that had saved Britain and France from defeat, but the USA had declined to become the guarantor of Europe's peace. Not that all European statesmen had particularly wanted it to be: Europe for the Europeans. Much American opinion subsequently thought that intervention in Europe had all been a mistake. It should not be repeated. The mood of 'isolation' took over. Yet no examination of the multiplicity of

American contacts with the world could for a moment take such a concept literally. Further, it was not infrequently conceded in 'old Europe' that the USA had become the engine of industrial civilization. Some said that it was the only truly independent country in the world. Its seemingly endless capacity to absorb new immigrants and create 'one' out of 'many' made it a kind of social laboratory for the world. It was still Europe itself from which most 'new Americans' came. Some firmly banished it, for good reason, from their minds. Others still felt a strong sense of their 'roots'. The American world blend was evidently complex.

'Imperialism' evoked different responses in the USA. On the one hand, the country had itself come into being by revolting from the British Empire. Anti-imperialism, in this sense, was culturally embedded, notwithstanding the 'imperialism' of its own subsequent internal expansion. Alongside opposition to 'empire', however, a sense of its 'manifest destiny' had taken the country into the world. The 1898 Spanish–American war was a specific example of that 'destiny'. In the aftermath, Spanish 'misgovernment' came to an end. Cuba became independent, though still under US protection while, on different bases, Puerto Rico, Guam and the Philippines were ceded to the USA. By 1943, therefore, for nearly half a century, the country, by such territorial expansion, had become a kind of empire, though, mysteriously, not like others. At the turn of the century, Filipino insurgents had unsuccessfully fought against the American presence, but by 1935 a Philippines 'Commonwealth' had been established. More self-government would at some point follow. However, Japanese forces captured Manila in January 1942. The following year, President Roosevelt announced that the Philippines would be granted independence after the defeat of Japan. America's brief foray into formal empire would therefore come to an end. Formal empire, however, was not the only expression of American global outreach.

'Europe' also evoked different responses in the USA. For all its European heritages of language and cultures, however, America was not Europe re-erected. It had its own internal wounds, arising from slavery and its legacy, and from a civil war more bloody than the world had ever known. Its conception of itself required constant reinvention. As visitors never ceased to report, in its different cities and states, the USA was almost as diverse as the world itself. Pluralism was rampant. It was the very embodiment of 'modernity'. It offered itself as a beacon of light, but that light did not shine everywhere. Uprooted Africa, too, was in America. Some 10 per cent of the US population at this time was classified as black. Most blacks still lived in the states of the old Confederacy. Optimism about the American future had been dented but not destroyed by the Great Depression. Naturally, given this complexity, outsiders saw in America what they wanted to see: threat and inspiration, bully and benefactor. This ambivalence was present in all European countries, particularly in Britain. It was an ambivalence Churchill himself experienced. He had an American mother and an English father. He visited the USA more frequently than he did any other country. His historical mind dealt with 'the English-speaking peoples'. Yet 'Pax Britannica' was probably passing away and a 'Pax Americana' might be rather uncomfortable. Others sought a kind of mid-Atlantic society in which, optimistically, a common language, or almost a common language, united Old and

New in a partnership which would dominate the world (for its own good) . Together – H.N. Brailsford, a well-known British left-wing journalist had written in 1940, encouraging American intervention – the two democracies might give the Western Hemisphere security and Europe peace, freedom and work. All these things might be true but, in the process, the British would lose their place in the world.

The 'Atlantic Charter' agreed by Churchill and Roosevelt during their Placentia Bay conference of August 1941 nevertheless set out, in eight points, a view of the world that was 'Anglo-American'. Neither country sought aggrandizement. Any territorial changes should be with the consent of the people concerned. All people had the right to choose the form of government under which they would live. Victors and vanquished, subject to some limitation, would have equal access to the world's trade and raw materials. Economic co-operation would be encouraged. The high seas could be sailed unhindered. People would be able to live out their lives in freedom from fear and want. All nations were to abandon force. The Soviet Union later indicated that it adhered to these objectives. To declare that all people had the right to choose their governments, as the British recognized at the time with some alarm, had wide-reaching ramifications. In South Africa, for example, in December 1943, the African National Congress adopted 'Africans' Claims in South Africa'. They were presented as a direct application of the Charter's precepts. What was therefore put forward in August 1941 as a commitment to restore what had been trampled on in Europe, might in fact, in time, destabilize the existing world.

In 1943 Roosevelt had every right to be regarded as the voice of America. He was the only one of the 'Big Chiefs' present to have a personal electoral mandate. It was the war, not a general election, which had shunted Churchill into power. An election in the future could remove him. Roosevelt, beginning in 1941, was now on his third term of office as president. There was every likelihood in 1943, afflicted by polio though he had long been, that he would stand again. Such endorsement gave him an unchallengeable world stature. He had not achieved this status, however, because in his manner of life he was 'a typical American': far from it. Yet he did seem to understand what 'ordinary people' needed in times of depression: a New Deal. He told 'all the American people' that he sought constantly to look into their hopes and fears. It had indeed been the internal condition of his country which had preoccupied him. Yet he could not avoid the deteriorating international situation. The reviving country did not seem to want to get involved beyond its borders. Roosevelt seemed to be saying that he would not take the USA to war. Lending and Leasing to Britain in January 1941 seemed to be a way of keeping the island-empire in the fight but also of keeping the USA out of it. It was wrapped up by its designation as a programme to support the 'Four Freedoms' in the world. They were identified as freedom of worship and speech and freedom from want and fear. It seemed that only Americans could crystallize aspirations so simply. Shielded by rhetoric, however, Roosevelt played his cards close to his chest. There was obfuscation beyond the normal level. It would not be acceptable to fight to save the British Empire as then constituted, but it would be disastrous if Britain were defeated.

It is not surprising, therefore, to find discordant strains beneath the heartfelt intimacy of this 'odd couple', Roosevelt and Churchill. The 'arsenal of democracy' was providing some 60 per cent of the Allies' combat munitions. US war production, within a year, would be double that of Germany, Italy and Japan combined. That mattered.

Scholars could discern, at all levels of American society, mood swings between 'isolationism' and 'internationalism' which made prediction of future American conduct difficult. A country saddled with a sense of mission was burdened with doubt about exercising it. It awkwardly stressed both its particularity and its universality. For a century, there had been speakers who had uttered variations on the theme of Secretary of State William H. Seward in 1846 when he engaged to give the people possession of the American continent, together with 'control of the world'. What 'control' meant, however, and whether it was other than the naked expression of self-interest, had been, and continued to be, endlessly debated. This was not just a matter for White House insiders or academic analysts of foreign policy. It engaged those who wrote for a large audience troubled by the dilemmas of ethics and policy. One such writer was the commentator/theologian Reinhold Niebuhr, who wrestled in the 1930s with the perils of American power. As the world's wealthiest nation, the USA had become 'the real empire of modern civilization'. His fellow-Americans, he thought, were trying, unsuccessfully so far, to manage their wealth and the world with the same economic and informal methods which had created their riches. Eventually, however, a 'world community' would emerge from America's awkward form of empire. It would do so, however, only if economic and military power were kept separate. The more economic power was supported by military strength, the greater would be the temptation to act in defiance of world opinion. Animosities against it would then multiply. Now, however, ever waxing military strength was what the USA had, and what it needed to have if the war were to be won.

The issue was whether, and on what basis, the 'Anglo-American world', with its exceptional wartime 'joint planning', would survive, or perhaps thrive, in probably very different post-war circumstances. There was a sense too that this world, in major part at least, was 'the Christian world'. The two men singing hymns on board a warship off Newfoundland in August 1941, in an interval in the drafting of their joint 'Atlantic Charter', were not expressing profound personal Christian conviction. The sense that this was a war for 'Christian civilization', however, had strong resonance on both sides of the Atlantic. The two countries had different arrangements as between 'Church' and 'State' but, at this juncture, could still talk about their common 'Christian values'. There might later be space for a 'Christian counter-attack' in a Europe which seemed to have abandoned them. So, in summary, while the two men, as their two countries, seemed in so many respects to see the world as one, that was not the complete picture.

Cairo had been the occasion for Britain and the USA to listen to China. Chiang was under the impression that most of his demands on 'the West' had been met. All his country's lost territories in the north were to be restored, though quite how was not clear. Roosevelt and Churchill went on to meet the embodiment of another world view, Josef Stalin. This time the destination was Tehran.

Tehran, November–December 1943: Stalin's stake

It was not a quartet that assembled. Chiang Kai-shek had gone home. The location again had its inner significance. No more than Casablanca or Cairo, was Tehran being visited by the Big Three because an indigenous government had to be consulted. It happened to be a place which suited a man of steel who was not a conspicuous traveller. Stalin had no wish to see the Anglo-American world at first hand. So the same ambivalence obtained in Iran as it did in Egypt. The Great Powers intended to confer among themselves: the Iranian view of the world would not feature. Both British and Soviet troops had arrived in Persia/Iran in 1941. To Iranians, the presence of these two powers scarcely constituted novelty. True, both before 1914 and after 1919, Persia had maintained its independence, but its geographical position always exposed it to Russian/Soviet and British attention. It was perceived to be a 'backward' country, but, as elsewhere in 'the Middle East', the discovery of oil, so important to the Western world, had brought about lopsided development. Churchill himself, as pre-1914 British First Lord of the Admiralty, had seized on the importance of oil-fired ships for the Royal Navy, and the Anglo-Persian Oil Company, in which the British government had taken a majority shareholding, was agreeably coming on stream. Oil and diplomacy, from the outset, were all mixed up. Whether Iran was really in 'the Middle East' could be argued over. Was 'the Gulf' Persian or Arabian? Iranians were not Arabs. It was an Islamic country, but Shi'ite not Sunni, with consequential ramifications. Its language and culture had long fascinated some European elites. Anthony Eden, the British Foreign Secretary, shared it, having studied oriental languages at Oxford – but he was not visiting Iran to gratify his cultural sensibilities.

The two Great Powers had forces on the ground because they believed the Shah of Iran to be consorting with German intriguers. Reza Khan was an army officer who had come to power in a coup in 1921 and had reigned as Reza Shah Pahlavi since 1925. 'Modernization' began, that is to say an expanded army and road and railway construction. In 1941, however, he was forced to leave the country and his 22-year-old son, who had been educated in Switzerland, was installed as Shah. Iran was used to outside intervention. Back in 1907 an Anglo-Russian Convention had delimited the 'spheres of interest' of the two countries. Tehran in 1943 personally was unknown territory to all the 'Big Chiefs', but the British and the Russians brought much historical baggage with them. The Americans, as yet, had only travelled light, though in Persia, as elsewhere in the Middle East, there had been 'oil wars' between British and American companies, and their governments had not been merely bystanders. Properly subordinated, Iran was simply the place where the immediate fate of the world was being shaped. There was no slot for the young Shah. Roosevelt, however, did accord him a short meeting. He expressed proper sympathy when the Shah complained about Britain's economic grip on his country's oil and mineral deposits. The young man wanted the British and Russians out of his country as soon as possible. Form required such a meeting, but the purpose of the conference was the future of the world.

The first meeting of the Big Three could not fail to have its moments of discordant drama. The strains of their gathering did not disappear simply because of moments of vodka-inspired bonhomie. There was hard talking between the principals and between their subordinates. Roosevelt thought that he could make more headway with Stalin than Churchill could. Churchill thought he could make more headway with Stalin than Roosevelt could. Stalin doubted whether Roosevelt could last the pace. Churchill looked a crusty enough old warrior. Intelligence Stalin possessed about disagreements between his 'partners' could be put to advantage. High on the agenda was the Soviet demand for clarity on the timing of 'Overlord' and 'Anvil', codenames for the operations into France that would create war in Europe on two fronts. He thought that there had already been too much prevarication on this matter, particularly from Churchill. Eventually he appeared to get the assurance he wanted. An Allied landing would be before the end of May 1944 (in the event it was 6 June). Stalin harboured the suspicion, denied by Churchill, that the British in particular still wanted some kind of Germany to survive and thus obstruct a Soviet advance into Western Europe. The Soviet Union, in its titanic battles with the German forces, was bearing the brunt of the fighting. Its westward advance in turn brought into sharp relief the future of Poland. The British handed over to Stalin a 'Sword of Honour' from their king, one struck to commemorate the Battle of Stalingrad. Stalin, perhaps slightly surprised, expressed gratitude. Perhaps, after all, 'Uncle Joe Stalin' was really avuncular: the terror that had ravaged the Soviet Union in the 1930s had perhaps been unleashed without his knowledge. He could steal the show.

Stalin's personal power was clearly different from either Roosevelt's or Churchill's. No ballot box would unhorse him. What Stalin really wanted was a mystery, perhaps to himself. His war aims, like all war aims, were fluid. Here were entangled, perhaps inextricably, the 'Soviet Union' and the 'Russian Empire'. The 1936 constitution of the former set out what Stalin had constructed. It ratified the Communist Party's hegemonic role in the state and saw this not as contradicting democracy but as confirming its very essence. What the regime was actually like was another matter. Its demonizing of class enemies, and constant capacity to discover them, could suggest a fundamental commitment to social equality. Its stipulated atheism could suggest a commitment to a rationalism that was scientific. Here was a package which could appeal equally to 'workers' and 'intellectuals' across the world. The Soviet Union was thus the scene of a new civilization. It was a success. By definition, it was 'international'. 'Socialism in One Country' might only be a temporary expedient owing to the failure of 'world revolution' to materialize at the appropriate moment. The relationship between the two had of course been the subject of much ideological strife. The Comintern, which had given, under Soviet 'guidance', expression to this 'internationalism', had for the moment been dissolved, but there could surely be no permanent abandonment of the missionary impulse.

Yet what was the 'One Country'? Stalin, the Georgian-turned-Russian, earlier as Commissar for Minorities, and subsequently, had set his face against any reduction in the Russian Empire's boundaries. There could be some cultural gestures but no place, within ostensibly autonomous republics, whether in Georgia or elsewhere, for political nationalism. As for the Baltic states, their twenty-year independence would be shown to be an aberration. The Finns, too, would pay a price – the loss, substantially, of Karelia, the territory over which two wars had been fought with the Soviet Union, in 1939 and 1941 – for their wartime misalignment. In practice, therefore, all roads and railways had led, and would lead, eventually, to Moscow. There would be no compunction about transplanting peoples deemed suspect – such as Chechens – to different 'secure' locations. The German advance eastwards, as in the Great War, might have been greeted, momentarily at least, as 'liberation' by some peoples, but that was now over. The Soviet Union, in short, would perpetuate a Russian hegemony. At Tehran, talking about 'the four policemen', three of them, the Soviet Union, the USA and Britain (with China at the margins), envisaged themselves in a position to shape the world. Continents were compacting together. Yet, as this chapter suggests, these 'four policemen' by no means straightforwardly expressed 'continental' perspectives.

3
Outcomes and Anticipations

Europe: beyond recovery?

Coming out of war, the future of Europe was obscure. There was no one to 'speak for Europe' or who could put forward a 'continental perspective'. The British and the Russians might both, perhaps, be judged to be Europeans, but they were rather peculiar ones. Europe was not going to 'arise' in any spontaneous sense. It was going to be 'liberated' from both west and east. Military reality in the present therefore shaped the future. In October 1944, in Moscow, Churchill and Stalin openly discussed 'spheres of influence'. In Poland, Romania and Bulgaria and also Hungary, the Soviet influence was to predominate. Italy and Greece would go the other way. It looked like, and in large measure was, an 'old-fashioned' carve-up of the continent. Such arrangements were difficult to square with the language about liberty and democracy to be found in the 'Declaration on Liberated Europe' made when Roosevelt, Churchill and Stalin subsequently met at Yalta in the Crimea in February 1945. What was precisely entailed by 'predominance' was soon a matter of disagreement. Both the behaviour of the British in Greece, in backing the royal government against Communists, and of the Soviet Union in Poland, in rounding up Home Army fighters, evoked criticism from the 'other side'.

Conflicting concepts of 'democracy' were soon evident. This was no moment, however, for protracted academic disputation. There were old scores to be settled. Moving out of violent and dangerous 'resistance' into a world of parliamentary debates and resolutions was never going to be easy in any part of Europe. Since there were different views on what had caused parliamentary democracy to 'fail', different views about its re-establishment were inevitable. Some contrasted a 'failed' bourgeois democracy with the Socialist democracy that was to come. The 'percentage' agreement presupposed the continuance of separate states in Europe – with the exception of the Baltic states absorbed within the Soviet Union. 'Restoring' states, however, was complicated. The Czechoslovakia of 1938, for example, had lived through the war in two guises – as a German Protectorate of Bohemia and Moravia and a notionally independent Slovakia. It looked likely that their German populations were going to be driven out altogether. Further, re-establishing relations between Czechs and Slovaks would not be straightforward. Germans living everywhere in 'Central Europe' would be likely to have the same fate as the Germans of

Czechoslovakia. The nation-state, it was argued, was 'natural': ethnic minorities created tension and instability. Population transfer was simply happening and could not be stopped. 'Poland' was going to exist with new frontiers, gaining in the west some compensation for what it lost in the east. The pattern of Central Europe was going to be far less kaleidoscopic than it had been in 1939. There was one particular difference. Jews had suffered savagely and could no longer play the part in the life of Central Europe that they had done. Could one still speak of 'Central Europe'? Peoples and countries which had conceived themselves to be lands between East and West looked likely to be absorbed into one or the other.

After the German surrender, British influence over Europe appeared to return, but appearances might be deceptive. It was not a British field marshal but an American general, Eisenhower, who was the Supreme Allied Commander as Germany had been driven back in the West. It was one sign, among many, that the fate of Europe would not simply be decided by Europeans (supposing the British to be Europeans). It was a world issue. The 'German question' was at the heart of the matter. Publicly and privately, in the USA and Britain, many 'solutions' had been canvassed, including the possible 'pastoralization' of the country. There were those who held 'National Socialism' and those who held 'Germany' responsible for the war. The former drew attention to the plot to kill Hitler in July 1944. It had been unsuccessful but indicated the existence of 'another Germany'. The latter were not convinced. This time, a ruined Germany would have to be occupied, controlled and 'denazified', whatever that precisely meant. These were matters which the Big Three intended to keep to themselves. The questions asked by enemy governments were of course ones which the German people, in their defeat, had to ask themselves about their past. Not everything could be blamed on Hitler. It was hard to welcome defeat, but there was much in defeat to be welcomed, at least for the future if not in the present. No answer could yet be given to the place which 'Germany' might assume in the European future. The ex-Kaiser's expectations of victory in 1940 now seemed far away. The Anglo-Americans were in Berlin. The continent had not been closed off. The Netherlands, to which he had been exiled, had been liberated from German occupation.

'France' reappeared. De Gaulle entered Paris in August 1944. He might have made himself the embodiment of French resistance but he was not a well-known figure in the country itself. There were pressing questions about the basis of his own authority and about the kind of governing institutions France should have. He was determined, however, that 'Europe' should not be settled without France. A Franco-Soviet pact had been signed after de Gaulle visited Stalin in December 1944. He hoped that it would give him leverage against the 'Anglo-Americans' (and also appeal to the French Left). It was a disappointment. It was Stalin as much as Roosevelt who excluded de Gaulle from the Yalta conference. The Big Three were not persuaded that France should detach the left bank of the Rhine from the rest of Germany – a Germany that France wanted to be 'decentralized'. They were not prepared, in negotiating these matters, to treat France as an equal partner. Some, but not too many, sops would nevertheless have to be given to acknowledge its *grandeur*.

There was, however, an unresolved and uncomfortable issue for Europe. It lay in the fact that, in country after country, not insignificant elements of the population had at least acquiesced in a 'Europe under German domination'. It was hardly a 'United States of Europe' which had been entered into freely, but it did hint at how structures might be devised 'continentally', whatever ideology prevailed. Even in Britain, there was talk of 'Federal Europe', and it might not be idle. It might need an 'Other' to weld it together. The USA might be that 'Other', though, paradoxically it was the USA which was making possible any kind of Europe. It was sometimes asserted that nobody in Europe believed in the American way of life: private enterprise and that kind of thing, as the English historian A.J.P. Taylor put it at the time. The immediate priority looked to be the reconstruction of individual states on a new social base. Whatever did emerge, and however 'recovery' came, European states would probably have to think about themselves in a new way. Those with substantial extra-European possessions might only be able to cling on to them in the short term. Europe would withdraw to itself. The outcome, however, might depend upon Stalin.

The Soviet Union: turning the world around?

Defeating Germany drove the Soviet Union deep into Europe from the East even as Britain/the USA drove into it from the West. The German surrender at Stalingrad in February 1943 had been followed by 'roll-back' in a protracted series of battles. The Red Army recovered Kiev in November 1943 and Leningrad was relieved in January 1944. It entered Romania in April 1944, Warsaw in January 1945, Budapest in February, Vienna in April and Prague and Berlin in May. When the military men from East and West met the greetings they exchanged were wary ones. What would happen next? Was there to be, in effect if not in name, an enlarged Soviet Union or, to put it another way, a Russian Europe which would extend over Central/South-Eastern Europe?

The Soviet hand was a strong one. 'The Great Patriotic War' had brought great suffering and loss of life. In the end, however, it was bringing a great victory. Stalin would not let slip the opportunity to assert Soviet predominance and ensure the security of the Soviet state against any future 'Europe' to its west. It was the kind of policy which a nineteenth-century Russian diplomat would understand. It might simply be a reiteration, with new uniforms, of 'Tsarist' strategies and Pan-Slavism. The mind of Stalin was not, and is not, easy to read. While Russian patriotism had been very evident, it was a victory for 'Soviet civilization' and showed its superiority. The civilization should lead the world. It was a noble cause, not 'the expansion of Russia'. The Soviet state, on this analysis, was still, fundamentally, the agency for a world revolution. It incarnated 'Communism' as Stalin had created it. It was not a system which publicly fostered debate on 'war aims and objectives'. The way things were, populations did not stand around discussing whether the Red Army was the agency of Russian imperialism or of Soviet Communism.

This part of the world stank of death – a grim catalogue of killing grounds. Liberation, in Poland, for example, could hardly be anything other than ambiguous. The 'liberator' of 1944–45 had taken Polish territory in 1939.

Polish officers – the class enemy – taken into captivity then had been murdered in the following year in the Katyn Forest. If the Nazi–Soviet Pact had lasted much longer it has been argued that the Polish nation would not have survived in a recognizable form. The Warsaw Rising came to a heroic but abortive end in October 1944. The city was destroyed, and with it, the cadres of old Poland – the latter outcome being agreeable to Moscow. During the process of 'liberation' it was abundantly apparent that the form it would have would be shaped by those who complied with Moscow's wishes. The Red Army was not going away. The Soviet Marshal who had masterminded liberation was himself of Russian–Polish parentage. A Poland would be reborn but it would be inseparably bound to the Soviet Union.

There was, of course, a particularly troubled history of Polish–Russian/Soviet relations which lay behind these events and gave them particular emotional and cultural salience. Now, however, each country in East–Central and South-Eastern Europe had to come to terms with changing external masters. Individual states would remain, but were they vassals, satellites or even partners of the Soviet Union? The power vacuum and economic chaos often to be encountered provided an ample opportunity for eager, confident and well-organized indigenous Communists to accumulate power. Hungarian Communists had a rallying anthem – 'We shall have turned the world around by tomorrow' . That was an attractive prospect. Communists in Italy and France sang similarly. Stalin, however, did not urge revolution on them. They should follow the parliamentary path to power. There was, therefore, to a degree, a pan-European 'working class' – very variegated in practice – which wanted this turnaround. Where the Red Army was present, that pointed in the direction of a particular kind of economic planning and control, the establishment of Marxism–Leninism as the ruling ideology, a total change in the political elite and the eradication of political pluralism.

The Soviet 'world' presented Stalin's Communism as the template with universal application. That turned the spotlight back on Stalin, a man at once awful and awesome. No amount of expressed inter-Allied rhetoric on the subject of 'free elections' could really hide the fact that the Soviet Union, viewed from London or Washington, was a baffling phenomenon. It had a continuing attraction for those devoted to its supposed egalitarianism. Against the stories of the pillage, rape and plunder which accompanied the advance of the Red Army went admiration for the wartime heroism of the Russian people. So long as Stalin lived, he would dominate his empire to a degree no transient elected Western politician could. That was a fact. The Anglo-American world had defeated 'fascism'. Yet, some scholars argued, for all their apparent mutual antagonism, Fascists and Communists shared a fundamentally similar 'totalitarian' mindset. For those who thought that there was such a similarity, 'Victory in Europe' settled little.

East Asia: resuming the old order?

The Anglo-American agreement on a 'Europe-first' strategy had relegated the Pacific War to the background. Of the 1,887 British official films made during the Second World War, only 14 dealt with the Pacific War. The Soviet Union had not been engaged in hostilities with Japan. With the defeat of Germany, however, that of Japan moved into its final phase. Ever since the Battle of Midway in June 1942, maritime supremacy rested with the Americans. The weight of American war production began to tell. Even so, as was shown in the battles to capture Iwo Jima (February–March 1945) and Okinawa (April–June 1945), the resistance of Japanese garrisons was fierce. The Americans had driven north from Australia and westwards across the Pacific. Australia, its then Prime Minister, Curtin, had famously declared in 1941, looked to the USA. It had been to Australia that General MacArthur had come, in the month after the fall of Singapore to the Japanese, to begin preparations for the eventual counter-offensive against Japan. Australia was therefore making its entry into Asia in the wake of the United States. The British Fourteenth Army, however, played its part in reconquering Burma. Australian and New Zealand forces were active in the Pacific theatre. Stalin had agreed at the second wartime summit meeting with Roosevelt and Churchill held at Yalta in the Crimea in February 1945 that the Soviet Union would join within three months of the defeat of Germany. The Red Army swept into Manchuria and advanced into Korea. Soviet participation was important to the other Allies since it would mean that the Soviet Union would not separately support Japanese conditions for an armistice. The corollary of intervention was of course Soviet participation in the peace settlement with Japan. Stalin would want to recover what a defeated Russia had lost to Japan in 1905. At Potsdam on 26 July the Allies defined what they meant by Japan's unconditional surrender. The country would be stripped of its empire and trans-formed into a peaceful nation. The future status of the emperor was left unclear. If the Japanese government did not accept this basis it was threatened with utter destruction. On 6 August 1945, the first atomic bomb was dropped on the Japanese city of Hiroshima, followed, three days later, by one on Nagasaki. On 2 September, on board the US *Missouri* in Tokyo Bay, Japan formally capitu-lated to the American commander, General Douglas MacArthur. Notwithstanding the contribution of others, the defeat of Japan was an American affair. The USA had become, by virtue of its impending occupation, a kind of East Asian power. But what might the new 'East Asia' be?

At first sight, it might not be very different. The British, French and Dutch were all determined to resume as colonial powers: 'Europe' was not withdraw-ing from South-East Asia, at least not immediately. Yet much had changed in the interval and could not be erased from memory. The brief period of Japanese control saw an independence which was spurious in its scope but potent in its appeal. Ba Maw and Aung San had declared Burmese independ-ence in August 1943. Aung San commanded a Japanese-trained and equipped Burmese National Army. In April 1945 it defected to the British. Early in 1943, leading Filipino political figures, summoned to Tokyo, were told that independence would be granted. Later, in September 1944, though apprehen-sive about the future consequences, they declared war on the USA. Filipinos had been told by their occupiers to assert themselves as an oriental people. Whether the returning Americans would forgive these collaborators remained to be seen. Achmad Sukarno (b.1901), a founder of the Indonesian National

Party in the then Dutch East Indies in 1927, left it until 17 August 1945 formally to declare 'Indonesia' independent. He did so, allegedly, with a pistol pointing at his head. The circumstances were revealing. Ten days earlier, he had accepted the chairmanship of a Japanese-approved committee to prepare for Indonesian independence. Those with their fingers on the trigger, however, did not believe independence could be 'granted' by anybody. It had to be seized. Elsewhere, the Vietnamese revolutionary Ho Chi Minh (b.1890) entered Hanoi and declared his country an independent republic. Neither the Dutch nor the French concurred. So these declarations might merely be empty gestures, only made possible by Japanese conquests. Sukarno had even been decorated by Emperor Hirohito in Tokyo in November 1943. Ho Chi Minh – busily organizing 'Viet Minh' guerrillas against Japan – received no such imperial award. It could be assumed that 'Korea' would regain the independence from Japan which it had lost in 1910 but how it would do so was obscure.

Looking further ahead, once independence had been achieved, in whatever precise circumstances, East Asian leaders, often self-appointed as such, would have to position themselves in the world. Their education and their travels, together, had often given them a blend of cultural influences and personal alignments. They were all fluent in the European languages of their colonizers, as well as in their own. Ba Maw of Burma, for example, from a scholarly family, had written a Ph.D. in France on Burmese Buddhism. Entering politics, he had become prominent in the Legislative Assembly which the British had latterly allowed in Burma. Ho Chi Minh had been away from Vietnam for many years. He spent time in England and France, the Soviet Union and China. In France not only had he been a founder member of the French Communist Party but, at one point, had boldly protested against the corruption of the French language by the importation of English words. Sukarno claimed to be at least comfortable in the Dutch, German, English, French, Arabic and Japanese languages, though his claims probably fell short of reality. Whether members of Communist parties or not, such men stressed that 'social justice' and 'nationalism' belonged together. Sukarno set forth 'Five Principles' of unexceptionable quality: nationalism, internationalism, democracy, social justice and belief in God. The vocabulary of the West, whether of Washington or Moscow, was now being uttered in very different cultural and religious contexts, Buddhist, Christian and Muslim, where nation-states, Western-style, might be precarious. Sukarno wanted to create an East Asian world that would, above all else, be as 'modern' as he thought himself to be.

The other side of this Japanese patronage of 'independence' was exploitation. No amount of rhetoric about 'partnership' could disguise the extent to which it had to fit Japanese requirements. If Japan had really succeeded in sealing off an Asian world, a more equal relationship between occupier and occupied might conceivably later have emerged. The reality was that there were Asian peoples whose hostility towards Japan was scarcely less than that evident, amongst sufferers, in Britain and the USA. There was the uncomfortable paradox – as with Germany in Europe – that Asia's most 'modern' country had also been its most aggressive and 'barbaric'. Post-war, there was probably 'another

Germany' which would re-emerge, but was there 'another Japan'? Ian Nish, a leading British scholar, likens Japanese government in the 1930s to a three-legged race involving civilians, army and navy, all pulling in the same general direction but staggering awkwardly as they argued over whether Japan was strong enough to go it alone or whether it needed an ally if it was to make its mark in the world. All, however, had ended in disaster. It was likely, post-war, that some Japanese would say that European or American criticism of Japanese expansion was hypocritical. But that was just a debating point. The deeper question was whether the elements so intrinsic to Japanese self-conception could be unpicked and repackaged to present a 'modern' Japanese identity acceptable to its neighbours and the wider world. The status of the emperor – which had so complicated the issue of possible Japanese surrender – was the key point. Neither Americans nor Europeans could suppose that an emperor was divine. But Japan needed an emperor if it was to remain 'Japan'. To allow the existing but now de-divinized emperor to remain was therefore an acceptable compromise, even though it complicated the possible prosecution of war criminals. The Americans – and also for some time a 'British Commonwealth' military presence, including an Indian contingent – found themselves entering difficult cultural terrain (as of course did the Japanese).

Japan, in theory, at the end of the war, was handing China back to the Nationalist government. China was surely now poised, as a 'Policeman', to become the 'voice of Asia' in the new world order. No other country could match it as things stood. The fate of 'British India' was still unclear. It was not only China 'proper' which gave it this scope but also the influential communities of 'overseas Chinese'. The reality, however, at the war's close, was a country which looked likely to resume a civil war, with the future settled on the battlefield, rather than perform as a global Great Power. On paper, both in terms of manpower and supplies, it looked as if Chiang Kai-shek's Nationalists were in the stronger position. There many ways of looking at what was at issue. Was it not arrogance to suppose that the USA could 'direct' China's future? The public reputation of Chiang in the USA remained high. It was the smiling pictures of Chiang, his wife and Joseph Stillwell which lingered. Chiang evidently did not understand by 'democracy' what Truman thought he understood by it, but why should Americans have a monopoly? China was China.

So it was also for the farmer's son from Hunan, Mao Zedong. As a young student, it is said that he had read, in translation, a cocktail from Europe: Montesquieu, Carlyle, Mill and Ibsen. He had been introduced to Marxism during his time in Shanghai and Beijing in 1918–20 and joined the Communist Party. A quarter of a century of precarious activity had followed. That China needed revolution was obvious, but would it be carried out by the urban proletariat or the peasantry? There were ideological and real battles to fight. Unlike some of his colleagues, Mao did not eagerly trek to Moscow to imbue and then transmit the orthodoxy of the Comintern. Mao evidently did not understand by Communism what Russians understood by it. From the outset, therefore, whether it was the Soviet or the American system that triumphed, China, eclectically, would go its own way.

The USA: making 'one world'?

As the war drew to a close, the USA, with its Canadian neighbour alongside, had played a decisive part in determining its global outcome. Yet the North American experience of the war could not be the same as the European or East Asian. The wars had taken place 'over there'. No American city was in ruins (though there had been the experience of Pearl Harbor). The loss of life suffered by the USA (260,000) was lower than that of any other belligerent country (and, unlike other countries, it suffered virtually no civilian deaths). Worldwide, approximately 50 million deaths had occurred. The continental distribution of those deaths was a reminder that 'the world' had in reality suffered to different degrees, in different ways and for different durations. 'Europe', the Soviet Union and 'East Asia', not surprisingly, recorded the largest number of deaths. In Europe, German deaths (5.25 million) far exceeded those of Britain (386,000), France (563,000) and Italy (330,000). Polish deaths (if the USSR-occupied regions are included) reached 6.02 million. Holocaust victims were in the region of 5.6 million. At 20.60 million, deaths in the Soviet Union exceeded the rest of 'Europe' put together. In East Asia, Japanese deaths were 1.80 million, Chinese 4.30 million and the Philippines 1 million. In such a context, the American experience of 'world war' and what war brought with it was modest. One fact, however, ensured that the USA was fully involved in its destructive acts. The bombardment of cities on the European continent, climaxing over Dresden in February 1945 – with 34,000 deaths – had been trumped by the atomic bombs dropped on Nagasaki and Hiroshima. Even before the dropping of the atomic bombs, states had used 'conventional' bombing with scant or no regard for the distinction between 'civilian' and 'military' casualties. Deaths from the 'conventional' bombing of Tokyo in March 1945 were even greater. The implications of the atomic bombs might not have immediately sunk in but the reality was that, in any future war, whole populations (and countries) could be wiped out.

The atomic bombs had been American bombs. As things stood, of course, only the USA had this weapon of mass destruction. It was a unique badge of its world status. How, or indeed if, such weapons could be 'cashed', in terms of international relations, was not clear, but the world was entering a new era. Not all states were likely to accept the USA as 'world trustee'. No state, however, could perhaps be deemed a 'Great Power' without such weapons. Were they to be the exclusive preserve of the 'Four Policemen' (supposing they all wished to, and could, develop them)? But it might not be possible to sustain a simple distinction between 'atomic powers' and 'the rest of the world'. Many states, in time, might make an atomic bomb. The scientists who had worked on the project in the United States were not all Americans. Nuclear physics was scarcely an unknown field in either Germany or Japan, and a different set of circumstances might have produced such bombs in those countries. Whether proliferation, were it to occur, would make war between states less likely could only be speculated upon. If it did occur, it could lead to death and destruction on a scale without parallel in human history.

The outcome of the war, therefore, left the USA both trapped and attracted by the possibilities before it. At the end of the first 'world' war, US forces had just packed up and come home. The USA had not taken part in the League of Nations. In 1919, it seemed as though the world, and Europe in particular, would have to sort itself out. Would history repeat itself? A new president was in office. Harry S. Truman (b.1884) took over on the death of Roosevelt in April 1945. He had himself served in France as an artillery captain during the previous war, but that had not produced an appetite for foreign travel. Like most Americans, he had stayed at home. Were not 'the Americas' world enough for Washington? Could or should the Western hemisphere maintain itself as a secure world apart?

The partnership with neighbouring Canada had been largely straightforward and intimate. In 1945 a Canadian historian, J.B. Brebner, published an influential book which described the two countries as Siamese twins: they could not separate and live. Yet, in speaking of 'the North Atlantic triangle' the author also highlighted how Canada related itself both to Washington and London. In certain circumstances, it could act as a 'go-between'. Canada was one with the USA in sending its forces out into 'the world' to fight. However, it cherished its position within the British Empire—Commonwealth, one reciprocated in London. Canada was in Churchill's eyes, 'the Great Dominion'. Its Prime Minister, Mackenzie King, attending in London in 1944 the first gathering of Dominion prime ministers for five years, spoke strongly to the British Houses of Parliament about 'the spirit of freedom'. So long as all its members shared it, there was no need ever to fear for the strength or unity of the Commonwealth. Even so, every Canadian decision about the war had been made by the Canadian government. Canada did have ties that bound, though these were 'spiritual' ones and not to be confused with any reactionary notion of imperial centralization. Nor were the ties only anglophone. That found another expression. De Gaulle came to speak to a large crowd on Parliament Hill, Ottawa. French Canadian and French soldiers were now fighting side by side once more. Such links did not suggest imminent hemispheric withdrawal on the part of the Canadian government.

Latin America was a different matter. Its states had had no desire to be drawn into the war or take a leading role in shaping the peace. Yet their detachment had not been complete. The British–German naval 'Battle of the Atlantic' raised issues of port access – local legislation tilted in favour of Britain. Yet some states – notably Argentina, Brazil and Uruguay – had substantial numbers of first-generation immigrants from Germany and Italy, some of whom were attracted by Nazi propaganda. After 1940, the uncertain position of the French and Dutch possessions in the Caribbean and north eastern South America raised at least the possibility of a German presence. These factors contributed to an acceptance by most South American governments of an American lead in the coordination of defence. That is not to say, however, that agreements to provide the USA with bases were easily negotiated. US military and naval missions did go south, however, to assist with defence preparations. South American officers received training in the USA or the Panama Canal Zone. At the conference of foreign ministers in Rio de Janeiro in January 1942 only Argentina and Chile held out against severing diplomatic relations with the Axis powers. An Inter-American Defense Board was established in the same year. Such nomenclature, however, did not disguise the fact that it was the strategic requirements of Washington which held sway. Bilateral relations with political and military elites in particular countries were more significant than the formal intergovernmental consultation mechanisms. By the end of the war, some 100,000 US troops were located in what were deemed strategically to be the most significant states in South America.

As it drew to a close, therefore, 'the Americas' as a whole viewed the war at a remove. That hemispheric reality, however, did not in itself entail a common perspective on the external world. North America stood in a different place. Internal hemispheric questions, for the USA, would still require exceptional attention as a sphere set apart, but the USA could neither orchestrate a common sound from 'the Americas' nor restrict itself to that sphere. In the short term, at least, there was no way in which the USA could 'come home' in 1945. No country was better placed, as the war ended, to make the world a better place. It was time to think of 'one world'.

Such optimism had found expression in the book published in March 1943 under the title *One World* by Wendell Willkie, the defeated Republican candidate in the 1940 US presidential election. Its publishing success in the English-speaking world was enormous, striking a chord with millions of readers, and had echoes beyond. In late August 1942, with Roosevelt's blessing, Willkie had taken off from New York on a 'world tour'. Returning home nearly two months later, he had become convinced that the world had become small and completely interdependent. He had talked to hundreds of people, including 'many of the world's leaders', in more than a dozen nations. Many matters, in the middle of the war, were still obscure, but now, he thought, was the time to plan for peace 'on a world basis'. Peering down from his four-engined bomber, converted for transport services, he had a new sense that continents and oceans were only parts of a whole. Instancing England and America; Russia and China; Egypt, Syria and Turkey; Iraq and Iran, he stressed too that countries were only 'parts'. There could be no peace *anywhere* in the world unless its foundations were secure *everywhere*.

'Making one world' was a tall order. Willkie travelled 31,000 miles, but there were many parts of the world he did not visit. There were many 'leaders' he did not meet. There were many millions whose hopes and fears he could not know. He was excited by his air travel and the vision it gave him. In 1914–18, not a single plane had flown across the Atlantic. Now that ocean was a mere ribbon. Europe and Asia (there was no allusion to Africa) were at the very doorstep of America (and vice versa). Now was the time to create a world in which 'there shall be an equality of opportunity for every race and every nation'. He sensed a global mood – and in turn contributed to spreading it. Men and women everywhere, he wrote, were 'on the march', physically, intellectually and spiritually. The 'Western world' and its presumed supremacy were now 'on trial'. Men and women in Russia, China and the Middle East knew that for the first time many of the decisions about the future of the world would lie in their hands. A great process, as he put it, had begun.

Not every person Willkie met on his travels shared this vision. When he and de Gaulle met in a Beirut room stacked with busts, pictures and statues of

Napoleon, de Gaulle complained that some people did not have France's glorious history in mind. De Gaulle had it very much in mind, and would not let Americans forget. When he dined in Egypt with the British naval commander in the Eastern Mediterranean, Willkie found that the officers round the table had no idea that the world was changing. They had read about an 'Atlantic Charter' that talked of 'self-determination' signed by the American President and British Prime Minister in November 1941, but did not suppose that it had any relevance for them.

'Uncle Joe' had laughed and laughed when Wendell Willkie, stopping off in Russia, told him that if the Soviet leader continued to educate his people in their splendid Soviet schools Stalin would educate himself out of a job. Stalin put forward his own educated world-view. He called for the abolition of racial exclusiveness, the equality of nations and their territorial integrity, the liberation of enslaved nations and the restoration of their sovereign rights, and the right of every nation to arrange its affairs as it wished. He urged economic aid to suffering nations to improve their material welfare. He looked to the restoration of democratic liberties and the destruction of the Hitlerite regime. It was an impressive list. Willkie recognized that it might not be believed. Stalin was a hard man, perhaps even a cruel one, but he was very able. The American could understand why many among the democracies feared and mistrusted Soviet Russia, but such fear, Willkie now thought, showed weakness and was wrong. Russia, he wrote, was a dynamic country, a vital new society. It constituted a force that could not be bypassed in any future world.

Willkie's excursions outside Moscow brought home to him just how diverse this 'Union' was and how huge its land mass. He suspected that there were places – instancing Sinkiang (Xinjiang) – where 'Russia' and China might in future clash (though could not know that it would be under a Chinese Communist government that, decades later, this clash would indeed occur). Stalin himself had reminded Willkie that this particular 'Russian' had begun life as a Georgian peasant. A Georgian republic, under differing political auspices, latterly Menshevik, had emerged in the wake of the collapse of the Russian Empire. In 1921 the Mensheviks were driven out of Tbilisi, the capital, and the Soviet Socialist Republic of Georgia was announced. The most perfect socialism in Europe, in the eyes of a visiting British delegation at the time, had come to an abrupt end. That, however, was not something now to dwell on. On his return home, Willkie expressed the fervent hope that Russia and America, 'perhaps the two most powerful countries in the world', would work together. It showed lack of faith to suppose that, in any possible contact between Communism and democracy, it was democracy that would go under.

When he was in China, contemplating Asia, Willkie thought a Japanese victory would result in an empire occupying one-third of the earth and ruling half of its total population. The prospect of the possible triumph of their opponents welded together, at least for the duration, states not otherwise identifiable as 'natural' bedfellows. They would all have a common interest in rooting out the ideologies and individuals, in Germany and Japan, responsible for war. What that would involve was another matter. He told his readers that they must not expect Chinese ideals of personal liberty and democratic government to be exactly the same as theirs. Americans ought to grasp that in Chinese eyes some American customs appeared ridiculous and even distasteful. If his fellow-countrymen were wise they would direct forces in the East toward a world co-operative effort for peace and economic security. If these forces were flouted or ignored they would continue to disturb the world.

In China Willkie had penetrated to parts he and his fellow-citizens had never heard of. He flew into Xinjiang from Tashkent 'in a single day'. He found the scene extraordinary. Even in 'remote' regions, however, it was possible to meet Chinese men who had graduated from the Columbia School of Journalism in New York. Any man who had run for president was used to crowds, but the crowds that greeted him in Chongqing were exceptional. Most of them, he suspected, did not know who he was. Surely, Willkie wrote, Americans could see the handwriting on the wall. The opening up of the new China, in world historical terms, would be like the opening up of the American West. The difference was that the former was starting not with locomotives but with 300-mile-an-hour aeroplanes.

All this, one might say, was the empty humanitarian optimism of a failed US presidential candidate. What did Willkie, now the president of a New York utility company, really know about the world? Dying in 1944, he did not live to experience the hard gap between his vision and reality. That vision was necessarily an American one. Politicians and commentators from other countries, as they lumbered their way across a world still at war, had emerged with different perspectives. Their uncomfortable machines conveyed contrasting messages and meanings. The world's travellers saw it from the same sky, but interpreted it differently. Visions of 'world loyalty', much rehearsed in certain quarters, were being busily refurbished for the present. The path to 'One World', however, was not easily traced.

Some thought a world based on a 'balance of power' between Britain, America and the Soviet Union (whatever might happen to China) would be a disaster worse than anything which had yet happened to humanity. The British High Commissioner in Canada, Malcolm MacDonald, said as much to a Canadian audience in 1944. His was not a solitary voice. The League of Nations, the first attempt at a 'world body', had been broken-backed, partly, it was said, because it lacked coercive capacity. Therefore, a new world organization would have to involve all states in discussing international questions. Such a body could in turn make representations to an executive body composed of the four 'policemen' and probably six other countries selected to give a global reach. It would, however, be the Big Four who would have the power to take effective action. Here, perhaps, was a model which rehearsed the notion of a 'world' which had a collective interest in security. It was an understandable and agreeably simple conception. The notion of a 'war to end war', in the light of all that had happened since 1918, was a dubious one to revive but, surely, this time, it would be true?

Yet, even as a 'grand design' evolved, the war was throwing up questions about the likely behaviour and aspirations of 'the Four' themselves, and, beyond them, what 'the world' as a whole would think. A United Nations Organization, if that was what it was to be called, was predicated upon an illusory global propensity to 'unite'. For the moment, however, it did appear that 'the Four' did 'represent', broadly, if somewhat lopsidedly, and without 'consultation', the continents that then 'mattered', namely the Americas, Europe and Asia. 'One World' had emerged as aspiration, but there were worlds within worlds. Whether the continental cross-currents identified in this part of the book would produce a world significantly different from that which existed either in 1937 or 1939 had now to be put to the test in the 'post-war' decade. Part Two will reveal the answer.

Part 1 further reading

Bosworth, R.J.B., *Explaining Auschwitz and Hiroshima: History Writing and the Second World War, 1945–1990* (Routledge, London, 1993).

Brivati, Brian and Jones, Harriet, eds., *What Difference did the War Make?* (Leicester University Press, Leicester, 1999).

Davies, Norman, *No Simple Victory: World War II in Europe, 1939–1945* (Viking, London, 2007).

Dear, I.C.B. and Foot, M.R.D., eds., *The Oxford Companion to the Second World War* (Oxford, Oxford University Press, 1999).

Dower, John, *Japan in War and Peace* (HarperCollins, London, 1993).

Grigg, John, *1943: The Victory That Never Was* (Eyre Methuen, London, 1980).

Heuser, Beatrice, *The Bomb: Nuclear Weapons in their Historical, Strategic and Ethical Context* (Pearson Education, London, 2000).

Parker, R.A.C., *The Second World War: A Short History* (Oxford University Press, Oxford, 2001).

Sainsbury, Keith, *The Turning Point: Roosevelt, Stalin, Churchill, Chiang Kai-shek, 1943: The Moscow, Cairo and Teheran Conferences* (Oxford University Press, Oxford, 1985).

Weinberg, Gerhard L., *A World at Arms: A Global History of World War II* (Cambridge University Press, Cambridge, 1994).

Willkie, Wendell, *One World* (Cassell, London, 1943).

Part 2
1945–1955:
MAKING A COLD PEACE

It seems natural to refer to the ten years after 1945 as 'the post-war decade'. The world war still lived on in the minds and memories of millions. Demobilizing, literally and metaphorically, took time. It was one thing, however, to receive surrenders and cease fighting, but another to make peace. The victors, this time, had been determined to demonstrate their victory beyond doubt. They were in occupation. There was not even the semblance of a negotiated settlement. There could be no room among the defeated for allegations that negotiators had signed away what had still been a strong position. In this respect, 'unconditional surrender', in principle at least, brought a superficial clarity to 'post-war'. The victors would impose their peace, and be on the spot in doing so. This new world would not emerge after protracted diplomatic haggling between victor and defeated. It would reflect the will of 'the United Nations'. There was a conscious effort to avoid the disaster, as it was portrayed, of peacemaking in 1919.

Yet 'unconditional surrender' by no means solved everything. Indeed, as will be seen, it did not quite mean the same thing in all circumstances. Occupiers soon found, in practice, that they could not run their territories without some re-entry into general civil life on the part of defeated populations. But that, in turn, raised awkward questions about the recent past and the degree of complicity of such populations in the deeds of the defeated regimes. If there was no such re-entry, however, there was the prospect of the heavy administrative costs of indefinite direct occupation. Sooner or later, under whatever constraints, states would resume their 'normal' sovereignty and alien occupiers withdraw, at least substantially if not completely. Only then could the war be said to have been fully brought to an end and a new set of relationships emerge. The timing of this transition, in Germany, Japan and elsewhere, is a common aspect of this decade. Peacemaking, in this respect, stands as shorthand for a host of slow adjustments by which enmity was transmuted into an adequate 'working relationship', if not friendship. Along the way there was bitterness, recrimination and resentment. Such emotions did not necessarily vanish simply because time passed. The desire for revenge and the demand for reparation did not disappear. Old scores had to be settled. On the other hand, a lesson from 1919 had appar-

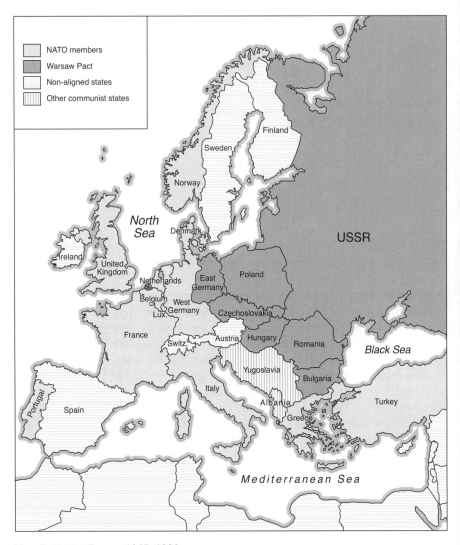

Map 2 Aligning Europe, 1945–1990

ently to be learnt if there was to be an enduring peace: harsh pursuit of reparations would be counterproductive and breed an endless cycle of violence. Or so it was said. How all this worked out in practice varied from country to country, not only as between victors and defeated but within countries, such as France and Italy, which were not unambiguously one or the other.

Examining 'making peace', however, is not simply a matter of looking at how the victors imposed a world on the defeated. It is to realize that a straightforward polarity between the two slipped away swiftly. The previous part of the book highlighted a war in which two wars conjoined and unexpected alliances crystallized, spurred into existence by the perception of a common enemy.

Given these facts, one interpretation sees nothing surprising in the pattern of the post-war decade. There never had been common interests, either national or ideological, amongst the victors and 'settling' Europe and 'settling' East Asia involved very different considerations. On this reading, the best that could be hoped for was the creation of a 'cold peace'. That is to say that the rivalries, animosities and suspicions, well founded – or not, in particular instances – could be contained for an indefinite duration and, perhaps, eventually issue in a harmonious world. Another reading, however, works in the opposite direction. While not discounting ideological differences between the victors, it sees at least the elements of a transcending desire to create a world without major war. The UN was a symbol of this desire. Yet, manifestly, within a few years, the international atmosphere was very different. It was not so much a cold peace that was being forged as a cold war that was being waged. So, much effort was devoted at the time, as ever since, to explaining the deterioration in terms of the aggressive behaviour and imperialist ambitions of either the USA or the Soviet Union, with a little help from their friends.

The confrontation was indeed real and enduring. It came, in fluctuating intensity, to dominate the decade. The rhetoric of 'one world' faded and commentators again saw the world in terms of blocs, spheres of influence and zones of occupation. It seemed a far cry from wartime talk of great policemen harmoniously patrolling the world. The story of international relations, some concluded, after all, is one of incessant conflict, only ever partially mitigated. So 'realists' sometimes said, puncturing that hope for a fresh start and enduring reconciliation that existed alongside the lasting hostilities engendered by the horrors of war. It was only with luck, on this reading, that another worldwide war was avoided.

It was not merely, however, that the Big Three were soon at loggerheads. China's unconvincing elevation to make a Big Four came to an end almost as soon as it had been contrived. The country was engulfed in the civil war which resulted in the Communist victory in 1949. That outcome could be variously interpreted as another leap forward for 'world Communism' or as an essentially continental development, another manifestation of a changing Asia. The Asia of 1943 was very different a decade later: India, Pakistan and Indonesia newly appeared on the map as independent countries. How Asian states related to each other had a profound bearing on what Asia might signify in the world.

The following three chapters, therefore, explore further, in different locations, these legacies and aspirations of 1937–45. Global implications and ramifications emerge from the particular. It was a decade in which, taken as a whole, the world neither succumbed to war nor found an agreed peace: cold comfort at best.

4
European Alternatives

A burnt-out case?

It was in Europe that the apparent division of a world growing out of war was most obviously evident. The speculation about the continent's capacity to recover, evident in the latter part of the war, continued. Its condition seemed parlous and its erstwhile global eminence precarious at best. No state in 1945 could 'speak for Europe' at the new UN. Some supposed that a continent – perhaps it was a civilization – had finally destroyed itself. The second struggle for mastery in Europe had perhaps fatally undermined the supremacy, indirectly or directly, which the continent collectively had exercised in and over other continents. The Europe of 1945 seemed to the British Prime Minister, Winston Churchill, to be 'a rubble heap, a charnel house, a breeding ground of pestilence and hate'. In wartime New York the exiled French Thomist philosopher Jacques Maritain had counselled against slick solutions. The world was too sick for its sickness to be easily cured. He wrote against the 'anarchic individualism' which he believed to have ruined the vital principle of democracy. The democracies had not only to triumph over Hitler but also over their own self-contradictions in the social and spiritual realms. It was a stance which he and others pursued in France, the Low Countries and in circles beyond the confines of 'Catholic Europe'. Such anxieties seemed well founded. 'Western democracy' needed safeguarding.

At this juncture, however, what united Europeans was not a civilization but their common experience of food, fuel and housing shortages. Economies were wrecked. Cities – Leningrad, Warsaw, Hamburg, Dresden and many others – were shattered remnants of their former selves. Material deprivation was bad enough, but the European spiritual crisis was even more grave. In time, though probably a long time, economies would recover, food would be grown or imported, and homes rebuilt. What was less certain was that 'European civilization' could be rebuilt. European philosophers, functioning within their national traditions, fell to discussing 'the European Spirit' and pondered its possible resuscitation. Some sought refuge in a notion of 'absurdity'. These were weighty reflections, if of limited currency beyond their own circles. Historians from victorious Western Europe, guided by the British scholar Sir Ernest Barker, settled down to considering the totality of the European past. Since they naturally took their time, neither policymakers nor publics could await such summations. Interpretation in this work, and in others produced elsewhere in similar vein, naturally differed, but Europe's singular combination of bestiality and brilliance had to be wrestled with.

It was all very well, in academic detachment, to ponder over 'Europe' in this way. In a general sense, a malaise might indeed be afflicting the continent as a whole, but responsibility for what had happened before 1945 could be firmly identified. The Allies in 1943 had declared that the perpetrators of war crimes would be tried and punished. From the autumn of 1945 onwards, before Russian, American, British and French judges, 'major war criminals' were found guilty and sentenced to be hanged or given varying terms of imprisonment. This International Military Tribunal held at Nuremberg was naturally open to the charge that it constituted 'victors' justice'. A charge of conspiracy to commit crimes against peace might be thought applicable also to the Soviet Union's invasion of Poland in 1939. But, however much blind eyes were turned, the tribunal was asserting that, in principle, 'war crimes' could be disinterestedly assessed The US prosecutor grandiloquently called the submission of their captives by the victors to 'the judgement of the law' one of the most significant tributes that Power had ever paid to Reason.

Within individual states, the identification and punishment of individuals, with or without due judicial process, was a familiar post-war process. The separation of sheep from goats was more easily accomplished in some countries than others. Wartime conduct under occupation could always be differently presented. The behaviour of King Leopold III of the Belgians, much debated, ran on for years before his eventual abdication. Quisling, the collaborator, was executed in Norway. The Romanian wartime dictator, Antonescu, was sentenced to death. So was Mihailović in Yugoslavia. To use the French term, this was *l'épuration* (cleansing) in full swing. Even the British managed to find two collaborators to hang.

This was justice of a rough kind. At its basis, generally, lay the assumption that the guilty persons had betrayed their nations. Indeed, local courts in Czechoslovakia levied charges against more than a hundred thousand people for offences against 'national honour'. For their part, the carriers of 'national honour' did so confidently, particularly in countries like Czechoslovakia and Yugoslavia where 'the nation' was contested and 'brotherly coexistence' not always conspicuous. In France, control of the national honour was taken by de Gaulle. In great speeches, he praised the resistance, allegedly, of the entire nation. Whatever appearance might suggest, de Gaulle insisted that the country's essential *grandeur* was undiminished. Monuments commemorating local Resistance martyrs appeared. They would help banish more complex memories. The 'Vichy' regime could not be accommodated in the national renewal but neither could it altogether be obliterated. A French army had to be patched up after its splintered existence. Pétain, sentenced to death, was in fact allowed to die in prison (in 1951). The French historian, Fernand Braudel (b.1902), later much admired, saw France in a *longue durée* and knew in his wartime imprisonment in Lübeck, North Germany, that it would endure eternally. Here spoke a Frenchman born in Lorraine when it had been incorporated into the German Empire.

'Germany', Britain and France: creating (Western) European unity?

How could Europe be restored, if indeed the notion of 'restoration' was the right one? To begin with, it seemed that the British role would be pivotal. Churchill, speechmaking in various European cities after the war, urged a united Europe on his audiences, though without giving much detail of how this was to be achieved. Franco-German reconciliation, he said, was key. The difficulty was the past and, even more, the fact that a single 'Germany' did not then exist, and a decade later seemed might never again exist. There were many questions about Germany. The European 'search for a usable past' was naturally most complex, contentious and protracted when it came to the German past. Much of the paper ration had been used up in wartime Britain in expounding 'the problem of Germany'. Historians remained busy across the world. In the Library of Congress in Washington, a few weeks after the German capitulation, the German novelist Thomas Mann spoke in English on 'Germany and the Germans'. He highlighted the extent to which recent German history had been influenced by the Middle Ages – the Reich myth. Hitler's rule has been seen by the German historian Heinrich Winkler as the pinnacle of Germany's rebellion against the political ideas of 'the West'. The question, post-war, was where Germany 'belonged' – not that there was one 'Germany' to answer it. Its rein-vention would take place under the control of its victors, the four occupying powers with their respective zones of occupation (which included Berlin). Britain, France and the USA constituted 'the West' in Germany and the Soviet Union 'the East'. The fate of the capital, a ruined relic of its former self, could not be settled by any one of the victors. Each occupier had a determination that Germany should never be in a position to dominate Europe again. Whether that entailed its permanent 'neutrality' was another matter. Each had a view, a differ-ent view, of what 'reparation', 're-education' and 'denazification' should entail. All Europeans had an interest in 'the German question'. This time, however, it was not theirs alone.

The Berlin 'blockade' crisis began in June 1948. The three Western zones in occupied Germany were prevented by Soviet forces from supplying West Berlin (the city was divided) by rail, road and water. Supplies could only be flown in, chiefly by the Americans and the British, thanks to the fact that air corridors had been designated at the Potsdam conference in 1945. US B-29 bombers arrived in England. They could reach Moscow. It could be speculated that they carried atomic bombs. In the event, though tension remained high for months, the Soviet Union lifted the blockade in May 1949. It had brought the Western Powers closer together. West Berliners, to their own surprise, began to feel that they too were 'Western' and find themselves accepted as such. Western diplo-mats, who had been saying that the airlift was 'untenable in the long run', need not have been so depressed.

The Berlin crisis arose out of the unresolved 'German question'. It acceler-ated a 'solution' which had in fact been developing, on the Western side, since 1947. Meetings between the Western Powers themselves, at various levels, or between the Western Powers and the Soviet Union, invariably had 'Germany' on the agenda, but no agreement on how Germany might be united had been reached. The Soviet blockade had been a response to the unification of the three Western zones and the launch of a new currency, the Deutschmark. The Western Powers announced plans to hold elections for a constituent assembly which would prepare a 'basic law' for a new German state. The decisive step had been taken. Whether this enforced 'turn to the West' would work was another matter. A westward-looking Germany found itself a western capital in modest Bonn. Berlin was not legally part of the country. Outside observers, seeing a situation in which neither of the two main Federal German parties had an over-all majority, feared instability. Relaunching 'democracy' might be a precarious business. The craving for 'strong leadership' so evident earlier in Germany (and elsewhere in Europe) might linger.

In the event, leadership came from a septuagenarian Catholic from the Rhineland, Konrad Adenauer (b.1876), leading a new party, the Christian Democrats, which sought to appeal both to Catholics and Protestants. He had only a few words of English and found the British difficult to deal with (an experience reciprocated), but with France it might be possible to 'think European'. The Federal Republic was coming to be perceived as 'West' Germany. Social Democrats hankered after a different socio-economic order and for an 'all-German' future, but there was no alternative to reluctant acceptance of division, though not too quickly. The final step in this 'innovative restoration' came with rearmament and the admission of West Germany into NATO in 1955 on a basis of equality. Its army, once formed, would be placed under an integrated NATO command. The designated number of divisions would boost the conventional force capacity of the West confronted by a numerically superior Soviet Army. Behind this decision there had been much controversy within and without Germany. A project for a 'European army' within a European Defence Community had earlier failed, after much discussion. By 1955, therefore, it could be said that the 1939–45 war had at last become 'history'. The remaining limitations on West German sovereignty were removed. Two years earlier, the acting British Foreign Secretary, Selwyn Lloyd, admitted that while Adenauer, the Americans, the French and the British all publicly supported a united Germany, on suitable terms, they really thought that a divided Germany was safer for the time being. It was just not advisable to say so openly because of the effect upon German public opinion. Lloyd also thought that the Soviet Union had reached this conclusion. There were two Germanies and they were going increasingly separate ways.

Churchill's immediate post-war speeches urging Europe to unite only spoke of the UK supporting such a course, but he did not commit himself to joining in the process. Having been defeated in the 1945 election, however, he could not deliver a 'United Europe', nor could he do so after 1951 when he returned to power. It had fallen instead to a Labour government in 1945 to construct its map of Europe (though Prime Minister Attlee talked of making a success of the UN as his first priority). Britain was a Great Power. British troops were still in Germany. The country had the prestige which accrued from 'standing alone' in 1940. The government's leading figures, however, did not approach 'Europe' as enthusiasts. Attlee, educated at a school founded by the East India Company, knew more, and at first hand, about the politics of India than he did about France. 'Dominion affairs' had been one of his wartime ministerial responsibilities. After the war, as will be seen, there were ample non-European issues for a British government to concern itself with. Bevin, the new Foreign Secretary, had first encountered the outside world when unloading ships on Bristol docks. As a trade unionist before the war, there were few years in which he did not visit conferences in Western and Central Europe. He had a substantial network of European contacts. A 'turn-up in a million' (his own self-description), his speech was blunt and direct. He well knew that there were vast post-war problems all over Europe, BrItain included. It might be that pre-war standards of living could never be regained.

It has often been asserted that in these years the UK lost that 'leadership of Europe' which was there for the taking. Much depends, however, on what at this juncture 'Europe' is taken to mean. In reality, 'Europe' was only shorthand for a complex set of orientations on the part of individual states, large and small: economic, military, political and cultural aspirations did not all point them in the same direction. There was no 'Europe' which could manoeuvre between the Soviet Union and the USA: maybe there never would be. Britain and France sometimes did attempt to flex their global muscles but found them flabby. Only if these two countries could find a common voice, never an easy task, might 'Europe' manifest itself. Their two foreign ministers, after a bracing stroll along the beach at Dunkirk in March 1947, a beach, inevitably, with 1940's evacuation in mind, which they could 'read' in different ways, moved inside to sign a treaty. The country against whose possible aggression they were preparing themselves, at least so the Treaty of Dunkirk said, was Germany. This looked like old Europe again, with its alliances and alignments. Officials reflected on where they thought their countries stood in the world. Unknown to each other, they both spoke of the USA and Russia as being 'giants'. Close neighbourly co-operation between London and Paris was essential. The two countries surely had so much in common. They were both great colonial powers. In the long run, whenever that might be, their political interests were the same. A year later, in March 1948, Britain, France and the Benelux countries signed the Treaty of Brussels, pledging themselves to mutual aid in the event of an attack on any one of them in Europe. Its signature was facilitated by the Communist takeover in Czechoslovakia in the previous month. There was little doubt that it was from the Soviet Union rather than Germany that any attack would come. It was unclear, however, whether this 'Western Union' portended a wider 'spiritual foundation of the West' (with US participation) or the nucleus of a 'Western Europe' standing between the superpowers.

Looking across the Channel, in the first decade after the war, for British governments, the American presence was a fact, a welcome fact. Yanks should not go home. War had brought exceptional intimacy and it was still cultivated. That did not mean, however, that the 'special relationship' which the British, at least, believed to exist between the two countries was free of tension. The British pressed ahead with an independent decision to develop their own atomic bomb. Australian governments obligingly made testing facilities available. Official London felt a loss of status but, for the most part, did not share the hostility to American 'meddling' in Europe to be found in France in particular. Back in 1944 de Gaulle, with scant success, had tried to revive the Franco-Soviet relationship as a means of countering the American presence. France surely would also want to possess an atomic bomb. Jean-Paul Sartre and Simone de Beauvoir, the cream of French intellectual life, did not admire what they found when they crossed the Atlantic. Somehow, Europe had to find its own voice. Officials could reflect thus in offices which were just about warm enough to work in, but it was very cold outside. Blizzards raged in 1947. It was thought to be the coldest winter on record in Britain. A fuel crisis and a weather crisis brought the country almost to a halt. The harsh environment spoke of a 'Europe' which could not survive on its own: cold winter, cold war.

Economic co-operation, from a British perspective, was important, but should be approached pragmatically, not with an identified goal of 'European integration' in mind. Even so, as Bevin warned his Cabinet colleagues, the formation of the Organization for European Economic Co-operation (OEEC) in April 1948 might have far-reaching consequences. The British would try to stop them being too far-reaching. The OEEC was in fact set up in Paris and its first Secretary-General was a Frenchman. Its most useful progeny was the European Payments Union, which facilitated intra-European payments. Planning was supposed to be 'in the collective interest'. There was no ambition to tangle with plans which had an explicitly supranational political element. In 1948 Britain would be associating with 'partners' whose political condition was judged by Bevin to be 'unstable' (not least France). Negotiators, in these years, had to tread carefully. 'National sovereignty' was a delicate area. The issue was whether 'economic co-operation' expressed a deeper political consensus amongst participating states. 'Sovereignty' might cease to be sacrosanct. This 'Europe', by no means homogeneous in its political institutions, nevertheless rested on a common understanding of 'democracy'. Political parties contended for power on a basis of free elections (whatever electoral system was deployed). Beyond that, however, difficulty arose for all potential members of a European 'Union'. Was Western European democracy 'neutral', as between the world's contending socio-economic ideologies? Could it be 'capitalist', 'socialist', or express a 'third way'?

The Soviet Union: creating a people's Europe?

This tentative 'Western' Europe had an alternative facing it. The outcome of the war left the Soviet Union in a position to create its own Europe. The wartime conferences had made the contours of the Soviet sphere broadly explicit. Agreements had purported to set out the respective percentages of interest East and West should have in a series of Eastern European countries. They had clarity, however, only on the back of an envelope. The Soviet Union would soon proceed to translate 'spheres of influence' into direct control. There might be some variation in the means adopted to this end, but no doubt about the end itself. Brute force would not be eschewed, but there were favourable factors. Representative democracy in East–Central Europe between the wars had not been a great success. It had not been lauded as the only way in which civilized people should be governed. Post-1945, therefore, there was no democratic system that had a deep purchase on the popular mind. Something new might not be bad. During the war, President Beneš of Czechoslovakia, in exile in England, having received certain assurances from Stalin, predicted the growth of a new Soviet Empire in the spirit of a new popular democracy, as he put it. It was the job of the state to create good citizens rather than the job of citizens (some of whom were undoubtedly bad) to create the state. Political parties, in such a scenario, could have a new basis. Such an outlook, in his case as in others, favoured what might be described as top-down democratic coercion. Talk of a Communist takeover was deprecated.

Communist parties in Eastern Europe were everywhere minority parties, although, as in Czechoslovakia itself, not without growth and increased confidence. They campaigned, after all, to the beat of history. Groups of intellectuals in many countries, particularly if young, were not averse to joining the vanguard. Well-nourished exiles, suitably groomed, returned from the Soviet Union to harness support, sometimes ousting or even eliminating home-grown Communists insufficiently saturated with the Soviet style. Step by step, at different paces and using different tactics and titles, the transition to a People's Democracy was engineered. People's Militias and People's Courts played their encouraging part. The pace and precise form of implementation varied between countries, but there was no doubt about the ultimate outcome. It could look as though there was some master plan, and perhaps there was. The event perceived globally as a turning point came in February 1948 with the Communist takeover of the Czechoslovak government. Beneš had in the past told Americans that his country was the godchild of the great and glorious republic of the USA. In the aftermath of the takeover, however, Czechoslovakia's self-designated status as a 'bridge' between Eastern and Western Europe was at an end. The body of Jan Masaryk, the foreign minister, son of the country's founder, was found beneath his office window. The appearance of constitutionality was put in place in Czechoslovakia, as elsewhere. General guidance and control, however, rested with the party. The organs of the state were principally concerned with practical administration and management. The bourgeoisie, where it significantly existed, was dethroned. Education was a priority, its primary purpose being to inspire the coming generation with the teachings of Marx, Engels, Lenin and Stalin. Recalcitrant cardinals of the Catholic Church were consigned to remote monasteries to repent of their perceived reactionary attitudes.

Beneš, in wartime, had also acknowledged the Soviet Union's leadership of the Slavs. Here was another historical message which still had resonance. It was one that could be rolled out to give Soviet hegemony a kind of authenticity. That races had certain characteristics was still widely believed. An English historian, Agnes Headlam-Morley, had taken the view in 1929 that in hours of national danger Slavs displayed heroic patriotism but ordinarily they were indifferent to public affairs. Such a view suggested a great solidarity amongst Slavs. The image of the Soviet Union as 'protector' of Serbs and Bulgarians lingered on from old Russia and was politically useful. Much of this, however, was myth-making and ignored real animosities. Czechs had not forgotten what Poles had done in 1938 in invading and detaching the region of Teschen from

Czechoslovakia. Poles did not forget the treatment they had received from the Soviet Union from 1939 onwards. Slavs though they might be, Polish Catholics looked west not east. In 1948, a young priest, Karol Wojtyła, returned to Poland from Rome to find the Church under systematic attack. A concerted effort was being made to undermine the influence of the Catholic hierarchy. A little later, church property, other than churches themselves and churchyards, was confiscated. There was little, it seemed, that an obscure priest could do to stem the oppression except to feed his flock. The post-war era, in theory, had no room for ethnic squabbles, but the reality was rather different. Generalizations about an 'Eastern Europe' as 'Slav' had only a limited strength.

What was true, however, was that the region was largely denuded of that German presence which has been so much a part of its history. Germans were sent 'back'. Their expulsion, coming on top of the Holocaust suffered by Jews during the war, combined, not without sad irony, to transform the ethnic and cultural life of East–Central Europe. The Soviet Union, in turn, could draw some benefit from the argument that, without its support, Poles and Czechs would find the Germans returning. A divided Germany, with the regime in East Berlin in the Communist camp, offered similar reassurance. There a Socialist Unity Party had been formed in February 1946 from the enforced fusion of Socialists and Communists. The fatal division in the German working class was being overcome. It was an era of 'anti-fascist democratic transformation'. Denazification in the Soviet zone was more comprehensive – in terms of the removal of people from offices – than in the Western zone, though there were 'specialist' exceptions. The man who pushed for the establishment of what became the German Democratic Republic in October 1949 was the SUP Secretary, Walter Ulbricht. The 'Eastern' aspect of the regime was emphasized in various ways. Russian became the compulsory first foreign language in schools. Comradely good relations were sealed by recognizing state boundaries and preventing refugees and expellees from forming interest groups. The new state laid no claim to being the successor to the former German Reich. In theory, therefore, there was an internal transformation greater than any occurring in the German Federal Republic. No state tried harder to define itself, in cultural terms, as a working- class state. It was all the more staggering, therefore, that in strikes and demonstrations in the summer of 1953, so many 'socialist heroes of work' turned against 'their' state. It was an anti-militarist state that was, however, pursuing its objectives in a highly militarist manner.

History still left 'People's Europe' with some not insignificant diversity, but the trend was firmly towards uniformity. Its countries should show ever greater Socialist solidarity. At the prompting of the Soviet delegate and meeting chairman, Zhdanov, a conference of Communist parties in February 1947 agreed that it was time to bring all comrades into line in a common cause. The Communist Information Bureau (Cominform) was set up with headquarters in Belgrade. Its purpose, however, was to do more than to take telephone calls from enquirers. The Yugoslavs, Kardelj and Djilas were given a starring role in this new body but, before a year had elapsed, Yugoslavia was expelled. Its leader, Marshal Tito, former Red Army soldier, wartime Partisan commander and now at the head of the new post-war Yugoslav Federal Republic, was attacked on the grounds of his ideological deviation. Subordination, however, did not appeal to Tito. If the Soviet Union sent forces into his country in order to bring it into line, he would fight. No such forces were sent. Tito and his regime survived. He was himself, however, no stranger to ruthlessness. Internally, his Communism did not welcome deviation. His strong line, arguably, was the only way to sustain his country's precarious unity. In other Eastern bloc countries grips were tightened. 'Titoists' were tracked down and punished. As each year passed, while Stalin was alive, it seemed that another union was hardening. Unlike in Western Europe, however, where its states stuttered towards some kind of unity without any single orchestrator, in Eastern Europe there was Stalin and the Soviet Union. That was a not inconsiderable difference.

Stalin: still policing?

Stalin bestrode the Soviet Union and his world position, after 1945, was unique. He was the only one of the wartime 'policemen' who exercised his power continuously – pre-war, wartime, post-war – until his death in 1953. Old Churchill was back in office after 1951, attempting to wield world influence and seeking to end the Cold War. There was Eisenhower, a general when they met in Moscow in August 1945, but President of the USA in 1952. Stalin then thought him a great man, not only as a soldier, but because of his human, friendly, kind and frank nature. It was still possible to think of Stalin as a great man, the saviour of his country in the late Great Patriotic War. Anyone who knew of or suspected his murderous record over the previous quarter of a century, however, might not find him so admirable. As ever, he manipulated his inner circle. Molotov remained Soviet Foreign Minister until 1949, but his melodious mandolin – his favourite instrument – then fell out of favour. Policy could not be made without reference to others, but Stalin, as all knew, maintained the upper hand. He had the power of life and death. How 'the world' looked to the Soviet Union in effect meant how it looked to Josef Stalin. There was no public debate. Aleksandr Solzhenitsyn, for one, later famous as a writer, was arrested in 1945 for making derogatory comments about Stalin. He was to spend the next eight years in a labour camp. Biographers, then and now, seeking to penetrate Stalin's 'inner man', eschew simplicity. The strands in his past – identified in Part One – still came together confusingly. One thing, however, comes through strongly. The war had been won, but at great cost. Soviet success showed the world that its system worked. The state's twin elements – carrier of the Russian past and exemplar of the world's future – continued to coexist confusingly. There was so much to be proud of. The security of the state should never again be put at risk from the West, from Germany in particular.

Stalin had raised a glass in May 1945 to the nations of the Soviet Union, but above all to the great Russian people. World war had not turned him into a cosmopolitan (a term of abuse with more than a tinge of anti-Semitism). He would not be seduced from the intoxicating liquor on which he relied by bottles of Coca-Cola despatched for him by the US President. The modern literature he read was not foreign. The intelligentsia in the Russian past, he thought, had abased itself, without justification, before foreign culture. Soviet patriotism could stand on its own feet. His own researches led him to emphasize the continuity of the Russian language. Yet his love affair with the language he had made his own had its limits. Apparently, though not in a way that was clearly explained, in the world socialism of the future, national languages would disappear. A global language would evolve. The Orthodox Church, as a Russian institution, had received a recent mild blessing, but its leaders were soon made aware that this was only a temporary stay of execution. Religion, even if it was Russian, would still be eliminated. When he looked at a map, Stalin was quite content with what he now saw. The Baltic region, which consisted, he thought, 'of truly Russian lands', was again 'ours' – he was speaking to the Georgian Communist Party boss. The Belorussians and Ukrainians were again 'living with us' (and no doubt contentedly). It might indeed be, in time, that what was 'ours' would really extend from Vladivostok to Berlin. Perhaps, for the moment at least, it was better to consolidate this 'Soviet Empire' rather than to strive for a truly global extension of Socialism. There was rich scope here, as in the past, for theoretical debate. What Marx, Lenin and Stalin themselves had to say on these matters went into the mix. It was only Stalin, however, who determined what 'real life' required. *Realpolitik* and missionary impulse coexisted, without final resolution.

Alternative conclusions

After Stalin's death, there was inevitable speculation, in Europe and beyond, as to whether a new era had arrived. How much of what had happened in Europe since 1945 could in fact be directly attributable to Stalin himself? To this and allied questions no immediate answer could be given, and perhaps still cannot. The departure of such a man inevitably left issues of leadership and direction hanging in the air. Some observers detected signs that the Soviet system was sclerotic. Others thought this far-fetched. Was there a 'thaw'? Winston Churchill, as his last attempt to lift the nuclear monster from the world, as he put it, thought at this time that a quiet word between the men that mattered would suffice. He resigned on health grounds in April 1955, without having succeeded. A generation at the helm of world affairs which had grown up in the 1890s was passing away. New prospects might be opening up. The foreign ministers of the occupying Four Powers met in Berlin in February 1954 for the first time since 1947 to discuss the German question yet again. Their talk led nowhere, but at least they talked. In May 1955 the Four Powers did sign a treaty which re-established Austria as a sovereign state (and one which would never seek either political or economic union with Germany). They agreed to withdraw their occupying forces from the country by the end of the year. The Austrian Parliament declared the country's perpetual neutrality. A decade on from 1945, the treaty might be signalling a relaxation of tension in Europe. However, it was immediately followed by the signature of the Warsaw Pact. Under its terms, in pursuit of their collective defence, the Soviet Union, Albania, Bulgaria, Czechoslovakia, the German Democratic Republic, Hungary, Poland and Romania pledged mutual consultation. A unified military command was set up with headquarters in Moscow. The mould might still be set.

Was Europe's division home-grown and peculiar to itself, or was the continent just the site of a worldwide clash of civilizations? In September 1947, Stalin's friendly general, Dwight Eisenhower, wrote in his diary that he was witnessing a battle to extinction between the two systems. No American president had ever had the on-the-ground experience of Europe that Eisenhower possessed. There was a sense in which he was 'at home' there. Russia was out to communize the world, he had added. Europe was the central arena of 'the Cold War'. His 'Free World' confronted 'the Communist World'. Breaking that down into particulars was not straightforward. At root, was there not a fundamental confrontation between two different systems, and the beliefs which undergirded them? It could happen anywhere. It was happening everywhere. The values in contention transcended particular continents. Nothing less than the future of the whole world was at stake. One or other civilization would be doomed.

Our civilization – the then much-read British historian, Arnold Toynbee, told his American readers in March 1947 – was not inexorably doomed. He was turning into a prophet with no mean sales for the abridged version of his multi-volume *Study of History*. His vision could be shaped into paragraphs for *Time* magazine. He commended indications of American commitment to Europe. Later, in 1952, he foresaw a coming American world empire. That would be lucky since, as empires go, it would be a good deal more lightly exercised than those of Russia, Germany or Japan (the alternatives). The 'Western World', crystallizing around the USA into something like a single community, could mean a new and promising chapter in world history. What he regarded as 'civilization', hitherto confined to small minorities, would extend to much wider circles, including, 'sooner or later, the depressed peasants of Asia and Africa'. Toynbee's conception of a 'single community' dissolving Old World/New World antitheses took things rather further than many other contemporary commentators.

'The world', taken as a whole, might not be as concerned about the threat to 'Christian civilization' that Churchill identified when, as will be considered in the next chapter, he came to the USA after the war and delivered his Fulton speech. Whatever he quite meant by this expression, he clearly located that civilization in Euro-America. The Vatican, for its part, necessarily looked on the world from Rome. The Pope, however, did not travel to meet 'the world', although, before his election in 1939 Pius XII's office as secretary of state had taken him to France, Germany, Hungary and Argentina. Unofficially, he had visited both the UK and the USA. His wartime role became intensely controversial. After the war, his hostility to Communism was strong. 'Christian Democracy' became a feature of the new European politics, though not easily placed on the political spectrum. Some strands were emphatically 'conservative' and not altogether purged of a certain authoritarian corporatism, but others were avowedly 'progressive', with a strong trade-union element. Some but not all Christian parties stressed independence from Vatican influence. The advantages secured for the Church by accords with Salazar's Portugal (1950) and Franco's Spain (1955) could be taken to show the kind of 'Christian Europe' which the Vatican wanted to see. Yet, to harp on too much about 'Christian Europe' risked the danger that Christianity be thought European. The same difficulty confronted non-Catholic churches. When the World Council of

Churches came into operation in 1948 its first assembly was held in Europe, in Amsterdam. Clerical/anticlerical culture wars had long been a feature in modern European history. They remained alive, as did Catholic/Protestant frigidity, though both did so in a less clear-cut fashion. It was inevitable, however, that the 'Christian' label carried with it the imputation that other parties were non-Christian and might indeed be anti-Christian. Some indeed were, but even though state or 'established' churches remained in Protestant Scandinavia and in parts of the UK, liberal democracy was uncomfortable with any privileging of Christian faith. The general drift appeared to be in the direction of a 'public space' that was 'secular', a word with many meanings.

The parallelism of two 'worlds' thus seemed complete. There were two Germanies confronting but not recognizing each other. There were two Europes which seemed, politically, economically and culturally, to be moving steadily apart, accentuating other and earlier continental faultlines. Governments in Ireland or Switzerland, Sweden or Spain might, for different reasons, resist this simple duality, but it appeared generally compelling. If the status quo continued indefinitely, a space called 'Europe' would fade away. There were two military alliances facing each other. Nuclear weapons were available to both sides. Europe, however, for all its centrality, currently, as the place where 'the two systems' directly met, was not the whole world. The 'rest of the world' would put Europe in its place. It was to North America now that attention shifted, home both of a Great Power and a Great Hope.

5
The United Nations and The United States

The UN: organizing

If the world needed a new start, it needed a new world body. To this end, representatives of 50 states, 45 of whom had signed the UN Declaration of January 1942, met in San Francisco from 25 April to 26 June 1945 to determine the 'International Organization' of the future. They drew together earlier proposals and sought to resolve contentious points. 'The world' had never before been considered so comprehensively. The 'United Nations' was obviously the successor to the 'League of Nations', but that lineage required careful handling. The League had 'failed', however that failure was explained. Simply to replicate the League, therefore, would carry the stigma of past failure. The wartime discussion, as we have seen, therefore emphasized 'realism'. The Great Powers could not be wished away. The new Security Council (China, France, the UK, USA and USSR, plus six temporary members) recognized that fact. These were apparently the only states that really mattered. When an issue was before the Security Council, the General Assembly could not also consider it. Ideally, the permanent members would be in accord, but the veto each possessed recognized that this could not be guaranteed. It was 'realism' to accept that the world could not be 'policed' in the teeth of opposition from a Great Power, though it was realized that constant use of the veto might render the Security Council ineffective. It came to be accepted that abstaining, in relation to a resolution, was different from vetoing it. In the decade up to 1955 the veto was used once by China, twice by France and 75 times by the Soviet Union. Neither the UK nor the USA used it.

Too much emphasis on 'realism' in creating the new body, however, risked making perfectly respectable states mere spectators, doing little more than voting in the General Assembly (which all member states attended) at the behest of one or other Great Power. The resolutions of the General Assembly, usually passed by majority vote, were recommendations rather than mandatory instructions (with the exception of budgetary recommendations). They could not be enforced. That upset those individuals who believed that the United Nations

Organization should be 'the Parliament of the World' in which all states, great or small, had a voice. The new body, however, like its predecessor, deliberately used the word 'Nations'. It was nations, apparently, who spoke peace. States and their governments could not be relied upon to do so. Yet the world did remain a world of states. Governments decided how much 'unity' there might be. Defining a state was normally unproblematic but Stalin tried in vain to get all the Soviet republics admitted. In the end, only Belorussia and Ukraine were accorded seats. A UN in which *nations* were represented would have embarrassed multinational states. Of course, inevitably, the new 'world structures' could only be 'the world' of 1945/6. Nothing thereafter would be static, since the founding Charter spoke of the right of peoples to choose their own form of government. Twenty-two of the fifty-one founding states came from the Americas and fifteen from Europe. The founding conference took place in San Francisco and the headquarters of the new organization were to be in New York. Europe, which had given a home to the League, was displaced, although the leader of the Norwegian delegation, who had been his country's foreign minister in exile in London, emerged as the first 'Secretary-General'.

Reconstructing and developing

It would not be enough, however, to consider political structures. It was time to create a new world trade order. Again, the initiative came from the USA. The existence of closed trading systems, it was argued, had been one of the major factors leading to war. The answer was a more open system with lower tariffs and convertible currencies. That it would be of particular benefit to the USA at this juncture did not escape notice, but the ambition reflected more than self-interest. Forty-four states had attended a conference at Bretton Woods in New Hampshire in July 1944 to establish the ground rules for post-war economic global life. The Soviet Union, New Zealand, Haiti and Liberia – scarcely a coherent alternative combination – dissented from the outcome agreed by the majority. The goal was to establish stable exchange rates. Each signatory would maintain its currency at a rate measured in relation either to gold or a convertible currency (in practice that meant the dollar) at a fixed rate of one ounce to $35. No currency other than the dollar, at this juncture, could be as universally convertible. That this was a particular advantage to the USA could not be helped. Two new organizations resulted: the International Monetary Fund (IMF) and the International Bank for Reconstruction and Development (the IBRD, or 'World Bank'). Each member state of the former would pay a subscription according to its economic capacity. In turn, from its reserves, the Fund would allow countries with balance of payments deficits 'drawing rights' to meet immediate contingencies. Reconstruction would be financed through the World Bank, with a huge sum available, raised initially by subscription from member states. The World Bank, with Presidents who were in fact American, though not required to be, was based in Washington. One further body was mooted, an International Trade Organization, but that proved not to be acceptable to the US Congress (in 1947, however, 23 states concluded a General Agreement on Tariffs and Trade, GATT, an agreement which spawned an organization based in Geneva to facilitate and extend implementation).

'Reconstruction' would give way, over time, to 'Development'. Development was a portmanteau expression. The world, it was suggested, consisted of countries in various identifiable stages of economic development. Developed countries knew that they were developed. There were others, however, that were 'under-developed', an advance, in public at least, on their blunt categorization as 'backward': a hierarchy was presupposed. It was indisputable that the USA headed the field, at least for the moment. A clear attempt to 'think globally' was being mounted. Fostering 'Reconstruction and Development' might, over time, eliminate or at least substantially reduce the gap between the 'developed' and the 'under-developed' worlds. The problem was that the 'developed world' might yet develop faster than the 'under-developed': the gap might widen, not disappear. Besides, while the attempt to create such institutions represented a 'world advance', they left the impression that 'development' was really only a matter of 'economics' narrowly defined. 'Developed countries' naturally supposed that they constituted models. The path to a 'modernized' and, by implication, increasingly homogenized world could be set out in steady and predictable stages. Economists were on hand to point the way. It was, in any case, in the immediate aftermath of the war, difficult to map the developed and the under-developed worlds precisely. Were countries that needed massive 'reconstruction' likely, as a result, in time, to be more 'developed' than those which needed little? To think beyond economics took one into the complex intermeshing of government, 'civil society', culture and religion. 'Development' was in fact Janus-faced. It might in reality be experienced as 'Destruction' or 'Disintegration'. At issue was the nature of social progress. How was one to compare the 'happiness' of a socially harmonious, culturally cohesive but materially 'backward' country with the 'happiness' of a materially prosperous but culturally confused and socially dysfunctional one? There were examples of both to be found. The 'standard of living' might be susceptible to measurement, but the 'quality of living' was perhaps another matter.

Declaring human rights

There was, however, some recognition that political, economic or commercial structures were intimately bound up with social and cultural values. A common understanding of what they were was elusive. On 10 December 1948, however, the General Assembly of the UN proclaimed the Universal Declaration of Human Rights. It called upon member states to publicize, disseminate, display, read and expound the Declaration. Its thirty articles asserted the rights to which all human beings were entitled, alongside duties they owed to the community. That the General Assembly was meeting in Paris was no accident. The new Declaration stood in linear descent, with elaboration, from the 'Rights of Man' as set down by the French revolutionaries of 1789 and which in turn found expression in the 'Bill of Rights' in the USA.

Each article began with the words 'Everyone has the right ...' followed by a comprehensive set of assertions. Moving beyond generality, however, their precise implications were far from clear, whether in relation to the family, property, education, work and other areas. Everyone had the right to freedom of religion, for example, a right to be expressed in teaching, practice, worship and observance, but how was 'worship' to be defined? Or, to take another example, it was asserted that the family was 'the natural and fundamental group unit of society and as such entitled to protection by society and the State', but different cultures and beliefs (religious and non-religious) viewed 'families' and their 'protection' differently. Everyone had a right to a nationality, but who defined 'nationality'? 'Declarations' along these lines emerged from Euro-American thinking as it had evolved over centuries. This Declaration, however, claimed to be the 'foundation document' of the *world*. Its reception outside Euro-America would be problematic. It might be the world's 'foundation document', at least in embryo, but it bore scant relationship to the world as it actually existed. The General Assembly also adopted a 'Convention on the Prevention and Punishment of the Crime of Genocide'. Genocide was identified as being a series of listed acts whose intent was to destroy, in whole or in part, a national, ethnical, racial or religious group. Post-war ethnic expulsions, however, had already taken place.

Other organizations looked at 'the world' from a different perspective. The UN Educational, Scientific and Cultural Organization (UNESCO) was founded in 1945. It grew out of the League's Intellectual Co-operation Organization. Education ministers, Chinese and Soviet, as well as American and European, had met in London during the war to establish the basis for post-war cultural exchanges. UNESCO could be disparaged as a talking shop, but 'culture' in a wide sense did need to be talked about if the world was to understand itself. Less contentious were other bodies, not subject to UN direct control – the Food and Agriculture Organization (FAO, 1945), the World Health Organization (WHO, 1948), the World Meteorological Organization (WMO, 1950), and the International Children's Emergency Fund (UNICEF). The first Directors-General of both UNESCO (Julian Huxley) and the FAO (John Boyd Orr) came from Britain. The remit of these bodies was worldwide, but their initial membership sprang essentially from Euro-America. Such new institutions emphasized the sharing of information and contrasted their methods of working with the confrontational styles of 'politics'.

Naturally, the emergence of such bodies, and the funds and programmes that flowed from them, also saw the appearance of a cadre of 'international civil servants'. How should they be appointed, and to whom were they responsible? Such questions, relatively modest at the outset when bodies were small, led to further issues of funding and control. Even agencies 'running the world' were not likely to ignore their own particular interests. There was, however, a much more fundamental question. How could disregard for the 'Universal Declaration', or 'rogue' interpretation of its articles, be dealt with? There was no short answer. The continuing assertions of sovereignty and the rejection of 'outside interference' meant, it seemed, that infringement might only be censured. Diplomatic pressure, exerted through 'the usual channels', might or might not have effect. In this respect, therefore, the new world, despite the rhetoric, did not look very different from the old.

Creating security

Security was what the *Security* Council existed to provide. Reflecting on the 'failure' of the League of Nations, there had been some initial talk of a UN Army established by agreement between the Security Council and consenting states. It would be commanded by a committee of Chiefs of Staff from the Council's permanent members. Article 25 of the Charter required member states to comply with the decisions of the Security Council. However, the army was never created on this basis. The failure pointed to the paradox of the whole conception. 'The world' needed to avoid another global war. Another *global* war would only be likely to be precipitated by one or other of the Great Powers. Such a possibility, while no doubt undesirable, and hopefully unlikely, could not be ruled out. The fact that it could not be ruled out, however, precluded the possibility of creating the envisaged army. In this, as in other respects, the UN, in all its manifestations, hovered uneasily between fantasy and realism in its conception of the world. In reality 'the world' was still not willing or able to think globally. Embryonic notions of 'policing the world' coexisted with the continuance of continental cleavages, national sensitivities and ideological alignments, all jumbled up together. They resulted in the very alliances and alignments that, in theory, the creation of the UN rendered redundant. The permanent 'pillars of security' either seemed likely to fall on each other or to be found, on inspection, to be no pillars at all. It was in these circumstances that much depended on the USA.

The USA: assuming global responsibility

The USA after 1945 had a global presence – commercially, culturally and militarily – unmatched by any other country. Its policymakers found themselves engaged almost everywhere. The scope of that involvement in the world beyond its borders at this juncture arguably exceeded that of any other power in history. Yet the nature of that involvement eludes easy categorization. The USA, the voice of 'America', was at the heart of 'Uniting the Nations'. It was the primary sponsor and principal supporter of the UN. The capital of the USA was in Washington; the 'capital' of the world of the post-1945 world was in New York. Whereas, in 1919, the USA did not join the League of Nations harboured in Geneva, in 1945 it hosted the headquarters of the new world body. Two ways of looking at the world existed within its borders. Its government in Washington was arguably emerging as the most influential in the world. There it powerfully shaped a perspective that was national. The UN Organization in New York was an untried instrument which expressed a global aspiration. The two might clash or work together, but their relationship was likely to prove one of the key elements in whatever world order emerged.

Its most immediate geographical relationship was with Latin America. The Americas were for Americans. Latin America's 'isolation from the rest of the world', as it is sometimes put, continued after the war. It remained a part of the world where, almost uniquely, it made little domestic sense to think in terms of pre-war and post-war. It was also distinctive in another sense. Arguably, alongside the reality of a set of independent states, South America, moulded by Spanish/Portuguese/Catholic culture, possessed a greater trans-state unity than that which, for example, existed in 'Europe'. Even so, that culture was less homogenous than was often supposed. Architecturally, Buenos Aires, the capital of Argentina, might give the appearance of smart 'modernity' but it was no more 'typical' of South America than Chiang Kai-shek's Nanjing was of China. Even though, as was noted, South America remained largely aloof from the world war, nevertheless it had brought about some greater hemispheric intermingling.

US attempts, on occasion, to 'involve' Latin American countries after 1945 in 'the wider world' rarely succeeded. A few years later, for example, Brazil would not send troops to fight in Korea. It might have been different, its government said, if a recovery plan for Latin America (not offered by the USA) had matched the Marshall Plan for Europe. But what had Latin America got to 'recover' from? An examination of the post-war decade, therefore, has little place for 'Latin America' as an agent in *world* affairs. Its focus must be on inter-American relations. From the US perspective, however, those relations had the primary objective of ensuring that both Central and South America accepted its view of the world. The 'Americas' had special internal relationships. The Organization of American States (OAS) was formed in Bogotá, Colombia, in May 1948. Its Charter set down that the territory of member states was inviolable. Any 'situation' which might endanger 'the peace of America' would require intervention. The question was what degree of 'support' the USA should provide to prevent such 'situations' arising.

In the early 1950s the USA concluded military agreements with ten Latin American countries. The likelihood of 'conquest' coming from overseas, however, was remote. Eisenhower's brother told him that the problem would be subversion. One by one, highly disciplined groups of Communists would undermine free institutions. He had the situation in Guatemala in mind. The USA, the country's Foreign Minister protested, seemed to regard every manifestation of nationalism or economic independence as 'Communism'. The USA, in reply, detected the real prospect of a Communist takeover. It claimed not to be simply serving the interests of US companies. A shipment of arms from Czechoslovakia sealed Guatemala's fate. A coup was mounted in which the USA was clearly complicit. Even the possibility of a 'third way' for its southern neighbours seemed, in this episode, to be being ruled out. Here and elsewhere the USA locked itself into regimes which buttressed the existing social order and also, often, buttressed American economic interests. The defence of 'freedom' brought unconvincing allies. Guatemala had appealed to the Security Council. The USA did not want the issue to appear on its agenda. Britain and France, initially inclined to allow it, were reminded that if they took an independent line on this issue the USA could do the same in relation to Egypt and North Africa. Spheres of influence, in other words, should be respected. Washington had managed to get most Latin American states to agree to a resolution in March 1954 that the extension into 'this Hemisphere' of the political system 'of an extra-continental power' would endanger the peace of all America. Just think what it would mean to us if Mexico voted Communist, Eisenhower put to his Cabinet at this time. What indeed.

Geography made the North/South relationship in the Americas special. The totality of its relationships with other parts of the world was not easily described. Some talked about the 'American empire', but if so, it was the empire of an anti-imperial state – with all the contradictions that entailed. After 1945 a truly global foreign policy was both necessary and possible. Presidents Truman and Eisenhower and their Secretaries of State did not shrink from statements which implied that the USA had a global responsibility exceeding the mere pursuit of national interest. Other countries issued reminders. Churchill – no longer prime minister but a man with a world audience – visited the USA in February/March 1946 and endeavoured, as he put it, to place before the American people certain facts about the current position in Europe. His Fulton, Missouri, speech, broadcast throughout the USA, identified an 'Iron Curtain' descending across that continent, from Stettin in the Baltic, to Trieste in the Adriatic. He, like his listeners, thought of Stettin – its German name. It was now Szczecin, a Polish city. He listed capitals and countries not only subject to Soviet influence but increasingly to Soviet control. His focus was on Europe, but it was 'throughout the world' that Communist parties or fifth columns constituted a growing challenge and peril to Christian civilization. If the Western democracies stood together, however, with military strength, no one was likely to 'molest' them. At the same time he welcomed 'Russia' to her rightful place among 'the leading nations of the world'. The speech caused a storm. President Truman denied, falsely, that he had seen it in advance. He knew that American opinion was not yet entirely receptive to standing together globally. In fact, however, a baton was being passed by 'dear old England'. Churchill's daughter, Sarah, wrote to her father that he had contributed to 'the World Cause'. It remained to be seen quite what that was.

Showing exceptional leadership

'History', at this juncture, seemed to be bequeathing to the USA a particular commission which made global 'involvement' or 'intervention' acceptable and necessary. It was much assessed to this end. The USA would not spurn the role of the world's leader and the world could not do without it. Such thinking, and the language in which it was encased, now pushed 'isolationism' to the margins. Instead, the US population, increasingly internally distributed heavily towards the west and south-west, found itself involved in distant regions whose cultures were beyond its comprehension. The world could not receive at American hands finely tuned attention or subtle appreciation of its diversity. The globe's complexity could only be handled from Washington by broad-brush characterizations and simplified, even vacuous, slogans. A superpower was not run by supermen sensitive to their fingertips about the nuances of life in Cairo, New Delhi, Jakarta, Tokyo or Shanghai – and who then shaped their policies accordingly. An American 'brashness', that so much upset intellectuals in Europe, had a positive side. It showed self-confidence. 'Capitalism' was imperfect, but always capable of adjustment. It was nothing to apologize for. The contemporary theorist Peter Drucker thought that the USA was creating a new society which moved 'beyond Capitalism and Socialism' and transcended both. Terminology, here, as elsewhere, was problematic when the USA was viewed from outside. Europeans could not make much headway with American party labels (and vice versa). They noted that Eisenhower, elected as a Republican, might conceivably, earlier, have accepted a Democratic nomination. American labor was different from European labour. The absence of a 'working class, solidly Left in orientation and unionized', puzzled outsiders. They thought it might be the issue of 'race' which made the USA different from whatever they thought 'normal' in 'democratic' countries.

Matters of race were indeed coming to the fore. In 1952 the USA had in Eisenhower a president who had been brought up in a small and entirely white town. He had served in a segregated army. He had his prejudices, but equally saw that change had to come, but wanted it to come gradually and was suspicious, on general grounds, of federal intervention. The decision of the Supreme Court in May 1954 in the *Brown v. Board of Education* case that in public education the doctrine of 'separate but equal' had no place, put him on the spot. He made no public statement of support. His acceptance of the principle of desegregation went hand in hand with a great reluctance to seek to enforce it. Domestic racial policy, however, as he knew, had to be seen in the context of the world struggle between freedom and tyranny. Who could say where the convulsions of change would end? The world of protests, marches, demonstrations, occupations and confrontations was not far away. America's problem, in microcosm, was the problem of the world as a whole.

Projecting hope, feeling fear

In the 1950s, however, the USA, taken generally, was exhibiting a prosperity which was unprecedented. It was dynamic and 'classless'. The 'American dream', put on hold during the Great Depression and the war, was back. The mass media drove home the message that buying was good for you. 'Immediate gratification' pushed out 'pleasure postponed'. The USA was happy again, even 'singin' in the rain', with Mr Sinatra. Such an image of contentment, no doubt, was too simple, given the particular issues alluded to above, yet, viewed from a distance and as portrayed on screen, it was the home of glamour and an enviable prosperity. Eisenhower (b.1890) was a genial president. Behind him lay Victory in Europe. From his lips came words about co-operation and compromise. He had the most famous grin in the world. Pictures now mattered more than ever. He won in 1952 in a landslide, taking 39 states and winning 55 per cent of the popular vote. There were contradictions in capitalism, the President admitted, but they could be resolved in a kind of corporate commonwealth by men of goodwill and patience. 'The Communist menace' had been identified very readily under his predecessor. The National Security Act of 1947 had created a new Department of Defense, a National Security Council (NSC) and a Central Intelligence Agency (CIA). Loyalty boards sniffed out disloyalty. The House Un-American Activities Committee (HUAC) found evidence of Communist activity in Hollywood. The Communist Party was still legal, but most Americans, when polled, wanted it banned. Spies might be everywhere.

For a couple of years after 1950 the 'Red Scare' was in the hands of Senator Joseph McCarthy of Wisconsin, who hit the headlines with the claim that the State Department contained no less than 205 Communists. Secretaries of State Marshall and Acheson, he asserted, were part of a conspiracy to betray their country. The 'loss' of China had been treason. No institution in the USA was safe from his accusations. In 1954, J. Robert Oppenheimer, the nation's most famous physicist, had his security clearance withdrawn. In the same year, however, after hearings into the charges McCarthy was then making against army leaders, the senator's popularity dropped away and the vehemence went out of the Red Scare, though fears on which McCarthy had drawn did not disappear overnight. This period of political repression blotted the image of the USA as a free society. Fear of Communism's contempt for freedom sapped American freedom. That explains, for example, why the American Civil Liberties Union (ACLU) took a less than full-hearted stance against McCarthyism and did not offer much support to its victims.

The USA presented the appearance of a strongly Christian country. Church building raced ahead in the decade after 1945 and church membership soared. Pollsters eagerly sought to discover how important Americans thought religion was in their lives. In 1952 one poll found that 75 per cent considered it 'very important'. President Eisenhower let it be known that he found the song *I Believe* very moving. He inaugurated the White House Prayer Breakfast. He addressed the World Council of Churches, calling for prayer, when it held its second Assembly at Evanston, Illinois, in 1952. 'In God we Trust' became the nation's official motto. The Roman Catholic bishop, Fulton J. Sheen, clashing on the TV schedules with Frank Sinatra, drew a larger audience. An up and coming evangelist, Billy Graham, matched Sheen's success with his bestselling *Peace with God* (1953). The president of the new National Council of Churches (NCC) urged the churches of the USA to work together towards the goal of a Christian America in a Christian world. A Christian world, however, could only be distantly glimpsed, and 'Christian America' found itself operating in many different environments, welcoming and unwelcoming. The UN, assembling in New York, was not the USA writ large. Other 'worlds' presented themselves in its sessions. Most evidently, there was 'the Communist world' led by the Soviet Union. Perhaps it was being paralleled by a 'free world'. In Europe, the elements of confrontation crystallized.

Truman's Doctrine: guarantees without limit?

Harry Truman, the blunt occupant of the White House, addressed a special joint session of Congress on 12 March 1947. It was a carefully prepared occasion, broadcast on nationwide radio. The President declared that the USA would support free peoples resisting attempted subjugation by armed minorities or by outside pressures. A more comprehensive undertaking could scarcely have been given. The time had come, he said, when nearly every nation had to choose between alternative ways of life. It was a bold global statement that emerged from two confined if serious issues: Soviet pressure on Turkey, in relation to the Straits, and the civil strife in Greece. There was a sense too, that by saying – and perhaps deliberately exaggerating – their inability for much longer to maintain troops in Greece, the British were pushing the USA into a corner. In the years that immediately followed Truman's speech, the Royal Greek Army, with substantial military assistance from the USA – though not American forces – gained the upper hand over the Communists. British troops remained in Greece until 1954. The pressure on Turkey over the Straits likewise subsided. The immediate repercussions, however, were less significant than the long-term implications. Behind the speech lay much reflection within the State Department and elsewhere. In shorthand, it has come to be referred to as 'containment'. The USA should be patient and firm. The Soviet Union would be met with counter-force if it should encroach 'upon the interests of a peaceful and stable world', as George Kennan put it. Kennan, who had served as a diplomat in Moscow, was a little surprised, or so he said later, by the 'grandiose' language used by the president. The difficulty with Truman's language was its capaciousness. Its advantage lay in its potential flexibility. Washington would decide who 'free peoples' were and what constituted their possible subjugation. The 'doctrine' chimed awkwardly with the role to which the UN aspired. Notwithstanding this language, however, the possibility of American 'isolationism' could not be entirely discounted.

Securing the 'free world' went hand in hand with its sustenance. In 1947, Truman brought in George Marshall as US Secretary of State. Here, unlike the President, was a man who knew something of the world at first hand, particularly Europeans and Chinese. At the close of the war, having transformed the US Army from a force of 170,000 men in 1939 to one of 7,200,000, he was arguably the chief architect of the Allied victory. That army was being demobilized but it remained a massive force. It was still powerfully present in Europe, though there had been many voices in the States urging that it should come home. There were many in Europe who feared (and some who hoped) that it would. Back in 1919, serving as an aide to the American commander, John Pershing, Marshall had a keen awareness of the importance of the American contribution to the Allied victory in the First World War. American power had then been withdrawn. This time, perhaps, to put it as crudely as it was sometimes put, it was time to 'finish the job'. A new Europe had to be cajoled, or perhaps coerced, into existence on a basis that would endure. A stable and prosperous Europe suited the USA. It should not hesitate to use both its economic and its military power to this end. It was a responsibility which fortunately had economic benefit. There were, however, two complications. First, while Americans talked about 'Europeans', Europeans themselves seemed reluctant to do so. While Americans were predisposed to think about continents, they found that countries in Europe thought about countries. Secondly, Europe was not the only continent Americans were concerned about. There was, as always, question of balance. It was only in Europe, however, that Americans and Russians came directly face to face.

George Marshall was the man of the moment. He told a Harvard audience in June 1947 that the USA should do whatever it could to assist a return to 'normal economic health'. He had a few months earlier reported that 'that patient', by which he meant Europe, was sinking while the doctors deliberated.

The reaction of the British, French and the Soviets to his idea – it was not yet a 'plan' – would be key. The French Communist Party, still participating in government, had campaigned against French involvement in the Marshall Plan. Distrust and suspicion of the plan, particularly in France, went wider and included some Catholic circles. The policy, Marshall said, would not be directed against any country or doctrine, but against hunger, poverty, desperation and chaos. Whatever form that aid would take, the USA would try to treat 'Europe' (which would include the Soviet Union) as a whole. The State Department did not believe that the offer would be accepted on this comprehensive basis. By making it, however, the administration could wrong-foot states which declined to take part, that is to say, in reality, the Soviet Union. There was little expectation that the Soviet Union would take up the offer. However, Molotov, buttressed by a posse of economists, did arrive in Paris to find out more. However, he concluded that the implementation of the Marshall Plan would breach Soviet sovereignty. The Soviet Union would not participate, nor would the states over which it exercised effective control (including both Finland and Czechoslovakia).

The USA made it clear that it would not deal with bids from individual countries, though, following a collective agreement, it would make some specific undertakings on that basis. Belgium, Denmark, France, Greece, Iceland, Ireland, Italy, Luxembourg, the Netherlands, Norway, Portugal, Sweden, Switzerland and the UK did attend a conference, as did Canada and Turkey. Bevin was in the chair. From the State Department perspective, the British wanted the benefits while still maintaining the position that they were not wholly a European country. The states listed above, therefore, represented the 'Europe' which decided to attend, a mixture of former belligerent and non-belligerent states, but decidedly 'Western'. Spain had not been invited. The aid which was promised would come in kind. Over the four years of the programme, ending in 1952, Marshall Aid, nearly $13 billion, made a significant contribution to the economic recovery of the recipient countries. Britain and France were the chief beneficiaries, followed by the ex-enemy states, Federal Germany (as it became) and Italy, with the Low Countries in the rear.

Quite how significant, in relation to indigenous factors, differed from country to country and remains much debated. In aggregate the aid constituted about two percent of the gross national product (GNP) of the recipient countries. The motivation behind the entire initiative has also been contested. Congress had been successfully lobbied to the effect that Europe's huge trade deficit with the USA was going to be domestically disastrous for American exporters unless a way round it was found. In addition, the prospect of enduring European economic weakness might in turn trigger unwelcome political turmoil there and tilt the continent towards the Soviet Union. As things stood, on the world scale, Europe was the only place where that might happen. There had, therefore, to be a kind of Euro-America, or the entire continent would become 'the Soviet sphere'. It was vital to restore European self-confidence – within four years.

The signing of the North Atlantic Treaty in Washington in April 1949 was a step of a different kind, though no less significant. The USA and Canada were linked to the UK, France, Italy, the Netherlands, Belgium, Luxembourg, Norway, Denmark and Portugal. Iceland, modest but actually in the North Atlantic, made up the complement. An attack on any one member would be an attack on all. Each, after consultation, would take such action as was deemed necessary. At one level, such a partnership was a major global step. At another level, from the outset, as the 'Organization' unfolded, based in Paris – with Eisenhower back in Europe as supreme commander from late 1950 – the terms of the 'partnership' could become contentious. It was international rather than supranational. For the Europeans, the 'nuclear umbrella' was a necessary 'shelter', though possible American 'first use' was alarming. On the other hand, they were reluctant to increase 'conventional' defence expenditure. In the immediate context, what NATO could do, in the event of a Soviet attack in Europe, was unclear. Apart from the ability to deliver a powerful atomic blow, the USA and its allies would need time to build up their strength. The situation was fast-moving. Within months, the Soviet Union had an atomic bomb – the announcement being made in March 1950. The race was on to develop hydrogen bombs, weapons a thousand times more powerful than those which had been dropped on Japan. Three years later, Greece and Turkey also joined NATO. The mutual relations of these states were bad and membership might produce some amelioration. Both countries, in different ways, stretched the notion of a world region that was the 'North Atlantic'. Their admission also widened further the diversity of the political cultures and practices which existed within the alliance.

The North America considered in this chapter therefore presented a global puzzle. The USA, the voice of 'America', was at the heart of alliances that reached far beyond its boundaries in a divided world. It was also, however, the primary sponsor and principal supporter of the UN. The UN Organization, however, was an untried instrument which expressed a global aspiration. The two might clash or work together, but their relationship was likely to prove one of the key elements in the emerging world order.

6
The Middle East

Egypt, Syria and Iraq: Nasser stirring

On 23 July 1952 Egyptians were told by Cairo radio that Free Officers had taken control of the country. The King was required to abdicate and leave the country permanently. A Revolution Command Council, chaired by a young colonel, Gamal Nasser (b.1918), was going to give the Egyptians a new start. The 1923 Constitution was abolished. A Revolutionary Tribunal was set up to try old-style politicians. By the end of 1953 the monarchy was overthrown. Deep divisions then followed within the army, personified in two men, Neguib and Nasser, as to whether there should be a return to parliamentary government or a radical revolution. The latter outmanoeuvred his rivals, survived an assassination attempt, and took on or dissolved the old parties of Left and Right and the Muslim Brotherhood. A Liberation Rally was promoted as a national movement of revival. He was not anti-Islamic, but his modern Egypt was not to be theocratic. His own *The Philosophy of the Revolution* (1954) proclaimed an Arab form of Socialism with an Islamic tinge. He spoke to the people in an Arabic that was not superior in tone and vocabulary. Power came steadily into his hands. Here was the first 'indigenous' Egyptian to lead the people for two thousand years. Building the new Nile Corniche in Cairo gratifyingly removed the garden of the British Residence in the city. Cairo and Egyptians were going to travel on a new road.

More than a British garden had to go. There was the massive British base in the Suez Canal Zone. In October 1954 it was agreed that British troops would be withdrawn but that the base would be maintained by both British and Egyptian contractors. It could be reactivated in the event of external aggression upon any member state of the Arab League. In 1955 the Egyptian flag was raised over Navy House at Port Said. Egypt could at last be said to be truly independent. The status of the base had been in more or less constant discussion with the British government since 1945. There was talk, at one point, of it becoming the focus of a Middle East Defence Force, but this came to nothing. The new regime, however, did conclude an agreement with the British that the future of Sudan should be left to the Sudanese. In January 1956 the British and Egyptian governments had little option but to accept the independence which the Sudanese then declared. Who 'the Sudanese' were, however, was not a topic to be broached.

Nasser still saw Egypt with a place in Africa but it was as 'the Voice of the Arabs' that he proclaimed himself. Cairo radio broadcast the message that the Arab masses should join together to free themselves from imperialism and its collaborators throughout the Middle East. It was not a message which King Faisal, newly assuming full power in Iraq and guided by the veteran politician Nuri es-Said, wanted to hear. The early months of 1955 saw vigorous diplomatic activity in the 'northern tier' of the Middle East. In February, Turkey and Iraq signed a treaty of mutual support. Adnan Menderes, elected as Turkey's Prime Minister in the country's first free elections in 1950 (and again in 1954), had taken his country into the North Atlantic Treaty Organization (NATO). It had joined the Council of Europe in 1949. His alignment was firmly 'Western', but at the same time he showed himself more sympathetic to Islam than republican orthodoxy in Turkey had hitherto allowed. The call to prayer in Arabic ceased to be a criminal offence. A period of rapid economic growth ensued: governments appeared not to need to observe the financial disciplines to which private persons were subject. Neither Ankara nor Baghdad wished to give cultural or political space to their Kurdish minorities.

The Pact then broadened out. Britain joined in March, as, later, did Pakistan and Iran. Its ostensible purpose was defence of the region against the Soviet Union, but Nasser suspected that it was directed against him (though he had been invited to join). At any rate, a clear signal was given that Britain still intended to remain a Middle Eastern player. After a fabulous dinner in Baghdad, ten years earlier, hosted by Nuri es-Said, the itinerant Wendell Willkie had been impressed by the Iraqi's quiet determination 'to build the first really modern and independent state' in the Middle East. Es- Said had then said that time was on his side. There was no disguising, however, that Egypt had a population more than three times as large as Iraq's (and larger than that of other neighbouring Arab states put together). Egypt and Syria signed a defensive alliance in March 1955. Syrian (and Lebanese) independence from France had been secured, after a confused inner French struggle and British intervention, in 1946. The French mandate in the country had functioned on a basis of 'communal representation' for its diverse elements. The emphasis now was on a 'Syrian' identity. The alliance with Egypt was the latest twist in a Damascus political scene which had witnessed military coups, the longest-lasting of which came to an end in 1954. An 'Arab world', as a political reality, might yet be conjured up from Cairo.

Tunisia, Morocco, Libya and Algeria: standing up

The Egyptian capital had been the chief home, post-war, of Habib Bourguiba, leader of the Tunisian political party which was pursuing a new constitution from France. He set up a Greater Maghreb Office there. Earlier, during his time as a law student in Paris, he had married a Frenchwoman. Returning to Tunis in 1949, he launched a campaign for complete independence (abandoning the notion of a continuing but 'equal' relationship with France). His deportation in 1952 had been followed by an insurrection which French forces could not contain. An offer of internal autonomy was made in 1954 but was unlikely to be sufficient. A different process, but with the same imminent outcome, was taking place in Morocco. There the Sultan linked himself with the nationalist party, astutely appealed to the Atlantic Charter and earned himself deposition and exile to Madagascar. An attempt to make El Glaoui, the Pasha of Marrakesh, 'the voice of the Berbers' (the people of the interior), and thereby split and nullify Moroccan resistance, failed. By the end of 1955 independence for Morocco was more or less conceded. The Sultan returned and took the title of King Mohammed V. He showed that it was possible to ride with nationalism (the Bey of Tunis failed to do so). Yet creating 'Morocco' at once raised questions about its extent. The Spanish government, unlike the French, was not under military pressure in other parts of the world. It was not disposed to budge from its Sahara. Libya, after the departure of the Italians, was divided as a UN Trust territory and administered separately by Britain and France, becoming independent as a kingdom in 1951. The first monarch was Idris, leader of the Senussi, followers of a particular strand of Islam.

'The Algerian question' became steadily more acute and raised issues of greater gravity than anywhere else in North Africa. The French National Assembly passed a Statute in September 1947 creating an Algerian Constituent Assembly on the basis of two differently composed electoral colleges. It was nevertheless emphasized that Algeria was part of France. In May 1945 violence had broken out with a substantial number of deaths, both French and Muslim (figures vary). The 1947 measure tried to indicate a desire to 'reform' – the creation of a new Algerian ministry in Paris was another step – while not budging on the central principle. It seemed to work for some years, partly because Muslim parties were divided in their strategies. The position of Algerian communities in France and, of course, of the French *colons* in Algeria, prevented the relatively simple process of transition occurring in Morocco and Tunisia, yet change in these countries provided an inspiration – as did Nasser's Egypt. Violence broke out again in November 1954, bringing a severe response. The Front de Libération Nationale [National Liberation Front] brought together political parties convinced that the national movement was entering the final phase. That was not the view of a new governor-general, Soustelle, who, while stressing that Algeria would remain *dans le cadre français* [within the French framework], also promised that Muslims would play their full part. It had been an objective proclaimed before. It might be too late to make it a reality. The Bandung conference, to be considered shortly, expressed its solidarity with Algerians struggling to be free. Was the only way out the complete dismantling of 'French Algeria' and the 'return home' of French families and perhaps also of 'unpatriotic' Algerian Muslims?

Throughout the Maghreb, as elsewhere, the political issue was how distinct territories and tribal affinities coalesced and how the emphases of particular religious traditions could be accommodated: how traditional authority blended with 'modern' state building: how Islam (and traditions within Islam) and 'secular' politics functioned: how legal systems were integrated: how rival cities and their cultures could be balanced. All these issues echoed from Rabat to Basra, from Aleppo to Tripoli. It was also difficult to judge what lasting impact, if any, the languages and legal and administrative systems used by Britain and France would have. But these were not issues confined to one side of the Mediterranean. If Arabs struggled with their alignment, so did Europeans. The latter, lacking a common language and, at least uncomfortable with their common 'Christian heritage', found themselves, as we have seen, wrestling afresh with their historic diversity. The former, possessing, more or less, a common language and a holy text in which it was written, were nonetheless seeking to enhance a sense of individual nationality, while not ceasing to be Arab. The components of the Euro-Arab worlds, apparently colliding, or at least separating, were in fact each experiencing a crisis of identity.

Palestine and Israel: not giving ground

There was one issue on which, in theory at least, the Arab world came together: the Palestine question. In 1947, Palestine under the British mandate had a population two-thirds Arab, both Moslem and Christian, and one-third Jewish. British government was under severe pressure. Options for the territory's future were once again rehearsed. In February, the British government referred the matter to the UN – which set up a Special Committee. The majority report in August, which was adopted in the UN by a vote of 33 to 13 with 10 abstentions, recommended a three-way division: an Arab state, a Jewish state (though one in which Jews and Arabs would be approximately equal in numbers) and Jerusalem as an international zone. The British decided in September that they would terminate the mandate in May 1948. They had no solution. The last British troops left in the following month. It was an ignominious end to a thirty-year involvement. An internal war between Jews and Arabs was by then in full swing. The former were gaining the upper hand, pushing into mixed towns and areas designated as Arab Palestine. The state of Israel was proclaimed on 14 May. Truces came and went. Count Folke Bernadotte, the UN mediator, proposed that the Arabs should have the Negev and Jerusalem and the Jews Galilee. The proposal was unacceptable to the Israelis. In September 1948 Bernadotte was murdered by the Jewish Stern Gang and fighting resumed.

In theory, the intervention of the neighbouring Arab states should have tipped the balance in favour of the Palestinian Arabs, but there were divided counsels. Abdullah of Transjordan toyed with the idea of a Greater Syria, but settled for a crown for himself and the possible acquisition of Palestine. The plan did not appeal to other Arab states or to the Mufti of Jerusalem. Other states initially favoured supplying Palestinian fighters without directly involving national armies. The Israelis exploited these differences amongst their opponents and by January 1949, largely fighting a now committed Egyptian army, the Israelis were victorious. Young Nasser marched away with his own head held high but with national morale low. Abdullah did largely acquire what would have been Arab Palestine and also old Jerusalem (the Israelis held the new part). His kingdom now simply became known as Jordan. However, in December 1951 a murky plot led to his assassination in Jerusalem. A year later, succeeding a mentally unstable father, young Hussein, extracted from his education at Harrow, Churchill's old school in England, succeeded to the throne. Saudi dislike of the Hashemite dynasty on the one hand, and opposition from Egypt on the other, seemed likely to make Hussein's reign short.

The exodus of some 700,000 Arabs, whether described as being 'driven out' or 'fleeing' from Palestine, led to major problems, naturally for themselves, but also for the receiving states. Israel did not allow the exiles to return and they entered into a kind of perpetual stateless limbo. Receiving states would not make them nationals, partly because to do so would imply abandoning the prospect of their return. What it was to be a Palestinian had always been somewhat problematical, and the new situation made 'placing' them even more difficult. Attempts to find 'a final settlement' under UN auspices never even got off the ground. Arab states proved more resolute after defeat – though the war, technically, continued – than they had been before it. Egypt, for example, in defiance of Security Council resolutions, prevented Israeli vessels from passing through the Suez Canal. Threats and counter-threats followed. Further fighting looked likely.

The existence and expansion of Israel was a constant reminder of the Arab world's humiliation. It was also perceived to represent a fresh intrusion of 'the West', not that 'the West' spoke with one voice. London and Washington, for a time, were at loggerheads on policy. Bevin faced some accusations that he was anti-Semitic. President Truman, perhaps anxious to secure the Jewish vote in the presidential election in 1948, was very prompt to recognize the State of Israel. Jewish support for Israel existed worldwide. It was difficult for Western opinion, conscious of the Holocaust, not to feel some sympathy for Zionist aspiration that Jews should 'return home'. Arabs, in turn, invariably pointed out that the guilt of 'Europe' should not be expiated at the expense of Palestinian Arabs. The argument ensured that the Middle East did not 'belong' entirely to the Middle East.

Iran: Mossadegh muzzled

Iran provided a vivid illustration of this point. In November 1951 crowds turned out in Cairo at what was then still Farouk Airport chanting 'Long Live Iran'. From the aircraft stepped the Iranian Prime Minister, Dr. Mohammed Mossadegh, on his way back to Tehran after addressing the Security Council in New York. The city gave a grand dinner in his honour. Mossadegh, freshly elected by the Iranian parliament after the assassination of his predecessor, had a mission to nationalize the Anglo-Iranian Oil Company (in which the British government had a majority share), revoking its exclusive and not yet expired rights of exploitation and exploration in Iran's southern provinces. He had the power of the street behind him. The contest was protracted. It brought to a head a specific issue but it was also to be the symbolic moment. Iran was going to throw off subordination to the West, particularly to Britain. He perhaps hoped that American fear of Communism in Iran would cause the Americans to make Britain give way. The British Labour government, and its Conservative successor, however, regarded the Iranian move as illegal and wholly unacceptable. The company closed its Abadan refinery and orchestrated a boycott of Iranian oil. A bitter struggle between the two governments then ensued, both sides being determined to make no concessions. That was not the only struggle.

Mossadegh wanted to reduce the power of the Shah. The latter temporarily fled the country in August 1953. That same month, however, a coup, in which there was US CIA involvement, brought Mossadegh down. Some military and religious circles had their own reasons for wishing to see him removed.

Paradoxes abounded. Mossadegh (b.1882) was not, like Nasser, a youthful 'nobody' and emblem of a new generation. Son of a Minister of Finance under the previous dynasty and aristocratically connected, he had studied as a young man in universities in France and Switzerland. He was neither religiously conservative nor a Communist and, in certain respects, was 'Western'. The Shah, however, came out on top in the struggle and reasserted tough control. Constitutional politics, yet again, were in abeyance. He took his country into the Baghdad Pact. For Britain and the USA, despite some differences between them, what mattered was to secure the 'northern tier' for 'the West'. Mossadegh had not succeeded, but neither could the old Anglo-Iranian Oil Company regain its former position. Here, as elsewhere in the Middle East and beyond, Western governments and oil companies, whose respective perspectives and interests did not invariably coincide, had to begin to adjust to the new political realities which flowed from burgeoning oil production across the region.

7
South Asia

Dismantling the British Raj

'British India' was not the story of some short-term 'mandate' without histori-cal depth. A sentimental picture of 'progress' and 'development' under British rule, as imperially presented, no doubt masked exploitation and arrogance, but was nevertheless genuinely held, and beyond the retired ranks of the Indian Civil Service. The end of the largest and most populous empire 'possessed' by a European power was a statement about European power or European will (or a combination of the two). It did not, however, arise out of a concerted and coor-dinated decision in the capitals of Europe to 'end' empire. France and the Netherlands would have to live with the 'signal' that the British intention gave: European colonial empire, in all its varied manifestations, would have to end everywhere. Its implications for the British could be glimpsed, as in the previous chapter, in the Middle East. That region's importance had often been seen as 'safeguarding the route to India', but it had now to be reinterpreted. There would, in short, no longer be the same kind of passage to India, whether the voyage out was viewed literally or metaphorically. In a different way, the context of the British relationship with the small sheikdoms of the Arabian/Persian Gulf on the one hand, and its position in Aden (both Crown Colony and the Protectorates in the hinterland) on the other, also shifted. In the former, by virtue of nineteenth-century Exclusive Treaties, Britain was the protecting power but the sheikhs carried on their own internal government. Their signifi-cance began to change from being, as it were, Indian backwaters to significant small states with ill-defined borders, possibly predatory neighbours, and oil wealth.

Dismantling the 'Indian connection', therefore, from a British perspective, had both short-term and longer-term consequences, some perceived and some not understood. There was one aspect which seems to have concerned the British government. The long British–Indian *durée* still had meaning for the present. Could there be a way of mitigating the absoluteness of the impending constitutional rupture? The Commonwealth of Nations would surely be a means of ensuring a significant continuing relationship beyond the 'normal;' diplomatic relations between states. The trouble was that the adjective which prefixed it was still most frequently 'British'. That seemed not unreasonable as a term which 'white Dominions', at least formerly, had not been unhappy with.

The Indian subcontinent, however, was not populated by 'sort of' British. Any kind of allegiance to the Crown seemed to cast doubt about independence (a view being shared in the Irish Free State and which was to lead to the declaration of a republic in 1949 and the state's departure from the Commonwealth). India's Prime Minister, Nehru, initially did not want to have anything to do with a Commonwealth, certainly not a 'British' one, but changed his mind. By the time India became a republic in 1950 a formula had been found. The British monarch could be recognized as Head of the Commonwealth but no member state, unless it wanted to, was compelled to have the monarch as its own head of state. No one knew quite what this 'Commonwealth of Nations' would be or do. Its expansion beyond being a 'club' of Britain and the 'white dominions', however, indicated that even at a point of separation something worthwhile might be preserved or developed between West and East (and, later, North and South). There was a keen awareness of the precedent that was being set. Nothing could be made of a Commonwealth as an element in the world structure, beyond its existing nucleus, unless countries, on gaining independence, felt comfortable with the prospect of joining. Commonwealth membership, however, while it was a matter which bothered the British, was a minor aspect of transferring power. The fundamental issue was the nature of the India to which it would be transferred. A certain precarious unity had been sustained in opposing British rule. With its end in sight, it was the ensuing structures that mattered.

India and Pakistan: making and unmaking

The British had welded together, by divers means, a single 'India' of great complexity. It took a considerable lesson in constitutional history to understand what the government of India was. It had its multiple layers. It was obvious that an independent Indian state could not be the expression of an Indian nation possessing that linguistic/cultural homogeneity which Europeans had largely come to expect in a 'nation'. The real India was a patchwork, more like Europe (with which, in size, excluding Russia, it equated). The unity of the Indian Union had to be found in a set of principles or ideals which did not seek to eliminate existing identities but which went beyond them. The shorthand for this aspiration was to speak of a 'secular India' in which there was to be equality for all irrespective of religion, language, culture and class/caste. Governing such an India, initially at least, would no doubt substantially rest on that relatively small section of the population which could communicate in English on an all-India basis but which could also speak appropriate vernaculars. Outside the princely states, the Congress movement itself already operated more or less on this basis. Whether the existing administrative units of the Raj were maintained or modified – and on the assumption that the princely states would be cajoled or, if necessary, coerced into the union – India would have to be a federal state. Where the line should be drawn, in terms of competence, between the central organs – 'New Delhi' – and the constituent states, as in all federal systems, would be difficult to draw and sustain. The powers reserved to the President were used to intervene in the Punjab in 1951. Nehru argued that he had to stop 'the progressive rot' that was setting in locally. The Indian army, provided that it could itself stay aloof from them, would act as a counterbalance to whatever centrifugal pressures might from time to time arise. Such an India could not avoid being a major influence in Asia, and indeed in the world. It was the kind of India which Nehru wanted. It embodied ideas and doctrines, however, which were 'Western' in inspiration rather than 'authentically' Indian.

Some Indian critics complained about this 'secular' vision. It ignored 'the soul of India'. An aspiration to accommodate all traditions would mean, in practice, that the state could not embody the 'world-view' of any. In effect, and perhaps by design, it would exclude so much that was 'Indian' about India, namely its religious life and its bearing on 'the public sphere'. Some architects of 'secular India', for their part, were worried that their 'secular' vision would buckle under the weight of religious tradition. The predominant weight was that of Hinduism and the claim that its tenets and practices represented 'the essence of India'. That could not be said, Hindus argued, of any other religious tradition, certainly not of Islam or Christianity, which were 'extraneous' and therefore, arguably, 'non-national'. The spotlight had naturally and particularly fallen upon Muslims. British rule had recognized 'communalism' to some degree, something viewed either as a wise recognition of plurality or as a means to 'divide and rule'. The Muslim League, under the leadership of M.A. Jinnah, had drawn strength from the fear that, no matter what was said, the Muslim minority would be marginalized, perhaps persecuted. Sporadic inter-communal violence constituted a reminder that this was not a theoretical problem. Further, Muslim religious leaders realized that even if Muslims were treated fairly as 'a religious minority' throughout India, they could never achieve an Islamic state. Other religious minorities, most notably Sikhs, had similar concerns. However, partition into separate states, or some recognition of distinctiveness which stopped short of full separation, raised alarming problems. Where and how should boundaries be drawn? Could fissiparousness in India, once started, ever be halted?

In the end, however, in 1947 the Congress leadership, still suspicious in some quarters that partition was a British plot to weaken both successor states, had to accept it. The difficulty, as had long been recognized, was that religion would largely determine boundaries. An ensuing Muslim state would have two foci – West and East – with an India in between. 'Pakistan', itself an invented name, came into being in two halves. It was difficult to think of a greater recipe for instability. India 'inherited' the Raj, as it were: its capital, army and other central institutions, Pakistan had to start from scratch. The sprawling port city of Karachi compared poorly with the authoritative grandeur conveyed by New Delhi. Pakistan lacked both industry and money. It looked dubiously viable. It could not draw upon a long pre-existing loyalty, amongst its own disparate communities, to a physical area that was 'Pakistan'. A struggle between 'the centre' (itself not easy to define) and the provinces became a regular feature of Pakistani life in a more pronounced and debilitating way than occurred in India. Jinnah, 'the great leader' of Pakistan, died in 1948. There was no one to inherit this accolade. There were further complications. It might have been Islam which explained the existence of Pakistan, but that did not necessarily make it an

'Islamic state' in a total sense (whatever that was judged to be). So, from the start, there was a tug of war which not only affected the country's legal structure and constitution, but also its world orientation. The new Pakistan was a major addition to the 'Muslim world' of the extended 'Middle East' but it added its own variety of 'accommodations' to the already existing pattern. Further, as has been noted, the country was prepared to signal its 'Western' orientation by signing the Baghdad Pact (together with Iran). This, in turn, was a reflection of its fear of India and desire to ingratiate itself, to some degree, with 'the West'.

In contrast, India was more obviously a 'unity' in a geographical sense. Even so, the Muslim issue apart, it had its own tensions on linguistic matters: continued use of English, the status of Hindi and the extent to which the states in its federal system should be restructured on linguistic lines. Although the princely states were brought into the union without undue difficulty – only in the case of Hyderabad was a hint of the army necessary – some Sikhs and some Tamils pressed for special status. These and other similar aspirations did not disappear but could largely be contained. Rehearsal of the principles of the new India, on the other hand, did not in itself overnight destroy a caste system ('abolished' in the 1950 Constitution which turned India into a republic). Notwithstanding such enduring issues, an increasingly confident Nehru worked to entrench 'secularism' and strengthen 'unity'. This was a personal effort. In January 1952, for example, he reckoned himself to have been for two and a half months continuously on the move around the country, addressing some 35 million people. Religious and communal tension had certainly not disappeared but, perhaps paradoxically, the assassination of Gandhi in 1948 strengthened his position. Of course, Nehru, like many millions of Indians, mourned the death of 'the father of the nation', but in reality the nation which Gandhi might have guided, after it had been born, was not one Nehru wanted. Certainly, from his own eclectic standpoint, Gandhi was striving for inter-religious harmony and believed that a religious understanding of life was fundamental. Nehru did not want to think that it was.

The Prime Minister found it all the more important to emphasize that many millions of Muslims continued to live in India and were not debarred, as citizens, from playing their full part. So could Christians or adherents of any other religion. Such declarations, it scarcely needs to be said, were easy to make, but did not invariably accord with the unfolding reality. To have denuded India of its Muslims would, of course, have been impossible. Even so, what had happened in 1947, once the borders had been confirmed, had been a period of massive upheaval. Communities and families left – Muslims (some seven million) and Hindus and Sikhs (some five and a half million) – in opposite directions to escape incorporation in one or other of the successor states. It was, in all probability, the greatest refugee crisis of the twentieth century. A million people may have lost their lives. Families were separated and communities uprooted. The old Punjab, for example, was split in two. Accusation and counter-accusation followed, with a liberal use of stereotypes to explain behaviour (Muslim violence or Hindu treachery). The substantial numbers of the uprooted, in their relocations, were lauded as national heroes and heroines but were frequently seen as 'outsiders' in their new homelands and subsequently marginalized. The 'Transfer of Power' from Britain to the 'people' of the subcontinent may have been 'peaceful', but the aftermath was not. There was also bitter wrangling over the appropriate shares of financial assets of the Raj and other contentious 'inheritance' issues. Massive transfer of population had neither been planned nor anticipated by either government. Indeed the anticipated continued presence of Hindus in Pakistan and of Muslims in India had been seen in some quarters as a guarantee of 'good behaviour' in the successor states.

If 'partition' could have settled everything in one single upheaval, the scars of suffering might have gradually healed, but it did not. Jammu and Kashmir in 1947 was a princely state with a largely Muslim population, ruled by a Hindu Maharajah. He opted to join India. Pakistan was furious. Two armies – which had so recently been but one and whose officers had been friends – went to war. In January 1949, through the UN, a ceasefire was brokered. India retained two-thirds of the territory. In theory, a plebiscite to determine the wishes of the population was agreed, but India appeared to be in no hurry to implement it. There were strategic reasons – the headwaters of the Indus valley – but also anxiety that a Muslim population voting to join Pakistan would undermine its claim that 'secularism' safeguarded its Muslims. 'Kashmir' festered and constituted a sign that the two successor states regarded each other as their primary enemies. Pakistan, conscious of Indian opinion which opposed its very existence, felt most vulnerable. Thus the two new members of the Commonwealth hardly enhanced its harmonious cross-continental aspirations. Neither Britain, as the just-departed imperial power, nor the Commonwealth as a whole, could exercise much leverage in lessening tension and resolving disputes. Both countries sought support 'out of area'. The Treaty of Manila (1954) set up the South-East Asia Treaty Organization (SEATO), which had only three (out of eight) Asian members. Pakistan became a member. It was scarcely in South-East Asia, but it was the alignment with the USA that mattered. For its part, India looked to the Soviet Union for moral support, bestowing garlands on the somewhat bemused Soviet leaders, Khrushchev and Bulganin, on their state visit to New Delhi in 1955. An Asian antagonism therefore took two powers, in different ways, into worlds beyond Asia.

Nehru's world: between Cambridge and Delhi

Nehru always had pressing domestic problems, but he looked to the world stage. His background gave him every confidence in presenting himself for inspection. Ever since 1928, when he had headed the Congress's newly-formed Foreign Department, India's call for freedom was to be seen as only one aspect of a global struggle against colonialism. Congress in that year, for example, had sent 'fraternal greetings' to the peoples of Egypt, Palestine, Syria and Iraq as they sought emancipation from the grip of Western imperialism. In 1947, therefore, on the point of independence, there was an accumulated agenda. An 'Asian Relations' conference in New Delhi, attended by delegates from 28 countries, reiterated anti-colonial themes but also left no small intimation that India stood ready to lead Asia. Nehru told the UN General Assembly in November 1948 that 'We in Asia' believe that there should not be any country 'under the yoke of colonial rule'.

The British yoke was being lifted elsewhere in South Asia. Ceylon (later Sri Lanka), which also joined the Commonwealth, became independent in 1947. Burma (which did not join) became independent in the following year. Both countries, substantially Buddhist, could be said to lie within the orbit of its large neighbour, but the former had been administered since 1815 as a separate British colony. The latter, initially governed as a province of British India, had been detached from it in 1937. These countries, too, had their problems in establishing a unity that was national. In Burma, many Karens were disaffected. In Ceylon the balance between Tamils and Sinhalese was contentious. The island's Tamils were not newly arrived from southern India, but Tamils in India were not indifferent to their fate.

There might be a general sense in which, globally, Nehru could articulate what 'we in Asia' were thinking, but his three immediate neighbours did not see him as 'the voice of South Asia'. New Delhi forged a specifically Indian synthesis, projecting internationally the image which Nehru gave India: progressive, peace-loving, globally non-aligned, in a general sense socialist. Further, Nehru remained committed to parliamentary government and to maintaining India as a democracy. The Congress polled 45 per cent of the vote in the first general election on an adult franchise in 1952 and won 74 per cent of the seats: the turnout was 47 per cent. Mounting the election was a formidable operation, but Nehru regarded it as a tremendous experience for the Indian people. Yet no one knew whether a vast country with a huge population facing massive social and economic problems could make its democracy function. Paradoxically perhaps, Nehru's personal style and authority might be thought vice-regal. No one quite knew whether Congress was a 'party' or what its specific programme would be.

The Prime Minister believed that the new India, which had never had, in modern history, its own global 'voice', should make its international mark by refusing to align itself with either of the 'worlds' on offer. It should mediate from an acknowledged stature of detached disinterest. When it came to the Korean War, for example, Indian diplomacy was put to hard work achieving the end of hostilities. Disinterestedness, however, has not invariably characterized the international behaviour of great states. India was a great state. In the new era that was imminent, and had indeed partially arrived, it could not be other than a voice in Asia. It had to be compared with China. Equally, however, it was not a participant in the sense that China was a participant in the unfolding crises of North-East and South-East Asia. So, when it came to 'settling' Indo-China, India was not at the conference table in Geneva in 1954 (though the Indian Foreign Minister, Krishna Menon, proved willing to talk to anyone who would talk to him). It was symbolic that the homebound Zhou Enlai stopped off in Delhi to report on the conference. Nehru in turn reported to his colleagues in optimistic terms about Sino-Indian relations. Chinese troops had begun moving into Tibet in 1950, but Nehru did not seem greatly concerned. Indeed, in 1954, the two countries reached an agreement on Tibet. India set aside any influence it had inherited there. Exchange visits brought Zhou Enlai again to Delhi and Nehru to Beijing. The two countries moved to higher realms. They agreed on 'five principles: mutual respect for territory and sovereignty, mutual non-aggression, mutual non-interference in each other's internal affairs, equality and mutual benefit and peaceful co-existence'. The Asian course therefore appeared to be set fair.

8
East Asia

China: standing up

Zhou Enlai (b.1898) had been a man of the world for a long time when he became Prime Minister and Foreign Minister of the new China in 1949. He had come to France in 1920 on what was supposed to be a work-study tour. Already a Marxist, he spent the next four years as an organizer of groups of Chinese students and workers in France and Germany and ferrying some of them through to the Soviet Union for training in the art of revolution. Another young Chinese similarly active was Deng Xiaoping. On his return to China, Zhou found himself navigating the twists and turns of the relationship between the Kuomintang and the Communists in the 1920s and 1930s. It was Communism as perceived by the world of the Comintern which initially guided his path. However, he backed Mao Zedong – who had not been so trained – for the party leadership in the mid-1930s. That support is sometimes seen to have been crucial. After 1937, until the end of the war, he was most often found in Chongqing in a pivotal role handling Communist relations with the Nationalist government there. At the end of the war, too, he was a key figure in the talks which the Americans hoped would produce a negotiated solution avoiding civil war. In 1946, in China, General George Marshall worked hard to this end, but to no avail. Stalin had also lent a hand, concluding a 'treaty of friendship and alliance' with Chiang Kai-shek which also brought him territorial concessions. In 1947, judged by their clear superiority in men and materials a Nationalist victory looked probable. However, weakened by corruption, defection and loss of morale, Nationalists lost ground inexorably. Chiang took his government and as much of his army as he could manage to the island of Formosa/Taiwan (it had been returned to China by Japan in 1945). He still proclaimed himself to be the legitimate government of China and still occupied the Chinese seat on the Security Council. He had the support of the USA.

From the rostrum overlooking Tiananmen Square in Beijing on 1 October 1949 Mao Zedong proclaimed the new Chinese People's Republic. He himself was declared its Chairman (alongside his chairmanship of the Communist Party). A 'New Democracy' was being inaugurated. After a decade of intermittent war, and in circumstances of high inflation, there was much to be done. His message was that China had 'stood up'. This was a strong nationalist theme. Even so, those who did not wish to hear it from Communist lips fled to Taiwan or to the still British colony of Hong Kong, or even further afield. So where did this China stand in the world? Mao himself had never been a globetrotter and he was not going to change. It was with the utmost reluctance that he was persuaded to visit Moscow. His perspective was Sinocentric. The kind of 'tutelage' into the modern world offered China by the USA was dead. The people of China (and the stars on the country's new flag gave at least symbolic recognition to their diversity) would stand on their own feet. It would all take time and probably entail perpetual change. The land reform, by which at least 200 million acres were distributed to about 75 million peasant families, must rank as one of the largest appropriations ever. The structures of government in China would not be blindly copied from elsewhere. Tight control was needed to prevent the debilitating fragmentation of the past. It was difficult to unpick the messages. Was the 'light touch' supervision of business enterprise merely an initial tactic? Much was initially said about freedom, but it did not take long for 'unacceptable deviation' to be identified. Yet the precise ideological ingredients of orthodoxy were obscure and were determined by the immediate international context. China might now be standing up, but the feet of its security were wobbly. Could it really stand alone? Nine months after the proclamation of the new republic, war broke out in the Korean peninsula.

Korea: peninsular problem – global test-case?

Korea had received little world attention for decades. The 1943 Cairo conference had determined that, on the defeat of Japan, it should resume its independence. That seemed a straightforward decision, but it turned out not to be. The peninsula had been divided de facto at the 38th parallel. The Soviet Army had entered from the north and the American from the south. To bring about a unified state seemed just the job for the new UN. At American prompting, a UN Commission was appointed. However, in pursuit of its intention to hold elections for this purpose, it was not admitted to the North. Elections in the South returned a government, headed by Syngman Rhee, which claimed authority over the entire peninsula. A rival government under Kim Il Sung was then nurtured by the Soviets in Pyongyang. Kim Il Sung had come home after living for a time in Manchuria as a fluent Mandarin speaker and, also, for a time, a Red Army captain – all on top of a family Protestant Christian background. North Korea braced itself for a 'Great Leader'. When the 70-year-old Syngman Rhee arrived back in South Korea in 1945 he had been away for some thirty years, largely in the USA. He had become a Methodist and had acquired both a Ph.D. from Princeton and an Austrian wife. It is scarcely surprising that there was, it might be said, a certain contentious eclecticism about the democratic course of South Korean politics.

Both the Soviets and the Americans withdrew their armed forces in 1949, leaving in their wake a war of words between the two governments. On 25 June, North Korean troops crossed the border and captured the southern capital, Seoul, on the following day. It was an action which would test what 'the world' really meant. At one level, it was an armed struggle between rival contestants for control of a state which had not existed since 1910 (both sides agreed that there should be only one state). That did not in itself suggest a world war or perhaps any reason for external involvement. At another, however, success for the North or the South would be taken to be a victory for their respective backers. It could be assumed (and does indeed seem to have been the case) that the Northern attack would not have been launched without Soviet support. It may be that that support was given on the basis that it was best to strike first and forestall a possible Southern attack, and also on the assumption that Washington would accept a fait accompli. The US Secretary of State, Dean Acheson, had in fact just excluded Korea from the 'defensive perimeter' to which the administration was committed. Unless there was outside intervention, the South would swiftly succumb. However, a direct US intervention raised a difficulty. It would indicate that the new 'UN' was an irrelevance. The question, therefore, was whether the UN could make the North withdraw or, failing that, assist the South. The former having failed, a further Security Council resolution requested the latter. A UN force, commanded by the American, General MacArthur, reversed the tide of battle. South Korean and other forces crossed the 38th parallel in October and pressed on to the Chinese border. It could appear, at this juncture, that this was an endorsement of 'world order'. 'Aggression' was being defeated by the world 'in concert'. In fact, such world solidarity was only operationally possible because the Soviet Union, at the time when the relevant resolutions were being voted on in the Security Council, had absented itself. The People's Republic had no place in the UN. Particularly in terms of the states committing troops, this was far from being a textbook example of 'the world' teaching a solitary delinquent a lesson.

And it soon became clear that the delinquent was not to remain solitary. It looked as though General MacArthur was taking his forces up to the River Yalu on the Chinese border. That could be represented as accomplishing the unity of Korea, though this time under Southern auspices. What it also did, however, was precipitate Chinese intervention. There were strong memories in Beijing that it was from Korea that the Japanese had launched their attack on Manchuria in 1931. The Americans – the 'new Japanese'- might shortly do the same (their position in Japan, to be commented on shortly, reinforced that emotional linkage). MacArthur had paid a friendly visit to Taiwan on the outbreak of the war. It all fitted. The new regime was being surrounded and imperilled. China struck first. Mao was motivated more by concern for his country's integrity than by solidarity with Kim Il Sung of North Korea. The stakes became higher as Chinese 'volunteer' forces drove south. At the beginning of 1951, a Chinese offensive captured Seoul, though it then faded. Intermediaries unavailingly sought a ceasefire. A telegram from MacArthur to the US Senate seemed to suggest a direct strike on China and rule out a settlement on the basis of a return to division at the 38th parallel. Battles ebbed and flowed. MacArthur's continuing stance could be taken to imply a desire, if need be, to use an atomic bomb. On 11 April 1951, however, he was dismissed by President Truman. Thereafter, a protracted path eventually led in July 1953 to the signature of an armistice agreement – on the basis of a divided Korea. The war was over, although there was no peace agreement. There was no normality here. Kim Il Sung's peninsular adventure had led to the death of some four million people, amongst whom was a son of Mao Zedong.

Three years of intermittent and oscillating fighting, therefore, seemed on the surface to have produced a simple return to the Asian status quo of 1950. Only superficially, however, and in Korea itself, was this the case. The war had apparently given good grounds for the mutual suspicions entertained by all the countries, great and small. How 'East Asia' was conceived and how it related to the 'worlds beyond' remained unclear. China had certainly asserted itself. Yet, as its military leaders recognized, the part its soldiers had played in Korea was not evidence that China could defend itself against all comers. At least in the immediate future, that pointed in the direction of strengthening the links with the Soviet Union and 'modernizing' the army on Soviet lines. The imposition of a trade embargo on China also had the only too predictable consequence of dramatically increasing the proportion of Chinese trade being conducted with Communist states – thus reinforcing the notion of a 'bloc'. Such tendencies gave added impetus to the external perception, most notably held in the USA, of a strong Sino-Soviet bond. If there was a window, in the first six months after 1 October 1949, in which the new China and the USA might have groped towards a reasonable working relationship, the Korean War brought it to an end. From Washington it was even suggested (by Dean Rusk) that the Beijing regime was a kind of Russian colonial government. Mao himself entertained no such notion. Tilting for comfort in a Soviet direction did not commit him to copying all Soviet ways. The visit he paid to Moscow in 1949 did constitute a kind of recognition that the Soviet Union, or at least Stalin personally, was paramount in 'the Communist world'. When Stalin died in 1953 Mao did not bestow the same recognition on his successors – as Khrushchev was to find on a visit to China in 1954. Nevertheless, the perception of a Beijing/Moscow axis had taken root in America. The USA, in response, would ensure the security of the Taiwan regime though not, perhaps, that of other smaller offshore islands.

South-East Asia: departures, divisions and outside 'solutions'

The establishment of the People's Republic also had repercussions to the south of China. A few months earlier, abandoning an attempt to reach an accommodation with Ho Chi Minh, French colonial strategy in Indo-China took a different turn. An agreement was reached instead with the Emperor of Annam, Bao Dai, resulting in the creation of a new state, Vietnam, with himself as its head. It was proclaimed an Associated State within the French Union at the end of 1949. The same status was accorded Laos and Cambodia. France could not bring itself to concede complete independence. Ho Ch Minh, for his part, was not disposed to compromise. The presence of a Communist China to the north changed the context. Vietminh offensives began. A protracted, though fluctuating, military struggle commenced. From the French perspective, it was complicated by the rivalries – personal, ethnic, cultural and religious – which flourished in the three states. These served to expose the extent to which 'French Indo-China' had been a political fiction. French casualties mounted, but the French government could not be seen to give up, not least because of the message it sent elsewhere, particularly in Algeria. However, a new government in Paris in June 1954 saw no alternative but to seek a settlement. The previous month, a French garrison at Dien Bien Phu had suffered a humiliating defeat (covert US assistance had been given to the French). Paris looked to Washington for support in negotiating a settlement, not for an attempt to achieve victory. Some opinion in Washington did contemplate intervention, but concluded that that in turn might lead to Chinese involvement and perhaps a general war in Asia.

The time was ripe, therefore, to attempt to settle the two 'succession' issues in North-East and South-East Asia, respectively. A conference on Korea had already begun at Geneva in April. In the event, scant progress was made on Korea and it was the future of Indo-China which was supposedly settled. A glance at this conference indicates how 'the world' would deal with 'Asia'. France, Britain, the USA represented 'the West' , then there was the part-Asian Soviet Union, and 'Asia' in the form of the People's Republic of China and the two Vietnamese entities. The US Secretary of State, John Foster Dulles, did not accept the outstretched hand of Zhou Enlai. The two men did not even sit in the same room. The USA and the People's Republic did not recognize each other diplomatically (the UK and the People's Republic did). The diplomatic role the British Foreign Secretary was able to play had significance. Eden had made it clear, before the conference, that Britain would not give military help in Indo-China. Britain did not in fact have much military help to give. Its forces, over this same period, had been engaged in Malaya in coping with the insurrection which the Chinese-dominated Malayan Communist Party had launched in 1948. The difference was that by 1954 the counter-insurgency campaign there could be judged to be successful (though the state of emergency lasted a further six years). The British felt some satisfaction that, unlike the French, when they came to depart from Malaya it would be in an orderly fashion.

At this first awkward world appearance, Zhou could sense that 'the West' was not quite the solid edifice which it was supposed to be. The Soviet stance at this conference did not embarrass China, but neither did Moscow energetically support its position. The conflict had placed the USA in a difficulty. Its view that European colonialism should come to an end had, in theory, not shifted. Yet if French withdrawal opened the path to a Communist takeover, that too was unpalatable. Elusive, but desirable, was a nationalism which was 'democratic'. A direct American intervention, in these circumstances, might well be counterproductive. Only a direct Chinese intervention would precipitate it. The USA had no desire to become embroiled in a new Korean-style conflict, at least not if, as it thought latterly, it was furnishing 90 per cent of the manpower. Indo-China could be seen as a local affair of no vast significance to the 'free world'. The contrary position, however, also being suggested, stressed the 'domino' danger. Bit by bit, it was said, China would be in a position 'ultimately' to dominate the Western/South-Western Pacific.

Mixed messages emerged from the conference outcome. Vietminh aspirations were not satisfied in so far as another parallel (this time the 17th) drew a line between two separate states of Vietnam (though elections, proposed for 1956, were to lead to unification). It was not an outcome, however, which displeased the Chinese. Ho Chi Minh had been supplied in the field but not made to appear too important. Khrushchev had been told by Zhou in 1954 that if the French had gained the upper hand, Ho Chi Minh would have been left to his fate. Behind such sentiments lay a long historical past. Laos and Cambodia were also declared to be independent states. Zhou spoke positively about the neutrality of these two monarchies. The final defeat of France brought to an end a 'civilizing mission' which had lasted three-quarters of a century, but its cultural-political legacy still remained. Taken together with the de facto position in Korea (and, in Europe, in Germany) the world, it seemed, had to get used to a situation in which 'nations' spawned states that were ideologically distinct. The word 'democracy' was held, by both sides, and by their Great Power backers, to be what characterized their respective systems and ideologies. 'Models', from wherever drawn, were as much honoured in the breach as the observance.

Democracy might have many mansions, but Communism was held to be all of a piece. Its spread had to be contained in South-East Asia. The USA took the lead in forming the treaty organization based on the NATO model (Pakistani membership has already been alluded to). The only other Asian members were the Philippines and Thailand. The USA, Britain and France were joined by Australia and New Zealand. Earlier, the Australian government had shown conspicuous enthusiasm to send troops to fight in Korea. Both countries had signed a pact with the USA in 1951. Although the new British (and Australian) queen, Elizabeth, paid the first visit of a reigning monarch to Australia in 1954, and British emigration was flowing to the country, Australia seemed to be edging towards Asia.

Japan: *hors de combat*

Pre-1945, the most significant Asian power was Japan. Now, however it played no direct part in the shaping of Asia. Post-war, the shaping of Japan itself had been almost exclusively in American hands. It therefore experienced no zonal division between different Powers. The imperial system remained in place. Emperor Hirohito was neither displaced nor tried as a war criminal – though there were some war trials – but under a new Constitution drafted in 1946 (for implementation in the following year) under the eyes of the American Supreme Commander, MacArthur, he was turned into a constitutional monarch with ample opportunity to pursue his harmless interest in marine biology. A Japanese government remained in existence under the watchful superintendence of MacArthur. There was some 'purging' of the civil service, but there might have been more. Gradually a constructive symbiosis emerged. A path, necessarily contentious, was steered which edged Japan along a 'Western' road: votes for women, freedom of the press, recognition of trade unions. Some foreign voices, smarting from war experiences, thought that the Occupying Power's approach was too riddled with compromise in its desire to foster a 'reliable' Japan. On the other hand, too severe an assault on 'tradition' might bring about a backlash against the emerging parliamentary democracy. Economic recovery was key, though economic success would no doubt bring its own anxieties. It received a substantial stimulus from American orders for war supplies during the Korean War. Japan itself, however, for very obvious reasons, could not participate in that war. It only again became a sovereign state in 1951. The USA and the UK had invited fifty other states to a conference in San Francisco in September 1951 to conclude a settlement with Japan. It had been mooted, under various guises, for some time. The Soviet Union accepted but, in the event, refused to sign the ensuing treaty. Japan formally renounced Korea, Taiwan, the Kuril Islands and South Sakhalin.

The key figure, on the Japanese side, in this post-war decade was Shigeru Yoshida, who served as Prime Minister (and Foreign Secretary) from 1948 until he was ousted in 1954. He became the lynchpin of its post-war 'reincorporation'. In 1948 he was 70. He had entered the Japanese diplomatic service in 1906, the year of the Japanese-Russian war, when an 'Asiatic' power had defeated a 'European' power for the first time. The Anglo-Japanese alliance had been concluded four years earlier. His inter-war career took him to Rome and then to London. He was ambassador at a crucial period in Anglo-Japanese relations and an advocate, though an unsuccessful one, of a worldwide Anglo-Japanese agreement on economic and political matters. His role in Japan after his return in 1938 led to initial imprisonment in 1945. Even though it was with the USA that he had to deal at close quarters, his first-hand knowledge of one English-speaking world facilitated relationships over his years in office. There was also an unexpected final twist to his story. He had apparently been drawn to Catholicism, privately, for many years. He was baptized in 1967, in the year of his death. It was a development which exposes the unexpected cross-currents at work in Japanese society.

Article 9 of the Japanese constitution declared that the Japanese people forever renounced war, or the threat of it, as a sovereign right of the nation. For this reason, Japan would not maintain land, sea and air forces. It was a drastic step, arising as much from American insistence as from a wholesale Japanese revulsion. However, on the very day that the San Francisco Treaty was signed the USA and Japan concluded a separate treaty. The USA could maintain land, sea and air forces in and around Japan. Japan would have no say in their use to maintain 'international peace and security in the Far East'. It would defend the country against external attack. It would even, should the Japanese government request, use its forces against riots (supposing that they were instigated externally). The USA could exercise a veto should the Japanese government wish to permit any other Power to have bases or station troops on its territory. Japan therefore remained central to American thinking about Asia. In 1954, when there was talk of dominoes, Japan was spoken of as 'the keystone of US Policy in the Far East'. A China which brought both South-East Asia and Japan under its wing would represent a more formidable factor in world politics than the Japanese Empire had ever been. In the short term, at least, the soreness arising from the past precluded a 'cosying-up'. There was a bizarre, though understandable, aspect of the San Francisco signings. Neither 'China' had participated or signed. Absence was better than any presence. It was, however, an odd way to purport to settle the future of Asia. Equally odd, however, though equally understandable, was the position of a militarily hobbled Japan. It was apparently cocooned, without time limit, within a pan-Pacific world detached, at least as far as power politics was concerned, from an Asia for which , for half a century, it had been, alternately, magnet and menace. The Pacific was now a kind of American lake.

Third worlds and other worlds: bonding in Bandung

Material in this chapter, and in the two previous, has highlighted conspicuous but still incomplete withdrawals (or ejections) of European colonial power. To think in terms of 'the rest of the world', however, as was often still done, in varying degrees, in Europe, the USA or the Soviet Union, revealed a deep mindset which assumed that the real epicentre could not be in the Middle East, Asia or Africa. It was that very mindset which was now under challenge. It posed again old questions about 'the Arab world'. Africa, however, south of the Sahara, has thus far scarcely been touched upon in this volume. It had not yet 'stood up' in the world. By 1955, however, there was a sense, if not a complete one, that Asia had 'arisen'. We have noted the salient points: the dependent British India of 1945 had become an independent India and an independent Pakistan: China was a People's Republic: Indonesia, Burma and the Philippines were also newly independent states. Yet this was not entirely 'Asia for the Asians'. The future of 'Indo-China', as has just been noted, was uncertain. War in Korea in 1950 brought non-Asians into the peninsula. Japan remained under American tutelage. There were many other uncertainties about how 'Asia' might be configured in the new world – and indeed whether the 'Asian continent' was in reality a set of 'worlds' – perhaps South Asia, South-East Asia, East Asia – only tenuously and contentiously sharing common cultural or political perspectives on the world. It is these alignments, or lack of them, which are explored in this chapter. The European withdrawal (or ejection) had still some to time run, but the end was in sight. Individual questions of national or regional identity were linked to the general question of the collective alignment of all 'emerging countries'.

The changes that have been highlighted had their individual significance. Did they add up to a 'Third World'? An answer came from an Indonesia which had gained its independence from Dutch rule in 1949. Its President, Achmad Sukarno, called 'Afro-Asian' leaders to his country in April 1955 to consider their global alignment. He chose Bandung, a city in West Java, as the meeting place. It expressed, through its buildings in the 1950s, the blending of its and the country's pasts. Part of the city had been burnt in 1945 during fighting between insurgents and Dutch forces seeking to reimpose their colonial authority. Its climate and late nineteenth-century hotels and clubs had made it attractive for Europeans. It was nicknamed the 'Paris of Java'. The conference met in one such building, the former Concordia Club. Bandung was a 'showcase' city in which the young Sukarno had once studied. Whether its blending of Javanese and Dutch colonial styles could in turn facilitate an 'Afro-Asian' blending was another matter. 'Indonesia' was itself a precarious creation. These were 'Indian islands'. Chinese workers, too, had come in under the Dutch aegis to develop the infrastructure of Bandung . Chinese communities in other islands, also, were strongly present in commercial life. Tension between its component islands was endemic, reflecting in turn different cultural and religious balances. Arab traders had brought Islam, Dutch missionaries had brought Christianity (substantially Protestant) – both superimposed upon a culture which showed its Hindu origins. Mohammed Natsir (b.1908), head of Indonesia's largest party, Masyumi, urged an Islamic future that was neither communist nor capitalist.

'Pan-Islam' in itself would constitute a third world. The Indonesian mixture was rich and potentially explosive.

It had been after four years of struggle that Sukarno and his colleagues had gone to The Hague in the Netherlands in August 1949 to sign an agreement establishing the Federal United States of Indonesia. Dutch attempts to form a kind of condominium had failed but there was supposed to be a Netherlands–Indonesia Union which would sustain a continuing relationship. By the end of the year, however, it had become a fiction. The USA had played a not unimportant part in compelling the Dutch to withdraw, using the possible cutting-off of Marshall Aid to the Netherlands as a weapon. Looking to a world without European colonialism, it wanted to support Sukarno, whose forces had put down a Communist rebellion in Sumatra the previous year. Even so, with independence, there still remained what the new government regarded as unfinished business. The Dutch retained West New Guinea (West Irian), which they had administered separately but which Indonesia said it should incorporate. Portuguese rule in East Timor also continued.

Leaders gathering in Bandung, however, would not find their host drawing attention to his local difficulties. What gave the conference its rationale was anti-colonial solidarity, but for most of the participants 'nation-building', though not so described, constituted their common task – by whatever means. The conference was organized by Indonesia, Burma (later Myanmar), Pakistan, Ceylon (later Sri Lanka) and India. Present were leaders from the following states: Afghanistan, Bhutan, Burma, Cambodia, Ceylon, the People's Republic of China, Egypt, Ethiopia, India, Indonesia, Iran, Iraq, Japan, Jordan, Laos, Lebanon, Laos, Lebanon, Liberia, Libya, Mongolia, Nepal, Pakistan, the Philippines, Saudi Arabia, Syria, Thailand, Turkey, Vietnam (North and South) and Yemen. South Africa, Taiwan, Israel and North and South Korea were not invited. Even with this omission, to run through this list is to recognize its variety in the size, standing and alignment of the states in attendance. The Asian heavyweights who took centre stage were Jawaharlal Nehru of India and Zhou Enlai of China. The latter might never have reached Bandung in 1955. The aircraft on which he was due to travel was blown up. Had he not switched planes, he would have been among the casualties. It was very important that China should be there on this new world stage. It was a further step beyond the negotiations in which he had taken part, as mentioned, in Geneva the previous year in 'settling' Indo-China. By the time Nehru arrived in Bandung, India was proud to show that parliamentary democracy was not merely an alien Western irrelevance. It could work for the people – over time. Part, at least, of the moral authority and leadership which Nehru aspired to when in Indonesia rested on this claim. Whether its achievement thus far did indeed make it *the* example for Asia was another matter. Others might think differently.

A declaration of principle emerging from a gathering claiming to represent half of the world's population was to be expected. What kind of 'world' it really was, or could be, was another matter. There were so many different voices. The speeches and statements made at the conference were not short in aspiration. A ten-point charter proclaimed agreement amongst the participants on great principles. They included respect for fundamental human rights, for the purposes and principles of the charter of the UN and for the sovereignty and territorial integrity of all nations. The equality of all races was affirmed and, with it, the equality of all nations large and small. The participants would abstain from interfering in the affairs of other countries, from taking part in collective defence arrangements which would serve any particular interests of the Big Powers, and from exerting pressure on other countries. The 'Big Powers', it was evident, were primarily Western. It was anti-colonialism on which all could unite, though whether the Soviet Union engaged in colonialism was not certain. It was not an occasion for academic discussion of where colonialism began and ended. Zhou Enlai signed an article which declared that overseas Chinese owed their primary loyalty to the country in which they lived. Sukarno had stated proudly in his opening speech that this was the first international conference of coloured peoples in the history of mankind.

The emphasis on colour is noteworthy. The paradoxes of the moment did not escape the black ex-Communist American writer Richard Wright, now living outside the USA, who attended. In his book *The Color Curtain* (1956) he asked himself what these nations had in common and answered 'Nothing'. It was their common if varied relationship with 'the West' which gave them any coherence. The paradox was that the only language in which most of the delegates could freely communicate with each other was English. 'Non-alignment', however, seemed the only answer for what was now beginning to be called 'the Third World' – the term was probably coined in 1952. It remained to be seen, however, when Nasser, Nehru, Zhou Enlai and many others went home, whether 'anti-colonialism' could translate into something both distinctive and positive. The gathering in Indonesia was also awkward in its timing. It was a broadly 'Asian' gathering. 'Africa' was present in the form of three states – Egypt, Ethiopia and Liberia. The Africa they represented was scarcely 'typical'. No invitation was sent to South Africa. Given that there were no other independent states, the situation was not surprising – but that position was about to change and change rapidly. It will be explored in Part Three. The absence of 'Africa' from the conference, as from this part of the book, indicated how much more realigning lay ahead before that continent's significance impacted globally.

In the longer term, 'Bandung' might or might not signify that there really was a 'Third World' capable, as such, of playing its part, alongside the other two worlds, in guiding the world's affairs. For the moment, it could not be the case. A few months after the Indonesian conference, in July 1955, a very different conference took place in neutral Switzerland. It was a 'summit' involving four Great Powers: the USA, the Soviet Union, Britain and France. Churchill had hankered after such a meeting. His successor, Eden, who had known Eisenhower well since world-war days, swiftly pressed for one. A face-to-face encounter, such as had not happened at the highest level for nearly a decade, might offer a way forward. From the Soviet side, Eisenhower was a known entity. From the American side, it appeared likely that it was Khrushchev who really mattered in the post-Stalin leadership. Perhaps some kind of global 'fresh start' was possible. The tension between Washington and Beijing over the 'offshore islands' in the Formosa Straits had been sharp at the beginning of the year. Statesmen worried about the possible use of nuclear weapons. Eisenhower asked himself whether 'the civilized world' could really contemplate their use against China. The bombs available were a thousand times more powerful than those which had been dropped on Japan in the war. Soviet bombs and delivery capabilities had also 'improved'. There had been pessimists in 1945 who thought that the world, through the Great Powers, would destroy itself. A decade later, that had not happened. Yet it became ever more apparent that terms like 'victory' or 'defeat' made little sense in a nuclear conflict. The decision by Eisenhower to go to Geneva has been given great significance. It has been interpreted as meaning that any American dream of winning a war by military means was at an end. On and off, over the previous few years Secretary of State Dulles had talked not just of 'containment' but of liberating peoples from the tyrannies in which they were enslaved. He was thinking of Eastern Europe. When he met Bulganin in Geneva, he did not want to be photographed smiling in his company – for the signal that it would send that all hope of liberation was lost. His President, however, could not resist a grin. Not that that led to any substantive progress in reducing the arms race. Eisenhower floated, unsuccessfully, an 'Open Skies' proposal whereby both sides would overfly each other's territory and take military photographs (Eisenhower went ahead with overflying anyway). As the leaders left for home, something called 'the spirit of Geneva' was discerned by commentators, though it did not amount to anything concrete. 'Europe' as has been discussed earlier appeared to be 'settled'. 'The West' might hold the 'moral high ground' in relation to Eastern Europe, though it availed it little, but in the Third World it lost ground. What happened in the world of Bandung, as in the world of Geneva, and the interaction between the two, might provide the key to the world's future.

Part 2 further reading

Ambrose, Stephen and Brinkley, Douglas G., *Rise to Globalism: American Foreign Policy since 1938* (Penguin, Harmondsworth, 2012).
Archer, Clive, ed., *International Organizations* (Routledge, London,1992).
Ball, S.J., *The International History of the Cold War 1947–1991* (Arnold, London, 1998).
Bell, P.M.H., *France and Britain 1940–1994: The Long Separation* (Longman, London, 1997).
Boyle, Peter G., *Eisenhower* (Pearson Education, London, 2005).
Breslin, Shaun, *Mao* (Pearson Education, London, 1990).
Brown, Judith M., *Nehru* (Pearson Education, London, 1999).
Geppert, Dominik, ed., *The Postwar Challenge: Cultural, Social and Political Change in Western Europe, 1945–58* (Oxford University Press, Oxford, 2003).
Iriye, Akira, *Global Community: The Role of International Organizations in the Making of the Contemporary World* (University of California Press, Berkeley, 1999).
Irving, Ronald, *Adenauer* (Pearson Education, London, 2002).
Mitter, Rana, *A Bitter Revolution: China's Struggle with the Modern World* (Oxford University Press, Oxford, 2004).
Robbins, Keith, *Britain and Europe, 1789–2005* (Arnold, London, 2005).
Talbot, Ian, *India and Pakistan* (Arnold, London, 2000).
Vickers, Adrian, *A History of Modern Indonesia* (Cambridge University Press, Cambridge, 2005).

Part 3
1955–1965:
TO THE BRINK AND
BACK

World leaders in power in 1955, as indeed for some time thereafter, belonged to a generation for whom the war had been the central experience of their political lives. The world should never again endure a conflict that was global. A decade later, one had indeed been avoided, but world affairs had scarcely been regulated, if that is the word, on the lines being envisaged in 1945. The UN was still in existence and might grow in stature and effectiveness, but events seemed to show that it could not be *the* world authority. The circumstances of the Korean War had illustrated that there was no single 'world' able to act unanimously against 'aggression'. That is not to say, however, that its institutions, procedures and conventions served no useful 'global' purpose in a world of states, but it was indisputable that interstate or intersystem rivalry, as identified in Part Two, remained vigorous. National leaders, whether elected or unelected, defended 'national interests'. Global history substantially remained the history of specific countries, regions, continents and indeed civilizations, with their internally generated and historically conditioned concerns. In this sense, the framework of 1945 extends beyond the initial decade. Yet the intensity of hostility was never constant. Different incidents triggered different levels of response. The context was always changing.

The July 1955 Geneva conference, concluding Part 2, seemed to mark one such moment. The ice of the previous half-dozen years was breaking up. A 'spirit of Geneva' was identified as the USA, the Soviet Union, Britain and France talked over the major issues of the Cold War in Europe. Very little of substance in fact emerged, but participants talked privately of an improved 'atmosphere'. In this light, slowly, over the next few years we can detect a significant transition. The 'spirit of Geneva', however, was not the only one evident. Indeed, Part 2 opens with two crises in the following year – Hungary and Suez. They were different in nature. Revolution in the former, from the Soviet perspective, challenged the integrity of the 'bloc'. That could not be contemplated. It also revealed, however, that whatever might have been said about rolling back Communism, the Western Powers would do nothing to intervene.

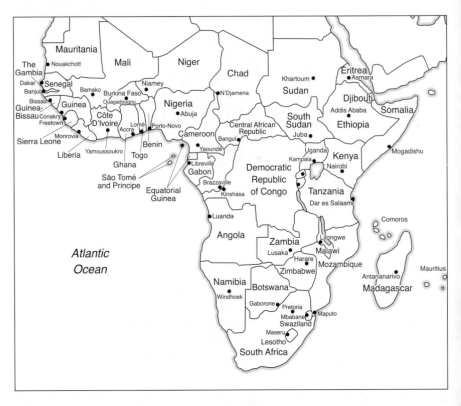

Map 3 Sub-Saharan
Africa, 2012

Map 4 Maghreb and the
Middle East, 2012

Whatever might or might not be done thereafter to resolve the question of Germany, a divided Europe had to be accepted. Suez, arguably, had more complex aspects: the capacity of Britain and France to act as Great Powers, their relationship with the USA, the status of Israel, Egypt and the Arab Middle East being among them. It was an episode that revealed unexpected cracks in alignment. The UN might be the agency through which peace could be restored. It had not been able to prevent conflict. The crisis also showed that the Commonwealth of Nations, with its 'new' and 'old' members, could not come to a common position.

The Cuban revolution added a further dimension. South America was now sharing in the world's ideological rift and posed fresh questions about 'the Americas'. There was a grave confrontation between the Soviet Union and the USA. Some contemporaries thought nuclear disaster was imminent. There was little scope for the allies or associates of either Superpower to influence the outcome. Washington and Moscow might be able to reduce the tension that had arisen by reaching deals in different parts of the world. The sense of their paramount power remained strong. The feature of the decade after 1955, however, was the emergence of Africa, that is to say the accelerating but still not complete liberation of its countries from European colonial rule. Each route had its particular characteristics, but in many instances there were common features: 'nationhood' within state boundaries which included different ethnic groups and languages, religious differences between Christians and Muslims, and the existence of European settler communities. Since state boundaries had been

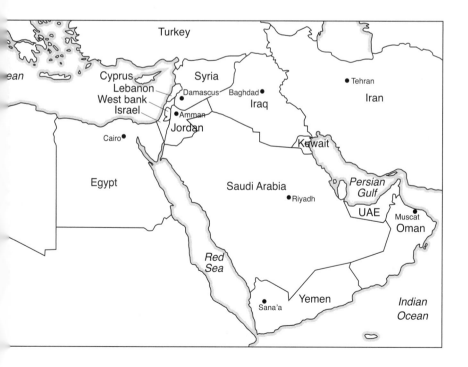

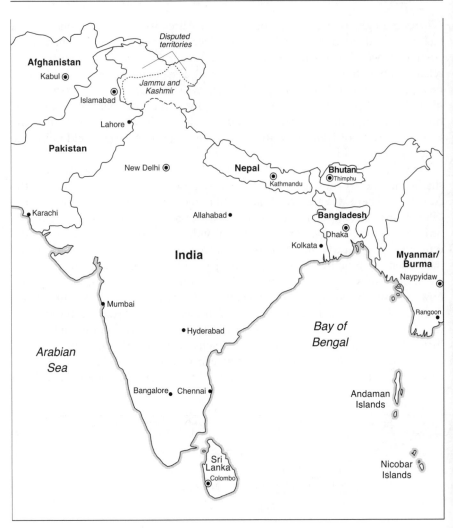

Map 5 South Asia, 2012

imposed by the departing Powers perhaps it was the moment, some African leaders said, to move directly to 'African unity', perhaps initially on a regional basis. The problems were legion and the outcomes as much influenced by external as by indigenous factors.

Problems of a similar character continued to be present in Asia. Manifested in Part Two, they could comparably erupt in this. Afro-Asian countries knew that at least some of their internal difficulties had been inherited from, if not caused by, a European colonial era. It generated, in certain circumstances, a solidarity of sentiment. Whether it was anything more, however, remained to be seen. To be non-aligned was a negative definition. Asia and Africa were very different, each with regional/national identities (and animosities) so strong as to preclude the notion that there was an 'Asian' or 'African' voice in the world.

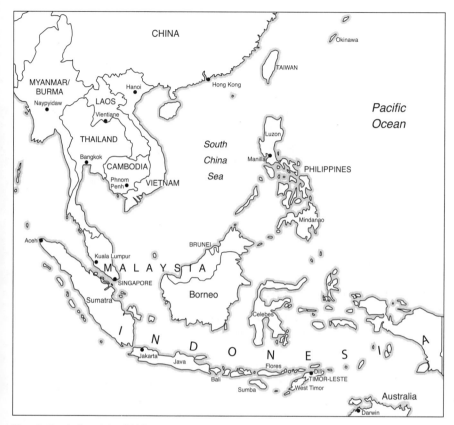

Map 6 South-East Asia, 2012

This part of the book therefore continues to explore, from different angles, both developments in the internal history of states and continents and their wider impact on the always ongoing rebalancing of the 'international community'. It was a decade where strains were apparent within the Free and within the Communist world, where continents 'emerged' into tentative prominence, and where fresh meanings were being given to 'West' and 'East'.

9

Superpowers and Subordinates: The Middle East and Europe

Suez, 1956: whose canal?

The last British troops left their Suez Canal base on 13 June 1956 in accordance with the 1954 British–Egyptian agreement. Within six weeks, however, Suez was once again the point where worlds intersected: Israel, Egypt, the Arab world, Western Europe, the USA, the Soviet Union. The origin, course and conclusion of the crisis revealed much about the mindset and preoccupations of the participants. The youthful Nasser had returned from Bandung feeling that the world was ripe for change. The 'non-aligned' world might not, as yet, itself be adequately internally aligned, but it gave him some potential leverage. He gained wisdom from Marshal Tito in discussions on an Adriatic island. He knew something about the balancing act required of those who inhabited the 'in-between' world. Both Washington and Moscow wanted friends. The trick was to accept their offers without slipping into subordination. Egypt's bid for meaningful independence needed to be taken a stage further.

A mention of Ferdinand de Lesseps – the canal's original builder – in a speech Nasser was giving in Alexandria on 26 July 1956 was the cue for action. Egyptian police and officials then took over the offices of the Paris-registered international company, with its large British and French shareholding, which owned the Suez Canal. This 'state within a state', as he put it, would end. The step was not rashly considered, though Nasser could not have envisaged all that would flow from it. Throughout its existence, the canal had a symbolic significance over and above its commercial role. It was 'an international artery'. It followed, therefore, that how the world reacted would reveal much about its current dynamics.

For Nasser, nationalization constituted a further escape from foreign domination. Egypt took a mere 7 per cent of gross profits and had few members on the board of the company. The lie would be given to haughty claims that Egypt lacked the capacity to run the canal efficiently. Its revenues could be used – although they were not in themselves sufficient – for other pressing purposes, notably building the High Dam on the Nile at Aswan. Early in 1956 Egypt had sought to negotiate large loans from the World Bank for this construction scheme. It would both enable more land to come under cultivation and generate power for an ambitious industrialization programme. A week before Nasser's Alexandria speech, the USA, Britain and then the World Bank had retracted their provisional agreements to provide funding. The former two had been regarding Nasser ambivalently. He might not, in practice, be as 'anti-Western' as his rhetoric had been suggesting, from Bandung onwards. However, in recognizing China and in acquiring Soviet arms through an agreement with Czechoslovakia, Nasser made clear that Egypt would go its own way. In March, British Prime Minister Eden had painted a stark picture: it was either him or us. Nasser should therefore be taught a lesson, but what? British Foreign Office Middle East 'expert', Sir Evelyn Shuckburgh, recorded in his diary that 'The time has come when we must show strength', and Nasser must be overthrown. If Nasser could have read this, he would not have been surprised. His own calculation, probably, was that there would be expressions of outrage from Western capitals (Washington, London and Paris) but, in the end, no use of force. Domestically, in Egypt, the step would be popular. In June 1956 Nasser, the only candidate, had been elected as president. This was 'our canal'.

Suez: disarray of the West

In official circles in London and Paris there was an understanding that Western Europe was at a decisive moment in its relationship with Egypt, and by extension, in all probability, with the entire Middle East. The British Chancellor of the Exchequer, Macmillan, suggested that if Nasser 'got away with it' it would be the end of British influence and strength in the region for ever. The 'lesson of appeasement' was apparently that unless dictators were stopped in their tracks they always came back for more. On this reading, Nasser – leaders of the major parties told the British House of Commons – was another Hitler or Mussolini. There was a nascent Caesar in Cairo who sought to rule from the Gulf to the Atlantic. France, struggling in Algeria, fully shared Eden's wish not to be 'kicked out'. Morrison, former Labour foreign secretary, thought Egypt was undermining international good practice. 'The world' had an interest. Unilateralism by any country could not be countenanced.

Twenty-two countries whose vessels used the canal were persuaded to attend a conference in London in August chaired by Britain and France. Although the impetus therefore came from those countries, it was a proposal for an international Suez Canal Board put forward by the US Secretary of State, John Foster Dulles, on which most of the participants agreed. The 'world', embodied in this instance in the Australian prime minister, together with the foreign ministers of Sweden, Iran and Ethiopia and a US Under-Secretary of State, took the plan to Cairo. It was rejected. The visitors were told that they were proposing a new form of imperialism. In turn, again meeting in London, the eighteen countries supporting the Dulles Plan agreed to form a Canal Users' Association. On 23 September, Britain and France took the issue to the UN Security Council. At its meeting on 13 October, after a week of discussions in which Egypt had also been invited to participate, the Council agreed with the British–French contention that the Canal was important as an international waterway. However, a Soviet veto blocked the specific conclusion that outside Powers should ensure that no constraints were placed by Egypt on the use of the Canal. It was evident that the UN, as such, would not be able to ensure 'internationalization' in a form which met British–French wishes.

France, in particular, feared that the USA would accept an outcome which would leave Nasser in control. Secret diplomacy went to work. French–Israeli and British–French meetings were followed by trilateral sessions on 21 and 22 October. The Israeli interest was to humiliate Cairo before it waxed stronger with Eastern-bloc arms. The Israelis were therefore to launch an attack which would 'threaten' the Canal and give the British and French the pretext for a military action which would 'protect' it. Israeli forces invaded the Sinai Peninsula on 29 October – to be greeted, the following day, by the expected British–French ultimatum that the advance should halt and pull back from the Canal. Israel indicated that it would comply in due course. Its progress, however, was so complete that the notion of 'separating the combatants' was almost redundant from the outset. Egypt, however, rejected the ultimatum that it too should pull back from the Canal (in what was its own territory). It also refused to countenance the temporary presence, as it was put, of British–French forces in Port Said and Ismailia. The substantial British cross-party unity collapsed in acrimony at this point. The Labour leader, Gaitskell, condemned an attempt to impose a solution by force, at least before the Security Council and the House of Commons had deliberated further. At this point there was a surprise. The USA put forward a resolution on 30 October calling upon Israel to halt its advance and withdraw behind its frontiers. For the first time, together with France, Britain exercised a veto in the Security Council. The following day aircraft from the two countries bombed Egyptian airfields. Eden talked of 'police action'; Gaitskell of 'reckless war'. The Egyptians sank ships and blocked the canal. On 5 November British and French paratroops landed at its northern entrance.

There could be little doubt that the immediate objective, whatever happened thereafter, was to topple Nasser. The British ambassador in Cairo, however, thought that while Egyptian forces could be defeated the difficulties would then start. Only an Egyptian government untainted by the occupying forces could last. The 'world' would surely understand that a British government was entitled to take the steps it was taking. 'Everybody', according to Eden, knew that the UN was 'not yet' in a position to take action. The British and French did have the forces available. They would not stay a moment longer than was necessary to produce an 'international solution' to the many problems of the area. The expression 'temporary occupation', unsurprisingly, had a rather hollow ring in Cairo. The British–French expedition went ahead – the French yielding command to the British.

There were paradoxes, at many levels, in this position. Here was a plot and an expedition launched by a prime minister whose entire career had been spent in dealing with foreign affairs. Perhaps he felt that this was the last throw of the dice for his country as a genuine Great Power. Some British diplomats thought

that he had lost his head (there was indeed some personal instability at this juncture). More generally, however, there was some deep foreboding in official
circles. Sir Ivone Kirkpatrick, the Permanent Under-Secretary at the Foreign
Office, thought that, Eden apart, the country had lost the will to live. Within
two years, Nasser would have deprived Britain of vital oil, the sterling area
would have fallen apart, no European defence against the further spread of
Communism would be possible, and unemployment and unrest would rise. The
British standard of living would be reduced – to that of the Yugoslavs or the
Egyptians. The tendency to exonerate that 'brigand' Nasser in sections of the
British press was incomprehensible. Sir Ivone thought that a country which
could not pay for its own defence would be 'finished'. The diplomatic manoeuvres at this time cannot be followed in detail here, but their rationale stemmed
from this widespread sense of imminent British doom.

Through the late summer of 1956 in the USA, Eisenhower was seeking re-
election. There was a lot to be said for playing the crisis long. He did not want
a military solution. The British seemed to suppose that they could act (with
France) on their own. Suddenly, in the correspondence between Washington
and London, there was an emptiness. There had been differences in detail, as
previously noted, but British–American global co-operation was the power-
house of 'the West'. Now there was a falling-out which exposed where, beneath
an apparently common world-view, power to act really lay. The US administration hated being kept in the dark by the Europeans – not that it lacked ways of
finding out just what was going on. Eisenhower, at this juncture, had powerful
financial and other levers and British diplomats found him 'unbelievably hostile'
in wishing to pull them. Sir Evelyn Shuckburgh, one such, could not believe
that Eisenhower would actually drive the UN to act so decisively and with such
speed. On 6 November the UN General Assembly endorsed the sending of an
Emergency Force. Troops from Canada, Colombia, Denmark, Finland, India,
Norway, Sweden and Yugoslavia now found themselves in an unfamiliar location. The British and French accepted a ceasefire (but would not withdraw their
troops until after the Emergency Force arrived). Their evacuation was complete
on 22 December. An expedition had been ignominiously ended. Nasser
remained in office. Eisenhower was re-elected on 6 November with a substantial
majority of the popular vote (though the Republicans as a whole fared badly).
The Canal did not return to 'internationalization'. A UN-sponsored fleet began
to clear the Canal so that 'the world's highway' could resume its normal business. The British Prime Minister sought the recuperative sun of Jamaica. In
January 1957 he resigned.

Suez: conclusions and implications

Many conclusions could be drawn – by the outside Powers most closely involved
and by Middle Eastern countries. There were implications for the UN and for
other bodies, such as the Commonwealth of Nations.

The specific conclusion in the Middle East itself seemed clear. President
Nasser was carried through the streets of Port Said in triumph. He was, as it
were, the 'son of Saladin'. He told his audiences how Arabs in the past had risen

as one man to repel the fanatic crusaders who had attacked them in Syria, Palestine and Egypt. Now the crusaders were being repelled again. Leading up to Suez, British ministers had frequently expressed alarm amongst themselves that 'Nasserism' would inflame the entire Middle East. Nasser's *The Philosophy of the Revolution* had argued that Arab and Egyptian history was a homogenous whole. 'Arab Unity' did not necessarily mean that all Arab countries should be combined into one country – but it might. The status Nasser had gained might take him anywhere. Yet there was something paradoxical about the situation. Events had combined to humiliate Britain and France in the region, undermining such of their erstwhile status as lingered. Egyptian forces, however, had undeniably been battered by the Israelis. The latter had withdrawn, under American pressure, but on the understanding that the Emergency Force would ensure freedom of passage through the Straits of Tiran (crucial for the Israeli port of Eilat). Egyptian forces did not re-enter the Gaza strip (from which, for a decade, irregular attacks on Israel now largely ceased). The Force would have to be withdrawn if Egypt, at some future date, requested it – that happened in May 1967 – but, for the moment, this was a real Israeli gain.

Some French opinion concluded that France had 'saved' Israel in 1956, but the country's fundamental insecurity remained. In the early 1950s thousands of Jews from Europe and North Africa had settled, a movement which received fresh impetus after 1956. They came from very different cultural milieux. Israel was undoubtedly 'democratic', but its electoral system and profusion of parties virtually ensured complex coalition government. Questions about its identity caused internal complications. Secular and religious definitions of Jewishness were in unresolved competition. Neighbouring Arab states did not accept that Jews had an unrestricted 'right of return' to Israel. The 'rightful ownership' of territory, if pursued on the basis advanced to justify the existence of Israel, would destabilize many states around the world. Israel's political leadership sought to strengthen ties with the USA. The two countries, it was claimed, had a common opponent. The 'Nazi–Communists' who were rampaging with their tanks in Hungary in 1956, as David Ben-Gurion, the most prominent Israeli politician put it, were arming Israel's neighbour, Syria. If necessary, however, Israel would fight on its own.

At another level, the inescapable conclusion for 'world order', as things stood, was that the UN could not offer a general system of collective security. The 'UN action' in Korea, in procedural terms itself something of a fluke, had been a serious war. It was not a fleeting 'police action'. There were other military contributions, but the burden had fallen on the USA, not on 'the world'. It was doubtful whether the Korean War constituted an enduring precedent for future UN action. To some minds, and for some governments, the UN, as 'the voice of the world', was no more than a façade. Effective power to act in particular situations still fundamentally rested with the superpowers. Their use of the veto kept a sense of realism about what 'the international community' could achieve. The veto's existence, however, did not altogether cripple the possibility of 'international action'. The 'Uniting for Peace' Resolution of November 1950 had made provision for the General Assembly to make recommendations for collective measures in the event of a lack of unity among the permanent members. It was this procedure which was used in 1956 against Britain and France. The Secretary-General gained increased prominence. Dag Hammarskjöld, a Swede following a Norwegian, took over as 'the keeper of the conscience of the world' in 1953. He wanted to raise the profile of his office. The fact that his predecessor had failed to gain Soviet support for reappointment was an indication, however, that one or other Power would always be liable to question the 'neutrality' of the Secretary-General. The UN might perhaps have an increasing role in 'keeping' rather than in 'enforcing' the peace. The 'rules of engagement' in such contexts raised thorny issues. So, while 'realists' considered the UN little more than a 'talking shop', this was to dismiss it too easily. The world could not do without it.

The role of the UN in 'clearing up' was indeed significant but it had not controlled the crisis. Britain and France had acted in what were perceived to be their own interests. The USA had brought them to heel. The Organization over the next few years continued to expand its membership and thus represent the kind of world that was coming into existence. Sierra Leone, in West Africa, became the hundredth member in 1961. Most new member states were themselves new. As an institution, however, it could not stand outside and above the world's tensions. It was structurally bound into them. The Security Council could not 'police' the world since one or other of its permanent members was quite likely to be involved, directly or indirectly, in any significant conflict. Such had been the case with France in Indo-China and in the case of Suez and, as shortly to be seen, with Hungary. There were 'anomalies'. Taiwan, not the People's Republic, continued to occupy the 'China' seat. The Security Council became somewhat unconvincing in so far as it was based on a notion of the equal standing of its permanent members, Britain, France, the Soviet Union and the USA. It was to be enlarged by the admission of two further non-permanent members and thus, to a degree, made more inclusive, but the impact of this step was for the future.

Other international bodies took stock. The Canal crisis tested the cohesion of a body like the Commonwealth of Nations with its own aspirations to link East and West. In the early 1950s it had been seeking to present itself as a unique organization at this juncture. Its members spanned the globe. Suez put its coherence and utility to its first serious test. The reactions of its widely separated membership provide clues about the way different worlds were moving.

In Ottawa, the Canadian government attached particular importance to the Commonwealth's role as a 'bridge to Asia' and wanted to see the dispute resolved through the UN. The Eastern Mediterranean, however, carried much more significance, some of it emotional, for Australia and New Zealand. The Australian Foreign Minister at this moment, R.G. Casey, a dozen years earlier, had been representing the UK government in Cairo. Menzies, the Prime Minister, happened initially to be in Washington when the crisis broke (and Holland, the Prime Minister of New Zealand, was in Los Angeles). Such locations in themselves testified to the lure of the USA. New Zealand, an Opposition Labour Party spokesman stated publicly, wanted the British lion to roar. Menzies too, as noted above, was prepared to involve himself personally and align Australia with the 'mother country'. Old reflexes, in both instances, remained strong, though not unchallenged. Some critical voices suggested that if all Canberra and Wellington had to do was to fall in line with London, their Foreign Affairs Departments and Ministers were redundant. It might even be that the Suez Canal was no longer as economically vital for the Antipodean countries as legend had long had it.

South Africa had another perspective. Since 1948, the National Party in power under D.F. Malan, and continued under J. Strijdom, asserted a strong Afrikaner standpoint. The notion of a 'British Commonwealth' had no appeal. However English speakers reacted, South Africa should cut off the lingering 'British' connection. But, while Afrikaner/English-speaking antipathies remained, all South Africa's whites might have to sink them in order to sustain their minority rule. That rule and the implementation of a policy of *Apartheid* was attracting some, though as yet limited, outside criticism. The South African government knew what was being said at Bandung. Earlier, it had noted the British withdrawal from the Indian subcontinent. In West Africa at least, Britain might before long withdraw from the African continent. Withdrawal would produce increased Asian–African pressure, however exerted, to bring about internal change in South Africa itself. In such circumstances, the Pretoria government might find 'world opinion' ranged against it. That point, however, had not yet arrived.

The Suez crisis had other African aspects. Nasser projected an Egypt which had a role within the Islamic, Arab and African worlds. Cairo was indeed a long way from the Cape, but Egyptian 'African' rhetoric was nevertheless perceived as a threat. A triumph for Nasser, therefore, would not be welcome. The African National Congress (ANC) affirmed that 'the people of Africa' would not allow themselves to be used against 'their fellow Africans'. On the other hand, from the South African government's point of view, any action against Nasser which was purportedly 'international' was an unwelcome precedent. South Africa wanted no intrusion in matters which it regarded as 'internal'. Further, there was at least the possibility that 'round the Cape' would lastingly prove a safer route for international shipping, with economic benefit to South African ports. The government made use of this unexpected opportunity to emphasize how important South Africa was to 'the West' in the global struggle against Communism. That positioning in turn presented Britain with a quandary.

No such lingering 'pan-British past' could be expected from the 'New Commonwealth', India, Pakistan and Ceylon, as they considered 'Suez'. Nehru reiterated, however, that as a principal user of the waterway, India had an interest. He sought a peaceful outcome and would use diplomacy to that end. There were more acute dilemmas for Pakistan. It had joined the 'Western' Baghdad Pact but recently and it feared India more than it did 'the West'. A rapprochement with Egypt, emphasizing a common Islamic heritage, had been attempted but made little progress. Nasser described Islam as the third of Egypt's circles, but the regime was certainly not clerical. In 1956 it closed Shari'a courts and, later, took steps to bring Muslim institutions under supervision and sometimes direct control. The Muslim Brotherhood was suppressed. Nasser's propaganda scorned the stance of the Pakistan government and its alliances. Egypt had the right to nationalize the Canal Company, the then Foreign Minister said, but he did not speak, as other Pakistani politicians did, of their brothers in Pakistan standing by the heroic people of Egypt.

The Suez crisis coincided with the outcome of a general election in Ceylon (Sri Lanka) which began to turn that country away from the firmly pro-Western orientation which the then defeated United National Party had adhered to since independence. D.S. Senanayake, until his death in 1952, had maintained close relations with Britain. Sir John Kotelawala, his relative, the third prime minister, had caused a stir at Bandung, and earned the epithet 'Donkey', for suggesting that not all colonialism was 'Western'. His fellow-Cambridge graduate, Nehru, rebuked him, though he was not himself happy at the recent Chinese 'colonialism' in Tibet. The Ceylonese election outcome ousted an often foreign-educated elite, judged 'insufficiently Sinhalese' and too accommodating, its opponents said, to Western needs (naval bases, for example). However, Solomon Bandaranaike, the new Prime Minister, leader of the Sri Lanka Freedom Party, also had an elite background and was an Oxford graduate. Bandaranaike's observations on the Suez crisis were in fact surprisingly restrained, but big change was in the offing. Sinhala became the official language and English was downgraded. Agreements with the British about the use of air and naval bases on the island were terminated. The world-view was shifting towards being 'non-Western', if not 'anti-Western'. Prominent families, from which both Kotelawala and Bandaranaike had come, had earlier not infrequently converted from Buddhism to Christianity. The tendency, now, was to revert, on the pretext that Christianity was 'Western'. A strongly Buddhist Sri Lanka, however, not only naturally upset its Christian and Muslim minorities but it also exacerbated the 'national' question. Were the regionally concentrated Tamils 'really' Sri Lankan? Bandaranaike's father had 'interpreted' Sinhalese opinion for the benefit of British Governors of Ceylon. His son was bringing the new 'Sri Lanka' into being. There was a certain irony, therefore, in that Solomon's death, only three years later, came at the hands of a Buddhist monk.

Taken in aggregate, therefore, these responses from the Commonwealth, as it was then composed, illustrate why it could not itself constitute a world of its own. It might be some kind of bridge between East and West, but not one to carry heavy traffic. Its members had their particular emphases. Nehru was critical of the Soviet Union, but it was 'colonial imperialism' in Asia which most aroused his ire. France had just agreed to relinquish its few coastal possessions in India but, to his annoyance, the Portuguese clung on to Goa. It would be an overstatement, therefore, to suppose that the 'lessons' drawn across the world from the Suez crisis were straightforward and easily applied.

'This is Hungary calling'

At the height of the Suez crisis, the Soviet Union threatened a missile attack on Britain and France, failing an immediate ceasefire and withdrawal of their forces. It seemed to Eisenhower to be a bluff. Even so, its intervention indicated to the Arab world an increasing Soviet interest in the Middle East. A friendship treaty had been signed with North Yemen in 1955. The arms agreement with Syria has just been mentioned. The Soviet Union and Egypt were both hostile to the

Baghdad Pact. The Soviet Union was apparently the stalwart opponent of 'outside intervention'.

It was, however, at this very point itself engaging in 'outside intervention'. The day before British paratroops landed at Port Said, Soviet tanks rolled back into Budapest. It was rumoured that conscripts from the Soviet Far East involved believed that they were in Egypt. The conjuncture of 'Suez' and 'Hungary', however, was extraordinary, giving rise subsequently to much fruitless speculation about what might have happened if these two crises had not occurred virtually simultaneously.

A 'new course' in Hungary had been promised, apparently with Soviet approval, by Imre Nagy as a new Premier in 1953. Two years later, after much party infighting, he was removed from the Central Committee. In June 1956, in part arising from Khrushchev's desire to repair relations with Tito, the Hungarian party boss Rakosí, a man widely loathed and feared, was replaced by Ernő Gerő. The new appointee did not believe that 'peaceful existence' globally entailed ideological concession domestically. On 23 October 1956, however, the huge statue of Stalin was toppled in Budapest. Solidarity with Poland was expressed. Demonstrators demanded the return of Nagy, the trial of Rakosí and the removal of Soviet troops from Hungary. Next day, Nagy did return as Prime Minister. Kádár, who had himself been a victim of Rakosí in the past, came in as First Secretary. Soviet troops were withdrawn from Budapest, where they had been under attack. Nagy promised in a radio broadcast on 31 October that his new government, which included prominent non-Communists, would end the one-party system. Hungary would remain socialist but would pursue a policy of international neutrality (which he wanted the UN to recognize). The country would leave the Warsaw Pact. This latter was a step too far. After hesitating, Moscow sent the Soviet Army back into Budapest, with an estimated 2500 tanks, to crush all opposition. Only after several weeks was that achieved everywhere. Figures vary, but perhaps some 22,000 Hungarians and perhaps 7000 Soviet soldiers were killed or wounded. Some 200,000 Hungarians fled the country. Some 100,000 were arrested, 26,000 of whom received prison sentences. Maybe 3000 were tried and executed. Nagy himself, two years later, was executed. The Hungarian revolution was over. The 'Soviet bloc' was saved.

'This is Hungary calling' had been the desperate cry over the radio asking for assistance from 'the West' in 1956. It had not been forthcoming. No arms or supplies were dropped to the Hungarian Freedom Fighters. Communists in Western European countries could not quite bring themselves to refer to 'Freedom Fighters' but some, in their disapproval, left the party. Eisenhower expressed anger and sympathy, but would not risk a direct military confrontation. Any talk of 'liberating' Soviet Eastern Europe had a hollow sound. In any future uprising the US cavalry would not ride to the rescue. Cynical observers soon came to regard events in Budapest as just another quixotic but necessarily doomed Hungarian revolution. Even so, a small country, linguistically on its own in the heart of Central Europe, hit the world headlines. Its treatment had implications way beyond its frontiers, just as its fate had been settled beyond them. The division of Europe was very apparent and, in the aftermath, its consolidation into West and East looked to be gathering pace.

Rome: European Community matters

In March 1957 six states – Belgium, Luxembourg, the Netherlands, France, Italy and Federal Germany – signed the Treaty of Rome which established the European Economic Community. The ECSC, widely presented as a progenitor, had been in existence since 1950. Two of these states, Belgium and France, at this point retained major colonial possessions in Africa. The preamble to the treaty spoke of the signatories seeking 'an ever closer union' but did not spell out what that entailed. The three small countries already had a common 'Benelux' relationship. Matters were more complicated for the big states. In the aftermath of both 1956 crises there was much uncertainty about the 'Europe' of the future. There was no simple linear path from the 'humiliation' of Suez or the stark outcome of Hungary to a 'new course' for Western Europe, but fundamental questions were being asked.

The British–French relationship, at this juncture, was critical. 'Suez' had been their joint operation. The two governments had acted in what they believed to be their national joint interests. They both had a long Eastern Mediterranean/Middle Eastern involvement. Perhaps it was time to make another attempt to give specific formal expression to their 'unity'. Guy Mollet, the French Premier, came forward in September 1956 with a proposal for Franco-British union. The British Foreign Office, its prudence undiminished, thought union would be unpopular and difficult to make work. The Americans, the Commonwealth, the Germans, the Scandinavians and the Benelux countries would all be upset – or so it was supposed. Nothing happened. Post-Suez, the idea was not revived. Combined operations in Egypt, therefore, did not lead to Western Europe's two major Powers agreeing to work out together the economic, and perhaps political, structure of their half of the continent. Instead, West Europeans went ahead on their own.

An Economic Community was certainly more than a free trade zone, but quite how much more might only emerge. It did not meet federalist aspirations. The members were states whose governments were elected by national electorates. From one perspective, therefore, this new six-state 'Europe' was a minimalist affair. Yet there might be deeper currents at work. The Rome treaty established a Commission, a Council of Ministers, a Court of Justice, a European Parliament and an Economic and Social Committee. Decisions in the Council would initially have to be unanimous, but there was an expectation that majority voting would come later. The task of the Commission was to make recommendations. It was not itself an executive body. Naturally some definition of their functions and ways of working accompanied the establishment of all these bodies, but it was neither possible, nor perhaps desirable, to be absolutely precise. Things would evolve. This was an event, but it was also a process. There was no perfect example to follow. What was not clear was the amount of political input required to make an Economic Community work. Deals had had to be done to create the Economic Community in the first place. They would inevitably continue. Community policy would only emerge after protracted discussion and eventual compromise. Enthusiasts for European 'integration' looked for a 'community spirit' which would transcend national haggling.

Sceptics feared a functionalist momentum which would prove unstoppable. In aspect after aspect, the prerogatives of states would be conceded in pursuit of 'union'. No one knew what the Economic Community would look like within a decade, but its creation, involving states which had so recently been at war with each other, was no mean political achievement. It was, however, not 'Europe', nor even 'Western Europe'. It did not include Britain.

A deeper and more extended Economic Community in a post-imperial Europe would surely require some new vision of Europe. Governments and their civil services might produce transnational arrangements which sidestepped thorny issues of 'sovereignty', but probably not indefinitely. Many academics in all Western Europe had come to dislike 'nationalist historiography' and indeed 'nationalism' itself. A 'nationalism' which destroyed 'empire' was laudable but otherwise there was little to commend it. It was a European invention from which 'Europe' should now emancipate itself. Yet it was not only in de Gaulle's Elysée Palace that 'a certain idea of France' was strong. A soft-pedalling of 'nation' in Federal Germany was only to be expected, and indeed desired. But was 'nation' really a wicked notion? Benelux notwithstanding, the participating countries had not lost their individuality. The signature of the 1957 treaty in Rome in one sense harked back to an ancient unifying Roman *imperium*, but something new was needed. The linking of Rome with the Vatican also had an appeal for governing parties at the time. The Economic Community was emerging in their 'Christian Europe'. Yet any description of Europe as Christian was rejected by secularists of varying hues and militancy. The 'New Europe' might be excluding all religion from 'the public space'. The collective message, in short, was mixed. Some kind of 'Europe' was being set in train but its scope and ultimate direction were unclear. Uncertainty about roles within 'the Free World' becomes more evident in the next chapter. The Soviet bloc might have been held together but shocks were coming in the Soviet Union itself.

Moscow: dropping Stalinism, preserving the Soviet bloc?

The struggle for power in the Kremlin, following Stalin's death in 1953, still rumbled on a few years later. Gyorgy Malenkov (b.1903) had been ousted from the premiership in 1955, having failed to 'solve' the problems of agriculture and industrialization (though he remained in the Praesidium). Perhaps more significant in his removal was his seditious view that world war between the Superpowers would destroy world civilization. Pursuing 'world communism' was therefore rather perilous: better simply to focus on the 'world' the Soviet Union did and could dominate. That 'Soviet zone of domination', however, compared to the world spread of the USA and its European allies, was still relatively modest. The USA and the Soviet Union, in short, were not world powers in the same way. Khrushchev (b.1894), metal fitter, wartime Party Secretary in Ukraine, and filler of many other roles, came mercurially to the fore. He defended Socialist orthodoxy. Marx, Engels and Lenin would apparently only be forgotten when shrimps learnt to whistle. There had, however, to be some shift of direction. Stalin, rather than Soviet Socialism, had to be criticized. Delegates at a special closed session of the Twentieth Party Congress in February 1956 heard the shocking 'news' that Stalin had not acted through persuasion, explanation and patient co-operation in his dealings with people. The 'cult of personality' had led to grave perversions of party principles. There would therefore be a return to 'socialist legality'. The system itself, listeners were told, was sound, and responsibility for perversion satisfactorily identified. There was no acknowledgement that the number of people who were killed or imprisoned ran into millions. The speech was not published, but its contents leaked out, within and beyond the Soviet Union. It was soon in the hands of the CIA.

It was in East–Central Europe that the significance of the 'secret session' speech was tested. Earlier, in June 1955, Khrushchev had apologized to Tito of Yugoslavia and talked of a mutual respect and non-interference which would now characterize Soviet policy. There might perhaps be different paths to Socialism. In October 1956, however, a furious Khrushchev arrived in Warsaw unannounced to confront the just-elected party First Secretary, Władysław Gomulka. For months, Poland had been disturbed, indeed had been so since the death of Stalin. Workers rioted in Poznán in June beneath banners linking 'BREAD AND FREEDOM' with 'RUSSIANS GO HOME'. Gomulka had had a chequered career within the party, including a spell in prison. Now was again the moment for 'national communism'. Symbolically, it was time for the industrial city of Katowice to abandon the name Stalingrad. The Soviet Army was to hand to intervene, as was a fleet in the Baltic, but a Khrushchev, critic of Stalinism, could scarcely unhorse a Gomulka who was another critic. Khrushchev was having to deal with a satellite Party Secretary whose appointment had not been vetted. This was not the last of the Polish 'peculiarities' with which to come to terms. Marshal Rokossovsky, Poland's Defence Minister, returned to the Soviet Union. Cardinal Wyszynski, the Catholic primate, was released from house arrest and some attempt at an accommodation with the Catholic Church began. The outcome, though still unclear in detail, constituted a kind of 'new beginning'. The 'Communist world' in Eastern Europe might be becoming variegated. Yet there could be no question of disintegration. No one could doubt that Gomulka was a Communist and the 'Polish route' might not in fact be very special. The Warsaw Pact would remain intact.

The ramifications of the speech inside the Soviet Union might, in time, be considerable, though Khrushchev did not have 'free speech' in mind. Nor was he abandoning the view that the world was witnessing a struggle between two systems, or that, in that struggle, Socialism, returning to a pristine Leninist purity, would triumph. It was rather that this competition should be 'peaceful', as principle rather than as tactic or reluctant acquiescence in reality. War was not inevitable. New forces in Africa and Asia would give the imperialists pause. It was time, therefore, for the Soviet Union to project itself globally in a new way – constructing an important steel mill in India, for example. The fact that it was the Soviet Union which in the end stepped in to support the building of the Aswan dam fell into the same category of extending 'influence'. It was time for the top team to travel the world and be garlanded with flowers.

Khrushchev and Bulganin had paid an ungarlanded state visit to Britain in April 1956. Malenkov had preceded them a few months earlier and had patted the heads of children. Khrushchev, however, found himself on the receiving end not of flattery but of a barrage of criticism – 'good humoured banter' – from British Labour leaders at a private meeting. He replied with an uninhibited tirade of his own. The Soviet leaders expressed no glowing admiration for 'the Western way of life', even after visiting Oxford University. The discovery of a British diver inspecting the sonar equipment of their Soviet cruiser docked at Portsmouth did not improve the climate. The incident was a reminder of the spying engaged in by states 'beneath the surface' or, as in the case of the American U-2 spy flights being authorized at this time, in the air. The old animosities between opposing worlds, evidently, were still very much present. In 1956, however, few supposed that the next major global point of intersection would emerge out of the Caribbean.

10
Cross-Continental Confrontations: Castro, Kennedy, Khrushchev

During the 1960s, the world witnessed interlocking crises. They involved the two Superpowers in the persons of a new boy and an old hand: Jack Kennedy and Nikita Khrushchev. They involved two 'Young Tigers', both testing their own 'New Frontiers': Fidel Castro and Jack Kennedy. The diplomatic scene shifted, as it had never before, between Havana and Washington, Bonn, Berlin and Moscow. There were experienced but largely impotent bystanders in Paris and London: Charles de Gaulle and Harold Macmillan. This was the way the world now was.

Cuban collisions: Castro and Kennedy

Fidel Castro (b.1927) entered Havana, Cuba's capital, in January 1959. Fulgencio Batista, ruler of the island for decades, fled, eventually to exile in Portugal and Spain. John F. Kennedy, during his 1960 US election campaign, had accused Batista – educated, long before, by American Quakers, of murdering some twenty thousand Cubans over seven years: under his corrupt regime Cuba had become a complete police state. Batista's departure was not, in itself, an event which shook the world. Castro's descent from the mountains, where his guerrillas had based themselves for several years, had turned out to be a straightforward operation. There was little initial suggestion that the message of Cuba would cross continents. The USA was inescapably nearby (the coast of Florida being some 90 miles away). It had leased Guantánamo Bay as a military base in 1903. Its sense of proprietorial hegemony in the Caribbean remained. The notion that Cuba would or could escape the American embrace was unthinkable, though adjustment might be possible. Indeed, a youthful, middle-class, Jesuit-educated Castro had an initial appeal. Fidel received star treatment from the press and public on his visit to the USA in 1959. An expert in these matters, Vice-President Nixon, who met him, thought him politically naïve. However, Nixon did not think Castro a Communist, though he could easily be manipulated by Communists.

If there was a honeymoon, it was brief. Eisenhower had thought it prudent to leave meeting Castro to Nixon. It was already clear that the new regime would hurt American interests. Stereotypes soon surfaced on both sides. Rejection of 'Yankeedom' lay at the core of the new regime. It was time to move fast in expropriating private property, some of it American, with scant compensation. There were show trials and executions. Here was the beginning of a comprehensive programme, firmly directed from the centre, which would create a new Cuban man (and woman) and emancipate the island from the enfeebling heritage of colonialism. Parliaments brought with them corruption and delay. Castro saw no need for them. What he wanted was disciplined development, and he deployed his charisma to this end. The precise nature of his creed at this juncture, beyond being a man of the Left, remains difficult to pin down. His message was mixed – as was Cuba's population and its tangled rhythmic music, chiefly from the Spanish and African worlds (the departed Batista, for example, seems to have been of mixed European, African, Chinese and Amerindian descent). At this juncture roughly three-quarters of Cubans were 'white', the remainder almost equally divided between blacks and those of mixed race. Emigration to the USA had long been a feature. It now began to accelerate (predominantly white and from the business and professional elites) as the revolution consolidated and dissent was stamped on. Cuban exiles claimed that the revolution was not popular and could be as easily overthrown as it had been accomplished. There was no lack of Cuban politicians in Florida who were, as the phrase has it, preparing themselves for government.

It was predictable that Castro would turn to another continent for support. In February 1960 a trade agreement was concluded with the Soviet Union which included Russian oil. US and UK refineries in Cuba refused to refine it and were promptly taken over for their pains. Che Guevara, Castro's Argentine-born principal lieutenant, was dispatched to Eastern Europe to drum up support. In May 1960 Castro established diplomatic relations with the Soviet Union. The USA even derived a mistaken comfort from such steps, supposing that they would make him generally unpopular at home. Since that did not happen, and the regime survived, it meant that 'next door' was a state avowedly in the Soviet camp. Khrushchev gave Castro a big hug – not an easy task – at the UN General Assembly in September 1960. The Soviet Union and its satellites would buy the Cuban sugar crop (the Americans stopped taking their normal quota). Guevara graced with his presence the great parade in Moscow on the anniversary of the Bolshevik Revolution. Soviet arms shipments began arriving in Cuba. Imperialism would be defeated in the Third World.

The youngest man ever to be elected President of the USA – the election result had been very close – was sworn into office in January 1961. Even so, Fidel Castro was junior to John F. Kennedy (b.1917) by nearly ten years. Their youth was part of their message to their respective worlds. Kennedy had served gallantly in the war – torpedoed in the South Pacific – but not at the level of high command. He was a Catholic – another 'first' – and nodded sentimentally towards Old Ireland. His period in London in 1939 acting as secretary to his father, the US ambassador (an isolationist and an appeaser), had made him an Anglophile. He had in these years visited both Moscow and Berlin. As a 23-year-old in 1940 he published a short book (with a little help from a friend) purporting to explain *Why England Slept*. He thought hard about dictatorship and democracy. The father had believed that the USA should never fight a war unless it was attacked first. The son thought this doctrine too simple. Two decades on from Pearl Harbor, there was perhaps a sense in which the USA was again sleeping.

Kennedy talked about a 'New Frontier'. The choice in the election, he claimed, had not merely been between two men and two parties but between national greatness and national decline. These words were almost an echo of the language about 'challenge and response' in the history of civilizations coined by the British historian Arnold Toynbee, then enormously popular in the USA. There was a sense in the country that the post-war circumstances in which the USA had successfully projected itself globally were changing. In London in 1939 the British Empire had been much less strong than a glance at the map suggested. In Washington in 1961 the American 'world empire' might also not be quite what it seemed. The presidential foreign in-tray was already full: Cuba was high up.

Kennedy's strong language about the Batista regime has already been mentioned. Its replacement, however, was not producing 'Democratic Cuba' (as Kennedy understood democracy). He allowed himself to be persuaded by the CIA that an invasion by a small force of Cuban exiles (with supporting US bombers being flown by Cuban pilots) would topple Castro. Such a force was to hand. However, the assault at the 'Bay of Pigs' in April 1961 was a failure. Kennedy had little option but to admit his own direct responsibility – for it had not required much persuasion by 'experts' to gain his support. Castro's forces, forewarned, dealt with the invasion very effectively. The new administration had bungled. A Great Power had shown itself to be incompetent. In other Latin American eyes, the expedition had proved that the USA could not wean itself off old habits. The president was personally humiliated. Castro proceeded immediately to announce that Cuba was now a socialist state in which, by definition, elections would be superfluous. Some tension thereafter between 'Castroists' and 'old' Communists inside Cuba never completely disappeared. Further, Castro's 'leadership style' was never quite what the Kremlin expected. Even so, the partnership with Moscow was clear. All of this, of course, had more international significance than a local victory for David over Goliath. There was the problem of Berlin.

Berlin walled in: Khrushchev and Kennedy

It was in Vienna – the heart of 'old Europe' – in June 1961 that Kennedy and Khrushchev had their first meeting. A century and a half earlier the Great Powers of Europe had settled the structure of the continent. Vienna now, however, was merely a suitable rendezvous for men concerned with the structure of the world. Kennedy and his French-speaking wife had first flown to Paris. A glittering banquet at Versailles reminded Americans of French civilization. De Gaulle was courteous but still committed to restoring France's position in the world. His view was that the Russians were bluffing over Berlin. 'Getting to know you' seemed the order of the day for statesmen in these years. In 1959 Nixon had been in Moscow and Khrushchev had spent ten days in the USA. The latter had made a family trip. It could not be said that either man gained a deep grasp of the 'other worlds' encountered on these occasions. Nevertheless the 'image' statesmen presented increasingly mattered before 'world opinion'. Confident in his own charisma, Kennedy needed no European to carry his bags in this encounter with Moscow. A summit meeting of this kind confirmed that there really was a bipolar world.

The president found, however, that the Russian's conversational style was pugnaciously direct. There was no substantive meeting of minds on any of the matters discussed. Khrushchev laid down terms. The Soviet Union would sign a separate peace treaty with the German Democratic Republic – which would then control access to Berlin – if by the end of the year there was no peace treaty with both German states. For several years, he had been demanding an end to Berlin's status as a city occupied by the four powers. The young man was bruised, though not battered. 'Cuba' and 'Berlin' were linked. Khrushchev taunted him about Cuba. Kennedy knew the former had damaged him and felt a need to show strength –but how and where? A man on the moon might be one indication of American vitality. Kennedy called on a rattled Macmillan on the way home and was advised to be cautious in his response to the Soviet Union. The British ambassador in Moscow, a little later, was warned by Khrushchev that there would be an atomic conflagration if the West tried to force its way into Berlin.

A kind of conclusion was being reached. On 27 July 1961, in a broadcast address, Kennedy reiterated that the Western Powers had a right to be present in the city, and stressed the necessity of free access and the freedom of its citizens. The emphasis, however, was on *West* Berlin. The leadership of the GDR, confronted by increasing numbers of its citizens moving westwards, wanted the escape route blocked. Khrushchev, still hoping that the Western Powers might be dislodged, was nevertheless persuaded to take action. In mid-August, in great secrecy and efficiency, a barrier of barbed wire was erected. When it soon became clear that the Western Powers would not intervene, it was made more substantial. The Berlin Wall – 'an act to secure peace' – imprisoned the East German population. Those East Germans who tried to get across it in the future would risk their lives. East Germans reacted with a sense of impotence (memories of what had happened in 1953 constrained any more dramatic response). The aged Adenauer, fighting his last election campaign, kept calm: excessively so, some Germans said. He did not go to West Berlin until ten days after the Wall went up. The situation was tense. Lucius D. Clay, regarded universally as the American general who had saved the city in 1948, returned. A complicated cat-and-mouse game ensued over the following months in which the Western Powers, led by the Americans, insisted on their access to East Berlin and on dealing only with the Russians in doing so, while the GDR, with East Berlin as its now designated capital, sought constantly to undermine the city's Four-Power status. 'Checkpoint Charlie' – the crossing point – was constantly in the headlines. In late October, when Soviet and US tanks with live ammunition faced each other, a showdown seemed possible. In the event, it seems through 'back channels', nothing happened. The wall, however, remained and became the most conspicuous illustration of 'divided Europe'. It also marked the end, so it seemed, of the spasmodic efforts to achieve German unification. The Federal Republic would be ever more firmly anchored in 'the West'. The incoming Foreign Minister, Gerhard Schröder, taking a more 'Atlanticist' stance and favouring British entry into the EEC, did not equate such anchorage with subservience, as de Gaulle did. Bonn did not attach the same 'European' significance to the Franco-German treaty of January 1963 as Paris. The GDR, for its part, took energetic steps to establish its own identity. Sheltered by the 'anti-fascist protective wall', with firm control of a workforce that could not escape, it would produce a socialist society. In world propaganda terms, however, a socialism that required a prison to realize its ambitions, was not very attractive. The USA did not fail to point this out. Yet, by 1962, though they did not say so publicly, 'the Wall' was a solution for both Superpowers, temporary or otherwise, to a vexed and sometimes dangerous problem. Khrushchev may have hoped still to prise the Western Powers out of Berlin at some stage (perhaps in his mind when framing his policy towards Cuba).

Cuba: blinking at the brink

The USA, meanwhile, had been maintaining pressure on Havana throughout the Berlin crisis. Over the next few years, a certain symmetry in the situations of Cuba and Berlin remained. Their fates were related as 'test cases' in a world struggle that went wider. A Communist Cuba was, as it were, an alien intrusion in the 'American world'. The presence of the Western Powers in Berlin was an alien intrusion in the 'Soviet sphere'. The USA was able to persuade the Organization of American States to expel Cuba from its membership in February 1962. An economic embargo was implemented. There was nothing secret about the American amphibious exercises which took place in the Caribbean. Another invasion would probably overthrow the Communist regime, perhaps by October 1962. The assassination of Castro appears not to have been ruled out. Would there not be something beautifully symbolic in his death by poisoned (Havana) cigar? It was hardly surprising, in these circumstances, that Castro sought a formal defence pact with the Soviet Union. Khrushchev, however, had a more devious assistance strategy in mind. In late September/early October 1962, Soviet vessels sailed for Cuba, stocked with intermediate-range missiles with nuclear warheads. Bases to accommodate them were under construction on the island. The package would be under Soviet control and protected by Soviet troops. It was a daring move, in part a genuine gesture of solidarity, but perhaps more fundamentally an assertion of Soviet status: the world was not 'zoned'. In April, US Jupiter missiles had been deployed in Turkey – thus in the Soviet 'backyard'.

A tense period of threat and counter-threat followed in late October. In a broadcast, Kennedy announced that the USA would impose a blockade to prevent the missiles being delivered. Khrushchev's actions were declared to be a threat to world peace. In the end, Khrushchev agreed to withdraw weapons 'regarded as offensive'. The Americans agreed not to invade Cuba. They also agreed, though privately, that the missiles in Turkey would be withdrawn. When the crisis was at its height there were those, perhaps particularly in Europe, who thought the end of the world near. It had not happened. Acute fear soon passed, but debate about nuclear weapons continued. Some thought that they had been shown to be a waste of money, but the two Great Powers, although they had 'stared into the abyss', still wanted both to expand the capacity of their missiles and increase defence against them. The spiral of expenditure seemed never-ending. On the other hand, by agreeing to direct communication between the White House and the Kremlin, the 'hotline', both sides recognized that chan-nels of contact, if not understanding, had to be effective and swift. Similarly, both sides quietly acknowledged that, by one means or another, the search for 'intelligence' about the other was inevitable.

The brinkmanship evident in the Cuban and Berlin crises has led to some different verdicts. Kennedy had been the diplomatic victor in the former. Khrushchev, who had tried a bold stroke 'out of area', had been forced to back down. He had only gained the American assurance that they would not invade Cuba – something which was anyway not now imminent. In the case of Berlin, however, the picture was not clear-cut. The Western Powers were indeed still resolutely in the city but they had not 'done something' about the Wall. Kennedy had stood by the Berliners but may have regarded the whole Berlin situation as an unfortunate historical hangover. He was not going to start a Third World War over it. It was not until June 1963, when the diplomatic temperature was lower, that he came to Berlin and said '*Ich bin ein Berliner*'. There were many people in the world, he declared, who really didn't under-stand, or said they didn't, what was the great issue between the free world and the Communist world. Let them come to Berlin.

Cuba, however, was still there: let the world come to Havana. Khrushchev continued to insist that the Soviet Union would defend Cuba. Welcoming Castro to Red Square in April 1963, he called Cuba a beacon of hope to all peoples of Latin America. Yet the internal politics of the island continued to show that Castro's actions and style did not make him an orthodox Soviet man. It was not only in the literal sense that Cuba was a world away from the Soviet Union. As things stood, Castro had no option but to seek such Soviet support as he could get, but he could prove a wild card (something which admirers of wildness in Western Europe and elsewhere welcomed).

Onlookers: holding breath and brooding

The 'outside world' could do little more than look on as this Euro-American crisis unfolded. The non-aligned world met for its first summit conference in Belgrade in September 1961. Previous preparatory meetings, particularly in Cairo the previous year, had attempted to set out appropriate criteria for admis-sion to its ranks. States were required to adhere to, or be favourably disposed towards, principles of coexistence and non-alignment. The latter principle entailed abstention from any collective military or bilateral alliance which involved the Great Powers. Military bases should not be offered to such Powers. It was axiomatic that non-aligned states supported liberation from colonialism.

At least some of these principles, however, offered plenty of scope for interpretation. The composition of the Belgrade conference meant that 'flexibility' was required. There were, in broad terms, 11 African states, 6 South or South-East Asian, 6 Middle Eastern, 1 Caribbean (Cuba) and 1 European (Yugoslavia). Three Latin American states (Bolivia, Brazil and Ecuador) were present as observers. Scrutiny suggested that a vaunted impartiality as between the Superpowers and between Capitalism and Communism, on their part, was not always evident. Almost all of the states had at one stage or another been the colonial possessions of Western European states. Some of them had had a pre-colonial 'national' existence; others were being busily created. Some were, in world terms, 'substantial'; others not. The emissaries who delivered the concluding messages to Washington and Moscow were not selected from Cyprus, Nepal or Yemen. Sukarno was posted to the USA and Nehru and Nkrumah to the Soviet Union. Their messages, drawing attention to the dangers of nuclear war, urged peaceful coexistence.

Non-alignment of this kind had no very clear concentration. It had still an Afro-Asian ring but this might not be its central dynamic. All of Afro-Asia might be on message with regard to colonialism but that unanimity could not disguise intra- and inter-continental disagreements. An 'Asia' in Belgrade which did not include Pakistan, China or Japan, to mention only the most prominent absentees, lacked a certain weight. There were European states more explicitly neutral than some 'non-aligned' states, but they chose not to participate. That the few Latin American states present were only 'observers' also carried a message. In addition, states purported to be establishing solidarity on the basis of negatives, on what they were against not on what they were for. Comments on the incoherence of this kind of 'world' could be frequently made. Even so, 'non-alignment' did constitute an assertion, increasingly attractive, that there was more to the world than bipolarity.

One thing was also clear. During this protracted and conjoined American/European 'world crisis' in 1961–63 there were really only two players: the USA and the Soviet Union. Britain and France were scarcely more influential than 'the non-aligned world'. Little that was said from London changed the US action. Macmillan, British Prime Minister and possessor of an independent nuclear deterrent, was no more than a sounding board. Where the Soviet Union and Berlin were concerned, a Warsaw Pact meeting had occurred very shortly before the Berlin Wall was erected, but the Kremlin gave no advance information to its partners. On the Western side, it was the formal status of the three Powers in Berlin which required some consultation between them. Even so, it was what the USA decided that really mattered. De Gaulle burnished his *Force de Frappe* [strike force] and talked about being tough to the Russians, but would not in fact risk war. The French and the British, however, were bound to reconsider both where they stood in the world and where it was going. De Gaulle and Macmillan both had long experience to draw on. They brooded.

The French President did not send mixed messages. De Gaulle spoke in set-pieces of great force. The drama of these occasions, sometimes deemed anachronistic by outside observers, conveyed the impression that France was still an exceptional country. The world in which it found itself, however, was not now congenial. Still with baggage from the Second World War, he disliked the predominance of 'Anglo-Saxons' in 'the West'. He also disliked bipolarity in the world as a whole. The following examples illustrate only some of his attempts to bring change. He suggested to Eisenhower in September 1958 that, within NATO, Britain, France and the USA should collectively take decisions on the use of nuclear force. Eisenhower would not agree. The following spring, de Gaulle withdrew the French Mediterranean fleet from NATO. In February 1966 he went much further. France was withdrawing from the command structures of NATO and requiring the USA to remove its bases and troops from French soil. The wholly national character of the French army, navy and air force was being restored – though France was not formally leaving the alliance altogether. It was 'subordination' to which France took exception. De Gaulle's reservations about America, however, did not entirely ignore the debt France owed to 'the American world'. Intellectuals urged the preservation of a 'French space'. Guardians of French culture vigilantly defended it against the infiltration of Anglo-Saxon words and some even more unpalatable cultural intrusions from across the Atlantic.

The British Prime Minister, Macmillan, gave Kennedy an avuncular but gloomy assessment of the world. He was 62 when he became British Prime Minister in January 1957. He had seen Europe as a Grenadier Guard in the First World War. He reputedly never subsequently found it easy to like Germans. The Second World War found him for a short time in the Colonial Office. He later conceded that his knowledge of the colonies was very limited. He then became British Minister of State in Algiers, much involved with inter-Allied politics, a remit which extended to the Eastern Mediterranean. After the war he had some involvement in the 'United Europe' movement which Churchill had launched in 1947. He attended the meetings of parliamentarians at the newly formed Council of Europe. He considered the Schuman Plan 'a major turning point in European history'. In the Conservative Party he passed as a 'European'. Briefly Foreign Secretary in 1955, he was suspicious of the meetings of 'the Six', did not participate in them, and did not like the direction they were taking. British responsibilities and associations, he declared, ruled out British participation in the Common Market. Trying to unite Western Europe would only cause divisions.

His priority as Prime Minister was not to embark on some European 'new course' but rather to repair relations with the USA and restore the 'special relationship'. It was galling for Britain to have been so conspicuously 'dumped'. This was not the moment, however, to let resentment fester. Macmillan's mother was American. He had worked with Americans in North Africa. Western Europe needed America. His predecessor's bones had famously once told him that they could never be European. Macmillan's were not so communicative. His antecedents and experiences, however, told him that it was Britain's task to build bridges across worlds which had clashed. The Free World could not be entering 1961 with great satisfaction. There had been few successes in the struggle against Communism and some losses. Its nuclear superiority had been replaced by a balance of destructive power. Reflecting on Africa and Asia he suspected that the long predominance of European culture, civilization, wealth and power might be drawing to an end. The British economy was balanced on a knife-edge. Changing an Empire into a Commonwealth was a difficult task. Further, there was the uncertainty about the new economic and possibly political state being created in Western Europe and last, but not least, was Britain, from the American perspective 'just another country' or 'an ally in a special and unique category'? On the last point, Macmillan hastened to try to ensure, by personal contact, that a 'special relationship' did survive. The Communist danger required the maximum degree of co-operation.

The personal chemistry between the two men helped. Macmillan came from a world Kennedy had known and liked in England two decades earlier. An elderly man from an old country offered wisdom to a young man from a young country: it was Greece to Rome, Macmillan liked to think. If, however, European global predominance was ending, as Macmillan suggested, was American culture, civilization, wealth and power also subject to the same decline? Was the USA, in its fundamentals, really an extension of 'Europe', or was it a quite distinct and still vibrant society? Aside from immediate issues on their agenda, these were matters on which alumni, respectively, of Harvard and Oxford could fruitfully brood.

Their weaponry, however, put the USA and the Soviet Union in a class of their own. They tumbled over each other, in these years, in the pursuit of technological mastery. They developed intercontinental ballistic missiles, anti-missile missiles, early-warning radars and other technical devices in pursuit of decisive advantage. There were complex arguments about the relationship between nuclear war and 'conventional' war. Some analysts thought that the possession of nuclear weapons would reduce, if not eliminate, the risk of war altogether. Others disagreed, or at least stressed that if war did begin use of nuclear weapons would be catastrophic. There was a fear of proliferation. If nuclear weapons became a badge of status, perhaps no Great Power could do without them. Any state 'sheltered' by its alliance with a nuclear power experienced two fears – either that the protector would not in the event protect or that it would act recklessly. These were issues, at this juncture, particularly for Britain and France. Their governments thought they needed an 'independent deterrent'. Some public opinion disagreed. In Britain, the first protests of what developed into the Campaign for Nuclear Disarmament (CND) began. The death toll in a nuclear winter was predicted to be fearsome. A sense of the insanity of the situation was universal. Medium-sized states asked themselves whether they could afford to develop nuclear weapons, which might never be used, and also maintain their conventional forces adequately. These were matters which also deeply troubled scientists. Were they not themselves responsible for this strange new world? Some of them set up an international conference – first held at Pugwash in Canada in 1957. They found themselves in an awkward place. Much funding of physics had a military end in view and took the discipline further away from the purely academic advance of knowledge. Scientists did not like being demonized.

The 'nuclear world', however, only intimately preoccupied those states which had the capacity, technical and financial, to enter it, either immediately or soon. Nevertheless, there was no hiding place anywhere. The human race was doomed, some claimed, to which a hedonism born of despair was the only sensible reaction. Yet future catastrophe might not in fact inhibit 'business as usual', that is to say the pursuit by states of limited goals for specific purposes – and a nuclear war might never in fact happen. A decade had passed in which the superpowers had come to the brink, but had then drawn back.

The tide of world affairs seemed sometimes to be running against 'the West'. Kennedy, in his inaugural speech, had pledged himself to assure the success and survival of liberty: stop. The fact was that America, in its own estimation, now stood in relation to 'the world' as no other country stood. Echoing Secretary of State Dean Acheson, McGeorge Bundy saw the USA as 'the locomotive at the head of mankind'. The rest of the world was a caboose (guard's van) being pulled along. Here spoke a Boston Brahmin, the brightest of the best, Harvard Professor of Government and a man called in to be 'special assistant to the President for National Security' to both Kennedy and Johnson (1961–66). The USA apparently had an umbilical responsibility for the world, but just how much could it pull along behind it? The 'burden of the world', made more demanding in Africa and Asia, might be too heavy.

11
Africa: Emergences and Emergencies

This chapter brings the African continent to prominence. It scarcely needs to be said, however, that it constituted no simple bloc. The routes to a flawed freedom were various. The sections that follow give glimpses of Africa's indigenous diversity, North South, East, West. Through and beyond the formal departure of European powers, the imprint of Europe remained. There were other transcontinental connections, with both North and South America, and into the Middle East. The interplay of relationships in these years was such that the sections that follow position themselves firmly in specific geographical locations. Emancipating Africa from the 'European world' – though there had never been a *single* European world – occupied centre stage.

Algeria: found and lost

In North Africa, the most savage and searing experiences were to be found in Algeria. France had a continuing fight on its hands there. In 1956, French paratroops moved straight from Egypt to fight in Algiers. British Prime Minister Macmillan, remembering his own wartime in Algiers, thought that the conflict was leaving France dazed. Only when Algeria was subdued, evacuated or conciliated, would it come round. There were approaching half a million French troops engaged in 'pacification'. The claim that Algeria was just as much part of France as Provence or Brittany was proving impossible to sustain. So, for long, was a 'civilizing mission' which engaged in torture. Settlers and the military in Algeria, on the other hand, were appalled at the complacency of Paris and feared that they were going to be abandoned. Intellectuals pronounced France sick. It was a country that had lost its conscience and its confidence. Civil war threatened.

In the end, it seemed, only one man had confidence: Charles de Gaulle. What his Delphic phrases, uttered both in France and Algeria at this juncture, actually meant for the future was another matter. On 1 June 1958, however, he was invested with full powers and embarked on a tortuous course. Violence came to France itself. In a broadcast on 16 November 1959 he announced that within four years of a ceasefire – which was defined – the Algerian people would be offered three alternative futures: independence, integration or self-govern-ment in close association with France. It was this third somewhat uncertain status which was massively endorsed in referendums in France and Algeria in April 1962. In July 1962 Algeria had an independent existence for the first time in history. French remained an official language alongside Arabic. Yet no amount of subsequent 'close association' could disguise how bitter and brutal this multifaceted conflict had been. Its legacy lingered. More than a million flooded 'home' to a France most of them had never known. A harsh fate awaited the Algerian *harkis*, those troops who had fought alongside the French. They were either killed in Algeria or set up in camps in the south of France. Bitterness, on all sides, was not swiftly assuaged.

Some interpreters of the times had seen in this savage encounter the ultimate confirmation that European civilization was rotten. It had trampled over other cultures and now, in the moment of its defeat, its own alleged superiority was being mocked. The most vitriolic *exposé* came from Frantz Fanon, a French-educated black psychiatrist from the Caribbean island of Martinique, whose *The Wretched of the Earth* (1961), appearing in this English translation in 1967, painted a picture of a Europe now in the grip of spiritual disintegration. Its game was over. Fanon had been a member of the inner circle of the Algerian National Liberation Front. He urged that a new country should develop a new man. The new man would be universal, the product of a dialogue between the colonizer and the colonized. An emerging Algeria, or any other emerging coun-try, could not revert to a myth of its past. The 'Third World' would create a 'world' such as had never before existed. It is not surprising that his book, which acquired a cult status, was furnished with an introduction by Jean-Paul Sartre. The whole articulated a vision of the universal deeply embedded in a style of conceptualizing which could only be French. What such a theory might mean for Algeria, in practice, was one thing. What it implied for Europe and for France in Europe, was another.

Ghana and Nigeria: African pilots?

In Britain's West African world, it was the Gold Coast (Ghana), the smaller territory, that achieved independence (1957) ahead of Nigeria (1960). But perhaps their boundaries would be short-lived. A black star in the person of Kwame Nkrumah had risen in Ghana and was piloting the way to a possible future. A symbolic black star appeared on the country's flag. African unity beck-oned.

The forts on the Gold Coast provided reminders of the Europeans – Portuguese, Dutch, Danes – who had all come and gone over a period of 400 years. Now, in 1957, the British, whose imprint had been deeper and all-perva-sive since they had declared the territory a colony in 1874, were also going. West Africa had its own external world, one created by the slave trade, a trade that had more or less been brought to an end a century earlier. It had, however, transplanted populations to the Caribbean and other parts of the New World. A 'black world' was waiting at the complicated point where West Africa, Western Europe, Brazil and the USA intersected. In addition, men from the Gold Coast, enrolled in the war, had been involved in the Burma campaign of 1943–45. That had been an Asian 'eye-opener'.

Independence came quickly. An ex-servicemen's march and riots in the capital, Accra, in 1948 indicated a new post-war mood. A small African elite, hitherto content to envisage a gradual transition, found itself outflanked by younger men demanding self-government now. It was in the environment of a black university in Pennsylvania that their leader, Kwame Nkrumah, had forged his vision of liberation. A civil disobedience campaign, waged against the limited franchise proposed by conservative Africans who had been asked by the British to draft a new constitution, led to an election on a universal franchise in 1951. Touring loudspeaker vans summoned large audiences. The election produced an overwhelming majority for the Convention People's Party, which had been formed in 1949. Nkrumah was released from prison and asked by the British Governor of the colony to form a government. Two years later the Legislative Assembly presented a motion requesting independence as soon as the necessary constitutional arrangements could be made. The British did not want to be stampeded into departure and took the view that, even in minutiae, these were matters which required protracted attention. Independence was something to be 'granted'. A period of tutelage in the arts of government would be no bad thing. It appeared that from 1953 'transition planning' between Governor and Prime Minister seemed harmonious, at least in externals. The new British Queen remained head of state.

Nkrumah (b.1909) was hailed as *Osagyefo*, a word in the Twi language meaning 'redeemer'. Such a style conveyed that what was happening transcended the niceties of constitutional construction. His father was a goldsmith and his mother a fishmonger. His early education had been at Catholic schools before proceeding to the newly founded elite Achimota College in Accra. 'That all might be one' was its motto (in Latin). Its aims were lofty – to develop all that was best in two cultures. It was the finest school in the country. Having then taught for a few years, Nkrumah departed for the USA. He enrolled in Lincoln University in Pennsylvania in 1935, graduating here and elsewhere in philosophy, theology and education. Lincoln was a black institution, many of whose students came from the segregated South. They too asked themselves where in the world they 'belonged'.

Jamaican-born Marcus Garvey, founder of the Universal Negro Improvement Association in 1914, gave Nkrumah one answer to ponder: blacks should go back to Africa. Garvey founded the Black Star Shipping Line to facilitate transportation within the African world. A Universal African Legion would expel the European colonial powers. It was not possible, however, to mobilize such a legion from the prison in the USA where he was serving a sentence, possibly 'political', for fraudulent use of funds. His career was extraordinary, taking place in many locations. Initially buried in London in 1940, his body was exhumed and returned, in triumph as it were, to Jamaica, several years after the island's independence in 1962. Garvey's 1924 poem 'Hail, United States of Africa' lodged in Nkrumah's consciousness, hence the black star on Ghana's flag. Nkrumah also struck up a lengthy correspondence with Trinidad- born C.R.L. James, who was living in the USA at this juncture and deeply involved in Marxist/Trotskyist theorizing (and its accompanying factionalism). James, in turn, introduced Nkrumah to 'George Padmore', a fellow-Trinidadian who was running the International African Services Bureau in London after a spell in the Soviet Union. Nkrumah, attending the Pan-African Congress in Manchester in 1945, was no longer quite the young man who had left Achimota College in 1930.

Given that background, change, for Nkrumah, could not stop at the frontier of Ghana. In December 1958 the All-African People's Conference assembled in Accra. There were only eight independent African states. Delegates from across the continent lamented the way in which imperialists denied Africans fundamental human rights. The exploitation of Africans should cease forthwith. It concluded its many resolutions by pledging full support for all fighters for freedom in Africa, whether by non-violent or violent means. A permanent secretariat was to carry forward the work of the Conference. Two years later, when Ghana became a republic and Nkrumah its president, the constitution provided that the country could dissolve itself into a union of African states. African unity came to dominate Nkrumah's mind. He started to promote his continental vision across the world. Internally, however, the rights of Ghanaian Africans became less conspicuous. The rule of the 'redeemer' became oppressive. He deemed it prudent in 1964 to make himself president for life both of the country and the party. In February 1966, while on a visit to North Vietnam and China, he was deposed in a military coup. He never returned to Ghana but continued to pursue his dreams in exile in Guinea. Traditional African society, he claimed, was founded on principles of egalitarianism. He could write, as fluently as the next man, about the need to work out 'scientifically' the social and economic policies. Equal opportunities for everybody should be guaranteed. Such rhetoric bore little relation to the political and social reality which Ghana, under his latter-day dictatorship, had experienced in a decade of independence. There was, to say the least, an irony in Nkrumah's assertion, on taking office, that 'the people' wished to manage their own affairs. Even so, it was Nkrumah who could be presented as the man who had 'broken through'. Africa's 'man of the millennium' was to be commemorated, later, by a large memorial tomb and park in the Ghanaian capital.

Nigeria, however, might take another path. Margery Perham, British biographer of the colonial administrator Lord Lugard, the man who had 'made' Nigeria, told her BBC audience in England in 1963 that Nigeria's 'successful eminence in world affairs' would be a most valuable assertion of the dignity of the African race, as she put it. The unity of Africa's most populous state, however, could not be taken for granted. It was a prerequisite if Nigeria were to become 'the voice of Africa' in the world.

In was in the Gold Coast, in Accra, in 1937, that Nnamdi Azikiwe, bright young product of a Methodist school in Lagos, founded and edited the newspaper *The West African Pilot*. He was the man who, on Nigeria's independence in October 1960, became its first governor-general, and, three years later, on the declaration of a republic, its first president. He was a man of the world. He too had recently spent years in the USA, obtaining degrees from Columbia and Pennsylvania and lecturing at Lincoln University. In 1943 he had been in

London with other West African journalists launching proposals for independence. They envisaged various stages over a twenty-year period. The British government did not then accept the timetable, though it turned out to correspond with what actually happened. The following year, he and others set up a 'National Council for Nigeria and the Cameroons'. It was not surprising, however, that Ghana had turned out to be the 'pilot'. The movement which 'Zik' launched aspired to be 'national', but what did that word mean in Nigeria? The British, as extra-continental outsiders, had come to the coast and then moved northwards from their Lagos colony. They had not conquered an existing entity called 'Nigeria'. Normally, power and authority in the region had extended southwards from a 'Saharan' world. It was in 'Nigeria' that 'South' and 'North' met, though one could not say precisely where. British rule could not obliterate historical faultlines. It recognized, on certain conditions, 'traditional authority' as the only way a colonial power could rule.

Assuming that Nigeria would become independent, the issue, both for Britain and 'Nigerians', was what kind of structure might work. The mere fact of having lived under alien rule for half a century may have created a certain sense of 'Nigerianness', but in a country with some 250 indigenous languages a unitary state never looked feasible (and perhaps in reality no single state was feasible). More than elsewhere in West Africa, the size and coherence of Nigeria's major linguistic/ethnic communities could make possible 'nation-states', as European understood the concept. The Hausa–Fulani in the North, the Igbo in the south-east and the Yoruba in the south-west constituted some two-thirds of the total population. The composition of the other third was variegated. Delineation of regions – East, West and North – was therefore inescapable, with a federal structure 'on top'. The North's population, however, approximately equalled that of the two other regions combined (its weight was increased by the decision of Northern Cameroon to join Nigeria). It might be difficult for a federal government to function effectively alongside three such governments. Constitutions might prescribe the division of powers, but powerful regions might ignore them. Whatever might be the theory, political parties had strong regional rather than pan-Nigerian bases. 'Nigeria' would function on the basis of the alignments and alliances struck between regional leaders. But the regions themselves might be too crude to survive. There would be demands for subdivision to meet the aspirations of particular groups. A larger (and weaker) set of regions, however, might make central government more powerful (supposing that to be desirable), but also opened the way to an almost endless fissiparousness. During the 1950s, constitutional conferences worked through these issues. Corruption and the threat of violence might play their part in determining outcomes.

'Expertise' on the subject of 'federation' at this juncture was to be found in the British Colonial Office in London (at a time when British governments viewed any suggestion of a 'federal' Europe with deep suspicion). Small territories and mixed ethnicities, the Office felt, might find it hard to survive on their own. Federation, in these circumstances, surely made sense. There was also a hope, no doubt incidental, that federation might find a little room for a continuing British 'facilitation', too. Considerations of that kind might apply in the

Gulf, the Caribbean, Southern Arabia and Malaya/Singapore. For a time, in the late 1950s, a kind of federal framework did exist in the West Indies linking the smaller islands in the Leeward and Windward groups with Jamaica, Trinidad and Barbados. The arrangement, however, was bedevilled by argument about budget contributions and the scope of central government. In September 1961, after a referendum, Jamaica announced that it would secede. Macleod, the British Colonial Secretary at the time, described it as a grievous blow to something which 'enlightened' West Indian opinion had been working towards for decades. It was not to be the only such scheme to fail. The omens for Nigeria, therefore, did not look good.

So it proved. Ethnic–regional disputes were endemic. Western Nigeria saw a power struggle between 'progressive' and 'traditional' forces in Yoruba society expressed in the rivalry between Chiefs Awolowo and Akintola. There was much argument about the population balance which a national census taken in 1962 purported to disclose. In the first federal general election of December 1964 only four out of an electorate of 15 million voted. The ethnic balance within the army was itself, as in other institutions, a matter of dispute. In January 1966, junior officers propelled General Ironsi, a Sandhurst-trained Igbo, to lead a rebellion. The Northern, Western and Federal premiers were assassinated. The Federal Cabinet handed over power to the army. In so far as there was clear intention at this juncture, it was to turn Nigeria into a unitary state. The old federal regime and its obsolete patronage were to be swept away. Igbos living in the North were massacred in thousands as the January events were presented there as an Igbo coup. A military counter-coup took place in July 1966 in which Ironsi was killed and the federal system restored. Subsequently further massacres of Igbos took place in the North. In turn at least one million Igbos, and probably more, fled back to the Eastern region. The country was on the brink of civil war.

Senegal, Ivory Coast and Guinea: implementing *négritude*

Leaders in francophone West Africa had a very different pedigree from the new men in anglophone West Africa. As Nkrumah prepared to immerse himself in the mid-1930s in the world of Black America, the future President of Senegal was launching a magazine at the Sorbonne in Paris, *L'Étudiant noir* [The Black Student]. Léopold Senghor (b.1906), son of a Catholic peanut farmer from a minority tribe in a largely Muslim country, started his lifelong quest for a *civilisation de l'universel* [civilization that is universal] at a school run by French missionaries. The priesthood beckoned, but those concerned deemed him unsuitable (he had objected to Africans being characterized as savages). Proceeding to Paris after his academic success as the solitary black pupil at the French *lycée* in Dakar, he and other young men from other parts of the Francophone world sought to develop *négritude* [black identity]. He began to write poetry. Later he found himself writing in a German prisoner of war camp – for he had identified himself with French resistance. In 1945, as a deputy for Senegal, he became a member of the French Constituent Assembly, called upon to check the style of the language of the new French constitution, a task he also carried out with its successor a dozen years later. But he was more than French.

His mind and his activity shifted back to his homeland in the late 1950s where he helped to organize a 'Progressive Union'. African ex-soldiers certainly wanted their pensions from the French state but, as one put it, unlike their fathers who fought in the earlier war they were not prepared to be treated like sheep. Also unlike their fathers, they had seen a France at war with itself.

The political solution which Senghor sought mirrored his very self-conscious habitation in two different worlds. Senegal should govern itself but in a close continuing relationship with France. He was an 'assimilated' Frenchman but one who resisted simple assimilation. Elected President in 1961 (in which year he published another volume of poems and was nominated for the Nobel Prize for Literature) he sought to promote *négritude* through cultural events such as the Third World Festival of Negro Arts in Dakar in 1966. Certainly such events put Senegal 'on the map', but it also built up an ever more expensive patronage system. In a country where peanut growing formed a major aspect of its economy, the son of a peanut farmer seemed to have forgotten his origins. An admirer of French democracy became steadily more authoritarian. By 1967, there was only one political party which was legal, his own.

In April 1957, Nkrumah visited neighbouring Côte d'Ivoire [Ivory Coast] for some straight talking with a man who was both President of its Territorial Assembly and a member of the Council of Ministers under Premier Mollet in Paris. Félix Houphouet-Boigny (b.1905) relished his different roles. Nkrumah's insistence that all the colonies of European powers should declare their absolute independence forthwith provoked him to insist that the relationship between the French and Africans was special. Interdependence should be now the watchword of the century. There could be a Franco-African community exuding *liberté, égalité* and *fraternité*. The two men discussed the relationship between economic and political independence. Houphouet-Boigny suggested that a meeting they would have a decade hence would reveal who had made the better decision. Such a meeting never took place. Houphouet-Boigny had obliged the conspirators who overthrew Nkrumah with a base for their operations. In 1967, however, he had no doubt that he had chosen the better course, or perhaps he had simply proved a smarter dictator. In 1958 he had accepted the 'Community' which de Gaulle offered. Even after the further shift to independence in 1960, the continuity of the French connection was expressed in the presence of French forces and French advisers at the heart of government.

Sekou Touré (b.1922) was younger than these other leaders. He soon found out the penalty for rejecting the 'Community' of 1958. An adept youthful reader of Marx and Lenin, he had achieved great prominence through trade-union activity. In 1956 he was elected Mayor of Conakry and Guinean deputy to the French National Assembly. The French withdrawal from his country was abrupt and comprehensive. Touré embarked on a domestic programme supposedly derived from Marxism. It was single-party rule. He shared Nkrumah's stances internationally and, after his deposition, made him Co-president of Guinea. Conakry became base for the all-Africa agenda. The country, however, was propelled forward to bankruptcy.

Jostling for space, therefore, both metaphorically and literally, was characteristic of these and other developments in West Africa. Patterns of social organization differed substantially. Ethnic/linguistic groups straddled boundaries (for example, the case of the Akan people in Ghana and the Ivory Coast). The dissolution of the two French federations – Equatorial and West Africa – left great uncertainty hanging over the subsequent units. Senghor criticized 'Balkanization' and hoped for a Federation of Francophone States. Others called this 'Senegalese imperialism'. Houphouet-Boigny would have none of it. There were, therefore, unresolved and interlocking issues as new states struggled to find sustainable structures and identities. What was true of the francophone states was also true of the small British colonial enclaves of Sierra Leone and Gambia.

Congo: brewing disaster

One of Europe's smallest states, itself falling into linguistic battles between its French- and Flemish-speaking regions, ruled a huge African territory, the Congo. Three months before Nigeria, it became independent, but the contrast in 'preparation' could scarcely have been greater, both on the African and European sides. In the mid-1950s, however, a new Belgian government could not fail to note what the British and French were apparently bent on doing. It was in French Brazzaville, across the river from Léopoldville (now Kinshasa), the Congolese capital, that de Gaulle had announced his 'offer' to French Africa in 1958. A 33-year-old director of a brewery, Patrice Lumumba, who had attended Nkrumah's Accra All-African Conference, founded the Mouvement National Congolais [Congolese National Movement] (MNC). He petitioned the Belgians for independence. After attending Catholic and Protestant schools, he had begun his working life as an assistant postmaster. A path into minor officialdom was not unexpected. In terms of African involvement, it was what Belgian administration in the Congo was geared to. Educational and health provision, with the aid of missionaries, made progress – but only up to a certain level. No cadres were being prepared for major executive responsibility. Lumumba forced the pace. Belgian administrators on the spot were fearful of what would happen unless the government in Brussels signalled change. A statement in January 1959 indicated that Belgium intended to organize a democracy in the Congo which would decide upon its own independence. Its assumption was that this would still be a gradual process. The notion of 'organizing a democracy' over the vast area of a Congo without electoral experience was ambitious. It was only after a conference in Brussels in early 1960 that the Belgian government realized that it was facing a virtually unanimous demand for immediate independence. It conceded at once. Even so, it was assumed that some Belgians would stay on – in the army, for example. African sergeants, who then realized that they would not immediately become officers, mutinied. Events, which cannot be traced in detail, got out of hand.

A movement might be called national but that did not mean that it was, or indeed that the term made sense. Moïse Tshombe, in Congo's richest province, Katanga, asked for Belgian help and declared independence. Belgian troops arrived and gave him and their own nationals support. Lumumba, whose party had gained the largest number of seats in the election and who had become

Prime Minister, though without an overall majority, scented a Katangan–Belgian plot. He wanted no truck with federalism. Kasabuvu, the President, was more sympathetic. The Belgian government now sought a confederal Congo, one which removed the economic power base from Lumumba. Kasabuvu and Lumumba fell out, the former dismissing the latter. Some aspects of what was happening suggested that Tshombe was a puppet in the hands of the mining companies who kept 'Katanga' afloat. Yet inter-ethnic tensions were real. It was difficult to tell where power in the country lay, as the Lumumba and Kasabuvu factions established themselves in different cities. 'Legitimate' government was difficult to identify. It did not look as though the Congolese army could defeat the Katangans and their supporters. In this confused situation Secretary-General Hammarskjöld perceived a role for UN troops – Lumumba had requested them. A largely non-Western force to suppress secession would show that the UN was not hamstrung by the Great Powers. UN forces arrived as 'peacemakers'. However, it became clear that Hammarsjköld was reluctant to use these forces actually to suppress the Katangan secession. Lumumba in turn called on the Soviet Union to send planes to transport his troops against Katanga. This prompted American (and Belgian) determination to destroy Lumumba. Arrested in October 1960, he was murdered in February 1961.

The crisis continued in acute form until late 1964 when the Congo, as of 30 June 1960, regained its territorial integrity. Throughout that period, convoluted political jockeying and spasmodic violence and killing continued. The hand of the Superpowers was sometimes visible and frequently suspected. General Joseph Mobutu received US encouragement to make the army the agency and focus of national unity. Not averse to such a prospect, he completed it by seizing direct power himself in November 1965. Four or so terrible years had come to an end, or so it might optimistically be thought. Blame could be generously distributed: the Belgian government had behaved with absurd precipitancy and subsequent malignancy; Lumumba had behaved with impetuous eagerness; the UN had only muddied the waters; Moscow and Washington had both, in different ways, unhelpfully inserted themselves. And so on. Two things, however, stood out. Under whatever auspices, the 'management' of the Congo would be a formidable task. Its 'tribal' differences, huge internal distances and poor communications exhibited, on a grander scale, what all new states were experiencing.

Ethiopia, Eritrea, Somalia and Kenya: dilemmas on the Horn

Eastern/North Eastern Africa presented an unusual but scarcely stable medley of states with competing and ethnic claims. Ethiopia was an African special, as indeed was its emperor. Haile Selassie (b.1892) had been a world figure for decades. In 1936, he had addressed the League of Nations in Amharic, his own language, in protest at the Italian conquest of Ethiopia. He spent his exiled years in the elegant English city of Bath, where his favourite reading, apparently, was diplomatic history. After the Allies defeated the Italians, he had returned home in triumph. His country had been occupied for a mere five years. Ethiopia's long independence gave it a distinctive status. The emperor now put his study of diplomatic history to good use. His country was a founder-member of the UN. It demonstrated, for obvious historical reasons, its attachment to 'collective security' by sending a clutch of soldiers to fight with the UN in Korea. It attracted the headquarters of the UN Economic Commission for Africa. It hosted, in 1960, the second conference of independent African states. These manifestations of 'modernity' (with large buildings to match) did not altogether disguise the fact that the emperor presided over an 'antique' government. There was a further twist. The emperor found himself revered 'out of area'. Rastafarians in the West Indies saw in him the Messiah who was to lead Africa and the African diaspora to freedom. His visit to Jamaica in 1966 saw some hundred thousand Rastafari assembled to greet him. He showed no sign, however, of wishing to lead them 'home'.

Ethiopia, however, had its own 'imperial' ambitions in the Horn of Africa. Eritrea was made a province in 1962, replacing the rather notional federal arrangement in place when the British departed. The British had had a Somaliland of their own but had also latterly been administering the former Italian Somaliland. This administrative change prompted an Eritrean struggle to secede. Ethiopia also maintained control of the Ogaden region, largely Somali-inhabited, an action bitterly contested by the newly independent Somalia. Somalia also made strong claims for the northern frontier region of Kenya with its large Somali population. It seemed likely that solutions, at some early point, would be sought by military action. Identifying Somalia as a threat, Kenya and Ethiopia would shortly conclude a Defence Treaty. The Somali government, somewhat precariously established, saw itself as surrounded. Various notions of federation were floated as a way of containing boundary disputes and promoting a common vision, but they petered out. It was perhaps difficult enough to weld the existing territorial units into 'nations'.

The Kenya which became independent in 1963 had many different ethnic communities which could be divided into the Bantu group and the Nilotic group. Nomadic herding communities, largely indifferent to frontiers, occupied its north-eastern area. Its passage to independence had been fraught. The Mau Mau 'emergency' had begun in 1952 and lasted until 1960. Kikuyu initiates, assembled in forests, swore an oath of an intricate kind to fight for lands seized by Europeans. A vicious many-sided struggle ensued in Kenya involving white settlers (less than one per cent of the population) and Asians (around two per cent), Kikuyu 'loyalists' and Kikuyu Mau Mau terrorists, non-Kikuyus and the British forces sent to deal with the situation. It was an ugly scene. Few holds were barred. Blind eyes were turned. The British government tried to argue, *pace* the expressed view of Nehru, that this was not a fight for freedom. Even those who thought that it was, however, were uncomfortable with the picture of Africa which Mau Mau conveyed. In all of this, the stance of Jomo Kenyatta was intensely contentious. Arrested, tried, convicted and imprisoned on a charge of oath-taking, no one could be quite sure where he really stood. Later, he was released and the tortuous path to Kenyan independence reached its conclusion, but opinion remained divided about him. Whether, in office, he could ride above the tribal divisions which had been so evident, and whether there was any future for Europeans and Asians in Kenya, remained to be seen. It was also very doubtful whether 'the Horn of Africa' would be peaceful.

Central Africa: breaking up

Early in 1960 the British Prime Minister, Macmillan, had spent nearly a month touring the African continent. His first discussions, symbolically, were in Accra with Nkrumah, the pioneer. He moved on to Nigeria where independence was then only months away. Back in London, the conference on the future of Kenya had at last got going. From British Somaliland (which would join ex-Italian Somalia) in the north-east to Sierra Leone in the west, the British would leave these African countries within the year. Whether in Sierra Leone or Somalia there were structures in place which offered a likelihood of 'good government' in post-colonial circumstances looked dubious. The worlds of Freetown and Mogadishu were not viewed affectionately in the hinterlands of these two capital cities.

The next stage in Macmillan's travels, Salisbury in Southern Rhodesia, took him to a very different context. Its name (now Harare) honoured one of his predecessors. It was now a handsome city far removed from the pioneer fort of just seventy years earlier. The constitutional situation he encountered, as he well knew, was complex and doubtfully durable. Since 1953 the three territories of Northern and Southern Rhodesia and Nyasaland had been brought together with a federal 'Central African' government and parliament placed on top of the continuing territorial administrations and assemblies. The northern territories remained British protectorates. Southern Rhodesia, on the other hand, regarding itself as 'almost a Dominion', had exercised substantial self-government for several decades. It was a self-government exercised by whites. By the time of Macmillan's arrival, African discontent with the arrangements was very evident. Should the federation be given independence more or less on its existing basis, or should it be broken up, with black rule emerging in all three component parts? But would white-ruled Southern Rhodesia secede? Violence was not far below the surface.

Macmillan appointed a commission in 1960 under Lord Monckton to seek a solution. Its proposed constitutional adjustments in turn led, over the next few years, to further conferences designed to adjust both the federal and the territorial constitutions. The British government was trapped. It could not grant independence without 'majority rights' for Africans but to do so would be unacceptable to a white electorate of Southern Rhodesia increasingly backing its conservative leaders. By the end of 1963 the Federation had collapsed. Nyasaland and Northern Rhodesia became independent in the course of 1964 as Malawi and Zambia, respectively. The government in Salisbury, now under Ian Smith, declared its own unilateral independence in November 1965. In the mid-1960s, therefore, 'British' Central Africa had changed, but not comprehensively. A hard struggle lay ahead.

The new states gave themselves new names, but how their leaders would seek to shape their societies, in the light of their own 'world-views', was unpredictable. Zambia had a Copperbelt. Malawi had no minerals. Neither Lusaka,

Zambia's capital, nor Blantyre, Malawi's leading city, possessed the civic style of Salisbury.

Hastings Banda (b.?1898) had returned to Nyasaland in 1958, having lived abroad since 1925. He had garnered financial support from various quarters to enable him to study anthropology, history and medicine at various institutions in the USA. He came to wartime Britain for further medical study in Edinburgh and afterwards practised as a doctor in various locations in England and Scotland. He had represented the Nyasaland African Congress at the 1945 Pan-African Congress in Manchester and kept in touch with politically active figures in the protectorate. Returning home to lead the African cause, his use of his native language, Chewa, after such a long absence, was very rusty. However, he proved an effective speaker. The support he received, together with the threat of violence, not always in the background, made an independent Malawi inevitable.

Kenneth Kaunda (b.1924), in contrast, had stayed at home. Before throwing himself into the fractious world of political organization, he had been a teacher. The Zambian African National Congress (ANC), which later turned into the United National Independence Party, was his foundation. Both Banda and Kaunda had spent short spells in prison. Both, in their early years, had come deeply influenced by Church of Scotland mission work (Kaunda's father was a Presbyterian minister). The influence of churches, in education and other spheres, remained strong.

Both men kept their countries within the Commonwealth. Such connections still pointed back to Europe and America. The immediate task, however, was to strengthen 'Malawi' and 'Zambia' as 'national' concepts in contexts where language use straddled frontiers. Later, one ironic aspect was the 'charge' brought against Kaunda that he was not a Zambian at all (his father had moved from Nyasaland). Both black men existed in the shadow of the 'indigenous' white and European-controlled regimes to the south – towards which, in the event, their leaders adopted contrasting attitudes and policies.

South Africa: resisting the wind

Macmillan, speaking to the South African parliament in Cape Town, told MPs that 'a wind of change' was blowing through the continent and that 'our national policies' had to be adapted in consequences. What this meant for Britain has been noted. What a new 'national policy' for South Africa might be, however, raised complicated and charged issues. The British might be abandoning their 'imperial mission' and retreating to their insular base, but the great bulk of the two white communities who ruled in South Africa were determined to stay in their 'homeland'. An Afrikaner-dominated government distrusted wisdom in these matters being generously dispensed by a visiting British politician. Afrikaners would make up their own minds, and perhaps find more English speakers sympathetic to their stance. 'White civilization' was what whites had in common. Within weeks of its delivery, Macmillan's message gained fresh urgency. ANC-organized protests against the pass laws operated by the state expanded. In the black settlement of Sharpeville, south of

Johannesburg, police opened fire on one such demonstration, killing 69 people and wounding some 200 others. An attempt to assassinate Verwoerd in April failed. Some thought revolution was imminent. The government, however, was determined to stamp out opposition with repression and appeared still to be confident of success. That there was 'international condemnation' was only to be expected but 'the world' was a frail entity. External connections and internal forces intermingled, complicating the prospect, one way or another, of an outcome acceptable to all in South Africa. Separate development would never be equal development. Robert Sobukwe, leader of the Pan-African Congress, talked in 1959 of Africans awaiting the call to reconquer their continent. It was time for armed struggle. The 'Azania' he envisaged would not be the multiracial country contemplated, with differing emphases, by white South African liberal opinion. The non-violent opposition, however, epitomized in the career of the black Albert Lutuli, awarded the Nobel Peace Prize in 1961, seemed to have little to show for its efforts. The ANC initiated a programme of sabotage. Nelson Mandela, a law graduate, went underground and set up a militant wing, Umkonto we Sizwe [Spear of the Nation]. Both Congresses were declared illegal organizations by the government. It took fresh powers to detain suspects and interrogate. Mandela was captured in August 1962 and, after his trial in 1964, was sentenced to life imprisonment on conviction of sabotage. The struggle, it seemed, would be a long one. The 1966 election gave the National Party 126 seats, the United Party 39 and the Progressives 1. Verwoerd appeared to be achieving a draconian stability approved by the majority of the white electorate. That stability was put in doubt, however, by his assassination in September 1966.

African mobilization in late 1959 had been in part a deliberate counter to the fiftieth anniversary celebrations of the 'Union' of South Africa, planned for 1960. Demonstrations would stress that the 'Union' did not in fact unite all its peoples. How its peoples should be described was fraught with linguistic complication. Could one speak of the population being divided between 'whites' and 'non-whites' or between 'blacks' and 'non-blacks'? Either way some groups would consider themselves misrepresented. Where did 'Indians' and 'Coloureds' fit? There was indeed no single South Africa. Cape Town was not Johannesburg and Durban was not Bloemfontein. So perhaps the country was a kaleidoscope of 'homelands'? In the year before his death, Verwoerd publicly acknowledged that the traditional policy of white rule over 'Bantu', who had no rights at all, could not continue. His mindset seemed to be changing – just a little. Instead, a patchwork of 'Bantustans' could be created which would embody or stimulate 'nations'. The 'High Commission' territories (Swaziland, Basutoland), surrounded by South Africa, for which Britain remained responsible, might join the assemblage. Even South-West Africa, which Pretoria had been controversially administering – originally under a mandate from the League of Nations – might also be accommodated. The 'Bantustan' scheme, unsurprisingly, was immediately dismissed as little more than window-dressing. Any African who accepted a client role would be denounced as a stooge. It would in any event be a work of art to draw up workable units. 'Independence' would be a sham.

Rivalry, not to say hostility, between different linguistic groups with strong 'identities', occurred within the ANC. It complicated its relationships with other organizations. At his April 1964 trial, in an impressive statement carried across the world, Mandela had set out his belief in equal political rights within a multiracial South Africa. The statement might still mean different things to different people. Black 'Africanists' had spoken in 1956 of regaining all the things that had been lost as a result of the white conquest of Africa. What might that entail in terms of 'traditional' government? Mandela himself was not 'just' a lawyer with a degree from Witwatersrand University. He was a member of a cadet branch of a royal house in the Transkei. Was South Africa's democracy, in which blacks had no part, a 'white system' and one which would be replaced by an authentically African one, or was 'democracy' a system of universal value, one for blacks and whites? The South African judiciary, on the whole, had exhibited, despite everything, a substantial commitment to 'the rule of law'. Mandela declared himself ready to die for what he believed in, but he had not in fact been made to die. It would have been his fate under many other regimes.

Cuba and Portuguese Africa: return of the native?

The resonances of the South African situation spread across Euro-America. US global perspective still identified the South African government as a staunch opponent of Communism. That government, for its part, continued to stress Communist activity in South Africa. The relationship between Communists, black and white, and the ANC was obscure. There was ample scope for disinformation all round. South Africa, however, could not simply be considered by the USA as a partner in the global struggle. 'Equal political rights within a multiracial country' spoke directly to the domestic politics of the USA itself. Cuba added a further intercontinental connection.

In December 1963, Castro's talismanic associate, Argentine-born Che Guevara, set out from Cuba for Africa to promote revolution. In the Congo and elsewhere conditions were judged to be ripe. Small groups aided by small Cuban units could galvanize popular revolution and defeat armies controlled or paid by colonial powers or settler regimes. They only *looked* more powerful. In April 1965 black Cuban soldier-volunteers sailed for Tanzania. The ensuing expedition into the Congo was worsted by mercenaries and withdrew. Another aspect of the Congo crisis also found Cuban soldiers in Brazzaville in the ex-French Congo, but it did not become the hoped-for base for revolution. A little later, however, black Cuban volunteers were able to give useful help to the revolutionary movement under Amilcar Cabral in Portuguese Guinea-Bissau. If, for the moment at least, global revolution exported from the Caribbean was of a modest dimension, there was a magic about the names of Castro and Guevara. If Cuba was indeed acting, in itself crossing continents, as a kind of Soviet surrogate, it was one of a rather special kind.

Portugal, however, showed little inclination to hurry out of Africa, whatever Britain and France might be doing. Still apparently in control, Antonio Salazar (b.1889), prime minister and virtual dictator since 1932, would have none of this changing world. He reiterated that his country, in Mozambique, Angola and Guinea, had a continuing responsibility to guide their backward peoples to civilization. Only a tiny percentage, judged by his criteria, was within striking distance of this goal. Salazar's Portugal was marginal in the 'new Europe'. Its colonies gave it a modest world status (and emigration to them was encouraged). The handsome civic, private and commercial buildings of Mozambique's seaport-capital, Lourenço Marques, complemented by a new university, with its communities of Portuguese, Ismailis, Indians (from Goa) and Chinese (from Macao), spoke rather of the 'Portuguese world' than of an African one. The city was scarcely typical of the hinterland. In 1962 the Frente de Libertação de Moçambique [Liberation Front of Mozambique] (FRELIMO) began its campaign in Mozambique. Increasing numbers of Portuguese soldiers were sent to contain it, as they were sent to other Portuguese territories.

A sense of crisis, therefore, hung over the whole of southern Africa in the mid-1960s. The interests and perceptions of the regimes in Salisbury, Pretoria and Lourenço Marques were not precisely the same, but if they held together they might survive. It was neither peace nor war in any complete sense of either term.

African unity: one voice, but many tongues?

The Africa that has been sampled in the preceding sections does not suggest a picture of 'unity', but contemporary rhetoric asserted that 'unity' and 'independence' belonged together. In May 1963, invited by Haile Selassie, African heads of state assembled in Addis Ababa to promote African solidarity. The objective was to create a single organization. The preceding few years had seen the emergence of what were, in effect, separate and competing blocs of states. Radical leaders of the states in the 'Casablanca' group did not normally welcome invitations from emperors, but this was different. The thirty-two states present did agree to create the Organization for African Unity. The inaugurated Organization had no specific security function. It envisaged an annual meeting of heads of state, established a secretariat and contemplated a commission which might mediate, conciliate and, if necessary, arbitrate in disputes between member countries. As with the UN, it was a task not easy to reconcile with the provision that members should not interfere in each other's internal affairs. The focus remained on ending colonialism – and on making Africa 'an influential force in world affairs'. It was not yet in a position to do so. Central and Southern Africa had still to be liberated. Africa had come onto the world stage, but not powerfully.

Creating an African voice went beyond organizational difficulty. It was the ex-colonial languages, English and French, which continued to be the means of communication across linguistically divided countries. These two languages kept alive continuing ready contact with Europe and North America. No single 'African language' could be 'the voice of Africa'. Neither could 'Africa' speak with a common religious voice. In country after country Islam and Christianity encountered each other, sometimes equably, sometimes tensely. From the Christian side, both the World Council of Churches and the Roman Catholic Church sought 'dialogue' with other faiths. The Second Vatican Council

(1963–65) expressed the Church's high regard for Muslims and made a plea for mutual understanding and the overcoming of past hostility. It was not easy, however, to find the appropriate Muslim body with which to engage in 'dialogue'. Countries which had Muslim and Christian populations, particularly when, as often, ethnic and linguistic aspects were involved, invariably struggled to maintain unity. Nigeria, from the moment of its independence, experienced this difficulty acutely, but it was not alone in doing so. It was sometimes suggested that Eritrea should be split in two, with Muslims going to Sudan and Christians to Ethiopia. Sudan itself, however, was divided between a Muslim North and a substantially Christian South. The relative strength of Protestant and Catholic was also sometimes important, very largely reflecting the religious balance of the colonial power back home. This 'European import', however, was examining its future path. African Christianity could perhaps be something new as it indigenized. There was work to be done in relating it to 'traditional' African religion. It began to look as if the balance in world Christianity was shifting. Perhaps African Christianity was more vibrant and dynamic than European.

Emerging leaders, too, had double heritages and therefore spoke with complicated voices. Two specific examples are selected, but their situation was paralleled throughout the continent. The pivotal position of Kenyatta in Kenya has been referred to earlier. The President of Kenya in 1964, he did not know where he was born or, with certainty, when. It was probably in 1893, the very year in which the British established an 'East African Protectorate'. A pupil in a Church of Scotland mission school, he converted to Christianity in 1914. His Kikuyu people, the largest of the thirteen tribes in what later became Kenya, formed what became a Central Association to defend land rights against white (British) settlers. As its Secretary, Kenyatta, set out for London in 1929, having promised to remain true to his tribe, not to marry a white woman and to return home. In London he watched the British King opening 'parliament'. Later, after a spell learning economics in Moscow, his study of anthropology at the London School of Economics led to the publication of his thesis as *Facing Mount Kenya* (1938). It attracted a good deal of attention. By the time Kenyatta returned home, without his then English wife in 1946, he had been abroad for fifteen years. It is hardly surprising that the path to power which he then began to tread could be interpreted in very different ways.

Ahmed Ben Bella (b.1916) was a very different character but one no less caught between worlds. In 1954 he founded and led the Front de la Libération Nationale [National Liberation Front] (FLN) in the armed struggle against France in Algeria. He was a former Marseilles footballer and French soldier (and a decorated one). Arrested in 1956, a spell in a French prison had enabled him to improve his rudimentary Arabic and work out a 'modern' Marxism. By the time of the 1962 Evian Agreement, and with those who had agreed its terms with France pushed aside, he had been out of the country for around a decade. As his country's first President he was determined that it would not 'go back' to some 'authentic past' before the arrival of France. He wanted Algiers to be the hub of revolution, and not only in Africa. It brought him into an immediate conflict with neighbouring Morocco. Two years later, he was deposed and exiled by a military faction led by Houari Boumedienne (b.1923). The new regime was equally committed to anti-colonialism in Africa and beyond, but the rhetoric still had a tinge of the French Left.

There were many tongues and nuances behind the fledgling African voice.

12

Asian Accommodations

Commentators in this decade, impressed by their size, frequently presented China and India as contrasting pathways to an 'Asian future', possibly even to the world's future. India was 'the world's largest democracy', as 'the West' understood democracy. Its elections, normally, functioned fairly. The Congress, however dominant as the governing party, did not exercise power as the Communist Party in China exercised power. India was attempting to operate a complex federal system – not without trial and error – whereas China was not prepared to risk it. In these respects and with central government in the hands still of an elite schooled in the political ideas and language of their former colonial masters, New Delhi had a 'Western' aspect not possessed by China. The balance between diversity and unity evolved under the British Raj was something which Indian central governments struggled to sustain. China, on the other hand, while it had been subjected to much outside European pressure, had not had a European presence defining its frontiers, map in hand. It was the lesson of the fragility of 'China' in the past which lay behind the insistence on a strong state, ruled out 'federalism' and produced assertiveness in border regions.

Yet evolving 'Asia' could not be reduced to a comparison between its two 'giants', emblematic though they might be. If the unity of evolving 'Africa' was problematic, so were the 'regions' of 'Asia': 'South', 'East', 'South-East', 'Asia-Pacific', not to mention the possibility that at least part of the 'Middle East' was better conceived as 'South-West Asia'. Subheadings employed in the sections that follow should not be held to foreclose the possibility of seeing different patterns of interaction between the countries and cultures which collectively made up 'the new Asia'. And intra-continental relationships were still themselves linked to inter-continental relationships. 'Asia' had many views on the world.

China: still at the margins?

'The world' and China, for a time, seemed to exist in different compartments. Beijing had not been admitted to the UN. 'China' in New York remained the Nationalist regime in Taiwan. The expanding UN did not yet yield a sufficient majority for change. In December 1961, for example, the Soviet delegate launched a fierce verbal attack on Taiwan in urging the admission of Communist China – so fierce that it was probably counter-productive. The USA remained firmly opposed and could still manage to organize a majority against change.

The British government, however, which had early established diplomatic relations with Beijing, voted in favour of its admission: 'realism' was required. The fiction that the government in Taipei really represented China on the world stage was absurd. Possession of its Hong Kong colony made Britain very well aware of Chinese facts. For the moment, however, in the formal eyes of 'the world' the voice of China came from Taiwan. Only the government there, however, had to live with the fiction that it was poised to 'resume' control of the mainland. Beijing sought to drum up support for its admission, but did so without great enthusiasm for what 'the United Nations' had hitherto achieved. The Chinese government had, after all, been engaged in Korea in a bitter and costly conflict badged as a 'United Nations' operation. Its possession of a permanent seat on the Security Council would surely make it impossible for 'the world' to be at war with China ever again. On the other hand, membership, whenever it came, would require China to take some more formal stances in relation to 'world issues'. Since, for the moment, it continued to be excluded, Beijing could function as a 'world apart'.

Soviet enthusiasm for Chinese admission, as evidenced by the 1961 motion just referred to, might seem only what was to be expected in 'the Communist world'. The previous half-dozen years, however, had raised questions about 'leadership' and 'solidarity' within that 'world' and they rumbled on. Who owned the copyright of 'Communism'? Could sacred texts be supplemented? Close watches were kept on doctrinal orthodoxy in both Moscow and Beijing, but such matters could never be divorced from geopolitical and cultural realities. Forging a viable Soviet–Chinese relationship was never going to be easy. The kind of primacy which Stalin had expected, and to some extent received, was not likely to outlast his death. There was, in a very limited way, an initial notion that Moscow's 'sphere' was Euro-America and China's was the 'underdeveloped world' – but it could not be, and was not, formalized. Even to contemplate the world in these terms succumbed to an 'imperial' mindset which characterized the Soviet Union as 'advanced' and China as 'backward'. What was meant by 'partnership', however, was inescapably problematic. China had made its own revolution. In their commerce, particularly in the development of some 'joint ventures', the Soviet upper hand was discernible, at least to the Chinese.

Thus, while the alliance made in 1950 remained in place and thereby established a massive single 'Communist world', there were divergences of interest and expectation from the outset. By the mid-1960s they were apparent. Any other outcome would have been surprising. Both countries had their own 'worlds' to contain, control and harmonize. Their long border threw up a number of contentious matters. The hand of history was heavy. From Beijing's perspective, treaty arrangements belonging to the past 'unequal era' were invalid and would be challenged. The present guardian of the 'Russian Empire' would not be exempted. Arguably, China had more boundary issues to grapple with than any other state in the world. Europeans remained in control in Hong Kong and Macau, though they would surely depart in due time. Taiwan was a special case.

One of the notable things about the 'new China' was the emphasis placed upon administrative unification. Here was a government determined to enforce its authority across the country and, unusually, it proved capable of doing so. Language as the instrument of unity was very important. Socialist construction in China was to go hand in hand with the political and economic unity of the Han people. That meant in practice, from the late 1950s onwards, the active promotion of Mandarin on radio in a modified version of the Beijing dialect. Cantonese or Shanghaiese still held local ground but it was clear that China, literally and metaphorically, would speak increasingly with the tones of Beijing.

In the west, China's boundaries were contentious. Matching the Russians within the Soviet Union in this respect, there were complicated relationships with minorities, in this case non-Han ethnic and religious communities. Tibet's fate attained much prominence. Chinese troops had invaded in late 1950 and showed no disposition to leave. Protests to the UN were to no avail, though there was much scope for discussing the legitimacy, or otherwise, of the Chinese action. India initially protested but then recognized China's sovereignty in Tibet in 1954. The Dalai Lama, the spiritual leader of Tibet, fled to India in 1959. A future as some kind of autonomous region of China, if it could be made a reality, seemed the only likely compromise. Obviously the Sino-Indian relationship was central in determining how the case of Tibet unfolded. The Soviet Union, for its part, remained anxious to assure 'Asian' Powers that it too had an Asian aspect and voice.

China and India: Himalayan rumblings

China's neighbours attached so much weight to boundary matters because their clarification had a bearing on their own complex identities. The Himalayan kingdoms of Nepal, Bhutan and Sikkim stood inescapably 'in between' their major neighbours. In Afghanistan, the king, ruling since 1933, found it increasingly difficult to maintain the country's precarious unity. The British in the past had played such a conspicuous part in its internal affairs and indeed had established his father on the throne, but they were not present. Tribal and linguistic affinities transcended the boundaries of 'Afghanistan' and 'Pakistan', rendering the division of peoples into 'Afghans' and 'Pakistanis' dubious. Kashmir, invariably described as a 'running sore', continued to fester. In January 1957 it was formally incorporated within the Indian Union over vigorous protest from Pakistan. In the previous year, Indian states had been reorganized on linguistic lines. The relationship between language, religion, ethnicity and statehood remained unstable everywhere in this Himalayan zone. The alignment of mountains and valleys, particularly for the major countries concerned, marched awkwardly with political alignments. Geography asked questions about 'leadership' in 'Asia'. China and India, as mentioned in Part Two, had agreed on 'principles'. They were now put to the test.

The flight of the Dalai Lama to India in 1959 put Nehru on the spot. Some of his colleagues thought that 'Chinese colonialism' should be denounced, but he would not be moved. He was well aware that the only way in which China would be dislodged from Tibet was by going to war, and that was not to be contemplated. Nehru was not absolutely opposed to the use of force. He had used it in 1961 to dislodge the Portuguese from Goa, thus removing the last vestige of European occupation in the subcontinent. The Indian army was, however, given increased responsibility in the northern border area. Fitful nego- tiations with Beijing took place, without resolution. It was evident, however, at this juncture, that China did lay claim to territory which India regarded as hers. In October 1962, with Cuba preoccupying the USA and the Soviet Union, Chinese forces successfully attacked Indian troops in one of the border areas, driving them back in disorder. The subsequent Indian counter-attack failed, with heavy casualties. Some thought a full-scale invasion of India threatened. On 21 November, however, China announced a ceasefire. It would withdraw to what it regarded as the correct frontier. Its point had been made.

China: east wind blowing?

The Himalayan crisis brought into the open deeper questions about 'worlds'. India had looked to the Soviet Union. In this instance there was very clearly no Soviet–Chinese accord. The 'Communist world' was falling apart. Back in 1957, on his second visit to Moscow, Mao had told students that it was the 'east wind' rather than the 'west wind' which was now blowing across the world. China would go its own way. It was about to take a 'Great Leap Forward'. It would move, by establishing huge communes, into a truly communist society, scything its way, in the process, through antiquated structures and values. Mao would show Khrushchev, and by extension 'the world', that his path to Socialism worked. Initially, all seemed to go well, but the vast endeavour then faltered. The great leap turned into a great famine by the mid-1960s, resulting in some 25–30 million deaths (estimates vary). There had been, amongst other factors, a disastrous overestimation of revolutionary enthusiasm. Soviet technicians and advisers were withdrawn. Relations between the two countries deteriorated further. The air was full of ideological recrimination. On the one hand, the Soviet Union was insufficiently revolutionary and on the other, China did not properly understand Marxism.

Zhou Enlai, no doubt echoing Mao, presented a picture of the world as it looked from Beijing. The superpowers occupied the top tier. Their political and economic systems contrasted and their rivalry was fluctuatingly intense, but their common possession of nuclear weapons paradoxically locked them together in their pre-eminence. Their signature of the Test-Ban Treaty in 1963 was taken in Beijing as confirmation – Khrushchev having 'capitulated' over Cuba – that the two powers had settled for the world pictured as a dyarchy. To be in this league, China would have to develop its own nuclear weapons, now without assistance from the Soviet Union – as indeed it proceeded to do. The second identified tier was that of the allies of the superpowers. The extent to which these allies were in fact inescapably subordinate varied, but their existence within the sphere of their masters (or protectors) shut China out. It was only through the non-aligned world, therefore, that China could achieve its place, whatever that place might be. Yet 'leadership' in this sphere was problematic. We have noted that the non-aligned world remained elusive and fluid. Events scarcely suggested that India would extend a welcome to Chinese leadership. It was far from clear that some other prominent non-aligned states, Egypt for example, would wish to rupture relations with the Soviet Union at Chinese behest. Beijing welcomed the fact that more Western European states established full diplomatic relations with it. It encouraged Poland to be more 'independent'. It was, however, within the third tier, as he defined it, that China could enhance its global standing while being vigilant for its own security against its potentially aggressive neighbours.

Zhou Enlai's frame of reference was not fully persuasive. To talk, as Mao did, about the 'East wind blowing' was appealingly extravagant but the wind had neither uniform strength nor direction. The 'west wind' could still be strongly felt. In fact, in this third tier, on 'China's doorstep', in 'South-East Asia', as in previous centuries, winds swirled about in many different directions. China might still be threatened, or perceive itself to be threatened, by the superpowers or their proxies, but it provided the 'east wind'. Whether nations and states in 'South-East Asia' would seek shelter from its growing strength, or blow along with it, was something governments and peoples everywhere pondered over. State-to-state relations with China could operate at one level, Communist Party-to-Communist Party relations at another. There was always an uncertain duality. In its emerging post-European form, South-East Asia remained a mixture, at different social levels, of linguistic, religious and cultural heritages. It was an open question whether historical contacts and connections, now being released from their European casing, retained their vitality. The 'Buddhist worlds' of Burma or Thailand, the 'Christian world' of the Philippines, the 'Islamic worlds' of Malaysia and Indonesia – all might crumble before the onslaught of a Communism that transcended these ancient moulds.

Yet, as the previous section has suggested, Communism's own 'globalism' was already patently compromised. Indigenous Communist parties, seeking external support, could not tap into a common Moscow/Beijing source but had to choose between rivals. An atheistic ideology was in practice no more immune from ethnic fears and prejudices than the religious traditions it sought to eliminate or marginalize. The fundamental Cold War convictions, in the USA and, to greater or lesser degree, in Western Europe, straitjacketed political movements and aspirations into simplified categories, perhaps inevitably. The other way round, European languages, specifically English, kept South-East Asian elites, and sometimes wider segments of populations, in lively touch with 'the Western world'. But there was always China 'in the background', not least because of the presence of Chinese minorities, sometimes substantial, with their own complicated attitudes to a 'homeland' under Communist government. Alongside these linkages, at once both 'external' and 'internal', ran a powerful impulse to 'nationalize' indigenous languages and insist that they too could function as fully as any alien and originally imposed import. 'East', 'West' and an often problematic 'nation' both collided and coexisted.

India: new principles, new principals?

The Indian–Chinese confrontation in the Himalayas placed post-independence assumptions in New Delhi under scrutiny. The 'five principles' that allegedly defined Sino-Indian relations had been shown to be flimsy. At the moment of crisis, Nehru sought and received modest British and American military supplies. It was a step which suggested that *in extremis* India was prepared, if unwillingly, to be more flexible, despite its studied 'non-alignment'. In the aftermath, the government saw no alternative but to increase the defence budget substantially, a step with inevitable consequences for other aspects of Indian development. All of this dented the vision of 'non-alignment' so central to Nehru's world-view. It was somewhat galling, from the Indian perspective, that a group of non-aligned states which attempted mediation after the Sino-Indian ceasefire did so in too determined a non-aligned manner. It came to nothing. An Indian claim or aspiration to be some kind of global arbiter looked precarious in these new circumstances. Nehru's discomfiture was not without its pleasing aspects in a 'West' accustomed to his criticism but, on the whole, the Indian view that China was the incontrovertible aggressor was accepted.

The while episode was a blow to Nehru's understanding of the world – and to his own effectiveness. Two years later, in 1964, he was dead. Here was a major point of transition. Nehru had come to 'represent' India. His vision, 'majesty' and firmness had kept the country together. The Congress which he had led had dominated, though not to the total exclusion of other parties. It was an open question whether his passing would cause Congress to fall apart. It might also upset the intricate balance between New Delhi and the states. However, there was one further aspect of his death. Nehru might indeed have represented 'India' to the world, but he was not a 'representative' Indian, if one can speak in those terms. Lal Bahadur Shastri, his diminutive successor, did not possess cosmopolitan charisma. His mind had been formed entirely within India in very different circumstances from his predecessor. What his notion of a 'socialist democracy' might amount to can only be speculated upon. Eighteen months later, he too was dead – in Tashkent, in what is now independent Uzbekistan. Some suggested he had been poisoned.

Pakistan: military direction

Shastri had been meeting the President of Pakistan, Muhammad Ayub Khan. Of much the same age, both men naturally had grown up in British India. The difference in their bearing, as they talked, however, had a more than personal significance. Ayub Khan, from a middle-income Pushtun family, had been commissioned at Sandhurst in 1928. He had fought in Burma with the First Assam Regiment during the Second World War. He had become the first Pakistani Commander-in-Chief in 1951, doubling as Minister of Defence a few years later. He and other soldiers came to have a vice-regal contempt for the corruption and incompetence, as they saw it, of politicians. Parliamentary government was indeed crumbling, exacerbated by the tensions between West and East Pakistan. In October 1958 a military coup took place. Ayub Khan deposed the president. Political parties were banned and an assault launched on black-marketeers and smuggling. A year later he promulgated what he termed a system of 'Basic Democracy'. Martial Law was formally terminated in June 1962 and a new constitution came into operation. The president continued to take the view that party politics had ruined Pakistan. His perspective was that of an administrator. His control of the machinery of government remained firm. The legitimacy of the regime, however, was strongly questioned, particularly in East Pakistan. For its part, the government made much of its efforts at land reform and industrial development. Any reform which touched property and inheritance inevitably touched differences between Sunni and Shi'a interpretations and practice, and indeed the more general question of the relationship between Islam and the legal ethos of the state. All of this was against the background of provincial tension within West Pakistan, whether in the Sind or Baluchistan, and between the two halves of the country.

In 1964–65, after some moments when an accommodation on the question of Kashmir seemed faintly possible, the issue flared up in August–September 1965. Pakistan seems to have thought that Kashmiri Muslims would rise up and that India would confine any military response to Kashmir. Both assumptions proved incorrect. Pakistani forces, crossing the ceasefire line in Kashmir, presumably hoping for a decisive military victory, had initial success, but then India invaded Pakistan. Fierce tank battles took place, but then petered out. An imperfect ceasefire followed (later consolidated at Tashkent). Both sides tended to suppose that the other was being favoured by outside powers – whether the Soviet Union, the USA, Britain or China. The ceasefire, of course, did not provide a solution. In 1963 Ayub Khan had appointed as his Foreign Minister the eloquent Zulfiqar Ali Bhutto. The two men clashed in the aftermath of failure and Bhutto resigned, telling cheering crowds that the struggle for Kashmir would go on, if need be, for one thousand years. Arguing that the ceasefire had been too quickly accepted, Bhutto claimed that Indonesia, Turkey and Saudi Arabia expressed strong support for the Pakistan case. If so, he was mobilizing a kind of Muslim world, though not to much effect. Once again, what was at issue was the basis of state formation. An Indian objection, being a secular state, to a plebiscite in Kashmir was that it would hinge on religion. Bhutto himself had been educated at Bombay Cathedral School and the universities of Oxford and California (Berkeley). The horses he rode, in his own environments and experience, pulled in different directions.

Japan: returning to 'normal'

The quarrels of the subcontinent seemed very exotic when viewed from Japan (though a watchful eye was always kept on China's stance in relation to them). In December 1956 Japan was admitted to the UN. Key to that admission was the 'normalization', in October, of diplomatic relations with the Soviet Union. Tokyo and Moscow had also then signed a trade pact. Even so, however, despite protracted negotiation, a full peace treaty had not been signed. Ownership of the Kurile Islands was a stumbling block and territorial questions were 'parked' for the time being. 'Normalization' was the key word, in a variety of contexts, used to describe Japan's experience of the subsequent decade. Yet was its dependence upon the USA 'normal'? It was an issue which moved steadily to the fore in domestic politics. The US–Japan Mutual Security Treaty was due for renewal in 1960. Some amendments, to which Washington agreed, failed to satisfy opponents of the government. Mass demonstrations led President

Eisenhower to call off his visit in June planned to mark the anticipated ratification. The Japanese mood was frequently described by commentators as 'anti-American'. Its most vehement expression came from the Left but was not confined to it. Yet to speak simply of rampant 'anti-Americanism' is misleading. The 'American Way of Life' had not taken over Japan, but neither had its impact been fleeting and insubstantial. Since the mid-1950s, when the two main political groupings – the Liberal Democrats and the Socialists (with the former being dominant) – had been consolidated, Japan seemed firmly set in a democratic mould. Outside observers, be they European or American, found its democratic politics puzzling – the apparent interchangeability of bureaucratic and political roles, for example – but democracy was a house with many mansions. Japan, to put it succinctly, had adopted a way of conducting itself that was 'Western' but had also adapted it. The 'American shield' in this sense was both boon and burden. Yet the 'artificiality' of this US–Japanese 'co-prosperity sphere', stemming from its imposed character, perhaps relegated rather than removed the nagging issue of the country's global orientation. The Sino-Japanese relationship, with its fraught baggage, was put into cold storage. Tokyo, at the American behest, recognized Taipei, not Beijing.

On the other hand, it was arguably the overarching American presence which facilitated the 'normalization' of relations between Seoul and Tokyo which occurred in 1965, accompanied by Japanese promises of economic aid. Korean sensitivities with regard to any sign of a continuing Japanese 'colonial mentality' were strong. Yet there were ironies in the situation. The regime in Seoul stemmed from a military coup staged by Major-General Pak Cheng-hi in 1962. Syngman Rhee's corrupt regime had been brought to an end by student protests in 1960, but the ensuing government had been 'weak'. Pak managed electoral victories but ensured that he and the military had the real power. Ironically, he had been trained as a soldier under Japanese rule. His style owed more to that past than to the 'Western' democracy of Tokyo with which he negotiated. Pak 'copied' new Japan, however, in embarking on rapid economic expansion. Japanese ministers had not only been promising transforming growth, they were achieving it. Seoul would follow. The two countries stood out in the early 1960s for their high level of adult literacy – Japan almost total and South Korea some 75 per cent (as against, for example, Pakistan at just under 20 per cent, India at around 30 per cent and Indonesia at around 40 per cent). The past – and the present – however, cautioned against envisaging a strong Korean-Japanese symbiosis. Christianity, in myriad Protestant and Catholic forms, had become a major and growing, though not dominant element in South Korean life. The Christian presence in Japan, however, was much smaller and static. Observers found it difficult to identify a dominant strand at all in the 'mindset' of Japan at this juncture. The great shrines of the now abolished State Shinto religion had become tourist attractions, or so it seemed. Local shrines still had their appeal. Buddhism, in its various forms, less entwined with the national myth, was frequently, but understatedly, pervasive. Tokyo café intellectuals, British historian W.G. Beasley reported, immersed themselves in English or French literature. Japanese musicians could be seen playing 'Western' music to perfection. But had such music been fundamentally 'absorbed'? Urban cultural eclecticism to some minds showed the open-mindedness of the new Japan. For others, however, it avoided a direct engagement with the recent past and a definition of the 'essential Japan' in the emerging world. Becoming a 'consumer society' infatuated with sophisticated gadgetry might be another way of 'parking' the problem of its identity. It was a sign that Japan had been 'accepted', however, when the world came to Tokyo in 1964 to take part in the Olympic Games. For their part, prosperous Japanese began to manifest themselves as 'world tourists'. They could leave aside the complications of their current domestic self-image.

The extraordinary dynamism of the Japanese economy could not fail to attract global attention. It was explained by reference to the 'liberation' made possible by small defence expenditure, by the interlocking, at the highest levels, of business, bureaucracy and politics. There was a ruthless focus on technical and managerial innovation which led to massive growth in shipbuilding, automobiles and electrical goods across a wide spectrum. It was an expansion watched in Western Europe and the USA with a mixture of admiration and apprehension. A prospering Japan, pursuing a doubling of living standards, would not be 'aggressive'. It was a premise which had permitted a degree of foreign acquiescence in Japanese protective tariffs. On the other hand, as industries in other parts of the world forfeited their accustomed dominance, apprehension mounted. The relationship between economic power and political power came to the fore.

The Japanese government emphasized that it had no intention of seeking to dominate South-East Asia. These were years in which it was engaged in paying compensation arising out of wartime occupation. Negotiation, however, was never straightforward. It was not helped by the occasional use, by Japanese politicians on overseas visits, of the term 'Co-Prosperity Sphere'. It was explained that all that was being meant, if such a term ever slipped out, was that Japan could not help but have a common interest in prosperity with its South-Eastern neighbours. That was indeed true. Japan might be neutered, and willingly neutered, as a Great Power, but it was inescapably part of East/South-East Asia. The anxiety about Japan's future intentions stemmed from the past rather than arose out of new tendencies.

Searching for 'South-East Asia'

Historically China, India and Japan had loomed over 'South-East Asia' to different degrees and in different ways. Where did its countries now stand in the world and on what 'principles? There was sad irony in the career of first Asian to be Secretary-General of the UN, the Burmese U Thant, in office since 1961. He was an English-medium 1930 history graduate of the University of Rangoon. His own country illustrated common problems. It was a fragile entity. It had a complex historic relationship with its Thai neighbour. Buddhism, Christianity and Islam all had adherents, though neither geographically nor ethnically in uniform strength across the country. Its Prime Minister, U Nu, had written an anti-Communist play, but nevertheless struck a determinedly neutral note. He and U Thant were very close. Both men were Buddhists (though apparently U Thant had both Muslim and Buddhist forebears). When U Thant had succeeded Hammarskjöld, the Soviet Union had at first pressed for a tri-person solution, one from each of the world's blocs, but the attempt failed. By 1966, however, when he was reappointed for five years, his performance aroused no Great Power opposition. He transcended blocs. The civilian government in Burma, however, had been supplanted in a military takeover in 1962. The new regime had no place for him in his homeland. When he died, in 1974, it was in New York, an event officially ignored at 'home'.

The road on which foreign embassies were to be found in Kuala Lumpur was named in honour of U Thant. Burma spindled down near to, but did not adjoin, Malaysia. A bloc of Thailand separated the two countries. It was a world where Islam and Buddhism met, not without tension. Whether, beyond, there was, or was not, some kind of 'Malay world' was problematic. The 'emergency' being over, Malaya became independent in 1957. Its historic diversity still had some constitutional recognition in the rotating kingship of the country exercised by the hereditary rulers of its individual states. It did not join SEATO. Singapore, with a population some three-quarters Chinese, became substantially independent two years later. Proximity suggested union. The complication was that in a united state there would be more Chinese than Malays. Malay opinion, anxious for national enhancement, wanted a state with a Malay ethos. The educational status of the Malay language, Bahasa Melayu, had to be improved. The Malay element in a unified state could be increased by adding the territories on the island of Borneo, North Borneo (Sabah) and Sarawak, which had become British protectorates. Brunei, an oil-rich sultanate, also under British protection, withdrew its initial agreement to join. Such a Federation of Malaysia came into existence in 1963. Two years later, Lee Kuan Yew, who took Singapore into the federation, took it out, or perhaps it might be better to say that he and the island were ejected. Malaysia was not going to accept a Singaporean Chinese as a future prime minister. However, at the time, on the island and elsewhere, an independent republic of Singapore seemed a risk. What about water supplies?

The careers of the two political figures chiefly engaged in producing these outcomes – Tunku Abdul Rahman (b.1903) and Lee Kuan Yew (b.1923) – illustrate in microcosm the way in which their personal world paths, both convergent and divergent, impacted on the region. Rahman, a son of the Sultan of Kedah, one of the Malay states, had taken degrees in England, in Cambridge and London. He then became active in the politics of the United Malay National Organization and led the various negotiations in London for Malayan independence. An erstwhile playboy, his adherence to Islam became steadily more pronounced. Lee was born as a fourth-generation of prosperous Singaporean Chinese. Learning Japanese during the Japanese occupation, he worked in the Japanese 'information' department, though he apparently also prudently operated a private black-market business selling tapioca-based glue. He also improved his Chinese language, for his family had given him the name 'Harry' and he had gone through English language schooling. Like Rahman, though after the war, he had come to study in Cambridge, where his academic record as a law student was brilliant. Back home, he and others formed the People's Action Party in 1954 and he rose to the top.

Lee Kuan Yew, therefore, personally embodied what the new state might become. Here was a kind of China beyond the People's Republic. Here too was a kind of English world, though certainly not as found in Cambridge. There were traces of India. Singapore would not be exclusively one thing or another. It would be an East–West city state existing with a majority Chinese population (speaking different dialects) alongside Indians (speaking various Indian languages) and Malays – the whole wrapped up in administrative and business English. Whether such a medley could work, and on what basis, remained to be seen. Similarly, whether Malaysia could work was also problematical. The detachment of Singapore made the state more Malay, but was there not something inherently unstable and unconvincing about it? It was a country, governed centrally from Kuala Lumpur, which stretched across the South China Sea to the north tip of Borneo, an island the great bulk of which was part of Indonesia.

All Malays were presumed to be Muslim. Islam was declared the official religion of Malaysia in 1960 though, acknowledging diversity, the state was also to some degree 'secular'. Indonesia was arguably the most populous Muslim country in the world – though one with Christian minorities which were locally significant. Malaysia and Indonesia were 'Islamic states' but neither in the same way nor to the same degree. The 'nearby' states of Thailand and the Philippines, largely Buddhist and largely Christian, respectively, nevertheless contained Muslim minorities in their southern regions or islands.

From the standpoint of Sukarno in Indonesia, and Macapagal in the Philippines, 'Malaysia' was bogus. It was the British, in their rather extraordinary presences along the north-east of Borneo, who, as it were, had provided a link to Malaya (though it had not been an administrative one). That it should be formalized as they were departing (or perhaps they were not really departing?) was absurd. Sukarno immediately launched a 'confrontation'. The British embassy in Jakarta was burned in orchestrated rioting. The Philippine government, too, claiming Sabah, broke off diplomatic relations with Kuala Lumpur. Confirmation that Malaysia was really a device for continuing 'colonialism' seemed to be provided by the fact that the Malaysian government turned to Britain and Australia for military support – support which did keep the state successfully afloat.

'Confrontation', however, raised the issue of 'Indonesia' itself. Here was a state, some said, of 13,600 islands, large, small and tiny, and 726 languages. As such, it was 'boundaryless'. Looked at from the southern Philippines, Borneo seem a 'natural extension' of *its* territory. The departing Dutch had insisted on staying on in 'West Irian' – the west of New Guinea – arguing that there was no political or cultural reason why its inhabitants should be thought 'Indonesian'. Witnessing Dutch preparations to hand over to 'West Irians' in 1961, Indonesia stepped up pressure. As a result, the territory, after an interim UN administration, was handed over to Indonesia in May 1963, pending a subsequent 'free choice' by the inhabitants. The Portuguese, governing the eastern half of the island of Timor, proved obdurate. And in New Guinea, Indonesia had to deal with an Australia that was never going to remove itself geographically. Whatever culture and history might suggest, it might become 'regionally active'.

In these circumstances, producing a coherent Indonesia was the central preoccupation of government. One key element was clearly language. The Dutch, for reasons that are disputed, had used their own language administratively far less extensively than the British had used theirs in Malaya. They had eventually settled on a kind of Malay as their 'service' language. They had equipped it, though only at the beginning of the century, with a Romanized spelling. It was this language, officially described as Bahasa Indonesia, which was adopted by the Indonesian state. Yet many millions more Indonesians had Javanese, in its various forms, as their first language than spoke Bahasa Indonesia. The resulting problems could not be easily solved. The country needed English to speak to India and Australia, not to mention the further 'West'.

Sukarno, with his swagger stick, ample wives and mistresses, and apparent immunity from assassination, sought to conjure a modernity that was not 'Western'. His image postage-stamped itself over a potentially fissiparous 'nation'. Replete with new monuments and hotels, Jakarta bloomed into a true state capital (despite some flirtation with the idea of a new city built in the jungle of Central Kalimantan). Sukarno had looked in the past to China for support and generally received it. When he took his country out of the UN in 1965 in protest against a resolution condemning Indonesian aggression against Malaysia, he linked arms with an excluded China. The notion of a Beijing–Jakarta axis, however, only looked impressive if one ignored the febrile situation inside his 'guided democracy'. He had tilted towards the Communist Party of Indonesia – which could count on the support of around one-fifth of the population – but he was not its creature. A false rumour of his death in September triggered a putsch. As in many such matters, its instigation, course and outcome (botched) remain contentious. General Suharto emerged as the dominant figure and old scores across the country were settled on a massive scale – perhaps half a million deaths. Chinese living in Indonesia, sometimes over as many generations as Lee Kwan Yew's family had lived in Singapore, were often picked out. Popular hostility towards urban and allegedly exploitative mercantile Chinese sat uneasily alongside the state's tilt towards China. The Sukarno era, however, was virtually at an end. If Indonesia tilted to 'the West', that is to say towards an eager USA, it was because that country had presciently gained credit in 1962 by putting pressure on the Dutch concerning the future of West Irian. The country's significance within 'the Muslim world' remained and might grow.

'Indo-China' was another kind of South-East Asia. The last French troops left in May 1956. What followed, from one point of view, was a 'war of succession', the unpicking of 'Indo-China', with struggles for power and identity both within and to some extent between the peoples of Cambodia, Laos and Vietnam – the Khmers, the Lao and the Vietnamese, respectively. What kind of state could flourish in a poor, mountainous and ethnically diverse Laos (in which the Lao people constituted a bare majority)? The political, cultural and economic basis on which the Khmers of Cambodia and the Lao of Laos would create successful states was unclear. Three factions struggled for supremacy in Laos over a period of years. Throughout the region, French education, indigenous language and culture, Buddhism, Catholicism and Marxism pointed in confusing directions. In addition, Vietnam displayed its capacity to produce indigenous syncretic religious–political cults of its own.

'It is impossible, quite impossible ... for you Westerners to understand the force of the people's will to resist and to continue', remarked the Premier of North Vietnam in 1964. Pham Van Dong (b.1906) was recorded as saying that Westerners would never understand the force of the people's will to resist. The Premier of North Vietnam's career demonstrated that he did know about both 'West' and 'East'. Born in the original capital of the Nguyen dynasty, Hué, he had been educated at the French *lycée* there. During a brief period in China, he had fallen under the spell of Ho Chi Minh. Subsequent revolutionary activity led to years of imprisonment. The world war had been spent in China. It was inevitable, after 1949, that there should be strong links between Chinese and Vietnamese Communists in the struggle ahead, but the Vietnamese had no intention of being swamped by Chinese power. In 1954 Pham Van Dong came directly to Europe for the first time. He was in Geneva as head of the Democratic Republic of Vietnam delegation to the peace talks (and became premier in Hanoi a year later). The division of Vietnam accepted at Geneva was to be 'temporary', pending elections to be held in July 1956 to decide the future. Meanwhile, the division of the country placed Pham Van Dong's birthplace in the South.

Ngo Dinh Diem Dim (b.1901) was also born in Hué. His father, like Pham Van Dong's, was a mandarin counsellor in the emperor's service. Likewise, both fathers had been angered when the French, in 1907, deposed the emperor, allegedly on grounds of insanity. These two sons, however, in their hostility to French rule, took very different courses over the subsequent decades. A Catholic, as his family had been over many generations, his convoluted course found him in the USA in the early 1950s, patronized by Cardinal Spellman. He said he opposed both the Vietminh and the French. In 1955 he was in a position to proclaim himself President of Vietnam, though he failed to evince much enthusiasm for US-style democracy. Instead, in an unbusinesslike manner, he ran an extended family business which included racketeers, controllers of private armies, an ambassador and the archbishop of Hué. American pressure to 'reform' was metaphorically and literally 'out of place'. He struggled to contain the Vietcong guerrilla movement, strongly backed from the North, which had emerged in 1957. For their part, Buddhists, the majority of the population, took no pleasure from Diem's dedication of the country to the Virgin Mary. The peasant population had a historic dislike of the great ruling family from which he came. The elections planned for 1956 to decide the future of 'Vietnam' never took place. Ho Chi Minh, Pham Van Dong and the inner circle in Hanoi, meanwhile, could get on with Stalinist state-building in the North: elections were unwanted. Ngo persuaded the Americans that he was state-building in the South: elections were unwanted. Both regimes could blame the other. Ideology, as in Korea or Germany, required two states.

It had been France which had cobbled together its distinct elements into an 'Indo-China'. It was now the USA which worried about 'Indo-China' in the context of South-East Asia as a whole. Washington administrations had not specialized in the cultural nuances of Indo-China. Kennedy, then a mere Congressman, visited Saigon in 1951 as he broadened his view of the world. The trip left him without enthusiasm for French colonial rule there, or indeed anywhere. In 1954 he spoke out against the view that the USA should take part in 'united action' in Indo-China to bolster France. Pouring money, materials and men into the jungles of Indo-China would be 'dangerous, futile and self-destructive'. The prospect of a French 'victory' looked remote. He seemed then to accept a Ho Chi Minh takeover of Vietnam with some equanimity. In 1956, however, again visiting Saigon, the now Senator John F. Kennedy claimed that the country (South Vietnam) was 'a proving ground' for democracy in Asia. It was perhaps an encouragement to his fellow Catholic, Ngo Dinh Diem, being a man regarded in Washington at this time as 'our best hope'. In December 1959, late in his presidency, Eisenhower embarked on a world tour. He seemed to be well received in such diverse places as Rome, Ankara, Karachi, Kabul, New Delhi, Tehran, Athens, Tunis, Madrid and Casablanca, but he did not extend to Saigon or Vientiane. Laos, however, was much on his mind. A year later he reiterated, in the face of Pathet Lao guerrilla activity, supported by China, the Soviet Union and North Vietnam, that the USA would not allow Laos to fall to the Communists. It was key to Southeast Asia – too big a slice of the world to write off. Here was the 'domino' view of the world. It was soon to be put to the test. In March 1960 the Vietcong, with their political arm, the National Liberation Front, began the struggle in the South.

As noted above, Kennedy, now president, had himself seen the danger of being sucked into Indo-China, but, given the wider international situation he faced, the imperative to prevent Vietnam as a whole falling under Communist domination seemed important, if something still of a sideshow. His Vice-President, Lyndon Baines Johnson, was dispatched to Saigon early in 1961 to see for himself. His conclusion was simple. The USA had either to help South-East Asian countries or 'throw in the towel' in the area. It would have to pull back American defences to San Francisco and build 'Fortress America'. It was a Texan view of the world which seemed to overlook the substantial presence of American forces elsewhere in East Asia. To run away from Diem, Johnson concluded, would tell 'the world' that America deserted its friends. There was no lack of American visitors armed with advice, but Diem, perhaps encouraged by the suggestion that he was the 'Winston Churchill of Asia', was his own man. The internal situation deteriorated in 1963. The self-immolation of a Buddhist monk was carried in pictures across the world. The US administration was not taken in by the suggestion that assaults on pagodas, carried out by special forces loyal to Diem's brother, were really the work of the Vietcong. So how could 'independence' be sustained in such circumstances? Generals in South Vietnam, who overthrew the government in November 1963, knew that that the USA would not intervene against them. Diem was executed. The notion that what would replace him would be a broad-based and militarily effective regime proved, over the next few years, an illusion. Many millions in the South did not want Communism, but what they did want was unclear. Kennedy, however, did not live to see the outcome of the process which he had initiated. In the month that Diem was executed he was assassinated.

Johnson, his successor, was given authority by Congress in August 1964 to take all necessary measures (an incident in the Gulf of Tonkin, if there was an incident, having been taken to be an act of open aggression on the high seas undertaken by Hanoi). Johnson, as a now elected new president, had to ask himself whether any government in Saigon could resist a Communist takeover. He could not quite decide the answer. Involvement deepened and dragged on, as the next part of the book will consider, for a decade. Kennedy had talked of his country's willingness to pay any price. It turned out to be a heavy one – and even more for the people of Vietnam.

Part 3 further reading

Balfour, Sebastian, *Castro* (Pearson Education, London, 1995).

Barr, Michael D., *Lee Kuan Yew: The Beliefs behind the Man* (Georgetown University Press, Washington, DC, 2000).

Birmingham, David, *The Decolonization of Africa* (UCL Press, London, 1996).

Clapham, Christopher, *Africa and the International State System: The Politics of State Survival* (Cambridge University Press, Cambridge, 1996).

Cooper, F., *Africa since 1940: The Past of the Present* (Cambridge University Press, Cambridge, 2002).

Davies, Norman, *God's Playground: A History of Poland. Vol. II: 1795 to the Present* (Oxford University Press, 2005).

Kyle, Keith, *Suez* (I.B. Tauris, London, 2011).

Lendvai, Paul, *One Day That Shook the Communist World: The Hungarian Revolution and its Legacy* (Princeton University Press, Princeton, NJ, 2008).

Legge, J.D., *Sukarno: A Political Biography* (Praeger, Washington, DC, and New York, 1972).

Lodge, Tom, *Mandela* (Oxford University Press, Oxford, 2007).

Louis, Wm. Roger and Bull, Hedley, eds., *The 'Special Relationship': Anglo-American Relations since 1945* (Oxford University Press, Oxford, 1989).

Pells, Richard, *Not Like Us: How Europeans Have Loved, Hated and Transformed American Culture since World War II* (Basic Books/HarperCollins, New York, 1997).

Young, Marilyn, *The Vietnam Wars, 1945–1990* (HarperCollins, New York, 1991).

Part 4
1965–1975:
OLD PATTERNS AND NEW PERMUTATIONS

In 1967 a German historian, Arno Peters, designed a new map of the world. He presented it at a Press Conference in Germany in 1974, creating a major controversy, splitting cartographers in angry debate. The basic principle of the map was that areas of equal size on the globe were equally represented. The outcome was visually to 'weight' countries and parts of the world in a different fashion from 'normal' maps in general use, which owed ultimate obeisance to Mercator's sixteenth-century projection. All maps, however, as the debate made plain, contain strengths and weaknesses when trying to represent a round earth on a flat surface. They have hidden messages. The consequence of the Peters map was that it gave additional prominence and 'weight' to countries whose affairs did not form part of the mainstream contemporary global narrative. In itself it was both a product of and a further impetus towards new ways of envisaging the world. Redrawing the map, however, had to coexist with remembering the past.

'Remembrance' of what the world had come through to reach 1945 still occupied a significant place in public life across the globe. Complicated memories of war still lingered in 1965 and beyond. This book has initially been divided into decades which take 1945 as their reference point. It has deliberately avoided talking about 'the Forties' or 'the Fifties'. It now also avoids 'the Sixties'. Too much haggling over dates is pointless, but many historians, Arthur Marwick for example, already agree, in any case, that 'the Sixties' lasted from 'about 1958 to about 1974'. Often, however, this only means the 'Western world' (taken to be Western Europe, the USA, Canada, Australia and New Zealand). There a youthful generation seemed to be seeking a different 'new beginning'. Other 'cultural revolutions', however, taking place elsewhere in the world, had different origins, carried different implications and moved to different rhythms. The 'characteristics of a decade', therefore, wherever we begin and end, are rarely universal. The world both was, and was not, 'joined up'. Minds set by their experience of the war lived alongside minds for which it was already history.

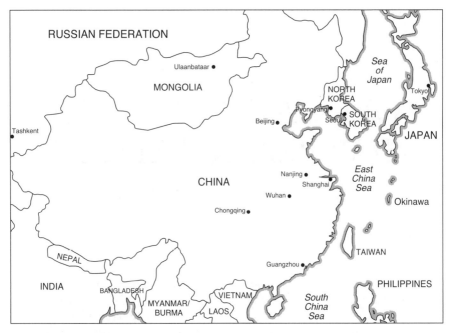

Map 7 East Asia, 2012

In the mid-1960s, as examples in the following chapters illustrate, erstwhile 'world figures', through death or deterioration, slipped from the scene. Men born in the latter decades of the nineteenth century, nurtured in a European imperial world, died or stepped down. Antonio Salazar, virtual dictator of Portugal since 1932, incapacitated in 1968, died two years later. In January 1965, a decade after resigning as Prime Minister, Winston Churchill died. Around 400 million people worldwide watched his funeral on television. Churchill had long since had his finest hour, but for Britain, his death symbolized the passing of an era. Charles de Gaulle, who came to the funeral of his wartime friend and opponent, was then in his seventh year as President of France. Five years later, however, having resigned his office in 1969, he too was dead. Robert Menzies, champion of global empire, a man physically distant from Europe but at home in London, Prime Minister of Australia in 1939–41 and since 1949, stepped down in 1966. In October 1939 he had declared that Australia had maintained its independent existence primarily because it belonged to a 'family of nations'. The war, putting it gently, had exposed some 'family disagreements'. After 1949, when again Prime Minister, Menzies stuck by his earlier convictions. It was only fitting that on his retirement, he became a Knight of the Thistle. No future Australian prime ministers would be Knights of the Thistle, indeed knights of any kind. Australia's view of itself and its place in the world was changing. In 1970 the world's 'senior' figure, the Emperor of Ethiopia, Haile Selassie, had been emperor for forty years. He provided a unique link, at this juncture, with the world of the 1930s. However, having survived one attempted military coup in 1960, he was formally deposed and confined to his palace in 1974. The monarchy was then abolished. The following year he was dead. Ethiopia was to be directed by a committee of junior military men. Addis Ababa – and Africa – suddenly looked very different.

In Taiwan, through the 1960s, Chiang Kai-shek lingered on, supposedly planning to 'regain' China. However, he died in April 1975 in the twenty-fifth year of his presidency. Global attendance at the funeral in Taipei did not match that assembled in London in 1965. The late departed had long since ceased to be a colossus on the world stage, if indeed he really ever had been. Taiwan itself, however, survived and was reshaping itself as a thriving but insular economy, clinging on to its claim to be 'China'. Across the water, Mao Zedong was still alive, but at this point, crippled by disease, not visible. No one could say what effective authority, if any, he still possessed. In 1971 an American table-tennis team arrived to play in China. That, as will be seen, was only the start of an extraordinary sequence of Sino-American developments over the next few years. In September 1976 Mao died (Zhou Enlai had died earlier in the year). Other Chinese veterans of the same vintage also passed away. In their wake, factionalism was rampant. There were more than ping-pong victories to play for within and beyond China.

Prominent 'non-aligners' departed the world scene. Nasser of Egypt died in 1970. His successor, another soldier and his exact contemporary, Anwar Sadat, had been no less hostile to the British presence in Egypt. He had been imprisoned in the world war for 'pro-German' activity. He had served in various offices under Nasser. This was therefore a transition from within the regime. There were those who thought that Sadat would not last long (in fact he remained in office until his assassination in 1981). Some sections of Egyptian opinion thought he looked 'un-Egyptian' (his mother was Sudanese). His face was a reminder that Egypt belonged to different worlds – Arab and African. Whether he would retain a 'Nasserite' perspective remained to be seen. Sukarno of Indonesia, who also died in 1970, had been finally edged out of power in 1967. General Suharto (b.1921), another Javanese, who succeeded him, was twenty years younger. As a young man, Suharto had served in armies under Dutch and then under Japanese command. He knew about changing worlds. What was latterly significant, of course, was his prominent role in the Indonesian army. He promised, after years of crisis, a 'New Order'. Military control would be strong.

In Pakistan, Field-Marshal Ayub Khan's eleven-year rule came to an end. He was succeeded in 1969 by another soldier, Major-General Yahya Khan. Although a civilian government was then formed under Z. Ali Bhutto in 1971, the first since 1956, its existence looked precarious. Military rule, whatever it precisely entailed, was becoming 'normal' in many parts of the world. The pluralist democracy of North America or Western Europe, apologists suggested, was not a universal model: a competitive party system, in which power alternated without violence, only worked in countries where the state itself was not in question. However, in the post-colonial world, it often was. The military, in such circumstances, kept order and directed government for 'the common good'. Critics, however, noted that the military interpreted the 'common good' rather widely. Some regimes did permit parallel institutions which provided some degree of 'democratic' involvement, but power still fundamentally lay with them. That was the case, for example, in Burma. After a referendum held in the previous year, the country became a single-party Socialist Republic in 1974, with a unicameral legislature. Military control was codified, but the codification was the product of the militarily directed political party.

There was, however, some continuity amidst new world faces. The Shah of Iran and Marshal Tito of Yugoslavia were two prominent veterans from the world-war era. The Shah, however, was no longer the callow ruler of 1941. Buttressed by a domestic security apparatus, significant armed forces and oil wealth, he was determined to create a 'modern' Iran. He would extricate his country from the humiliation he had himself experienced. Iran would come to 'count' in the world. In Belgrade, Tito also oscillated, though in very different circumstances, between 'East' and 'West', beholden to neither. Under the 1953 constitution, which he had organized, he had been made president on five successive occasions. In 1974, reality was recognized. He became president for life. Probably he alone could effectively manage, by whatever means, the prickly national sensitivities of his federated country. Another man fortunate enough, in 1975, to arrange to have himself elected as president for life was Habib Bourguiba. He had now, with increasing autocracy, ruled Tunisia in the first two decades of its independence. A third long-term survivor from 1939–45 continued to hold power in Madrid until his death in 1975. Francisco Franco had kept his country out of world war, but the characterization of his regime as 'Fascist' meant that even in an anti-Communist Western Europe Spain remained an outsider, if not quite an outcast.

With only occasional exceptions, it was men who came to power. Golda Meir, however, became Prime Minister of Israel in 1969 and served for five years. Sirimavo Bandaranaike of Ceylon/Sri Lanka had become the first woman prime minister in the world in 1960. Losing office in 1965, she came back again in 1970 and was still in office in 1975, by which time the country had both changed its name and its constitution. In India, Indira Gandhi became Prime Minister on the death of Shastri in 1966 and was still in office in 1975. Woman she indeed was, but she was Nehru's daughter. She too had been to school and university – Oxford, not Cambridge – in England. What difference, in India or elsewhere, gender and generation would make was not clear.

The cumulative impact of these changes was considerable. Too much generalization, of course, cannot be drawn from the arrival or departure of particular individuals. There was clearly no simple co-ordinated global exodus from power of an entire generation. Nevertheless, in these and other instances, since their successors were frequently younger, sometimes by a generation, their lives had been framed by different events and contexts. They saw the global environment differently and took new directions. The chapters that follow examine the consequential mutations in different geographical locations, all taking place under the watchful eye of the Superpowers.

13
Asian Variations

Indian democracy: a state of emergency?

The future of India had undoubted global significance. When Indira Gandhi became Prime Minister, there had been much comment, at home and abroad, on the fact that India was 'the world's largest democracy' (in 1967 the electorate stood at 250 million – with a turnout of 61.3 per cent). If democracy should fail in India it would signal that it had no future in the 'developing world'. On one occasion Mrs Gandhi publicly said that interpreting India to the outside world was difficult. The outside world, in turn, was not sure whether her elevation was a sign of continuity or the beginning of a new trend. No short-hand depiction of 'India', externally or internally, was ever adequate. Indira had been a minister in Shastri's government at the time of her father's death. Pushed forward by Congress notables, she defeated Morarji Desai in the subsequent election by roughly two to one. In itself the contest had opened up different Indian worlds.

Desai was a 70-year-old (Mumbai)-educated Congress veteran with jail experience under the Raj. He was vastly experienced in the politics of Bombay – the country's financial and increasingly industrial centre – before moving into all-India politics with ministerial responsibilities for commerce and industry and finance under Nehru. He was not a global traveller. His India differed from that presented by his opponent. He combined a strict personal Gandhian asceticism – though one with public application – with a belief in business and free enterprise. His public belief in the merits of urine therapy was not something shared by Western political leaders, though its merits were apparently vindicated by the old age to which he subsequently lived. His western Indian base was significant. He knew 'on the ground' the political aspects of the country's linguistic tensions. Maharashtra, with Bombay as its capital, was a state set up in 1960 to meet the agitation of Marathi speakers. It was the second most populous and economically one of the most prosperous states in India (the range between the most and the least was a very considerable one). By 1971 the state's population passed 50 million and it constituted one of India's most prominent 'voices'. Desai became Deputy Prime Minister and Minister of Finance, but broke with Mrs Gandhi in 1969. He moved into the assorted medley of groups which constituted the Opposition. In 1975 he was one of those arrested under the State of Emergency (to be considered shortly).

Language mattered in India, particularly at this time. In the south-east of the country Tamil voices vigorously opposed the promotion of Hindi as *the* national language. The creation of the state of Tamil Nadu, with Madras (Chennai) as its capital, however, gradually moved the region's politics away from a secessionist direction. After 1967, however, here, as in other instances elsewhere at state level, government was not in Congress hands, a development which perhaps challenged India's capacity to function cohesively. There happened to be the additional complexity, in this particular case, provided by the Tamil population of north-eastern Sri Lanka. After a further electoral victory in 1970, Mrs Bandaranaike equipped the island with a republican constitution. The drive to make it 'more Singhalese' continued. Would there in turn be a 'pan-Tamil' response, and how would Delhi also in turn react? India was a country of many 'provincial' voices, too many to enumerate. They were often growing in self-confidence. So, despite diversity, was India 'essentially' Hindu? Was it religion which kept it together – if it was possible to say exactly what 'religion' was? As a political party, Jana Singh polled badly before 1967, but a variety of organizations continued vociferously to press the case for India as a Hindu state or perhaps nation. It was, however, not easy to combat or advance this notion without entering into the thicket of defining 'Hinduism'. As a totality, Hinduism might even be a construct of Western scholarship. Its emphasis on 'religious activity' rather than on creed made it possible for hundreds of millions of Indians to be Hindus 'of a kind'. This same elasticity made it difficult to say precisely how nation and state would play out in Mrs Gandhi's India. As 'centre' and 'state' jostled for position and control, political scientists found it difficult to describe how the country actually functioned. Her father, Nehru, had declared that the 'nations of the world' would admire the extent to which the Indian constitution had 'kept no room for communalism'. In practice, however, communalism had not disappeared.

In 1947, not yet quite 30, Indira had been present with her father at that midnight hour when Indian independence had been declared. Before and after, she had been his unofficial aide, travelling with him both in India and abroad. No one had been closer to his notion of what India was and what its role in the world should be. Now, after nearly three decades, the commitment to democracy, which had seemed so to distinguish India's development in Asia, appeared precarious. In the contest for the succession, Gandhi had successfully made a pitch for Congress's Left – not that a Left/Right dichotomy fully explains the factors involved. The magic of her father still counted to some degree: like father, like daughter. She too – on her wartime return to India – had spent time in prison. Yet this quasi-continuity expressed by her appointment inevitably functioned in changing circumstances, both internally and externally. Quite apart from her time at Oxford, three decades earlier, Mrs Gandhi was no stranger to the world beyond India. This cosmopolitan background naturally set her apart from most Indians. The succession to Shastri had split Congress and the division scarcely healed. The story of the intervening years was one of crisis for the Congress and for the subcontinent's place in the world: internal and external came together. In the Nehruvian elections up to 1962, Congress had held some three-quarters of the seats in the Lok Sabha, the all-Indian parliament. In 1967, however, although it still had a majority, it lost nearly 60 seats. Was this the beginning of the end? Time was perhaps running out for a body which had been so central to the achievement of independence. Decades on, 'normal' political differences arising from contemporary issues scarcely came as a surprise. While in a number of African instances, 'the party of independence' had proceeded to eliminate or incorporate other parties, independent India had seen the continued existence of Socialist and indeed Communist parties. It was about to witness even greater plurality. The Congress split, with both segments, led respectively by Gandhi and Desai, claiming to be 'the real Congress'. After 1969, the Prime Minister ruled with the support of the Socialist and Communist parties. Banks were nationalized. The Socialist ethos of the administration was confirmed. India did not jettison its 'neutral' stance but was conscious that it was now a kind of Great Power. It had to deal with the world's other Great Powers on as near a basis of parity as it could manage: it had to develop internally. The focus of Mrs Gandhi's activity and energy was on the subcontinent itself, though there was no formal withdrawal from global 'non-alignment'.

Matters came to a head internally when, on 26 June 1975, the President of India declared a State of Emergency in his country, being careful to act under a specific article of the constitution. A fortnight earlier, the Prime Minister had been found guilty at Allahabad High Court of electoral corruption. The case had been running for four years, having been brought by her Socialist opponent in the 1971 general election, Raj Narain. The verdict should have entailed Mrs Gandhi's removal from parliament, together with a ban on running in elections for six years. The Prime Minister, however, announced that she would appeal to the Supreme Court and would continue in office pending its outcome. She persuaded the President to act because of the disorder following the Allahabad verdict. Under a Maintenance of Internal Security Act, political opponents were arrested and press censorship imposed. That was only the beginning. India was not, or was not yet, a police state, but central government expenditure on the police had been rising very rapidly over the previous few years, outstripping, in the number of police per head, the growth of population (and what the Raj had required). The 'world's largest democracy' was now in disarray. Some said that India was becoming more like Pakistan – not a remark intended as a compliment.

Pakistan/Bangladesh: dissolving union

Pakistanis were offended by such remarks, but it could not be denied that Pakistan's governance, since 1947, had been problematic. However, after its period of military rule, elections were held in December 1970, envisaged as part of the process of transition to civilian government. The previous month the Ganges delta had been hit by a tidal wave which resulted in several hundred thousand deaths. This had caused the elections to be postponed. The outcome revealed the extent of the cleavage between West and East Pakistan. In the latter, the Awami League led by Sheikh Mujibur Rahman (b.1925) swept the board, but had no representation in the West. He had recently been imprisoned for allegedly collaborating with India to bring about the secession of the East. Bengalis, for their part, claimed that the East, though more populous, was a virtual 'colony' without a significant part in Pakistan's military–bureaucratic elite. Mujibur's Six-Point programme envisaged Pakistan becoming a loose federation. Zulfiqar Ali Bhutto's Pakistan People's Party was dominant, but not so dominant, in the West. Mujibur's party had an overall majority in the new National Assembly but that body did not speedily assemble. Negotiations between the two ambitious party leaders made little progress. The president, Yahya Khan, and the army by no means stood idly by. The country drifted towards civil war. In March 1971 demonstrators and troops clashed in East Pakistan. The basis on which some kind of agreement might be found constantly shifted. Conditions laid down publicly by Mujibur virtually amounted to a declaration of independence. They were unlikely to be met. A brutal army crackdown followed. Mujibur was arrested and taken to West Pakistan. Ethnic violence between 'Pakistanis' was only too evident. Some semblance of order was restored, but guerrilla activity and public hostility made it precarious. The attempt to get civil administration going again could only rely on non-Bengalis.

India could not fail to be involved. Figures vary, but perhaps ten million fled from East Pakistan into adjoining Indian territory, seven million of whom were Hindus. The influx put a severe strain on Indian administrative resources and there were maybe six thousand deaths in refugee camps. In West Bengal a Communist-led Naxalite/'Maoist' terrorist campaign was already making the region unstable. From April 1971 a 'Bangladesh" government-in-exile was established in Calcutta. The Indian army trained a Bengali 'liberation force' (though not one with great political coherence). Would Delhi go further? By November, envisaging direct Indian intervention either as an exercise in 'border containment' or as the prelude to a full-scale attack to capture Dhaka, Pakistan launched a pre-emptive but unsuccessful air assault on North-West India. The Indian military response, both in the West and in the East, was highly successful. In two weeks of fighting Pakistan probably lost half its navy, a third of its army and a quarter of its air force. The consequences were profound.

India was confirmed as the dominant power in the subcontinent. The military pretensions of the Pakistani army had been exposed. Delhi was in no hurry to repatriate the large number of Pakistani prisoners of war or to return territory taken in the Punjab and Kashmir. It was not until July 1972 that Bhutto and Mrs Gandhi, meeting in Shimla, reached an agreement on these matters, though it was another year before repatriation occurred. In effect, though not in so many terms, Pakistan recognized the existence of Bangladesh but could not accept that there had been a 'war of liberation'. Bangladesh was admitted to the Commonwealth in 1972 – a step which caused Pakistan to leave. The Commonwealth had no capacity to prevent its two largest members going to war with each other. On his release, the British government had provided an RAF aircraft to take Mujibur home to Bangladesh – he had come to see the British Prime Minister in London – but had not made any major diplomatic contribution. Bhutto and Mrs Gandhi agreed that the Kashmir problem should be settled by diplomacy. Hardliners in Delhi had argued that India should have taken advantage of its strong position to insist on a 'final' Kashmir solution there and then. Both at the time, and subsequently, the motives for the Indian intervention have been debated. India could scarcely not be 'involved', but invasion was another matter. That some Indian opinion saw in the crisis the opportunity to inflict a grievous blow on Pakistan is evident, but whether this desire drove policy remains uncertain. A grievous blow was in fact delivered. A single state, even though it was Islamic, with parts separated by a thousand miles, could not and did not work. There was also a question mark over the (West) Pakistan that remained. The rump might become more manageable, sandwiched between a complicated 'Islamic world' to its west and India to its east, but it might not. Complaints about 'Punjabization' had not been confined to the East. Ethnic and linguistic issues might tear the truncated country further apart and even 'eventually' end the 'absurdity' of the 1947 partition. But even as this point was being made, with some satisfaction, in Delhi, India itself was experiencing ethnic and linguistic conflict.

There were immediate questions to be addressed about how Pakistani government functioned. No one could look back at Pakistani decision-making processes, and decisions, between December 1970 and December 1971 with any admiration. If they had been better, a single Pakistan might have survived, albeit a different one. In a rare moment of sobriety, Yahya Khan resigned as President and found himself placed under house arrest. He was succeeded by Bhutto – the latter reverting to the title of Prime Minister two years later. Although the pride of the military had been dented, it remained an inescapable political factor. The creation of a new Greek-planned and truly 'national' capital at Islamabad had been going ahead since 1960. The intention had been to draw in a well-educated population from different parts of the country, and create an ethos in the hinterland which was different from that of the port city of Karachi. It was designed to show the unity of a modern state – but Pakistani self-confidence was shaken, at least temporarily. The 'Green City' expressed aspiration. It did not reflect reality.

As far as the new state was concerned, it did not take long for Bangladeshis to realize that independence did not solve their problems, even if a treaty with India guarded it against potential aggressors (who were difficult to identify). The promise of a 'Golden Bengal' looked a long way off in circumstances of widespread poverty, hunger and unemployment. Mujibur Rahman, plagued by ill health, vacillated between a secular Socialism, an 'Islamic Socialism' and a purely Islamic emphasis. This amalgam was dignified by the label 'Mujibism' but, however interpreted, it did not swiftly unlock the path to progress. Parliamentary government crumbled and Rahman became more dictatorial. He was murdered in the aftermath of a military coup in 1975. The leader of the coup suffered the same fate months later. It was not an auspicious start to statebuilding.

China: cultural alienation, diplomatic accommodation?

No one could doubt that China 'mattered'. By the time Chairman Mao took himself, at the age of 73, for a celebrated 65-minute dip in the River Yangtze near Wuhan in July 1966, however, the country seemed to be swimming away from the world's 'mainstream'. Its 'cultural revolution' was not an incorporation into the Western 'cultural revolution' as identified at the opening of this part of the book. It looked more like a peculiar 'reign of terror', a period of self-absorbed madness, as European or American minds, struggling to understand, often categorized it. China was clearly, for the moment, so locked into its internal world that no map could adequately disclose its global 'weight'. Its internal preoccupation, too, made a wider 'East Asia' difficult to envisage. No city in China, before 1949, bore more imprints of China's relationship with the outside world, and of the presence of different foreigners, in its midst, than Shanghai. The 'restoration' of its pre-1937 pattern of commercial and financial relationships after 1945 had, however, been short-lived. After 1949, the 'outside world' had substantially disappeared. It was a Chinese city, bereft for the time being of its imposed 'cosmopolitan' aspects. It was the city in which Jiang Qing (b.1914), to use only one of her many names, third wife of Mao, operated. She was acting a new part in a life which had seen much acting. Mao himself was living in Shanghai in 1965. In January 1967 workers with determinedly egalitarian objectives set up the 'Shanghai Commune'. Over the following weeks they tried to collectivize property in the city. Their zeal had to be reined back by central party intervention. Even so, their continuing organization proclaimed that they had raised the red flag of Mao Zedong's thought and brought about a new phase in the Great Proletarian Cultural Revolution in Shanghai. The workers, in using the word 'Commune', had the Paris Commune in their minds. There was, however, something paradoxical in such a model – for part of the energy of the moment sprang from the sense that new China should go its own way. Neither its own past nor foreign pasts should guide its future. The link with China's pre-revolutionary order was to be smashed (literally, in the case of temples). Foreign errors of every kind, whether 'Western' or 'Soviet', were pointed out everywhere. 'Revisionism Street', for example, was the name now given to the street in which the Soviet Embassy was situated. 'Polluted' intellectuals were persecuted and the foreign books or music found in their homes were removed. Libraries were destroyed. It was a risk to wear Western dress. Anti-imperialism, it was evident, could slip, without much difficulty, into xenophobia.

On an all-China basis, there was a Cultural Revolution Group 'in charge', with Jiang Qing as its deputy director. It was supposedly 'controlling' events, but 'letting things get out of hand' was an unusual way of exercising direction. There seemed no specific goal in sight. One event triggered another. From 1966 onwards, the violence of language, and sometimes of behaviour, suggested 'culture wars' of a depth and complexity beyond alien comprehension. China was a country not 'open to the world'. Foreigners were rarely seen. Interpretation, in these circumstances, was challenging both for contemporaries and subsequent historians. Confusion surrounded everything, not least Mao himself. The ageing icon was certainly not content to be marginalized. He saw the party succumbing to bureaucratization and the seductive attractions of the capitalist road. There had to be new revolution. The existence of a 'New Class' running a system, across the Communist world, with particular attention its own self-interest, had been detected by commentators, particularly by some who had themselves once been inside it. The thoughts of Chairman Mao, collected in the *Little Red Book*, appeared in English in 1966 and attempted to lay down a new mass line. It was very pertinent to repeat what had been said in 1948, namely that without a general policy Communists would be blind, half-baked and muddle-headed revolutionaries. Revolutionaries, however, muddle-headed or not, thought that Mao had given a red light to a reckless and wrecking iconoclasm (why not change red from the colour for 'stop' to the colour for 'go'?). A new generation was emerging which had not known a China before Mao. There was no reason to believe, contrary to Chinese tradition, that age brought wisdom (except in the case of Mao himself). In late 1966, in ever-increasing thousands, equipped with little red books, youthful Red Guards paraded before him in Tianenmen Square. It may well be, however, despite his public blessing, that Mao never envisaged the scale of the chaos that ensued. Schools, colleges and universities, already with many organizational problems, ceased to function (for varying periods and in varying degrees). Eventually, it required special 'propaganda teams', made up of peasants and workers, to go in and compel a resumption of educational life. Red Guards moved around with freedom, something in itself which contributed to their enjoyment and which for some, in their mature years, explained the otherwise inexplicable. Perhaps some half a million people lost their lives in this upheaval. Neighbour had been set against neighbour. Some four million or so young people were sent away into the countryside. Taken in the round, therefore, the 'Cultural Revolution' characterized the decade after 1966. In August 1973, one speaker at the 10th Party Congress supposed that China would always be undergoing Cultural Revolution.

Nearly half a century later, it defies any single explanation. The upheaval did lead to some not insignificant subsequent purges in the Communist Party and thus met at least some of Mao's own original objectives, as did the new Revolutionary Committees established at every level throughout the country. These committees, however, found themselves deferring to the representative of the ever more prominent People's Liberation Army which sat in their midst. Yet it is arguable that the problem of 'bureaucratization' still remained. Educational and economic life had suffered great damage that could not be made good rapidly. In the aftermath, Mao himself also still remained, but the succession issue came to dominate political behaviour at the top of the party. His myth, however, had become as important as his person. Five years on from the revolutionary days of the January 1967 'Commune', as will shortly be seen, the city of Shanghai was the location for the release of a communiqué which would have seemed inconceivable, and abhorrent, to those then battling 'the counter-revolutionary black wind of economism'. The Chinese and US governments declared to the world their intention to normalize their relations.

Ever since the start of the Cultural Revolution, it had been difficult to draw firm conclusions about the message it was delivering concerning China's relations with the outside world. The recall of Chinese ambassadors to Beijing suggested, in those many capitals where it occurred, that there was a profound crisis of identity back home. In May 1967 mobs attacked the Foreign Ministry in Beijing and evicted the Foreign Minister, an associate of Zhou Enlai. They attacked both British and Soviet diplomats in the capital. A huge demonstration in Beijing protested against the continued British possession of Hong Kong and there, months later, a state of emergency was declared. In August 1967 Red Guards burnt the British quasi-Embassy in Beijing. Red Guards were known to be fomenting disturbances in Burma, Cambodia, Hong Kong – and even in Moscow. When continuing outbursts against the USA in relation to Taiwan and elsewhere are taken into account, it looked as though China was lashing out against all comers, if one could be at all confident about what 'China', at this juncture, was. Yet, perhaps, in its wider sense, the xenophobia evident in the 'Cultural Revolution' reflected fear. China was on its own, surrounded still, on almost all sides, by more or less hostile states. So, issues at the domestic heart of the 'Cultural Revolution' had an inescapable international dimension.

A critical world juncture had been reached. It still looked bipolar. Only Washington and Moscow, to different degrees, had truly 'global spread'. China did not have 'global spread'. It had dabbled in independent East Africa – a connection shortly to be taken further by supplying loans to Tanzania and Zambia to construct the 'TanZam' railway – but this was only a modest 'out of area' link. The solidarity expressed by Albania in 1968 – the country had been excluded from the Warsaw Pact in 1961 – was doubtless welcome but of limited value. If to be a Superpower was to possess a nuclear weapon, the matter was already in hand. China carried out its first nuclear explosion in October 1964 and announced its first hydrogen bomb in June 1967. That announcement, and its context in relation to the Cultural Revolution, signalled that China now had a new status (though a really potent nuclear capacity would still take time). Yet, as the other possessors of nuclear weapons were experiencing, in Vietnam and elsewhere, possession was of little direct utility whatever their general 'threat' value might be. So China had found when its forces clashed with Soviet forces at the River Ussuri in 1969. Both countries increased the military divisions stationed near their border. Subsequent talks in Beijing aimed at reducing tension made little progress. Elsewhere, China edged its way onto the world stage. In April 1971 the UK restored the telephone link with China (which had been cut in 1949). More Western states (Canada and Italy) established diplomatic relations in 1970. In November of the same year, the UN General Assembly voted to admit China, though still short of the required two-thirds majority, but that was achieved in October 1971. A US–Japanese motion to allow Taiwan to retain membership failed. Notwithstanding its enhanced status, however, for China to be at loggerheads, though in different ways, with both the Soviet Union and the USA was, to say the least, uncomfortable. Beijing was torn between glorying in a precarious isolation and seeking to reduce it. The state of Soviet–American relations would largely determine its options.

The issue went wider. New Delhi and Islamabad came into the picture. Over the decade, Indian–Pakistani relations always had a Russian–Chinese dimension. Governments in Islamabad and Delhi, if they were wise, could not take any significant steps in their mutual dealings without some kind of support from China and the Soviet Union, respectively. Indian and Chinese troops clashed briefly on the Sikkim border in September 1967. In due course (in 1974), to

China's displeasure, India tried to pre-empt further dispute on this question by declaring Sikkim an 'associate state' of the Indian republic, with representation in both houses of the Indian parliament. In June 1968 India accused Pakistan and China of aiding the rebels who were active in (Indian) Nagaland. Its Treaty of Friendship and Co-operation with the Soviet Union matched the domestic thrust of its policy. For their part, Pakistani administrations talked up the significance of their connection with China. In the vital circumstances of the East Pakistan crisis, however, it became clear that, words apart, there was little direct assistance for Pakistan. Some supplies arrived, but after the termination of hostilities. China had no intention of involving itself in a full-scale war with India.

'Asia' was not merely an Asian matter. The role of the USA, in its relations with the Soviet Union, China, India and Pakistan, was likely to be critical. Indian–American relations, broadly, were cool, and even the economist J.K. Galbraith, a sympathetic US ambassador, could not generate much warmth. Nixon and Mrs Gandhi were not naturally drawn to each other. Normally the USA sided with Pakistan. On 4 December 1971 it put down a Security Council resolution which called for an immediate ceasefire in East Pakistan. The Soviet Union vetoed it. Four days later, however, the General Assembly passed a similar resolution (its objective, of course, was to halt the Indian army's progress). Nixon dispatched an aircraft carrier to the Bay of Bengal which perhaps indicated to Delhi that the USA might intervene. He also persuaded Moscow to warn Delhi not to use the crisis to try to 'settle' the Kashmir question. He hinted that he might cancel the summit meeting with Brezhnev in the Soviet Union arranged for May 1972. Brezhnev wanted that meeting. So indeed did Nixon, but he had other stratagems. In mid-July 1971 he announced that he would be visiting China (which came about in February 1972). The Soviet invitation was a reaction to this announcement. Within the space of a few months, therefore, Nixon would become the first US president to visit the Soviet Union while in office and the first president ever to visit China. Some kind of turning point in world affairs was clearly being reached.

The visit to China, which lasted ten days, was a striking event. Perhaps only a president with as confirmed an anti-Communist record as Nixon possessed could have done it. It was Kissinger, through his favourite 'back channels', who set the whole occasion up. Pakistan was a helpful intermediary. There was much public shaking of hands. Officials, meanwhile, worked away at the content of the communiqué – to be released in Shanghai. It stated that neither country should seek hegemony in the Asia-Pacific region. Both would oppose any country or group of countries seeking to do so. Beijing reiterated that it was the only legitimate government of China. It was committed to the liberation of Taiwan, an internal matter. Washington stated that the island's future should be settled amongst the Chinese themselves. American forces would ultimately be withdrawn and withdrawal would commence as tension was reduced. Despite difficulties still to be overcome, China and the USA were entering a new era.

It was, however, essentially a diplomatic revolution at the top. Neither of the men shaking hands in front of the camera had acted with full-hearted domestic endorsement. Back in September 1971, Lin Biao, Mao's chosen successor, possibly fleeing to the Soviet Union when a plot against Mao had failed, met his death when his aircraft crashed in Mongolia. Perhaps he favoured the Soviet rather than the American option for China. More generally, the weight of mutual perception, deeply embedded at various levels, did not shift overnight. No American ballot in July 1971 would have backed Nixon's visit. There was no open public discussion in China. As things turned out, Nixon, Chou Enlai and Mao Zedong were not in a position to cement personal relationships. In this sense, 'the visit' was simply an unexpected coda to long careers. Whether Sino-American understanding could be reconstructed on a broader basis remained to be seen.

Japan: re-engaging and remodelling?

'The visit' could not be other than a shock in Tokyo. The ruling party in Japan had long been a loyal supporter of US anti-Communist policy in Asia. Many of its leading politicians had maintained contacts with Chinese Nationalist figures before and after they had moved to Taiwan (Japan's former colony). Little effort had been made, out of deference to the USA, to seek better relations with Beijing. Now Nixon had gone ahead, without prior briefing of his intentions. The context, in addition, was one of growing trade friction with the USA. The return of Okinawa, held by the USA since the Occupation, had been a topic of widespread if periodic agitation for some years. In November 1969 the USA agreed to hand it back in 1972, though still with provision for US use. Japan's 're-engagement' with the world continued to be carefully managed. Here an international exhibition (Expo 70 in Osaka), there an imperial visit (Hirohito to Europe in 1971) – the first by an emperor outside Japan in half a century.

It fell to Tanaka Kakuei (b.1918), appointed Prime Minister in July 1972 through the 'usual channels' by which his party operated, to sense that a new moment had come. Appropriately, he was himself a 'new man', a wealthy businessman, uncorrupted by the customary university education or bureaucratic routine, though possibly corrupted by money. The previous month a bestseller appeared under his name – *Building a New Japan: A Plan for Remodelling the Japanese Archipelago*. He reputedly remarked, in the light of its staggering sales, that it was a book he must read. Certainly, there was a big domestic agenda, but his eyes were immediately on China. After groundwork, he arrived in Beijing in September 1972 with his foreign minister. Zhou Enlai was again on airport duty. The two men produced a communiqué which was not very explicit in detail but set out the basis for improved relations in the future. Mao had little to say. All were aware of how much history there was between the two countries. As if to endow himself with the weight of the whole nation before he set off for Beijing, Tanaka visited all the surviving past Japan prime ministers and the graves of their deceased post-war predecessors.

In going to China, however, he was more than merely following obediently in the footsteps of Nixon. The global oil crisis of the time needs to be remembered. No major country needed energy supplies from abroad more than Japan. Its speedy statement of support for Palestinian self-determination will be recalled. On that occasion, Japan put its own interests first and did not fall in behind the USA. Tanaka travelled to Indonesia, Australia and elsewhere in pursuit of energy, aware all the time that commercial negotiations took place against a historical backdrop and against suspicion of Japanese economic hegemony. It was not that the post-war relationship with the USA was dead, but it evolved issue by issue. The USA and China might, in time, develop an 'Asia-Pacific' understanding, but, in a response to it, no Japanese–Soviet 'special relationship' was either possible or desirable. Tanaka did visit Brezhnev in Moscow but failed to obtain the return of a group of islands north of the Japanese island of Hokkaido. By the end of 1974, however, in the wake of criticisms of his financial dealings, Tanaka resigned. Neither domestically nor internationally was the Japanese 'remodelling' complete. How China and Japan related to each other was intimately related to the condition of Soviet–American relations at any given time. 'East Asia' was not a world apart, and it was increasingly important.

South-East Asia: associated – up to a point

In Jakarta in August 1967, Indonesia, Malaysia, the Philippines, Singapore and Thailand formed the Association of Southeast Asian Nations. Its official headquarters were in the city. It was not a political federation, its purpose being to stimulate economic development by promoting collaborations across many fields. It was rich in general aspiration. Cultivating some sense of regional identity through an annual meeting of foreign ministers, it was hoped, would promote political stability. It helped that all the member states had anti-Communist governments. The association was serviced by a Secretary-General (an Indonesian, still in post in 1975). Even granted its limited objectives, however, its survival and indeed its success were by no means guaranteed. Sovereignty over North Borneo was a source of friction between Malaysia and the Philippines. There was no particular congruence between the Buddhist monarchy of Thailand (and its military buttresses) and the Philippines. A Chinese-dominated Singapore had its neighbours to north and south prone to occasional popular bouts of violence against their Chinese minorities. These matters, however, did not lead to inter-state warfare.

Any such association, and even more the prominence of Indonesia within it, would have surprised any observer in the first half of 1965. It was an indication of how much had happened in a short time. Indonesia, as Asia's third largest country, was clearly key. Sukarno's, the hand that had guided its 'guided democracy', was in effect removed in March 1966. Six months earlier, though after a confusing and still puzzling bloody sequence of events, General Suharto had emerged in charge and been given a fig leaf of legitimacy. A violent campaign was triggered through the country, targeting Communists whose alleged coup intentions had justified the military takeover. Half a million people probably died in a bloodletting which saw many old scores being settled, not least against some members of the Chinese minority. Another military regime was thus firmly installed. It too gave promise of another 'New Order'. Externally the 'confrontation' of Malaysia came to an end and Indonesia rejoined the UN. The notion of a single 'Malay world' slipped away in relative Islamic harmony. Internally, no opportunity was lost by the new regime in Jakarta to claim that it saved the country from Communism. The language in which its own aims were elaborated was in an elevated Javanese Indonesian far above the commonplace language of the street. The government even sponsored occasional 'Festivals of Democracy', though the democracy being celebrated was some distance from Western notions. Its anti-Communism, however, met Western needs. It was not that elections did not take place but their outcome conformed to clearly stipulated requirements. Given that Western capitals had supposed that Indonesia might have 'gone Communist', it seemed only appropriate to turn blind eyes to the nature of the regime. It could be said, once again, that only military rule, decked out with certain trappings of democracy, could keep a collection of islands together. It was a view in 1975 that gave cover to the action of the Indonesian army in invading and annexing the eastern half of the Pacific island of Timor when it declared its independence from Portugal.

'South-East Asia', therefore, though ragged and contested at the edges, had established by 1975 a kind of regional identity in the shadow of India and China but not beholden to either. The struggle in 'Indo-China', and the nature of its conclusion, for the moment precluded the possibility of South-East Asia's wider extension, but one day its states might become members and the 'region' extend from Burma even to Australia. Australia's Labor government under Gough Whitlam did not remonstrate against Indonesia's takeover of East Timor. Its successor formally recognized Indonesia's sovereignty. Australia, certainly, was different, but in the evolving world, geography might not permit it to be *that* different.

Everywhere out of place?

Across the world, however, states found themselves becoming, to one degree or another, 'world states', with a diversity in their populations unparalleled in their history. Migration began to blur the identity of continents. New immigrants, with their different perceptions of the world, it was true, were unlikely to have an immediate impact on policymaking in 'receiving' countries but in time the coexistence within states of people with different global origins and perspectives might have profound consequences. It might complicate determining 'national' objectives and the capacity to implement them. Any consideration of Asia that considers it in terms of uniformly homogeneous countries, or supposes that there were not aspects of 'Asia beyond Asia', ignores much. 'Overseas Chinese' were to be found across the world, existing in complicated relationships with each other, with their co-citizens and with two 'Chinas', as has just been noted.

It was, however, both a historical legacy and present patterns of migration which took the Indian subcontinent to other continents. Independence in East Africa brought into contention the future of Indians, with considerable intercontinental consequence. The Kenyan government in 1967 and the Ugandan in 1972 both made it clear that Indians, so prominent in commerce in both countries, had to leave. It was evident that 'Africanization' left no place for Asians in East Africa. The issue of their resettlement became more of a direct issue for

London – forcing debate on what it meant to be 'a British subject' – than for New Delhi. Even so, India found itself, though at a remove, involved in 'India overseas' and thus became itself, though involuntarily, a kind of colonial guardian. The Indian government reacted to events in Uganda by breaking off diplomatic relations with Kampala. Here was a complicated triangular case. It was not only in relation to East Africa that the 'multicultural question' arose. It was present elsewhere because of the Indian diaspora originally under the auspices of a now vanishing or vanished British Empire. Independence came to Guyana (British Guiana) in 'Latin America' in 1966 after four years in which Cheddi Jagan and Forbes Burnham, with Indo-Guyanese and Afro-Guyanese support, respectively, struggled for post-colonial power. 'Amerindians' constituted a small minority in an English-speaking 'Latin American' country which had once been 'theirs'. Burnham, however, proved the victor. The significant 'Indian' population in South Africa was certainly not dominant, but, concentrated in Natal, it was somewhat ambivalently placed between the white government and African opinion – an intermediate and exposed position. In Fiji, independent since 1970, Fijians were in a majority in 'their' country, but the Indian minority was considerable and relationships were volatile. In Mauritius, independent in 1968, there was an Indo-Mauritian majority which, for many years to come, backed Sir Seewoosagar Ramgoolam (b.1900) as Prime Minister. The island, nevertheless, was ethnically, linguistically and religiously very diverse. In these and other instances, Indian subcontinent populations, Hindu and Muslim, through historical accident, had become significant 'out-of-area' locations.

In Britain, in the 1960s immigrants from the subcontinent were outstripping those from the West Indies, so that by 1971 the number born in the subcontinent was approaching half a million. This population, however, largely Punjabis, Gujaratis and Bengalis, was scarcely 'representative' of the subcontinent as a whole. There were some Sikhs from the Punjab and some Hindus, but the majority were Muslims. It might have been expected, after 1947, that the passage of time would only have seen the progressive weakening of the links between the subcontinent and Britain – and certainly not their renewal in this way. It was in the late 1960s that immigration and its implications moved to the fore in British politics. British governments, as never before, formally began to talk about 'Race Relations' in Britain. A new Commonwealth Immigration Act was passed. Integration, the then Home Secretary, Roy Jenkins, claimed, was not so much assimilation – which he described as a flattening process – as 'equal opportunity accompanied by cultural diversity'. Not unexpectedly, he presumed that this notion would take root in an atmosphere of mutual tolerance, though that was not always evident. It was probably in 1971 that the concept of a *multicultural* society was first employed in a British parliamentary debate. The subcontinent, as it were, was being transplanted. The England which Indira Gandhi visited as Prime Minister was no longer, in significant respects, quite what she had known as a schoolgirl and undergraduate. Such relocations, of course, were part of a wider picture. 'Receiving' countries changed course. Australia, for example, abandoned in this decade its hitherto 'White Australia' policy and opened its doors to Asian and other immigrants not of 'British stock'.

The full significance of population movement was for the future. What occupied the headlines, however, was the working-out of the two crises which saw troops of the two Superpowers operating beyond their borders: Vietnam and Czechoslovakia.

14
Superpowers Challenged

The world from the White House: the US mission

In 1965 the epic encounter between the 'Free world' and the 'Communist world' still seemed the world's dominant narrative. The difficulty of conducting a global policy was not to be underestimated, even in simple management terms. Distant global lenses were liable to ignore or misinterpret the peculiarities of local circumstances. Vietnam, from the east coast of the USA, was far away, geographically and culturally. Americans thought it scarcely conceivable that a country could voluntarily choose to become Communist. However, regimes in countries threatened by Communism did not necessarily share 'American values'. In turn, safeguarding 'freedom' from Communism might lead the USA down paths at variance with those values. The USA seemed to have an ample supply of self-belief, but it might not be endless. The Soviet Union, for its part, had a self-belief which rested on the certainty that history was moving in an identifiable direction. It was therefore necessary internally to stamp on any 'revisionism' which called any elements in the existing system into question. By 1975 the outcome looked straightforward: the USA had lost in South-East Asia and the Soviet Union had 'won' in Eastern Europe. A decade earlier, however, American globalism had seemed both manageable and domestically acceptable in order to contain Communism. In March 1965, however, US marines arrived in Da Nang, on the coast of South Vietnam and, a few months later, were deployed routinely in combat. Their president had declared in his re-election campaign that he was not going to send American boys 15,000 miles from their homes to do what Asian boys should do for themselves. The numbers, however, thereafter grew steadily. By early 1969 US forces in the country had peaked at just over half a million. In April 1975, however, all was different. The last US helicopter was taking off from the roof of the US embassy in Saigon. Indo-China, it seemed, had changed the world. It brought the USA up against its global misconceptions and the limitations of its power. That came back to the men at the top.

American presidents and their advisers inevitably brought the baggage of their pasts into the handling of the present. Where they 'came from', and how they had experienced 'the world', therefore mattered. Johnson (b.1908), Nixon (b.1913) and Ford (b.1913) came from the same generation. In the USA, a presidential candidate's view of America's role in the world could emerge, at least in general terms, during an election campaign, though it probably would not determine the outcome. Once elected, however, the president was on his own for his term, though always subject, to some degree, to 'public opinion' and, for resource, to Congress. Unusually, however, it was a decade or so in which two vice-presidents, one at the beginning and one at the end, found themselves unexpectedly catapulted into the White House. The electorate had not heard much about their views of the world. The presidential assassination in 1963, of course, had introduced an unpredicted element into policymaking. Kennedy had made much of the fact that he represented a new generation at the helm. Lyndon Baines Johnson, in succeeding Kennedy, was nearly a decade his senior. He was not a 'man of the world' – as Kennedy conceived himself to be – and had not globetrotted in his youth.

Johnson came from a modest but politically active farming family in Texas. Whereas Kennedy graduated from Harvard, Johnson graduated from South Western Texas State Teachers' College. After a spell teaching public speaking, he then went into politics, initially as a Congressman, in Washington. The world war took him to the South-West Pacific in June 1942. He glimpsed Australian hill country and thought it rather like Texan hill country. His rootedness in Texas found symbolic expression (though it was of course fortuitous) in his acceptance of office on Texan soil. Johnson did not appear greatly interested in the European origins of his fellow-citizens. Apart from a brief visit to Europe in 1945, he had not been to the continent until he became Vice-President. That office took him across the world, on average every three months. His preoccupations, until this juncture, had been domestic. He did not 'take naturally to international relations'. It was not the subject he thought about spontaneously while shaving, for example, as Henry Kissinger put it. He had simple foreign priorities. He was not going to be the President 'who saw Southeast Asia go the way China went'. Optimistically, in March 1966 he hoped that Americans would be remembered in Vietnam for their schools, not their cigars. 'We're going to turn the Mekong into a Tennessee Valley', he declared, alluding to a famous US New Deal project of the 1930s. The actual 'footprints of America in Vietnam', however, turned out to be rather different. De Gaulle found in Johnson a man who physically towered above himself, an unusual experience. Attending Kennedy's funeral, the Frenchman reputedly privately remarked that the late President had been America's mask, whereas the new man was the real face. America would still tower over the world. For his part, Johnson found that foreigners spoke odd languages. They could not be bullied on the phone – as his compatriots could be.

In 1968, however, Johnson did not seek re-election. The incubus of Vietnam fell upon his Republican successor, Nixon, from 1968, and again from 1972, though, as it turned out, not for a full term. Nixon's father, perhaps succumbing to mild anglophilia, gave all his sons the names of English kings. A poker-playing Quaker Californian law graduate, Nixon had served in the US navy during the war and had also ventured into the Pacific, though not in a combat role. His political career had waxed in vigorous pursuit of the Communist enemy within and without. As Eisenhower's Vice-President, he had fully shared that administration's view of the world. He was required to travel.

It had fallen to him, back in 1959 in Moscow, to engage in barbed banter with Khrushchev. He had experienced a good deal of hostility visiting some Latin American countries the previous year. He visited Libya. He visited Oxford. Defeated by Kennedy in 1960, however, his career had seemed to be over, but in 1968 he bounced back. Little in his world-view had apparently changed in the interval. Here was the first properly Republican president for more than three decades, one suspicious of liberal intellectuals who thought they understood the world.

In January 1969 Nixon appointed as his special assistant for national security a 45-year-old Harvard academic foreign policy specialist, Henry Kissinger. In September 1973 he became the first foreign-born US Secretary of State. Here was a man devoted, or so he proclaimed, to cold and dispassionate analysis of the structure of the world. History, he supposed, knew neither resting place nor plateau. Nor did Kissinger. His analysis of the world led him to pursue the 'linkages' which would establish a bargained stability. The USA, he believed, should be proud of its global post-1945 contribution, but he sensed that the domestic consensus on which it had rested was collapsing: increasing national self-doubt, even self-hatred. He thought he had a special feeling for what America meant, something which native-born citizens perhaps took for granted. Although not perfect, the USA embodied the hopes of mankind. There was a need, somehow, to articulate a new foreign policy for a new era, as he put it. That could only be achieved by questioning post-1945 assumptions about the world and America's place in it. A 'secret diplomacy', at variance with hallowed notions of 'open covenants openly arrived at', might establish a new international equilibrium.

In August 1974, under the threat of impeachment for his involvement in the Watergate burglary scandal, Nixon resigned, though Kissinger remained in post. Nixon was succeeded by his Vice-President, Gerald Ford, a man with a fine footballing pedigree behind him. In a fraught environment, it was no bad thing to be thought an ordinary American. He had little personal knowledge of the outside world. Like his immediate predecessors, his naval war service had been in the Pacific, but it had not triggered much curiosity about 'foreign affairs'. Ford talked about bringing the country together again. It was in this mood that he took the contentious step of pardoning Nixon. The American dream, however, was badly battered. Ford's speeches in 1975 talked about the need for America to recover the sense of national pride that existed before Vietnam. The tragic events there, he claimed, portended neither the end of the world nor America's leadership in the world.

The USA and 'Indo-China': entanglement and endgame

In 1975, following the fall of Saigon to the Communists, the city was renamed after Ho Chi Minh. Its colonial and vibrantly corrupt past was to be wiped out. Ho Chi Minh himself, dying in 1969, had not lived to see the day, but his objectives in founding the Vietnamese Communist Party in 1930 had been realized after fighting for thirty years. It had demonstrated, again and again, an amazing tenacity and willingness to shoulder disproportionate losses on the field of battle. Now Vietnam was one country under the control of its Communist

Party. Foreigners – French, Japanese and Americans – had all successively been removed (though help from other foreigners, this time Russian or Chinese, had made this possible). If they could, their defeated Vietnamese opponents fled the country – so forming vocal expatriate communities across the world. The USA was the largest 'receiving' country in the world at this time. Its 1965 Immigration and Nationality Act had scrapped the existing quota system and set the first limits on immigration from the Western hemisphere. From the early 1970s, the change meant that non-whites formed the bulk of immigrants coming into the USA, with preference being given to anti-Communist refugees, whether Cubans or, after 1975, from Vietnam and Laos. Exiles angrily complained that the USA had let them down.

The war had been at once local and global, literally fought out in the field but metaphorically through the world's media. There were, at its conclusion, as there had been throughout, conflicting views on what it had all been about. Was Vietnam 'another Korea'? The USA and its allies had prevented a Communist takeover of Korea and militarily sustained the South. It had been in many respects a brutal war. The peninsula still remained divided. The analogy, nearly two decades later, seemed pertinent. It was one given substantial symbolism in the readiness of the Seoul government to send troops to South Vietnam. Modest help also came from Thailand, the Philippines, New Zealand and Australia. Such flags were welcome in Washington, but the USA was the key supporter. The involvement of the 'Asian coalition', however, lent credence to the view that the future of South-East Asia was at stake.

At the beginning of 1968, in the 'Tet' offensive, Vietcong guerrillas and infiltrated North Vietnamese regulars overran most of the provincial capitals in the South and some public buildings in Saigon. These gains were subsequently reversed, but, even so, nothing was really secure. The military setback, even though temporary, persuaded much external opinion that the war could not be won. It was foolish, and perhaps wicked, to go on trying. Victory for Hanoi, protesters proclaimed in Europe and the USA, would be a victory for 'the people'. Their opponents denied this. It would be some time, however, before South Vietnam, presided over by Nguyen Van Thieu and Nguyen Cao Ky, soldier and pilot, respectively, functioned as the kind of democracy that Americans thought democracy should be. Time, however, was what Americans might be able to provide.

By 1969, the year of Ho Chi Minh's death, the ultimate Communist victory had yet to be achieved. After much wrangling, a four-sided peace conference had opened in Paris at the beginning of that year. Peace discussions, while Johnson was still President, led nowhere. The USA, South Vietnam, North Vietnam and the National Liberation Front (insurgents active in the South) took part. However, it made scant progress. It had not been President Nixon who had sent US troops to Vietnam but it fell to him to find a way of extricating them while also buttressing a non-Communist South. In July, on his second major foreign trip, Nixon, speaking in Guam on his way to the Philippines, put forth a new 'doctrine'. The countries of Asia should not so depend upon the USA as to drag it into Vietnam-like conflicts. Existing treaty commitments would remain but Asian nations themselves should take increasing responsibility for their own defence. That would mean 'Vietnamization' and its equivalent elsewhere. The equipment, expansion and training of the South Vietnamese army should make it capable both of containing insurgents within its own territory and coping with a formal invasion from the North. Correspondingly, US troop numbers would be steadily reduced. The formula was predictable. It hoped to reduce the domestic opposition, now very vocal, by clearly indicating a pattern of withdrawal. At the same time, however, it would be withdrawal 'with honour'. The South would successfully stand on its own feet. The doctrine also showed that the USA, on the ground, was not in it for the long haul. The North Vietnamese government had waited a long time. It could wait a while longer.

'Vietnamization' had some successes. Yet the strategy was only superficially plausible. It had to happen at speed, but it could not happen coherently at speed. The military emphasis failed to grasp the extent to which the winning of 'hearts and minds' would be crucial. A South Vietnamese army of a million sounded impressive, but it was spread thinly across the country. The presupposed cohesion amongst Vietnamese commanders was conspicuously lacking. Trust was in short supply. Americans and Vietnamese found co-ordination very difficult. The former found the family linkages and patronage systems of the latter hard to comprehend. This was not merely a situation in which 'West' failed to understand 'East'. Americans also found themselves at sea in dealing with 'European' Vietnamese who persisted in speaking French. In the spring of 1972, Northern and Vietcong forces again made inroads in the South, but also again inconclusively. The American response, by way of assistance to Saigon, was to bomb the North, including Hanoi and Haiphong, and mine the country's ports and harbours. It was sometimes, mistakenly, thought that this would be 'decisive'.

Outside the formal peace conference, Kissinger and Le Duc Tho had been spasmodically talking for many months. In October, just before the American election, they haggled themselves to a conclusion. A ceasefire agreement between the USA and North Vietnam was reached. US troops would withdraw completely and US prisoners would be repatriated. In effect, a veil was then drawn over what would happen in the South. Lifting the veil, President Thieu saw no future for himself and, with all the authority of a man who had received, unopposed, 94 per cent of the votes cast in the 1971 election, made his objections public. The Americans could not openly abandon their ally. Re-elected, Nixon responded by trying to put fresh pressure on North Vietnam. He ordered an intensive series of air raids on Hanoi–Haiphong as a Christmas present. They were very damaging, but American aircraft losses were high. It looked likely that the new Congress would cut off funds for bombing. In January 1973 Nixon called off the bombing and agreed to the ceasefire on a basis little different from what had been agreed in October – though it could be claimed that the air offensive had compelled Hanoi back to the table. Direct American fighting participation in Vietnam was over.

The Vietnam War itself was not over. The ceasefire, all round, was more honoured in the breach than in the observance. The International Control Commission appointed to monitor it looked impressive but was pointless. Thieu and his government assumed that US aid would continue to support his very large army. His forces initially regained some territory that had been in Communist hands at the time of the ceasefire, but by 1974 they were badly hit by desertions and lack of supplies. Corruption and cronyism were rife. Saigon purported to believe that American air power would be deployed if the Peace Accords were seriously violated. Such delusions misread the position of an increasingly beleaguered president in Washington. The North was now ready for the final push. Early in 1975, after Communist advances, Thieu decided to pull his forces back to allegedly more defensible lines. Once the retreat started, it did not end. The cities of Hué and Da Nang fell in late March and by the end of April the remnants of the South Vietnamese government unconditionally surrendered. Thieu departed into permanent exile, blaming the USA.

The Communist future elsewhere in 'Indo-China' seemed assured. Prince Sihanouk, who had tried to keep Cambodia 'neutral' for decades, was overthrown by his own Prime Minister, General Lon Nol, in March 1970. Nol wanted to deal with the North Vietnamese intruders. President Nixon announced on television that US and South Vietnamese soldiers would do the job for him. One 'incursion', it seemed, demanded another. Kissinger was able to explain that it was not an 'invasion', a view from which student activists in the USA vociferously dissented. Congress tried, in 1970 and again later, not altogether successfully, to cut off funding for further bombing. The administration's case was that expanding the area of conflict was a step towards an eventual peace. In a military sense, the operation had some success, though it caused considerable dislocation in Cambodia itself as populations fled the bombing. The population of the capital increased some threefold in five years. The Khmer Rouge, with North Vietnamese backing, steadily expanded and took control of the capital Phnom Penh in April 1975. US intervention had arguably helped bring about what it deplored. There had also been South Vietnamese 'counter-incursion', with American support, into Laos, but the North Vietnamese remained strongly entrenched there. From 1973, with much repetition of the mantra that 'all foreign troops must be withdrawn', attempts were made to form a coalition government in Laos. It collapsed in 1975, the same year as it was formed. The Pathet Lao took over by the end of the year and renamed what had been a monarchy as a People's Republic. It was, in effect, a client of Vietnam. The Vietnam of 1975 was a battered country, scarred and disfigured. The tonnage of bombs dropped on North Vietnam probably exceeded by three times the total dropped by the USA on all fronts during the Second World War. Making Vietnam truly one country would be a task undertaken by the victors with no great delicacy. The sufferers, in terms of death and injury, were Vietnamese. By 1973, around 200,000 South Vietnamese soldiers had been killed, and probably five times that number of North Vietnamese and Vietcong fighters. Military casualties may have reached a million, and civilian casualties a similar figure. More than 57,000 US forces were killed and roughly three times that number wounded. South Korean, Australian and New Zealand losses were much smaller.

Historians quickly got to work. One simple 'world-historical' observation was that a century, successively, of direct Franco-Japanese–American involvement in 'Indo-China' had come to an end. Independence for its inhabitants had required tenacity of purpose combined with an indifference to cost. Success had required assistance and support both from Moscow and Beijing. That dependence had come at a price. To some extent, in 1973 in particular, Hanoi was constrained by the contemporaneous three-way diplomatic manoeuvres between Washington, Moscow and Beijing. It could not control their outcome. What could not be judged, in 1975, was where the three countries, Vietnam in particular, would 'fit'. Successive American presidents had argued that if Vietnam 'fell' so would all South-East Asia: the domino effect. That was why they became involved. Now, in the event, despite American efforts, Vietnam had 'fallen'. Would others follow? If so, the USA seemed unwilling or unable – which was it? – to 'intervene' again. War was not what it was, military power had its manifest limitations and nuclear weapons were irrelevant. The limit of American globalism and the power of the presidency had perhaps been reached. So, it was time to call the boys home.

The world from the Kremlin: the Soviet mission

The Soviet Union did not have a 'Vietnam', but its problems were closer to home. Its ideological domination of its 'bloc' was again under challenge. The 'opposite numbers' of the American presidents in Moscow, if they can be so described, had worked their way up to reach their present eminence from peasant/worker households. 'Popular choice' had not played a part. The outside world called them 'Russians', but the picture was more complicated. The Soviet leadership tapped into many of the diverse strands to be found in the country they ruled. It too faced in many directions as it confronted the world.

The Soviet Prime Minister from 1964 was Alexander Kosygin. He was born and spent his early career in Leningrad (St Petersburg). He had survived, somewhat precariously, the machinations of Stalin. After the fall of Khrushchev, his global objective was to repair 'the Communist world'. A conference of world Communist parties was mooted for Moscow in May 1965 but the Chinese refused to attend. Kosygin visited China twice. His 'mediating' role between India and Pakistan in 1966 has already been alluded to. He clearly aspired for a time to be the outside face of the Soviet state, and its 'Asian significance' was to the fore. Relations with China, however, did not improve. The Soviet embassy in Beijing was attacked by a mob in 1967. Soviet 'world' pretensions, as expressed in Moscow's behaviour in Eastern Europe in 1968 (to be discussed shortly), were dismissed in Beijing. The following year, the two countries clashed at the River Ussuri and proceeded to increase their force levels. Subsequent negotiations at a high level produced no meeting of minds. Such a level of deterioration made talk of 'world Communism' increasingly empty. It opened up the possibility that new 'worlds' would be created. This crisis gave a reminder that the leadership in Moscow faced both ways: to Europe and to Asia (so, of course, did that of the USA).

Kosygin's prominence did not altogether commend itself to Andrei Gromyko, Soviet foreign minister since 1957 (and seemingly permanently occupying that post). The world Gromyko knew, at first hand, was different. He had earlier served as ambassador in Washington, New York and London. Born in what is now Belarus, and initially educated near Minsk, he had moved to the heart of the Soviet state. He offered the world another kind of Soviet face. His mouth said no very often. Leonid Brezhnev, too, who became General Secretary of the Soviet Communist Party in 1966, had moved, like Gromyko, from the periphery to the centre. He normally had a good working relationship with Alexander Kosygin. Brezhnev had also made a transition to 'Russianness'. As he got older and more prominent, he presented himself as a Russian rather than a Ukrainian, though it was in Ukraine that he was born. He had a technical training. He had served during the war as a high-ranking political commissar in the Red Army. He already wore medals with enthusiasm. Later came party posts in both the Moldavian and Kazakh Republics. Thereafter, he rose rapidly, helped by the patronage of Khrushchev – the man he had in the end played a part in ousting. Ultimately, Brezhnev's was the voice that mattered. By the end, there were few major foreign dignitaries he had not received. He travelled. He liked to be driven in foreign cars, generously given by appreciative foreigners. Approaching 70, nothing else foreign excited him. The workings of the USA were as mysterious to him as those of the Soviet Union were to Johnston.

By this juncture, however, exchange visits between American and Soviet leaders had almost become routine. Kosygin may perhaps have retained an abiding memory of Glassboro, the innocent small New Jersey town where he had met Johnston in 1967. Nixon was in Moscow for eleven days in May 1972. There were weighty issues to attempt to resolve arising out of the Strategic Arms Limitation Talks (SALT) which had begun in 1969. The agreement reached in May can be summarized, admittedly starkly, by saying that both sides agreed to the establishment of their own two sites on which to station defensive anti-ballistic missiles. Satellite observation would verify what was done. They further agreed on totals of offensive weapons. The numerical superiority of the Soviet Union was supposed to be balanced by the technical superiority of the USA. Specific agreements were accompanied by general statements. Normal diplomatic relations should not be obstructed by differences in ideology or social system. Ties and contacts could be strengthened in many fields. Brezhnev came to the USA in June 1973 and Nixon went to the Soviet Union in June 1974. As it happened, this was the last of their exchanges. Both sides had achieved 'mutual assured destruction', though one could argue, within that framework, about particular superiorities or deficiencies. Neither side, however, was committed to abandoning projects which might upset the rough balance that appeared to have been achieved. The sense of two Superpowers 'directing' the world – though in 1969 France and China had both declined to sign the Test-Ban Treaty – could transcend, though not eliminate, the tension between them.

The men at the top, in both countries, evidently, were not freewheeling cosmopolitans soaking up 'foreign impressions' with academic enthusiasm. That was not what their roles demanded. The states they governed embodied ideological standpoints. The 'Free World' and 'Communism' therefore remained, it seemed, absolutes, locked in perennial conflict. Gromyko, for one, became energetically anti-religious. The USA, however, while it separated church and state, was not anti-religious. Sooner or later, therefore, it seemed, the rest of the world would have to make up its mind which global 'offer' was more attractive.

The Soviet Union and socialist countries: solidarity without sovereignty?

On 24 September 1968 *Pravda,* the official newspaper of the Soviet Communist Party, formally set out the relationship between sovereignty and the international obligations of socialist countries: Czechoslovakia, Hungary, Bulgaria and Poland, as will be seen, amongst other states, had to toe a line. Non-Soviet socialist countries could determine the course of their development – but only so long as neither socialism internally nor the worldwide workers' movement were harmed. The Soviet Union would judge their behaviour and lay down the rules. It was this assertion of universal authority which Beijing had angrily rejected. The doctrine of limited sovereignty, while novel as a 'doctrine', was hardly a surprise. It gave a very strong signal. It reaffirmed that there was a working-class movement that was worldwide and that the Soviet Union was not just any state. It was the universal guardian of that movement.

It had been the complicated internal world of Czechoslovakia which had brought the Soviet Union to crisis and produced the formal elaboration of 'limited sovereignty'. At the June 1966 Czechoslovak Party Congress, Alexander Dubček, Secretary of the Slovak Communist Party, dismissed as a 'relic of the past' the claim that nationalism was the antithesis of international-ism. The country's 'National Day', banned since 1948 as bourgeois, was to be restored in October. Something was stirring in Prague. Quite what it was, however, was not clear. Czechoslovakia had arguably given least trouble of all the Soviet satellites. It had also stood surrogate for the Soviet Union itself in various external contexts. Dubček's claim, though, left vague what nation he was referring to. Was there a Czechoslovak nationality, or were there two nationalities, Czech and Slovak, uneasily, and in Slovak perception, unequally joined?

Leonid Brezhnev knew Prague. He had first come to what had been the capital of the German 'protectorate' of 'Bohemia and Moravia' in 1945 as a political commissar with Ukrainian divisions of the Red Army: the German forces surrendered. In December 1967, however, he was secretly back in the city in a very different capacity. He did not want the disaffection with the status quo to deepen. Antonin Novotny, the Czechoslovak Communist Party Secretary, who also had doubled for a decade as the country's President, was in political trouble and looked to Brezhnev for support. He did not get it straightforwardly or directly. Novotny, a man of Brezhnev's age, a veteran Communist and defi-nitely a Czech, had spent most of the war in the German concentration camp at Mauthausen. He had taken over in 1953 when Klement Gottwald had died attending Stalin's funeral. Stalinism, however, had not died. It survived in Novotny's 'cult of personality', though the cult suffered from his lack of person-ality. In the early 1960s the economy was in trouble and criticism of the rigidity of the system mounted. One target was the dual party/state role played by

Novotny. 'Reformers' pushed forward Alexander Dubček, a Slovak, and a man relatively unknown, as least in Prague. In January 1968 the Czechoslovak central committee unanimously elected him as party First Secretary, replacing Novotny (who remained President of the Republic)

Few then appreciated the worlds which came together in the person of Dubček. Chicago had received many late nineteenth-century Czech and Slovak immigrants, Alexander's family among them. His parents, however, came back to the new state called Czechoslovakia where he was born in 1921. A few years later, his father, inspired by enthusiasm for Communism, took his family off to Soviet Kyrgyzstan, though they all came back to Slovakia in 1938. Young Alexander therefore soon found himself living in the new state of Slovakia, subordinated to Germany, presided over by a Catholic priest, Josef Tiso. He joined Slovak partisans later in the war and was wounded. Post-war, having taken appropriate political studies in the Party College in the Soviet Union, his career inside the party apparatus in Slovakia developed until he reached the top in 1963. Now he was in Prague.

There was little reason to suppose that Czechoslovakia would precipitate a crisis throughout the Soviet world. 'Slav solidarity' was sometimes alluded to and, looking back to 1938, it seemed that Czechs congenitally made the best of a bad job (as also in 1948). Not for them the occasional German or Polish erup-tions or the heroics of Hungary. Such national stereotyping aside, the 'indige-nous' strength of Czechoslovak Communism had been evident in 1945–48. Comrade Brezhnev's men had been generally welcomed in 1945. Although Czechs (Slovaks more dubiously) were accorded a bold libertarian or demo-cratic streak in 'the West', Moscow, after 1945, had not insisted on the perma-nent stationing of the Red Army (unlike in Poland or Hungary). Some Czechs retained a sense of Prague's historic role, commercially and culturally, as a bridge at the heart of Europe. Could that role between East and West be resur-rected? The Czech Protestant theologian, J.L. Hromadka, for example, who had spent the war in the USA, inspired, from the late 1950s onwards, Christian Peace Conferences in Prague. They brought together 'East' and 'West'. Christians should escape from the prison of 'blocs'. But was a 'middle path' really possible?

Such perceptions of what Czechoslovakia was, or might be, swirled around in the spring of 1968. Economists in the country proposed some decentraliza-tion of economic management. There was substantial press freedom. Novotny resigned as President, being replaced by an elderly general whose surname, when translated, meant 'freedom'. Moscow, though, might be more reassured by the fact that he had commanded Czech forces in the wartime Red Army. It was unlikely to be content, however, by promises of elections and other reforms. 'Reformists' and 'Hardliners' battled for supremacy in Prague. Through the summer, fearing what might emerge from a proposed special Party congress, the Soviet leadership worried but vacillated. Warsaw Pact exercises were held – but it was still hoped that the contagion could be contained. Dubček might be persuaded, by one means or another, to rein in change. If he would do so, there were advantages in letting him stay in post. There were many meetings. In Bratislava on 3 August, with the Czechoslovaks present, the Soviet and other

Eastern European leaders apparently agreed that Prague could continue with its 'internal reforms' if it reiterated its intention to remain within the Warsaw Pact. Eventually, however, during the night of 20/21 August, Warsaw Pact troops invaded, meeting no resistance from the Czechoslovak army. Initially, Moscow dealt with a bullied Dubček in engineering the return to 'normal' in Prague, but he was elbowed out within a few months. In April 1969 a fellow-Slovak, Gustav Husak, became a compliant Czechoslovak Party Secretary. He had himself been imprisoned, as a deviant, both by the Tiso regime and by fellow-Communists, but he now eagerly stripped out 'reformist' elements. A year later, therefore, it seemed that the 'Prague spring' might never have happened. The Czech–Slovak issue rumbled on inside Czechoslovakia, but the regime installed in Prague posed no threat to 'Soviet Europe'. Just to make sure, however, Red Army units remained in the country and the Soviet Union accepted, with gratitude, a Czech contribution towards the costs it incurred.

Developments in Czechoslovakia had been closely followed in the Western world, but governments showed no disposition to intervene. Their condemnations seemed almost perfunctory. No Western capital expected them to make any difference. In Prague itself, students had shouted at Soviet tanks, but to no avail. Abroad, the lack of armed Czech resistance to the invasion was interpreted either as reprehensible cowardice or prudent common sense. Moscow exercised control over its 'bloc'. In early August, both Tito and Ceauşescu had flown to Prague to express some sort of support for Dubček. This step, far from deterring Soviet military action, had made it seem necessary. Even so, from Moscow's perspective, there were reasons to pause before invading. It would upset the West, even if only routinely and temporarily, at a time when concern about China suggested improved relations with the USA. Brezhnev did not rush. He may indeed have finally acted because he feared that 'hardliners' would call him weak – and oust him. It was virtually certain in advance, however, that the invasion would not be opposed. Yet the downside was arguably worse – for the external image of the Soviet Union, but perhaps even more for the future of Communism itself. Dubček may have been naïve, but he was tearfully sincere. He could not believe that a Soviet Union to which, as he stated, he had been devoted all his life, could behave like this. He did not see himself as a counter-revolutionary or as a tool of supposed Federal German *revanchistes*. He dreamed of 'Socialism with a human face' and a new kind of socialist democracy. The stark fact, however, was that there was no 'Third Way'. The self-immolation of the student Jan Palach in Wenceslas Square in January 1969 was a gesture of despair.

That was one reading of the situation. Another suggested that the Soviet system, contrary to the impression of powerful stability, was in inexorable, if still long-term, disintegration. No definite conclusion, however, looked possible at that juncture. The participation of troops from Warsaw Pact countries did give the appearance of bloc solidarity but that might be deceptive. Certainly, to different degrees, the leaderships in all the participating states had feared the spread of the 'Czechoslovak disease' (though Hungary had attempted some kind of mediation). In this sense, they were not coerced into participating. Walter Ulbricht of the German Democratic Republic (GDR), in particular, had warned that the Federal Republic (FRG) was attempting to create what he called 'economic dependencies' in Eastern Europe.

Attention, for obvious reasons, had been focused on Czechoslovakia. The party leaders in other countries had circumspectly been following their own 'reform'. In 1968, the Kadar regime in Hungary was itself tinkering with the 'command economy' and talked of a 'New Economic Mechanism' in language which resembled that coming from Prague. There were other 'liberalizing' gestures. Participation in the invasion of Czechoslovakia had the deliberate if paradoxical consequence that Hungary, having been 'loyal', could still follow a distinctive path. Hungary had seen some 'opening up'. In 1965 it received over a million foreign visitors, a quarter from beyond the Iron Curtain, and the numbers continued to rise. So too did the number of Hungarians travelling abroad. Only some fifteen per cent, however, travelled to 'the West'. Cautiously, the wily Kadar created what was sometimes described as 'soft Communism', though hardness was always in reserve. Some gentle tilting was also attempted externally. Urho Kekkonen, a Finnish 'cousin' – rather distant – of the Magyars, was welcomed in Budapest in 1969. He brought the message that neutral countries with different social systems could show the path to peaceful coexistence at the world level. The domestic Hungarian situation changed from year to year. There was only so far that Kadar either wanted or could go. He was happy to state, in Brezhnev's hearing, that no one could call himself a Communist and hold anti-Soviet opinions. On the 30th anniversary of the liberation of the homeland in 1975 the opportunity was taken in Budapest to reiterate Hungary's 'indissoluble fraternal friendship' with the Soviet Union.

Bulgaria was very different from Hungary. Support for the Soviet Union, intoned in an impeccably peasant accent, had been regularly offered by Todor Zhivkov, Bulgarian Party Secretary since 1954. Russophilia in Bulgaria was not the forced plant that it was in Hungary. His country, surrounded by 'unreliable' Communist states – Yugoslavia and Romania – and non-Communist Greece and Turkey, wanted distant companionship. Moscow was pleased to provide it. Zhivkov exuded loyalty. He developed a close personal relationship with Brezhnev. In the past, however, he had vigorously trimmed his sails as the circumstances warranted. A brief flirtation with the obscurities of the 'socialist market' gave place, however, in the wake of the 'Prague spring', to a strong reassertion of orthodoxy. A new constitution and party programme in 1971 reiterated that Bulgaria was now a socialist state of the working people. The party committed itself to a system in which all property and functional differences would disappear. The whole nation would, in effect, become working class. Despatching a contingent of troops to Czechoslovakia, it hardly needs to be said, had not been a problem for the Party Secretary.

Poland was not likely to be the same as Bulgaria. It was not an accident that it was in Warsaw that Brezhnev had chosen to formulate his 'doctrine'. It was a clear reminder of Poland's 'limited' status. Throughout the earlier part of the year, the country had been going through a simmering political crisis. There were cracks in the 'Polish road to Socialism'. Extraordinary political manoeuvring took place in which the Minister of the Interior, General Moczar, was heavily involved. One outcome of this bizarre phase, which had seen an attack on 'Zionist traitors', was the exodus of most of the remaining small Jewish population in Poland. Gomulka's wife was Jewish, and this may have been a factor behind the onslaught. Gomulka had to make a broadcast calling for national unity and identifying 'troublemakers'. However, he survived – for two more years – during which period, with the new Social Democratic–Free Democratic (SPD–FD) coalition in power in Bonn, he began exploring 'the German question'. In December 1970, however, the Christmas present of huge price rises announced by the government, triggered demonstrations and protests in Gdansk and other cities, leading to some loss of life. A state of emergency was declared. This time Gomulka had to go: the 'National Communism' associated with him had proved 'different' – but less different than some Marxist intellectuals had hoped for.

Gomulka was replaced as First Secretary by Edward Gierek, the party boss in Silesia, the region where a German past was, as it were, still present. His arrival, coinciding with the treaty with the Federal Republic (to be considered shortly), gave Poland what it had not had since 1945, namely security with regard to its western frontier. That in turn altered the sense in which Poland needed to 'put up with' the Soviet Union as its 'protector'. The new man had himself had an expatriate past in Western Europe – a part of that 'Poland beyond Poland' which always had a bearing on its internal life. He had been brought up in France and Belgium where his mother has taken him as a boy on the death of his father in a mining accident. Originally a miner himself, he had been active in the Belgian Communist Party. He had not come back to Poland until 1948. Although it was not a factor in his elevation, it was a curious conjuncture that there should be a 'Westerner' in Warsaw just at this time. The early 1970s witnessed some economic recovery under Gierek and the 'new men' he brought with him. There was a 'new Poland' in another sense. For the first time in its history, more people lived in towns than in the countryside. What did not change was the fundamental fact that all political life was controlled by the Communist Party.

The position in Poland also remained the case throughout 'the bloc'. The decade, as has been glimpsed, witnessed some modifications, or attempted modifications, in the manner in which that control was exercised, but only at the margin. The rationale for the state, and the party's control of the state, could not be questioned. The overarching presence of the Soviet Union was everywhere. It was, therefore, not foolish to speak of 'the Soviet bloc'. The Warsaw Pact looked, on paper, militarily formidable. It had acted in the only circumstance in which, as yet, it had been called upon to act. Leaders met each other regularly and 'fraternally'. Russian, as a second language, to a certain degree, created a community of communication. Consolidation was furthered by the extensive pattern of in-bloc trade, even if the Council for Mutual Economic Assistance (Comecon) fell somewhat short of its grand design. Further, pre-Communist East–Central Europe, as it had existed in 1939, itself scarcely idyllic, faded in the memory with the passage of time. By the 1960s, it was not a 'norm' which should or could be returned to. All of that seemed to point to an ever deepening division within Europe. At the time, therefore, it looked as if 'Soviet Europe' in 1975 had indeed been saved. The Helsinki Accords, to be considered shortly, seemed to seal the status quo. They reflected the 'lessons' which could apparently be drawn from the previous decade.

Some outside commentators, and some insiders, drew the conclusion that nothing on its 'periphery' would bring 'Soviet Europe' to a close. They argued that the end could only happen as the result of an upheaval of some kind in the Soviet Union itself. That seemed far-fetched. There were, however, writers who were proving thorns in the flesh of the Soviet authorities. One neat tactic they adopted was to demonstrate in favour of the Soviet constitution. Anonymous compilations drew attention to the UN Declaration of Human Rights, which the Soviet Union had signed. Pavel Litvinov, grandson of Stalin's foreign minister, drew up a protest addressed to 'world public opinion'. Some trials of dissidents did take place, but the publicity they aroused led to less public ways of restraining them. These, and other indications of dissent, expressed chiefly but not solely by writers, were not insignificant, but 'world public opinion', even supposing it could be identified, was not likely to be of much assistance. Some Western observers, ignorant of the historical role played by writers in articulating dissent, did not take it very seriously. For the moment, at least, it looked as though the Soviet system would and could take sufficient steps to enable it to survive.

In addition, the extent to which the Soviet Union itself, within its own frontiers, had to deal with the 'national' issues just identified in its 'bloc', became steadily more apparent. Was 'Russification', explicitly or implicitly, the aim of policy? Not that it was clear what 'Russification' meant. Speaking Russian did not necessarily turn Soviet citizens into Russians. Individual republics, and their First Secretaries, had their own perspective on such matters. There were particular tensions, to greater or lesser degree everywhere, surrounding the appearance of Russian 'immigrants'. It was claimed, in the Baltic republics and elsewhere, that incoming Russians never bothered to learn the local language and that 'natives' were pressed more and more to use Russian. The memory of independent statehood in Estonia, Latvia and Lithuania, snatched away in 1939 and never restored, had not disappeared. Elsewhere, in Stalin's native Georgia, for example, a street protest in Tiblisi led to a proposal to give Russian equal rights with Georgian being abandoned. Different nationalities had different birth rates. The overall ethnic balance of the Soviet state was changing. Then there were religious/national issues of great complexity affecting the position of Muslims and Jews. By 1975, though the Western media often continued to use 'Russia' to describe the Soviet Union, that was increasingly inappropriate. It might therefore be that the 'Soviet bloc', including the Soviet Union itself, was undergoing a systemic crisis, though a slow-burning one. Alexander Solzhenitsyn's first volume of *The Gulag Archipelago*, published abroad in 1973, reverberated widely. His account had different consequences and implications. It led to his own arrest and deportation in the following year. Bent at this juncture on 'détente' with Moscow, neither President Ford nor Secretary of State Kissinger thought it prudent to meet him. In Western Europe, however, its account of life in the camps put even the French Communist Party on the spot. Solzhenitsyn's revelation might be soft-pedalled in the White House, or become caught up in the internecine battles of the French Left, but Solzhenitsyn was not at home in either of these locations. He addressed a 'Letter to the Soviet Leaders', published in the West, which urged a revival of 'Russia'. It was likely, he thought, that it would need to be authoritarian. The Orthodox Church would provide the necessary spiritual revival. He loathed what the Soviet Union had been, and still largely was, but 'the West' also had little attraction. Even if its philosophy was not supposed to be materialist, its way of life was in fact shallowly materialistic. Old East, in other words, should not be replaced by new West: a Russian 'Third Way', in the long term, perhaps beckoned.

15
Security and Co-operation in Europe

The path to the Conference on Security and Co-operation in Europe held in Helsinki in July/August 1975 had been winding. Warsaw Pact countries meeting in Romania in 1966 had proposed a general conference on European security. The idea had been that all European states should confirm their acceptance of existing boundaries and political systems. The NATO countries did not rush to reply and, when they did, wanted to shift the agenda onto a discussion of force levels. Proposals were batted to and fro. Events in 1968 and after, as discussed in the previous chapter, did not suggest that the time was altogether ripe. Instability in that year, as will shortly be discussed, was not confined to the Soviet bloc. Events in France and the Federal Republic revealed the scale of dissatisfaction with the status quo that existed in some quarters in Western Europe. There was, however, a paradox. In the 'West' it was a 'liberal capitalism' which was being savaged. In the 'East' it was the illiberality of a 'rigid Communism' that was being attacked. In country after country across Europe political debate raged. Familiar concepts – Democracy, Communism, Socialism, Class, Culture, Consumerism, Christianity, Secularism, Capitalism, Freedom, Tyranny, Equality – were again fiercely argued over and paired in different ways. There was, however, no regime change. 'Order', though different both in substance and structure, was reasserted in Paris and Prague. The questions that had been posed, however, had not disappeared, even in the 'co-operative' conference chambers of Helsinki.

Eventually, however, in November 1972, a first meeting, at ambassadorial level, was held in Helsinki. It was agreed that the process should have three phases and levels of engagement. When the heads of government assembled in July 1975, therefore, it was to ratify an agreement which had been steadily worked at over the preceding two years. The successful outcome, however, only came about through the conjuncture of various interlinked factors: 'stability' in both Eastern and Western Europe and movement on the 'German question'. These inner-European issues, however, were also global. They could not be attended to without the concurrence of Washington and Moscow. American and Soviet signatures at a 'European' conference were therefore imperative. Brezhnev and Ford had the global situation very much in mind. The previous few years had witnessed a global diplomatic revolution which would not have been thought likely in 1966. China, of course, was not a signatory but had, as it were, a distant presence. The Americans were aware that Beijing thought that they had made too many concessions to the Soviet Union. For their part, the major Western European powers continued to have distinct and diverging perspectives on peace, security and on Europe's future.

France: upheaval and order

In March 1966 de Gaulle ended the integration of French forces in NATO and required all foreign forces to leave French soil. It would not be the end of French membership of the alliance, but it was as far as he could go without taking that ultimate step. De Gaulle had no intention of being dragged into the war in Vietnam. Sophisticated French minds knew that since France had not been able to win in Indo-China the Americans would surely fail. The war was detestable. More generally, however, de Gaulle's decision signified France's determination to throw off American 'hegemony'. It was all of a piece with a denunciation of the imperialist tendencies of the Superpowers which he had made in Latin America in 1964, the same year he established diplomatic relations with the People's Republic of China. He did not believe that the nation-state was obsolete. France could act independently, though still in a sense in the American sphere. He supposed that states in Eastern Europe could do the same within the Soviet sphere. That was a message which he conveyed to Moscow in person. It was time to unfreeze the world. It was a historical vision which was persuasive to a degree, but it did not carry the day either in London or Bonn. It was also one suddenly put into a different context, not only by the events in Prague, just noted, and their repercussions, but also by the domestic turn in France itself.

In Western Europe in 1968 it was not altogether surprising that France was the scene of destabilizing confrontation. Paris was a city familiar with revolution. The centenary of the 1870–71 Commune was approaching, though to 'celebrate' it would inevitably be divisive. It was the year of the tenth anniversary of the Fifth Republic. In May, as liberalizing reforms were being announced in Prague, Paris was in uproar. The university campus at Nanterre, where teaching had already been suspended, was closed on 2 May. Its sociology department had developed a specialism in nurturing revolution. The following day, police were ordered into the Sorbonne, which was also closed. Violent clashes between students and the police took place in the Latin Quarter. Tear gas filled the air. A week later barricades were being thrown up in the streets of Paris. The Sorbonne, reopened on the orders of the Premier, Pompidou, who had just returned from the tranquillity of Afghanistan, blossomed into a libertarian utopia. The sense of crisis mounted. By the middle of the month, students and strikers were occupying factories and holding protest marches – a total of 164 it was said – across France. Observers at the time, as subsequently, disagreed about mood and motivation. Was there not only a struggle between the workers and 'authority' but also one between these 'spontaneous' revolts and established trade unions, both Communist and non-Communist? Was the presentation of specific demands relating to wages, hours and conditions being replaced by a yearning to overturn the whole socio-political/industrial order – nothing less than self-management by the working class? Perhaps ten million people came out on strike. The state was certainly shaking. Tanks appeared on the outskirts of Paris. De Gaulle talked of a referendum on greater participation in the running of universities and of industry but otherwise kept a low profile. Other veteran politicians generously indicated their willingness to take over a tottering state. De Gaulle opted for a mysterious helicopter flight to the French army stationed in Baden, Germany. He learnt there that he had no military option. He returned, however, to find half a million French people massed in his support on the Champs Élysées. His spirits rose. The referendum was dropped in favour of a general election. The second round gave the party supporting him an absolute majority. The challenge had been defeated. Pompidou, to his chagrin, was made the casualty for his handling of events. The referendum was held in April 1969, but de Gaulle's proposals were defeated. He resigned.

The pattern of events, to outsiders, seemed 'very French', even though the invocation of Mao Zedong or Trotsky on the streets gave a kind of global backing to the building of barricades. Activists saw their actions as steeped in a national tradition of revolution. Mass social action would go hand in hand with 'progressive' thinking to bring about change. This, it seemed, was a generation in revolt, exposing the corruptions of bourgeois society. More than that, a whole new social order, it was thought, was tantalizingly close. Yet such a talismanic transformation did not happen. The Fifth Republic had not buckled in the face of the politics of the street. The silent, and not so silent, majority had spoken. So, was this outcome victory or a defeat for 'democracy'? The 'will of the people' became rather a 'will of the wisp' as Left, Centre and Right all claimed to know what 'the people' really wanted. The French Communist Party found itself outflanked, vulnerable to the charge that its 'orthodox' stance towards the events had betrayed the revolution. Daniel Cohn-Bendit (b.1945), the young Franco-German frequently taken to express the mood of the moment, wrote a book with his brother which described Communism as obsolete. For his part, Georges Marchais, within a few years to become the party's General Secretary, famously described Daniel Cohn-Bendit as 'a German anarchist'. Communists and Socialists – the latter in internal disarray – manoeuvred against and with each other. In the early 1970s, after protracted negotiation, a 'programme for government' was agreed by both parties. In essence, the Socialists committed themselves to a massive nationalization which would constitute a 'break with capitalism'. The Communists, for their part, backpedalled on 'the dictatorship of the proletariat'. Events in Prague put the ownership of 'Liberty' to the fore. The French Communist Party had expressed its surprise and disappointment at the invasion of Czechoslovakia, but only tentatively moved towards 'Euro-Communism'. A struggle for supremacy on the Left ensued, even as, in theory at least, the two parties looked forward to a period of government together. In the 1974 election, however, the Left failed to gain power.

The shadow of the war also still hung over French public life. Pompidou had lost his job as Prime Minister in 1968 but he stood waiting in the wings. He succeeded de Gaulle as president in 1969. De Gaulle had shaped a certain idea of France and its role in the world, but perhaps he alone could conjure it up. In 1971 Pompidou gave an interview in which he spoke of the irritation and loathing which the Resistance inspired in him. Was it not time to throw a veil over a time when the French not only did not like each other but killed each other? In fact, however, veils were still being uncomfortably lifted. Pompidou died in 1974. The new president, Valéry Giscard d'Estaing, was of a new generation and stood 'independently'. He had not been in the Resistance but had joined the First French Army as an 18-year-old in late 1944 for the invasion of the country of his birth – Germany (his father had been a civil servant during the French occupation of the Rhineland). He also had a grandfather who was a member of Vichy's National Council. Thirty years on from 1945 he downgraded VE Day from the status of a public holiday which it had formerly enjoyed. That might, or might not, have been solely a step to assist in furthering Franco-German reconciliation. Accommodating the French past in a manner which satisfied all France remained complicated.

'Germany': neighbourly relations?

'Germany', government lawyers in Bonn were declaring in 1965, was still a legal entity and the Federal Republic was the successor to the Reich. Any state (with the necessary exception, as it turned out, of the Soviet Union) which recognized the GDR as a state was committing an 'unfriendly act'. It would lead to the rupture of diplomatic relations with Bonn. Soviet bloc countries, therefore, had GDR embassies but not FRG ones (Romania, in 1967, as usual, managed to be the exception). In 1975, however, in Helsinki, Helmut Schmidt, Federal Germany's new Social Democrat Chancellor, and Erich Honecker, from the GDR, sat beside each other as they signed the Accords. Such a scene could not have been predicted a decade earlier. 'Ownership' of 'Germany' had become a stock question, though one in existence long before 1945. There had always been division and plurality in the 'German past'. A single 'united Germany' might have been an historical aberration. If so, two separate states might be conceivable, though ones not quite 'foreign' to each other. Thinking about a new *Ostpolitik* would match a domestic mood which wanted change. In Berlin and elsewhere in the Federal Republic, as in Paris, youthful protesters in universities and on the streets attacked 'fossilized structures' and 'everyday fascism'. In April 1968 Gudrun Esselin and Andreas Baader set fire to a department store in Frankfurt. They called such stores agencies of consumer terrorism. The attacks on government figures, captains of industry, bankers and US military installations, subsequently mounted by the 'Red Army Faction', could thus be presented as a kind of counter-terrorism. Some young people seemed determined, in their moral outrage, to expose the past political failings of their own parents. An 'extra-parliamentary opposition' offered an alternative world, one apparently in which Chairman Mao would feel at home.

It was in this climate that the Social Democrat/Free Democrat coalition government after the 1969 elections, with Willy Brandt as the first Social Democrat Chancellor, marked a significant change in a Federal Republic hitherto shaped by Christian Democrat governments. Since 1966 Brandt had been Vice-Chancellor and Foreign Secretary in the coalition headed by the Christian Democrat, Kurt-George Kiesinger. Kiesinger, who had spent the war in Germany, as had his predecessor, Erhard, had been a member of the Nazi Party – something he was never allowed to forget by his opponents. Ten years earlier, at Bad Godesberg, the Social Democrats in the FDR had decided that they were a party of the whole people rather than the party of the working class. Marxism had not been so much rejected as ignored. The problems of a modern economy, it seemed, were technical: suitable for research, not agitation. Another way of putting it was that ambitious politicians were not prepared to accept perpetual opposition – which otherwise might well be their fate.

At this juncture, therefore, as it happened, both in Bonn and East Berlin, there were men at the helm who had been imprisoned in Germany between 1933 and 1945 or had been living abroad. Brandt, had left Germany in 1933 for Norway – where he adopted a Norwegian name and took Norwegian citizenship. He returned to Berlin after the war and resumed his German citizenship in 1947. His past could not but have a bearing on the present. He had been born in Lübeck – a city which now directly abutted the GDR. As Mayor of West Berlin (1957–66) he had been 'at the front line', far away from 'western' Bonn and the conscious cultivation by government there of a Germany that was 'Western'. The Deutsche Demokratische Republik [German Democratic Republic](DDR) had been all around him in Berlin. There Walter Ulbricht, architect of 'Socialist Unity', held sway. Born in Leipzig, he had been elected in Westphalia (now in the FRG) to the Reichstag in 1928 as a Communist. Ten years older than Brandt, Ulbricht had lived in Paris and Prague from 1933 to 1937. He then moved to the Soviet Union and had returned to Germany after the war. During the civil war, he had spent some time in Spain seeking out, and arranging the elimination of, comrades who could be identified as Trotskyists or heretics of some other persuasion. The Partido Obrero de Unificación Marxista [Workers' Party of Marxist Unification] (POUM) needed to be reined in. A certain 'Willy Brandt' was a journalist in Spain at the time. Ulbricht's dominant tenure came to an end in 1971 when he was edged out as Party General Secretary by Erich Honecker (with Soviet backing). In August 1970, in a conversation with Leonid Brezhnev, Honecker had given his opinion that there were in reality two German states: a Socialist GDR and a capitalist FRG. A unified but Socialist German nation was not going to emerge. Honecker was originally a 'Westerner' (from the Saarland). He had been in a Nazi prison for ten years after 1935. In seeking to revisit 'the German question' at this stage, therefore, personal pasts, the nature of 'Socialism' and 'Democracy', together with the enigma that was 'Germany', all came together.

In December 1970 a dramatic picture flashed around the world. It showed Willy Brandt kneeling before the monument in Warsaw erected to the heroes of the Warsaw Ghetto. He was in Poland to sign a treaty whereby the FRG recognized the state frontier of Poland in the west as the Oder–Neisse line. It was, however, in theory at least, a matter which could only legally be concluded by an all-German government at a peace conference. On the Polish side, the initiative had come from the about-to-be-deposed Gomulka (though its conclusion did not cause his departure). Brandt's presence, and act of expiation, was one very public demonstration of 'change through rapprochement', the formula which encapsulated his *Ostpolitik* from the outset. It had seen meetings in March and May, in East and West Germany, respectively (Erfurt and Kassel) between Brandt and the DDR Prime Minister, Willi Stoph. Recognition of the Oder–Neisse line still upset some 'expelled' groups in the FRG. Their organizations had hitherto deterred Christian Democrat governments from tackling the issue, but Brandt realized that no progress could be made without such recognition. The treaty with Poland had been preceded, in August, by the critical treaty with the Soviet Union which had talked about the need to relax tension and renounce the threat or use of force. In terms of territorial integrity, it referred specifically to the Oder–Neisse line and the border between East and West Germany.

The conduct of these 'inner-European' negotiations inevitably took place with the weight of the area's past hanging over the participants. Yet it would be wrong to see this sequence of events in that context exclusively. The USA and the Soviet Union, because of preoccupations elsewhere, wished to see a relaxation of tension in Europe. If this had not been the case, nothing much would have happened. In March 1970 the four occupying powers in Berlin began discussions on the city's future which were concluded, subject to ratification, in September 1971. The agreement confirmed their existing rights. The Soviet Union would oversee traffic routes across East Germany and ensure that they were 'unimpeded'. It was also made clear, as had long been the case in practice, that West Berlin was neither a constituent part of the FRG nor of the GDR. However, Moscow accepted that West Berliners could travel abroad on Federal German passports and existing ties were to be respected.

The debate over the 'Eastern treaties' took place in the Bundestag on 22 March 1972. The fundamental division in the speeches on this occasion, though with other variations, was between those who took the Bismarckian Reich, as of 1937, as 'Germany' and those who did not. The Coalition carried the vote. The way was then open for direct and difficult negotiations between Bonn and East Berlin. Under the ensuing Treaty, signed on 21 December 1972, the two Germanies recognized each other, exchanged diplomatic representatives and were admitted to the UN. They affirmed the inviolability of the existing frontier between them and a desire to have 'neighbourly relations' with each other. In accepting that each state had no jurisdiction beyond its own territory, the FRG gave up its hitherto firm claim to represent the whole German people. The 'national question' was in effect put into cold storage.

The process was completed in December 1973 when a treaty was also concluded between the FRG and Czechoslovakia. The 1938 Munich Agreement loomed large in the protracted negotiation which led up to the treaty. Had it simply become meaningless with the passage of time, or was it, from the very outset, invalid? Eventually, mindful of legal implications, one way or the other, a form of words was found which both governments could accept. Its signature marked the end of a significant few years of diplomacy. The achievement was Brandt's though, ironically, he himself resigned in 1974 on the discovery that an important figure in his entourage was an East German agent.

Considering the whole process, commentators normally concluded that the question had been settled: two Germanies, two worlds. Europe, at Helsinki, moved forward on that basis,

Britain: coming home to roost?

British governments would not have been happy to have been lumped, from an American or other external perspective, into Western Europe, but that was where geography suggested their country was. It held on to its status as a permanent member of the UN Security Council. It had a 'nuclear deterrent'. No British government was going to disarm unilaterally. The British, as the Americans well knew, attached weight to the 'special relationship'. That was a little awkward. Kissinger, ahead of the US President's first official visit to London in February 1969, suggested that the thing to do was not to discourage a warm relationship but to elevate other countries to a comparable status. The British Prime Minister's way of demonstrating the intimacy of the 'Atlantic world' was to invite Nixon to attend a Cabinet meeting. Real foreigners, that is to say fellow-Europeans, did not get such an invitation. Harold Wilson – close to Nixon in age – had been in office since 1964. Since his youthful wartime days as a civil servant, he had been a frequent visitor to the USA. He was not instinctively 'European'. The government struggled with economic and industrial problems. In November 1967 it devalued the pound sterling. The 'spirit of '68' did not entirely pass the country by – though London was not Paris or Berlin. The voice of a new generation in revolt could be heard. Some said that the British role in the world was now played out. Devaluation of the currency was more than a matter of economics. It perhaps symbolized the country's loss of global value. Nixon could not find a Britain willing to lend him military support in South-East Asia. Since coming into office there had been many twists and turns in the Labour government's defence reviews. The rationale for distant British military presence seemed to be disappearing. Civil servants thought they saw a world emerging where almost all colonial or quasi-colonial traces were fast being removed. Yet, neither in Whitehall nor in the country at large was it easy to deal with the overhang of the vast past. Raw nerves were exposed. What world did Britain belong to? The decision to withdraw a military presence from 'East of Suez' by 1971, except for Hong Kong, was taken in 1968. A successor government was not going to reverse the decision. Royal Navy ships slipped out of harbours where, as in Malta, they had been stationed for very many decades. Prime Minister Wilson, despite pressure from a substantial section of his party, refused publicly to condemn American policy in Vietnam, but he also refused to send British troops in support. Some supposed that there was an element of 'payback' for the American actions in 1956 in this decision. Wilson's own efforts, through the Commonwealth, to facilitate a peace in Vietnam came to nothing. He did acknowledge 'a growing mood of isolationism' in his country at this juncture. It was not something which he welcomed or accepted, but it seemed, perhaps temporarily, that Britain was weary of the world. Nixon could not turn this tide in one visit. Dean Rusk, the US Secretary of State, was naturally prominent in Anglo-American discussions at this juncture. Thirty years earlier, he had been a Rhodes Scholar at Oxford, graduating in 1934. He could sense at this point how distant the 'British world' he had then known had since become.

An enhanced global British–American partnership was not on Edward Heath's agenda when he became Conservative Prime Minister in 1970. The same age as Wilson and, like him, also an Oxford student of politics, philosophy and economics, he had had a very different war from his predecessor. At its close it had taken him to Germany as a soldier. Reflection on that experience led him to a distinctive and strongly personal commitment to a 'European future' for the UK. It would not mean the rupture of the ties between London and Washington, nor would it mean dissolving the Commonwealth, but it would entail accepting, in world terms, that Britain was 'European'. Heath had played a major part in the unsuccessful negotiations of 1961–62. He knew the terrain intimately. There were many technical issues for the British negotiators again to wade through – from the fate of West Indian cane sugar to New Zealand butter. Then there was the question of the Community budget. What was likely to be decisive, however, was the attitude of the French President. The fact that he was not de Gaulle might make all the difference. Not that Heath and Pompidou were friends, nor even acquaintances. It was a commentary on the strange distance between neighbours that they had probably only met once – at de Gaulle's funeral. Pompidou had neither the style nor the ambition to carry on de Gaulle's public attempts to project France as an independent global voice (or, under French guidance, to give 'Europe' a voice). However, he was not deaf to the suggestions that the British would not really play by the rules so intelligently drawn up under French eyes. Colleagues raised the suspicion that Americans were hiding inside the British horse. There was also a fear that the French language would be displaced by English in the working of the Community. It was a sensitive issue, because the reach of its language beyond France (and, of course, not only in Europe) was a measure of France's world status. Other British politicians would not have been very convincing in conveying assurances on these matters. Heath, however, was – for he said what he actually believed. Pompidou was persuaded. Entry was fixed for 1 January 1973.

In Britain, debates in parliament, press and the country at large from 1971 onwards, as earlier, revealed mixtures of enthusiasm, hostility, suspicion and ignorance. Was entry 'merely' a matter of economics – weighing up the financial advantages and disadvantages – or would it undermine national sovereignty and lead to the creation of a 'Federal Europe'? Some, conditioned by history to think in such terms, thought that Britain would now 'lead' Europe. Others thought Britain was doomed to become a 'province' of this rapacious conglomerate – for was there not talk of economic and monetary union by 1980? The issue of membership was put to the UK electorate in June 1975. Of the civilian votes cast, 67.2 per cent voted 'yes' – 43 per cent of registered voters – and 32.8 per cent voted 'no'. It appeared to be a decisive result, but the appearance was deceptive. It was partly that the new Labour government, elected in 1974, was engaged on a 'renegotiation', but more because the language of the referendum campaign skirted some fundamental questions about the future. The whole issue, in party-political terms, had proved very difficult to handle. The 'pro' campaign took 'Britain in Europe' as its title. Even with the simultaneous accession of Ireland and Denmark, however, the Community which the UK was joining hardly constituted Europe. There might well be further accessions in the future but as things stood, however, this 'Europe' was only a segment, though a very significant segment, of 'Western Europe'.

Helsinki 'Final Act', 1975

Two months after the outcome of the British referendum, heads of state or government from 'all Europe' assembled in Finland. Their unique collective presence was a substantial diplomatic achievement. It had taken years to weave together an acceptable agreement, but it might be that thirty years on from 1945, a kind of peace was at last being achieved. Thirty-five states signed what was referred to as the 'Final Act'. All European states did so, with the exception of Andorra and Albania. They were joined by the USA, the Soviet Union and Canada. 'Europe' and the external, yet also involved, Superpowers had never before reached such an accord. The agreement came to be more generally known as the 'Helsinki Accords'. There was symbolism in the location of the conference. The capital of Finland advertised itself as a city where Eastern and Western (European) cultures met. Symbolically, it had two cathedrals, Lutheran and Orthodox, on its skyline. The city had three 'neighbours' – Stockholm, Leningrad/St Petersburg and Tallinn. Stockholm pointed to a past in which Finland had been a part of a now 'neutral' Sweden. 'St Petersburg' pointed to the nineteenth and early twentieth-century past as a Russian grand duchy while Leningrad was a reminder of the present proximity of the Soviet Union and of the loss to it of a large area of Karelia. Tallinn pointed to the cultural/linguistic link with Estonia, a country like Finland itself, which had embarked on independence in 1919 but which had lost it in the Soviet occupation of 1939. Both geography and history compelled Finland to be 'accommodating'. It had two official languages. It had had its own post-independence civil war, which lingered in the memory, and two bitter wars, 1939–40 and 1941–44, with the Soviet Union. Post-1945, Helsinki politicians had managed to negotiate an arrangement with the Soviet Union which preserved independence within a framework of neutrality. The precise implications of this status required constant consideration and both internal and external caution. Finland 'looked West' but was not 'in' the West. From time to time, 'Finlandization' was thought to offer solutions elsewhere in Europe and even beyond. The master of this diplomacy was Urho Kekkonen, its president (by no means, in his hands, a merely ceremonial post). In 1975, he was approaching his twentieth year in office. There was no better location and no better person to orchestrate European co-operation.

Ten principles were set out in the agreement: the sovereign equality of states; rejection of the use or threat of force; inviolability of frontiers; territorial integrity of states; peaceful settlement of disputes; non-intervention in the internal affairs of other states; respect for human rights and fundamental liberties, including freedom of thought, conscience and religious and other convictions; equal rights and self-determination of peoples; co-operation between states; fulfilment in good faith of obligations under international law. This new

'Decalogue' was accompanied by further 'confidence-boosting' sections which included the exchange of military information, the conclusion of trade agreements and increased cultural and educational contact. How all this worked out in practice was to be reviewed at a further conference scheduled for Belgrade in 1977. It was no surprise that the negotiations had been protracted. There was some surprise that they had been successfully concluded and some scepticism about future implementation. Different signatories naturally highlighted different features. Both in the USA and the Soviet Union there were doubters. In the latter, Brezhnev emphasized to his colleagues that the post-1945 boundaries in Europe had now been settled (although there had been no formal recognition of the incorporation of the Baltic States in the Soviet Union and there had been no agreement that boundaries were 'immutable'). Some of his colleagues did not like the provisions for cultural exchange. They could easily amount to that interference in the internal affairs of another state which had been specifically ruled out. It was true that the Soviet Union reserved the right to decide in such an instance, but the genie might have been let out of the bottle. In the USA, the opposite considerations applied. Critics disliked the extent to which the Final Act legitimated the status quo in Eastern Europe and ruled out the release of 'captive peoples'. They thought that, in return for recognizing state frontiers, the provisions for cultural exchange should have been more extensive. Ford was accused of 'selling out'. The future might be uncertain but 'Europe' looked to have come as close as was achievable to a formal peace settlement. It was what Europe's external 'protectors' were prepared to live with. In this sense, it turned a page. It seemed a settlement based on stable 'realism' rather than utopian and futile expectations of change.

16
Overlapping Linkages:
A Mediterranean World

Europe and the Middle East, not to mention Africa and 'West Asia', rubbed shoulders in a kind of extended 'Mediterranean world', one which in turn stretched through to the Gulf. An Algerian Foreign Minister in the late 1970s urged the world to think of Algerians as a Mediterranean people in an Arab context rather than an Arab people. Alternatively, he might have been prepared to say that Algerians were an Arab people, but in a Mediterranean context. There might often be disagreement about where the emphasis should be placed, but either way there was an underlying reality. Here was a duality, publicly expressed or not. It was also present, if with different elements, in the cities of Tunis, Tripoli, Alexandria and Beirut. Nor were 'Northern' Mediterranean people living in Nicosia or Izmir, Athens or Valetta without duality, a duality further complicated in the case of the islands by continuing Commonwealth membership, the substantial continuing presence of the English language and of British people, whether living as residents or visiting as tourists. An example of this ambiguity was Malta. The Oxford-educated Dom Mintoff, once the ardent but unsuccessful advocate of the island's integration with the UK, returned to office as Prime Minister in 1971. Malta had been independent since 1964 with the British Queen remaining as its head of state. Mintoff now moved in another direction. The island became a republic (though remaining within the Commonwealth) and, while seeking to extract what he could from NATO for use of the island's naval facilities, he increasingly looked across the Mediterranean. He presented himself in a rather different guise at the Algiers Non-Aligned conference. Malta's geographical position necessarily made it 'in-between', but policy now seemed to be trying to turn geography into politics. Europe, Africa and West Asia all lapped the Mediterranean. The Middle East/North Africa/Southern Europe/Asia Minor did indeed have their own distinct external linkages elsewhere but some events suggested, notwithstanding their distinctiveness, that they could be a loose 'region', albeit one with profound ambivalences. It remained blurred as different 'worlds' overlapped and intersected.

Arab worlds

The core and periphery of the 'Arab world' were not self-evident (and it was of course only partially 'Mediterranean'). It was questionable how much common perspective linked the inhabitants of such places as Khartoum, Kuwait, Tunis, Algiers, Aden, Baghdad, Tripoli, Rabat, Damascus and Riyadh. Each city, as each country, had its own individuality. The outside world saw the 'Arab world' as one with an intractable ambiguity in which professions of solidarity coexisted with intense rivalry and internal conflict. Perhaps it was not so very different in its diversity, however, from the 'Europe' of the previous chapter. Western Europe, however, had no common language such as Arabic (its variations apart) provided for the 'Arab world'. In a social context widely supposed in the 1960s to be 'secularizing', European Catholic/Protestant antagonism had substantially weakened, but in the Middle East Sunni-Shi'a antagonism seemed to be rising. The 'Arab world' – quite apart from the existence of its continuing Christian minorities – was of course not synonymous with the 'Islamic world'. The two states which contained the largest number of world Muslims, Indonesia and Pakistan, were of course not Arab. Nevertheless, because of the importance of Mecca and other sites in the Arabian peninsula, and because of the central authority of the Arabic text of the Koran, the Arab world, in a certain sense, still defined Islam.

However, the era of direct European control was now over. The last British troops left Aden in December 1967. It was not clear what was going to happen to the federal structure in South-West Arabia. British departure from its protective role in the Gulf proved more straightforward – with the independence of Bahrain, Qatar and the formation of the United Arab Emirates (Abu Dhabi, Dubai, Sharjah, Ajman, Umm al-Quaiwayn and Fujayrah), all in 1971 – but it was nevertheless uncertain whether this 'Gulf world' would survive. Theoretically, therefore, the 'Arab Middle East' was at long last formally 'settled' – except that the very concept remained problematic. There was only one state which called itself the 'United Arab Republic' – Egypt until 1971. This title was the lingering legacy of the failed attempt to create a working Egyptian/Syrian Union. The prospect of a single Arab state which would extend to the Tigris and Euphrates rivers was even more remote. In 1962 Nasser had sent Egyptian troops to fight in Yemen to support the new republican regime. It proved a financial drain. The troops were there for five years without conspicuous military success in difficult terrain lively with sectarian and tribal animosities. The royalist cause was supported by Saudi Arabia with money and arms (there was more than a suspicion in Riyadh that Nasser aimed to extend Egyptian control over all Arabia). Attempts to reach a negotiated settlement came to nothing. At another level, neither in Damascus nor in Baghdad was there any eagerness to accept Nasser's leadership. To say the least, Arab unity was elusive.

There was little prospect that 'the Arab world' would witness any conference which could be compared with the 'northern' ethos of Helsinki. Journalists frequently revealed that it was a 'perennial hotspot'. It became synonymous in their minds with 'oil' – not that this resource was by any means spread equally across all Middle Eastern states, a fact which was itself a frequent source of tension. Saudi Arabia had become the world's largest oil exploiter and, at this juncture, held roughly a quarter of the world's proven reserves. Discoveries in the Gulf and elsewhere radically and rapidly transformed the basis of economies, and in the process altered long-established local relationships and balances of power. The abundant resources of the Middle East, enhanced by fresh discoveries, supplied Western Europe, Japan and, increasingly, the USA. External purchasers looked for security of supply. It was not surprising that the terms of ownership and production moved to the fore. Further, the potential use of oil as a political weapon had not escaped attention. In these circumstances, no other part of the world was so endemically unstable and prone to conflict, conflict which, as before, drew in outside players. Internal issues and external pressures invariably intertwined.

'Palestine': war and its aftermath, 1967

Unity in the Arab world might only be found in a common strategy against the 'Other' that was Israel. In January 1964, meeting in Cairo, the Council of the Arab League States reiterated its support for the Palestinian people in liberating their homeland and determining their own destiny. It was easy to express such sentiment: action was more difficult. One sequel, however, was the Palestine Liberation Organization (PLO), founded in Jordan in May 1964 to co-ordinate the various Palestinian factions. A flag as the symbol of Palestine was also adopted. Yasser Arafat (as he became known) emerged as the leading figure, though never without rivals. He was a man of no fixed abode. He had been largely brought up in Cairo, with a father from Gaza and a mother from Jerusalem. He had fought in Gaza in the 1948 war but then returned to Cairo to complete a civil engineering course at King Fuad University. He then moved around, spending time in Kuwait and elsewhere. Fatah, the group which he had formed in 1959, launched its first raid in Israel in January 1965. It was styled as the beginning of a war of liberation. Disputes over control of the waters of the River Jordan added to regional tension at this time. Israel mounted counter-raids, particularly against Jordan. Relations between Syria, where a new regime had come to power, and Israel, deteriorated. A major air battle between the two countries took place in April 1967. The following month Syria informed Nasser of a large Israeli troop concentration before the Golan Heights (from which there had been Syrian shelling into Israel). Nasser was put on the spot. He was already being criticized – compared with Syria – for his 'inaction'. In mid-May 1967, reassured that, if required, the Egyptian army was battle-ready, he raised the temperature. Since the 1956 war a UN Emergency Force had been present, with the required Egyptian consent, in the Sinai Peninsula. Now the UN Secretary-General complied with Egypt's request that it be withdrawn. Nasser then ordered the blockade of the Straits of Tiran, at the mouth of the Gulf of Aqaba, at the head of which was the Israeli port of Eilat. By the end of the month, King Hussein of Jordan had placed his forces under Egyptian command.

Lev Eshkol, the Israeli Prime Minister, hesitated. In his early seventies, he had been around a long time, having reached Ottoman Palestine in 1914 from

Ukraine, where he had been born. Finally, he accepted military advice that a war was imminent and that Israel should strike first. The 'Six Day War' began on 5 June. It ended with the comprehensive defeat of Egyptian, Jordanian and Syrian forces in a succession of hammer blows. Israel occupied the Golan Heights, the West Bank (including east Jerusalem) and the Sinai desert. On 9 June, accepting responsibility for failure, Nasser announced his decision to retire. Public demand, evident in well-organized demonstrations, persuaded him to change his mind. Others at the top of his regime were made to pay the price. Egyptian troops were withdrawn from Yemen. Nasser's prestige slumped and, in failing health, he never regained his former stature.

In the short term, at least, Israel's military supremacy seemed assured. What to do in and with the occupied lands raised deeper questions. There was little domestic dispute in Israel about its formal annexation of East Jerusalem – which happened immediately, despite widespread world condemnation. The continued occupation of Sinai and the Golan Heights brought military advantages, but ones which might be bargained away, though at high price, at some future date. The West Bank was another matter. To some Israelis it was 'Judaea' and 'Samaria', and should properly be part of a 'Greater Israel'. Yet continued occupation brought a much increased Arab population if Israel/the Occupied Territory were to be considered as one unit. Maybe a third of that population consisted in turn of impoverished refugees from the 1948 war. The impact of such Arab numbers could only be mitigated by getting more Jews to come to Israel and by establishing Jewish settlements in these territories. Otherwise, demographics, in a run that might not be very long, might jeopardize the Jewish basis of the state. Further, whatever long past, a very long past, might be deployed in justification, occupation stemmed directly from fresh conquest. It pointed once again to the 'alien artificiality' of Israel. Abba Eban, Israel's foreign minister, a contemporary, in age terms, of Arafat, South African-born, English-raised, Cambridge-educated, and a brilliant linguist (including translation from Arabic), rejected that notion. He argued at the UN and elsewhere not only that Israel had a right to exist, but also that it was an 'authentic' rather than 'alien' part of the Middle East.

Neither the USA nor the Soviet Union directly intervened in the war, though the latter, for a time, appeared to contemplate it. The Mediterranean Fleets of both countries steered clear of the conflict. That is not to say that the Superpowers simply sat by. It had been Soviet Intelligence, as much as Syrian, which had alerted Nasser to the supposed Israeli 'troop concentration' before the Golan Heights. Egyptian weaponry came from the Soviet Union (the USA stopped aid to Egypt in 1965). The USA, Britain and, until a late stage, France, had been supplying Israel. Neither belligerent could have fought without such external equipment. The USA would not countenance the destruction of Israel but did not underwrite its expansion. Ties were close. Eshkol had been the first Israeli Prime Minister to pay a formal visit to the USA when he went to Washington in 1964. 'Western' opinion, in the USA and Western Europe, to judge by opinion polls, substantially applauded the Israeli success. Friends of Israel, prominent in public and commercial life, urged their non-Jewish fellow-citizens to see Israel as a democratic country with 'Western values'. Such identification, however, highlighted Israel's 'peculiarity' rather than its 'Middle Eastern' character. Its portrayal as 'David' in a battle with the Arab 'Goliath' had considerable appeal, but the 'Arab world' existed and would continue to exist. The ties of the USA with Saudi Arabia were close. King Hussein of Jordan maintained strong connections with Britain, the country where he had been educated. Western governments did not regard the territorial outcome of the war as final.

It was in Khartoum, rather removed from the immediate conflict, that Arab heads of state came together in August–September 1967 to affirm the unity of Arab ranks. There was to be no peace with Israel, no recognition of Israel and no negotiations with it. They insisted on the rights of the Palestinian people in their own country. They recognized that oil could be 'a weapon in the battle' (though the war had been over too quickly for the embargo on exports to countries friendly towards Israel to be effective, and this conference lifted it). They agreed 'to strengthen military preparations to face all eventualities'. It would have been surprising if any other statement had been forthcoming.

Notwithstanding intransigence displayed both by victor and vanquished, a 'turning point' might have been reached, 'another moment of choice', as President Johnson put it. De Gaulle was not the only leader to link the Middle East and Vietnam as potential sources of a new global conflict. Rather than let a situation fester indefinitely, the 'outside world' should orchestrate a solution. The British drafted a Resolution (No. 242) which was passed by the Security Council in November 1967. It spoke of Israeli armed forces withdrawing from territories (there was no definite article used) which they had recently occupied. It called for the ending of all claims or states of belligerency. The sovereignty, territorial integrity and political independence of every state in the area should be acknowledged and respected. A UN Special Representative (who turned out to be a Swedish diplomat, Gunnar Jarring) was to press for the implementation of these principles (and further questions which stemmed from them). In the event, however, although Resolution 242 achieved the status of a hallowed text, regularly cited in the future, no direct consequence flowed from it. Ambassador Jarring occasionally expressed restrained optimism, but ultimately met disappointment.

In December 1969, US Secretary of State Rogers issued a comprehensive statement identifying the key issues of peace, security, withdrawal and territory on which he thought agreement would be possible. A solution of the refugee problem and the status of Jerusalem could follow. Peace, he said, in a resounding statement of the obvious, depended on the attitudes and intentions of the parties. That being so, little changed. From time to time, the Superpowers appeared not to be far apart in seeking a solution. Yet, neither was prepared to withdraw the backing given to their respective 'clients'. Soviet advisers and equipment (including missiles) flooded into Egypt to buttress a flagging Nasser. The Egyptian leader looked for financial support from Saudi Arabia and Kuwait in particular. Israel was able to receive continued American backing. Such reinforcement, by both Superpowers, could be interpreted as making a further round of fighting more likely, but neither wanted that to happen.

Yasser Arafat declared that it was time for Palestinians to take matters into their own hands. They could not suppose, in the light of the above points, that what they would regard as a just settlement would be imposed from outside. Nor could they rely on Arab states, formal professions notwithstanding, to put the issue of 'Palestine' ahead of any of their own individual concerns. The PLO, which he now chaired, convened a congress in July 1968 to draw up a revised 'National Charter'. It affirmed that armed struggle was the only way to liberate Palestine. It called upon 'the Arab nation' to help 'the Palestinian people'. 'The Palestinians' were defined as Arab nationals who had been living in Palestine until 1947 and those with a Palestinian father – regardless of their present location. Jews (small in number) who had normally lived in Palestine before 'the Zionist invasion' were to be considered Palestinians. A Jew, it stated, was the adherent of a religion, not the member of a nationality. The passage of time did not alter the fact that Israel had been illegally established. It violated the principles of the UN Charter.

Arafat's twin strategy, in so far as his rather ramshackle organization possessed one, was both to seek a degree of international recognition as a quasi-government representing 'the Palestinian people' and also to initiate terrorism, such as the hijacking of civilian airliners. The former eventually achieved some success when Arab heads of state, meeting in Rabat in October 1974, recognized the PLO as the sole legitimate representative of the Palestinian people (a warning to King Hussein not to contemplate a separate deal with the Israelis). That success was capped, even more significantly, the following month, when Arafat was invited to address the General Assembly of the UN on behalf of the PLO. Israel attacked this invitation, reiterating that 'Jordan is Palestine'. The General Assembly passed a resolution which reaffirmed 'the inalienable rights of the Palestinian people in Palestine'. The other part of the strategy produced the attack on the Israeli team's headquarters at the 1972 Olympic Games in Munich – an attack welcomed in Germany by Andreas Baader and Ulrike Meinhof. This killing became the most well-known example of 'anti-Zionist' terrorism.

Sustaining (or creating?) a 'Palestinian identity' with so many Palestinians living as refugees in neighbouring countries was inevitably difficult. There was no 'homeland' under Palestinian control. Their presence as exiles – perhaps approaching three million – in Jordan, the West Bank, Gaza, Lebanon, Syria and, in smaller numbers, in Egypt, Iraq and the Gulf countries – also tested professions of solidarity. This was particularly the case, at this juncture, in Jordan. The war had 'temporarily' deprived the state of its West Bank, its rump of Palestine. The equilibrium of the kingdom had always been difficult before, but now maybe a further two hundred thousand Palestinians had fled the fighting to enter 'East Bank Jordan'. Tension mounted between the 'incomers' and King Hussein (and the 'traditional' Bedouins on whom he relied to maintain his power). In September 1970, the king, unwilling to accept 'a state within a state' and entirely to abandon his claim to represent 'Palestine', declared martial law. He sent his army against the PLO camps. Heavy casualties ensued and, at one point, seemed likely to bring in Syrian assistance for the PLO. At a Cairo conference, Nasser attempted to achieve a deal between Hussein and Arafat. It caused his fatal heart attack. The following year, PLO forces and Arafat left for Lebanon. It had indeed been 'Black September'. The title of the gang – 'Black September' – responsible for the Munich killing indicated that Jordan, or any other government hostile or indifferent to the Palestinian cause, might also be attacked. Israel portrayed the PLO simply as a 'band of murderers'.

'Palestine': war and its aftermath, 1973

In June 1975, Nasser's successor, Anwar Sadat, formally reopened a Suez Canal which his predecessor had closed to shipping for eight years. The significance of the world's commercial artery, in a world of huge tankers and accelerating quantities of air freight, was no longer quite what it had been. Even so, its symbolism as the channel which linked 'West' and 'East' remained potent, as Sadat was well aware. This reopening, however, was only the concluding showpiece to an extraordinary sequence of events. Early on, in June 1971, Sadat had boldly declared that the 'Year of Decision' had arrived. One way or other, the battle for Palestine would be brought to an end. Initially, given his army's dependence on Soviet supplies, he had had little alternative but to sign, the previous month, a fifteen-year treaty of friendship with his supplier. In October, visiting Moscow, he told his Soviet hosts that force alone would end Israeli aggression. The Kremlin, pursuing detente with Washington at this juncture, was very cautious. In July 1972, however, Sadat abruptly changed tack. He ordered the departure of all Soviet military advisers – who, in the event, took their military equipment with them. The hope must have been that, in response, the USA would compel Israel to withdraw. The Israelis, for their part, thought that Egypt had little option but to recognize the status quo. It offered no concession. Sadat therefore turned to the Arab world – with Syria (and even, perhaps, on a lesser scale, Iraq and Jordan) providing significant forces and Saudi Arabia and other producers deploying the 'oil weapon' (though it would be unlikely to be swiftly effective). Then, on 6 October 1973, a two-pronged Arab attack began – the Syrians on the Golan front in the north and the Egyptians crossing the Suez Canal – and initially made good progress. Idi Amin, ruler of Uganda, subsequently, if implausibly, claimed that he was personally operating behind the Israeli lines and contributing to the Egyptian success.

The Israeli Prime Minister, Golda Meir, born in Kiev in 1898, looked to the USA, the country which had been her home for fourteen years before she emigrated to Palestine in 1921, for support. The Americans were warned that Israel's very survival was at stake. Language she used might be taken to imply that, in the circumstances in which it found itself, her country could deploy an atomic bomb. A hasty and substantial airlift brought her the additional weaponry she sought. The tide of battle turned. After several false starts, a complete ceasefire was agreed on 26 October. The fourth Arab–Israeli war ended more or less in a draw. Casualties, on both sides, had been high. The role of the Superpowers, as time passed, became critical. They became more involved than they had initially supposed likely or probably wanted. A possible Soviet military intervention in support of the Arabs had triggered an American 'war alert' (including a nuclear alert). It had taken tense direct contacts between Moscow and Washington before both countries could agree on the terms of a Security Council resolution.

The outcome was paradoxical. External 'meddling' had long been supposed in the Middle East to be one of the banes of the region. This time, however, if both Superpowers became active in seeking a solution, one could perhaps be found. It was not clear whether they would really do so in concert. The contemporary oil crisis, to be considered shortly, and the enhanced position of Arab oil producers, was another factor in the search for a settlement. In December 1973, Israel, Egypt, Jordan, the USA and the Soviet Union – though not Syria – opened discussions in Geneva. Kissinger subsequently undertook a very active diplomatic role, but saw little need for Soviet assistance. He could broker a deal directly between Israel and Egypt. Here, as on other matters, the presidential crisis in Washington added to the complications of reaching a settlement. So did the fact of a fresh Israeli government under Yitzhak Rabin from 1974 – the first Israeli Prime Minister to have been born in Palestine (in Jerusalem). His Cabinet witnessed a struggle between 'doves' and 'hawks'. In September 1975, after protracted negotiations, it was the US Secretary of State, offering increased US aid to both parties, who brought about an agreement between Egypt and Israel (although it was formally signed in Geneva). The Israelis withdrew further back from the Canal, creating a new buffer zone, and surrendered the strategically important Gidi and Mitla passes. That still left them, however, with most of Sinai. The Egyptians agreed to the passage of non-military Israeli cargoes through the Canal. The first article of the agreement stated that the conflict between the two countries should be resolved peacefully. This was not the language of the PLO. It might mean, however, that the 'Middle East' would undergo substantial change. What Egypt did next would be critical.

There were other contemporary events and shifting alignments, however, which made the shape of that 'world', extending almost all around the Mediterranean and its hinterlands, so problematic. The Sinai agreement was not paralleled by any resolution of the other contentious issues involving Syria and Jordan. That fact in itself highlighted the ambiguous position which Egypt again occupied in the 'Arab world'. Sadat also had to look south as well as north and west, though it could not be his central preoccupation. There, in Sudan, a coalition civilian government had ruled until 1969 but struggled to govern a state whose ethnic and religious divisions largely coincided with geography. A military coup then brought General Numeirl to power and, for a time, certain 'African' provinces in the south were allowed more autonomy. Egypt played its part in sustaining Numeirl in power. The two countries concluded a joint defence agreement. For the moment, the armed conflict between north and south in Sudan, which had spasmodically flared, came to an end. Sadat seemed to be preparing to put 'Egypt first' and risk hostility towards him in some Arab capitals. The latest Israeli war had indeed shown that the 'Arab world' did have some substance. However, the co-operation had been between Arab states whose regimes and rulers were in reality cool about any formal 'Arab unity'.

Greece, Turkey, Libya and Algeria: military orders

There were indeed, in this decade, some 'Mediterranean' developments which revealed marked similarities north and south of the lapping sea: Greece and

Turkey, Libya and Algeria. Perhaps chief among them was the increased presence of military men, directly or indirectly, in control of their countries. Even in Israel, though Prime Minister Rabin did not come to power in 1974 in a military coup, most of his career had been in the Israel Defence Force. In April 1967 a group of middle-ranking army officers seized power in Athens, claiming to have detected a Communist plot. It is likely that an election due the following month would have returned a radical government, though the pattern of Greek party politics made nothing certain. One issue was what direct power, under the constitution, the monarch retained. The civil war, in which, nearly twenty years earlier, Communists had been defeated, still hung over the Greek political scene. Young King Constantine reluctantly bestowed legitimacy on the new regime and then tried, but without success, to engineer a counter-coup. He fled the country in December. A new constitution was in due course produced which emasculated parliament and then abolished the monarchy. The actual business of government was steadily 'militarized'. Civil liberty was restricted. 'The Colonels' saw themselves as radicals with a mission of national regeneration, one to be carried out with exemplary censorship and, if necessary, brutality. Northern European countries, in particular, through the Council of Europe, expressed their displeasure at a military takeover in Europe (such things should not happen). Governments run by colonels, or some other military rank, assumed or otherwise, were therefore to be found on both sides of the Mediterranean. But perhaps the Greeks were 'a Mediterranean people in a European context'? The regime, however, kept going. Its commitment to NATO, and Greece's strategic importance to the alliance in the Eastern Mediterranean, ensured the turning of blind eyes in Washington. Indeed opponents of the regime supposed that it was the creature, even the creation, of the USA.

Military intervention was not new in the politics of Turkey. The army had 'retreated to barracks' after its intervention in 1960 but its leading figures still saw themselves as the rightful guardians of the republic. The new constitution had been implemented, under its watchful eye, in 1961. The subsequent decade saw accelerated industrialization, expansion of education and increased urbanization. Parliamentary democracy survived, but did not flourish. A division between Left and Right was only to be expected but it was constantly complicated by the underlying issue of the identity of the Republic and the 'sacred' legacy of Kemalism. One particular concept of Turkish nationalism left no room for a Kurdish identity in a pluralist state. The ambivalence of Turkey's position as both in and out of 'Europe' remained. In relation to the Palestine wars, some sections of Turkish Muslim opinion vociferously criticized Israel, and the USA as its protector. Yet Turkey was clearly not an Arab state, and its own international security remained firmly within the framework of NATO. Its democracy again faltered as the 1970s began. The political parties fractured and government failed. Some observers described Turkey in 1971 as being in a state of chaos.

In March, the military intervened once again, blaming the government led by Süleyman Demirel (b.1924), whose resignation it had forced, for driving the country 'into anarchy, fratricidal strife and social and economic unrest'. It looked to ending 'the current anarchical situation' but 'within the context of democratic principles'. Yet, having intervened, the military did not directly want to run the country. However, the 'Cabinet of national unity and consensus' which it oversaw proved incapable of delivering either unity or consensus. Terrorism and repression fed on each other. The country fell under martial law and over the next few years the power of the state was firmly asserted. Political factions grouped and regrouped, adopting new names but still clustering around charismatic individuals rather than programmes. Two parties, led respectively by Bülent Ecevit (b.1925) and Necmettin Erbakan (b.1926), came together, for a time, to make a shaky coalition government possible. However, their personal visions of Turkey's future direction were fundamentally different. As a young man, Ecevit had taken the unusual step of learning Sanskrit and Bengali. He had improved his English by studying in London. A poet himself, he translated the British poet, T.S. Eliot, into Turkish. He had spent some months in the USA. He was 'occidental', committed both to 'Europe' and NATO. Erbakan, almost exactly his contemporary, had a Ph.D. in engineering from Germany but his perspective was 'oriental' and emphatically Islamic. Turkey should align itself more closely with its Muslim brothers in the Arab world in the struggle against Zionism. Such divergence, accompanied by economic problems, ensured that Turkish politics in the early 1970s was both volatile and occasionally violent.

Greece and Turkey, of course, had a 'long past'. It had, however, become a commonplace to observe that their shared membership of NATO would restrain both antagonisms inherited from the past or contemporary quarrels concerning ownership of the North Aegean seabed. Such an assumption, however, reckoned without Cyprus. Relations between the Greek-speaking majority and the Turkish-speaking minority had rarely been other than fraught in the years since the island's independence in 1960. It had led to the arrival of a UN Peacekeeping Force in 1964. Archbishop Makarios, the island's president, survived several assassination attempts. In July 1974, however, he went into exile following a coup carried out by Greek-born officers of the Cyprus National Guard. The Athens government, which was implicated, saw at last the opportunity to bring about *enosis* [national unity]. It assumed that the Americans would block any Turkish intervention. It was a fatal mistake – one which led to the collapse of the regime. Britain, which still had a 'sovereign base' on the island and was supposedly a guarantor of the independence settlement, declined to get involved. Ankara therefore acted unilaterally, sending in troops in two expeditions in July and August. They occupied approximately 40 per cent of the island – in the north. They were not going to go away. Ecevit, transformed from poet into man of decisive action, became the Turkish hero of the hour – whereupon he resigned. Opponents blocked the general election which he had supposed would be forthcoming and which he would win handsomely. Instead, after much bargaining and distribution of fiefdoms, a four-party right-wing coalition was formed under the watchful eye of the military: the 'Nationalist Front'. In 1975, further violence was round the corner and the 'direction of travel' for Turkey unclear.

After the fall of the Colonels, Constantine Karamanlis, veteran Prime Minister of Greece in successive terms in the previous decade, returned home from his exile in Paris. With coalition partners, he set about restoring democracy (though not the monarchy, which was rejected in a referendum). The country's future orientation was reasserted. In the early 1960s Karamanlis had been able to conclude a preliminary protocol of accession to the European Economic Community (EEC). Brussels suspended this agreement during the era of the Colonels. Karamanlis wanted to reinvigorate it. 'Europe' would balance the strong influence of the USA in Greek life. There were also strong 'democratic' reasons for pursuing a 'European destiny'. So there were in Turkey. Both countries also, but particularly Turkey, had large numbers of their nationals working in Germany and their remittances were economically significant back home. Yet elements of similarity in the position of the two countries at this juncture did not create any 'common front'. Turkish–Greek antagonism disturbed the military partners they shared. What had happened, and was still happening, in Cyprus created a fresh obstacle to establishing a relationship which would facilitate the 'Europeanization' of both countries.

On the other side of the Mediterranean military men also took charge. A new regime was installed in Libya in 1969 with the bloodless overthrow of the monarchy. It was led by the 27-year-old Muammar Muhammad Gaddafi. He had abandoned the study of history at the University of Libya to go into the army. His Free Officers Movement echoed that of Nasser two decades earlier in Egypt. What had been the Kingdom of Libya became the Libyan Arab Republic. The change of title was significant but could not in itself solve the fundamental problem of identity. 'Libya' as a 'nation' had scarcely any significance. The monarchy which had been overthrown had itself been 'new'. Gaddafi, himself of a nomadic background, was difficult to tie down and seemed to like living in tents, at least sometimes. Only a firm exercise of power, it seemed, could bind this sprawling country together. Islam – in a form of which he approved – would integrate a society conspicuous in its 'tribal' divisions. Residence in England in 1966 to learn the English language and study advanced signals procedure had not led him to modify his pan-Arab Islamic agenda or his hostility to Western imperialism (and Israel). Oil had been discovered in Libya in 1959. It gave a new future to a country that had only a tiny proportion of land suitable for agriculture, a country capable of outflanking its more populous eastern neighbour, Egypt (whose nationals came seeking work). One of Gaddafi's early actions was to nationalize the oil industry. An Anglo-Libyan Treaty of Friendship, signed when Libya became independent in 1953, was formally abrogated in January 1972. The aborted historian turned now to devising schemes of political, social and economic organization which were claimed to have universal significance. This was 'Islamic socialism' Tripoli-style. Gaddafi possessed an eccentric image in the world. This may have been because he was eccentric.

Further west, Algeria too had large oil and natural gas reserves. By the early 1970s the Algerian government had taken a majority holding in all the oil and gas companies. For a time a Franco-Algerian economic war had ensued. The Algerian government went out to the world, without particular regard to ideology, in order to gain the technical know-how it needed to develop its resources. In April 1975, however, patching things up, President Giscard of France paid a state visit. A certain stability in Franco-Algerian relations was achieved. Yet a remaining ambivalence was obvious. Some 7000 French teachers came to Algeria under the 'cultural co-operation' provisions of the Evian agreement which had ended the war. But was this 'co-operation' something which more soothed French anxieties about keeping a 'francophone world' intact rather than something that helped Algeria shape its problematic new identity? Looking at the configuration of Algiers, however, the observer could still see in some of its buildings clear evidence of 'French civilization'. Statues of French conquerors, however, had been replaced by those of Algerian liberators. Many streets had been renamed. The Catholic Cathedral had become a mosque. The striking church of Notre Dame d'Afrique stood in sorrowful neglect. The city's population had roughly doubled over the previous decade and passed the million mark. Approximately half came from an Arabic-speaking background and half from a Berber/Kabyle-speaking background. The French language, however, was still very much present.

Oil's messages: Algiers, 1973

Building on the country's hydrocarbon resources, Boumedienne aimed to make Algeria the industrial hub of the Maghreb and, as a state-directed operation, it made strides, if somewhat unevenly. His wider vision, however, was for Algeria to assume a pivotal role in revitalizing the Non-Aligned Movement. It was in Algiers in September 1973 that more states (75) than ever before attended its conference, including, amongst other newcomers, such admittedly modest states as Bhutan, Oman, Malta and Mauritius. Also attending was Bangladesh, a state but two years old, which had achieved independence after the bloody war which destroyed the Pakistan of 1947. Whether that war could be described as a 'civil war' raised contentious questions. Whether, too, India's role had been that of a non-aligned bystander was also contentious. These matters apart, the conference expressed a general determination, as Boumedienne put it, to show such collective strength that 'they' [the rich countries] would understand that 'we' mean business.

The city of Algiers in November was also where Arab heads of state assembled after the 1973 war. There was a real sense of the Arab world's collective weight. Such rhetoric gained substance from the exercise of the 'oil weapon' in October–November 1973. Some Arab states raised oil prices significantly. Saudi Arabia, having had its request to the USA to stop arms deliveries to Israel disregarded, placed an embargo on oil supplies to America. So too did Libya, Algeria and most of the Gulf States. Cutbacks in overall oil production were also implemented. Recipient states were categorized as 'Hostile', 'Friendly' or 'Neutral' and their supplies were maintained or reduced accordingly. The impact on the Netherlands, for example, placed in the first category, was profound – though Belgium, placed in the second category, could help its neighbour out. Japan made diplomatic noises which enabled it to be listed as 'Friendly' rather than 'Hostile'. In three months, by the end of December 1973, the oil price had quadrupled. The 'oil weapon', however, had not been decisive in the war. It took time for the Arab producers to get their act together, and not all did. Some remained more concerned than others about their own loss of revenue from implementing a boycott. Yet, while granting how difficult it had been to create and maintain a united front, a point had emphatically been made. An Organization of Arab Petroleum Exporting Countries (OAPEC), now with its headquarters in Vienna, had been formed in 1968 by the Arab members of the Organization of Petroleum Exporting Countries (OPEC) formed in Baghdad eight years earlier. By 1973 this 'oil world' consisted of twelve members, only four of which (Venezuela, Nigeria, Ecuador and Indonesia) were outside the Middle East.

After the war crisis which had brought about the increase in oil prices was over, they did not plunge back and Arab and other producers began to see a significant rise in their oil revenues. The 'oil shock' seemed full of contrasting implications for producers and consumers alike. Economic turbulence rippled across the globe. Commentators detected a 'new world order' in which power shifted to the producers. So, in general terms, it did. There was much speculation about where a new equilibrium was to be found, for a market still remained. Additionally, within OPEC members, not to mention producers like Mexico outside its ranks, all had somewhat different perspectives on where the balance was to be struck. A common front would be difficult to sustain. The 'oil world' in its then geographical dispersion was an odd one, not easily aligned with any other. For their part, consuming countries in Europe, like Britain and Norway, which could exploit oil from the North Sea, pressed ahead rapidly in doing so. It was in June 1975 that oil from the North Sea was first pumped ashore in Britain. From the USA to Japan, countries at least looked to ways in which dependence on foreign oil could be reduced: by exploiting hitherto uneconomic 'home' sources, by thinking more seriously about reducing consumption, by developing nuclear programmes or at least by expanding their stored oil reserves significantly so as to have more security in a crisis. What difference all this in fact would make was not clear, but 'the world' now had a different feel about it. At the invitation of the French President, five other 'industrialized' countries – Britain, West Germany, the USA and Japan – met in November 1975 to consider possible common responses to common problems they were now experiencing. It was a kind of counterpoint to OPEC, but it was no more certain than it was with the latter that at the future annual meetings of this 'Group of Seven' (G7) – Canada was added in 1976 – the countries concerned would not still seek particular solutions to their difficulties. It did not escape comment that most of the world was neither in OPEC nor in the G7.

At the close of their conference, the Arab leaders declared that 'the Arab nation' would do its duty and be prepared for further struggle and sacrifice to obtain justice in Palestine. A renewed dispute between Algeria and its neighbour Morocco shortly afterwards, concerning the future of Western Sahara, cast another light on the Arab nation. So did the situation in Lebanon in 1973. Over its forty years as an independent state, its constitutional checks and balances to comprehend its complex blends of different Christianities and different forms of Islam had always been precarious. Beirut, for all its sophistication, was nevertheless a communal city. It was the arrival of a fresh tranche of Palestinians, driven out of Jordan, which caused its internal balance to snap. Congregated in camps, critics complained that Palestinians were once more constituting themselves a state within a state. Palestinian attacks across into Israel brought Israeli reprisals into Lebanon. A right-wing Christian militia, the Phalangists, attacked the Palestinian camps in April 1975 and inflicted heavy losses. Palestinians, in turn, received support from left-wing Muslim groups. It looked as though a 'civil war' was beginning. Such conflicts, present or emerging, put 'the Arab nation' in a different light.

The Shah's Iran: crowning achievement?

Oil brought Iran into the 'Mediterranean/Arab' political world which has been discussed in previous sections, though at a tangent. The power of Iran caused apprehension in that world, particularly, for obvious reasons, in the Gulf. The Shah of Iran 'as a colleague' took a leading role in pushing for the oil price rise, but he had his own reasons. His ambition was growing. In 1971 he had ruled for thirty years (he had taken the trouble in 1967 formally to crown himself) and had suitable arrangements in hand to mark that fact. By his good fortune his anniversary coincided with the 2500th anniversary of the Persian Empire. An expensive celebration was held in a specially created tent city amongst the desert ruins of Persepolis. Peacocks, the national symbol, were everywhere, on coins specially minted in France or, in dead reality, on the dinner plates of guests. The Shah was pleased to present himself as the successor, if not the descendant, of Cyrus the Great. Haile Selassie, a fixture at global celebratory gatherings, impe-rially outshone the other sixty heads of state present. The extravagant affair was simultaneously designed to demonstrate Iran's antiquity and modernity. One day the Shah was bowing before the mausoleum of Cyrus, the next he was greeting his guests at Shiraz Airport. 'Modernity' showed itself in a programme of land and educational reform, one bulldozed through in the face of religious opposition. It was made illegal for women to wear the veil. The Shah's addiction to supermarkets, though not as a customer, upset traditional traders. He had means of enforcing his view of modernity. Conciliation and incorporation were foreign to his way of proceeding. In the city of Qom, and then, from 1964 in exile in Iraq, following in a family tradition as an ayatollah, Ruhollah Khomeini poured out of a stream of work integrating Islamic philosophy, law and ethics, all from a Shi'ite perspective. He denounced the monarchist mythology of Persepolis and other indications of an attempt to curtail Islam (such as the imposition of a new calendar dating from Cyrus the Great rather than from Mohammad's *hijra)*. Naturally, he condemned what he saw as the Shah's subservience to the USA.

The relationship between the USA and Iran was indeed close. The former was content in the early 1970s to see Iran as the guardian of the Persian Gulf. The Shah, however, now did not see himself as a mere local adjunct of the USA. Iraq, and the rulers of the new states on its southern shore, bereft from 1971 of a British presence, thought the Gulf Arabian. They were less appreciative of Iranian guardianship, as was King Feisal in Riyadh (King Saud had finally been deposed in 1964). Statements were issued from Tehran which let it be known that Iran was on course to become one of the five great powers in the world. Tank manufacturers in the USA and Britain were kept very busy by the Shah's requirements. His visits to Germany, India, the USA and elsewhere – accompanied by a wife who was certainly not veiled – presented him as a significant world figure. Domestically, however, there was in reality no consensus about where Iran 'belonged' in the world. Hubris would have its nemesis. A new twist in the relationship between Iran and the Arab world and between Shi'a and Sunni lay not far ahead.

17
Africa's Worlds

Part of the message Boumedienne delivered from Algeria was that 'Africa' should assert itself. It was time, he said, to escape from a world which had been dominated by an East–West framework. Speaking in the UN in 1974 he spoke of millions of men leaving 'the Southern hemisphere' to go to 'the Northern hemisphere'. They would go, he said, not as friends but to conquer it. They would conquer it with their sons. The wombs of our women would bring victory. It was not a speech which was well received in the 'Northern hemisphere'. Yet, despite this belligerence, North African states, whose populations were increasingly concentrated in their Mediterranean littoral cities, dubiously spoke for sub-Saharan Africa which lay at their frontiers. Africa in reality itself had its own distinct spheres. It was difficult to know where Africa began and who spoke for it. Most African states, settling down to their first decade or so of independence, still heavily carried the imprint of their particular former colonial rulers.

Claiming identity: francophone *authenticité*

The anglophone and francophone African worlds were still very self-contained, though within each the same problems of 'unity' were encountered. In Chad, François Tombolboye (b.1914), its first President, a former teacher/trade-union activist from the south of the country, had been challenged repeatedly since the mid-1960s by the northern Front de Libération Nationale du Tchad [National Liberation Front of Chad] (FROLINAT). Direct military help to buttress his position had come from French paratroopers. In the early 1970s, however, Tombolboye changed tack, announcing a commitment to *authenticité*, that is to say, Africanization. To the north, the Libyan regime had its own perspective on what that meant. He himself took a new first name, Ngara. He also gave his capital, rapidly expanding in population, a new name – Ndjamena – displacing the name Fort Lamy given by the French to the small town they had originally occupied. Even so, in the university which opened in 1971 the language of instruction was French – another later one operated through Arabic. He imposed an initiation rite, though it was a very particular one to his own Sara people. His form of Africanization was not universally welcomed. In 1975 he was assassinated.

Chad's circumstances and its precise evolution to that date naturally constitute a particular history. Nevertheless, the task of balancing different regions, languages and peoples was common to all its neighbours, often compounded by poverty and internal migration. The cry for *authenticité*, in these circumstances, could not be other than complex. It was a word which fitted into a particular kind of French discourse, even if its objective was to revisit a 'real past' which was pre-colonial. By no means all writers or politicians thought in terms of 'rejection'. Many of the 'old guard' in power in this decade had received an education at the William Ponty School in Dakar. 'Frenchness' was part of their being. Modibo Keita of Mali had served for a time in the National Assembly in Paris. French governments did not much like his political orientation in office. Political arguments were still framed in French concepts. In Senegal itself, Senghor, who remained in office in what was at this juncture essentially a one-party state, continued to elaborate on this French–African world in elegant style. Dakar hosted the first world congress of black arts and culture – and it also serviced the French navy: a perfect symbiosis? For Houphouet-Boigny in the Ivory Coast, co-operation with France remained central. The country experienced economic success, largely through the expansion of cocoa and coffee production. Immigrants poured in from neighbouring states. He maintained a tight grip on power, stamping on any hint of internal secession and seeking to destabilize neighbouring uncongenial regimes, whether in Guinea or Dahomey. He dreamt of building a very big church. In Guinea, Touré survived, with increasing resort to imprisoning his opponents in notorious camps, but by the 1970s some of his revolutionary ardour had abated. He too began seeking a rapprochement with France.

Impatient both with elevated language and elevated buildings, critics, within and without, characterized the scene in large parts of former French West and Central Africa as being 'neo-colonial'. Notwithstanding 'independence', French advisers and businessmen were still present, sometimes within ministries. So, in a number of countries, were French troops, at the ready. Intervention in a crisis was by no means confined to Chad. While their involvement was by invitation, there were ways of inviting invitations. It was not so much 'independence', critics said, as 'dependency'. Even the fanfare which accompanied the two 'Accords' concluded at Yaoundé in 1963 and 1969, which financed infrastructure and agricultural projects in sub-Saharan Africa, could not disguise the reciprocal benefits which the European providers, France in particular, gained from the accompanying preferential trade arrangements. 'Fraternity' of a kind might be in evidence, but French embraces were not always brotherly.

'Liberty' and 'equality', however, did not seem greatly in evidence in the evolving political world. Younger military men were conspicuously moving out of their barracks in this part of the world, too. It was a young soldier, Moussa Traoré, product of a French military academy, who ousted Keita in Mali in 1968. Two years earlier, Jean-Bédel Bokassa embarked on a tyranny which might, at times, be taken for a farce. He had joined the French army at 18 in 1939 and was awarded both the Légion d'Honneur and the Croix de Guerre. He was the Central African Republic's army Chief of Staff on the country's independence in 1960. He mounted a successful coup in 1966. Here was another sparsely populated, ethnically diverse and land-locked country coming under bizarre control. Not content with making himself a marshal, he entertained imperial ambitions and, in title, was to realize them a decade later. In 1974, a military coup in Niger overthrew the single-party civilian rule which Hamani Dion had maintained since independence. These and comparable takeovers, evanescent or enduring, now seemed endemic. That was the way the world went.

Claiming identity: anglophone authenticity

The anglophone West African world was turning out not to be so very different. In 1962, a Ghanaian exile published his thoughts on *The Challenge of Africa*. Kofia Busia was spending time in an academic environment in Oxford and in the Netherlands. He had earlier written an Oxford thesis, published in 1951, on the position of the chief in the modern political system of the Ashanti – he himself came from a royal line. His Christianity had been formed by transplanted English Methodism. He had been one of the first Africans to enter the colonial administration in the Gold Coast, but had seen no future in that capacity. A sociologist, he became the first African professor at its university. No Ghanaian had reflected more on his country's post-independence life. After the three years of military rule following the deposition of Nkrumah in 1966, Busia became Prime Minister in a civilian administration. The economic problems he faced were daunting but the measures he took, which included a drastic devaluation, did not help much. Neither his intelligence nor his integrity was in question, but his suitability was doubtful. In 1972, while away in London, he was ousted by an army committee calling itself the National Redemption Council. Its chairman was another colonel, Ignatius Acheapong. Given the global economic picture, a swift economic transformation was unlikely. The Council believed that the country needed 'redemption'. One of its slogans was that Ghana should 'Keep Right' – a reference, not to politics, but to the abandonment of the absurd British habit of driving on the left. Busia was not really a politician and within a few years he was dead. His writing, illustrated in a sense by his life, wrestled with 'authenticity'. Colonial rule had brought both mental enslavement and liberation. Its impact, both for good and ill, could not simply be erased from the contemporary memory. He himself was as much at home in Oxford as in Accra. Now in the post-colonial world, how his society should function and what kind of democracy it could achieve constituted *The Challenge of Africa*. In fact, there were many 'challenges' and also many 'Africas'.

In January 1967 the then Ghanaian ruler, General Ankrah, had hosted a conference in Ghana to try to resolve the crisis in Nigeria and, initially, he seemed to have had some success. Since the first military coup there a year earlier, which had seen the murder of the then federal and northern prime ministers, Sir Abubakr Balewa, the Sardauna of Sokoto and others, a succession of military leaders had briefly held sway. The latest was Colonel Yakubu Gowon, a northern Christian. There were noises about a return to civilian rule. It was agreed, once again, to revisit the federal structure. Tension still centred on the fate of the Igbo people. Perceived, when outside their home Eastern Region, to be dominating, they themselves feared massacre. Odumegwu Ojukwu (b.1933), an Igbo, but born in the North, had been appointed military governor of the

Eastern Region in early 1966. He concluded that the Igbo people would only gain security by seceding from Nigeria and forming their own state. His father was a very wealthy businessman who had been knighted by the British. The young man had been sent to England to school and university (he had a history degree from Oxford). Later, back home, he joined the army and received rapid promotion. At the Ghana conference he appeared to moderate his wish to secede from Nigeria but in May, claiming endorsement by the Regional Assembly, he declared 'Biafra' an independent state.

The stakes were high. Looking at other states in West Africa, it could scarcely be claimed that a 'Biafra' was not viable. Yet if it did successfully secede, it would be likely to trigger other secessions and lead to the complete disintegration not only of 'Nigeria', but constitute an example followed elsewhere. Gowon undertook a major expansion of the Federal Army and a bitter civil war ensued. The participants resisted attempts by the Organization of African Unity (OAU) and others to mediate. A considerable propaganda war was waged. The British government came down firmly on the federal side and supplied it with arms (as did the Soviet Union). Ojukwu was disgusted. He received arms supplies from France and, as conditions deteriorated, other aid from Catholic charities worldwide. It was in the Ivory Coast, which had recognized Biafra, that Ojukwu found refuge when Biafran resistance ended in January 1970. Other West African states, very aware of their own multi-ethnicity, were content to watch and wait.

The outcome was an endorsement of the territorial integrity of states. Yet it still left Nigeria itself in a precarious condition, unfit for the moment for any 'world role' on behalf of 'Africa'. The Ivorian recognition of 'Biafra' was only one of a number of signs that French-speaking states were hostile to Nigerian 'hegemony'. Such sentiments made it difficult to develop 'West Africa' as a 'world site'. However, in May 1975, fifteen West African states created the Economic Community for West African States. In February, under the provisions of the Lomé Convention concluded between the EEC and a new bloc composed of former European colonies in Africa, the Caribbean and the Pacific, African countries gained a better trade deal than they had had under the Yaoundé Accords. A planned commodity stabilization fund looked likely to be especially beneficial. Even so, critics opposed the entrenchment of an outdated 'Euro-Africa' world view, one in which Africa was the weaker partner. Nigeria did indeed have 'leadership' potential. Its oil resources gave the state exceptional opportunities. They also, however, gave individuals exceptional opportunities – for corruption. Oil, as elsewhere, might be a domestic bane as much as a blessing. There were many other problems. The war bequeathed a swollen army and continuing debate about the appropriate federal–state balance. Gowon increased the number of states but population balance, ethnic or linguistic composition, and communication links rarely coincided. Census figures were always controversial. Gowon remained in control, so far as control was possible. Military rule, perhaps indefinitely, was the order of the day. So it was in Sierra Leone after coups in 1967 and 1968.

The result, by 1975, was that all four 'British West African' territories had departed, more or less substantially, from their forms of government at the moment of independence. Their dispersed locations and different sizes meant they scarcely constituted a 'bloc'. They had individual rather than collective points of contact with 'London'. Yet even the continued currency of the English language in Nigeria did not necessarily perpetuate a British–Nigerian axis (though a steady trickle of Nigerians began to emigrate to England). Commentators pointed to what they called the Americanization of Nigerian life. If, culturally and commercially, that was indeed happening, it was perhaps strange, simultaneously, to observe in Liberia the weakening hold on power of its tiny percentage of 'Americo-Liberians' in that exotic creation of an earlier world, as it now increasingly seemed. W.R. Tolbert, grandson of a freed slave from Charleston, took over as president in 1971. He had taken the trouble to learn one of the many indigenous languages of his country but its 'Africans' were unlikely to tolerate the dominance of the 'American clans' for much longer. A comparable issue existed in next-door Sierra Leone, where the original 'Colony' and the hinterland 'Protectorate' had been joined.

Rhodesia: unilateral pilot

In January 1966 the Commonwealth of Nations held a special conference in Lagos. It was the first time that it had assembled outside the UK. That in itself was symbolic. It assembled in Nigeria because an African problem was before it. In November 1965, Ian Smith, the Prime Minister of Rhodesia, declared independence 'unilaterally' for his country. Smith himself, Rhodesian-born to parents who had emigrated from Britain, had 'come back' to fly as a fighter pilot with the Royal Air Force during the Second World War before 'returning home'. Twenty years on, he had not changed, but the world had. His government, elected by the white minority – 5.5 per cent of the population, its maximum, in 1970 – would go its own way, whatever those who now piloted Britain thought. Britain refused to recognize the state and imposed trade restrictions and an oil embargo. African Commonwealth members wanted Britain to go further and put their points strongly in Lagos. Prime Minister Wilson ruled out the use of force and claimed that sanctions would be speedily effective, but there was no quick outcome. Talks with Smith, directly and through intermediaries, got nowhere. Years passed.

In March 1970 Rhodesia declared itself a republic and was still in existence five years later. It was now engaged, however, in a war with two guerrilla forces – the Zimbabwe People's Revolutionary Army (ZIPRA), the military wing of Joshua Nkomo's (b.1917) ZAPU (Zimbabwe African People's Union), latterly based in Zambia, and Robert Mugabe's (b.1924) Zimbabwe National Liberation Army (ZANLA), the military wing of the Zimbabwe African National Union (ZANU), latterly based in Mozambique. Their respective strengths were to be found amongst the Ndebele and Shona peoples, but rivalry between these two men was as much personal as ethnic. Schooled in a Marist college and a faithful Catholic, or so it appeared, Mugabe's African world was much more varied and extensive than Nkomo's. It was the period he spent in Ghana which made the greatest impact on his thinking. Nkrumah became a hero. In the decade after 1964, however, both Nkomo and Mugabe spent most of their time in Rhodesian prisons. The Rhodesian endgame had not yet been reached.

Commonwealth African states thought that Britain, under successive governments, had failed to take 'Rhodesia' sufficiently seriously. The issue awkwardly impacted on British opinion. It disclosed how much the world was changing and rendered policy incoherent. There was little support for direct British military intervention to bring down the government in Salisbury (Harare). There was some, but not a great deal of, support for 'minority white rule'. On the other hand, based on what appeared to be happening elsewhere in Africa, cynicism was developing about 'black majority rule' and the fate of constitutionally entrenched rights. The Rhodesian Royal Air Force pilot who had flown bravely for Britain in defence of 'civilized values', some of his generation felt, was being abandoned. A younger generation felt little sympathy. The failure of the UK government either to bring down the Smith regime or, as yet, force it to accept defeat at the negotiating table, continued to rankle with African members of the Commonwealth into the early 1970s. It placed the association itself under further scrutiny. It now had its own Secretariat in London and a Canadian diplomat was its first Secretary-General. He busily visited Commonwealth capitals. The curious could consult a *Handbook of Commonwealth Organizations*, published in 1965, which listed over two hundred bodies designed, in a wide variety of fields, to promote professional contact and personal friendship across the Commonwealth world. In Britain, however, any lingering notion that the Commonwealth was a body which would reflect the British perspective on the world was rapidly disappearing, if it had not already gone. The incoming Conservative government, with its 'European' trajectory, resented the extent to which, as it saw it, it was being hectored by African states. Another Commonwealth conference, this time in Ottawa in 1973, saw the British government reiterating that Rhodesia remained its responsibility and it would do what it saw fit. Talk of the Commonwealth breaking up, which surfaced from time to time, faded away, but there was a sharper realization in its many capitals that it had no 'world policy'.

Portugal in Africa: first in, last out

'Rhodesia' brought one 'Euro-African' history into focus; Angola and Mozambique brought another. Marcello Caetano (b.1906) became Prime Minister of Portugal in 1968. He had been a firm supporter of the 'New State' which Portugal had allegedly been for forty years. While there might be change at the margins, he would maintain an authoritarian stance. His publications on administrative law gave him academic distinction. It was, however, practical administrative and political problems which confronted him. Portugal had, in Angola and Mozambique, two territories which since the early 1950s it had designated 'Overseas Provinces'. That made them different, it contended, from colonies of other European powers which were en route for 'independence'. Until his death, Salazar was certain that his country's African mission was a civilizing one. Post-1945 Portugal had remained outside a consolidating 'Western Europe'. It struggled economically. Its empire gave its rulers reassurance that the country was not just backward and marginal. Emigration to Portugal 'overseas' offered some prospects for impoverished sections of the population. Unlike the British or the French in Africa, Portugal had controlled its African territories for centuries, though rather in fits and starts (and admittedly more tightly on the coast than in the interior).

Mozambique constituted a conduit through which vital supplies, notwithstanding the British naval blockade, reached neighbouring Rhodesia. The Smith regime needed an understanding with the Portuguese authorities in Lourenço Marques. They, in turn, were dealing with FRELIMO, the just-launched guerrilla movement which sought independence. Young men, often educated in Portuguese in Catholic mission schools, now enrolled under a banner which at least purported to be Marxist. A gulf separated the Portuguese-speaking world of a nurse like Samora Machel (b.1933), FRELIMO's leader, from that of Professor Caetano. Machel did not visit Portugal and Caetano did not know his 'overseas provinces' at first hand. It seemed at first, in the later 1960s, that Portuguese forces could contain the insurrection masterminded by Machel and his disputatious comrades. Hostility towards the enemy was more apparent than unity amongst the oppressed. It was again a situation in which forces which controlled the towns did not control the countryside, and vice versa. Conflict might go on for a long time. The same fundamentals also existed in Angola, although here, from the outset, there was an explicitly four-way struggle. The largest movements, the Movimento Popular de Libertação de Angola [People's Movement for the Liberation of Angola] (MPLA), the União Nacional para a Independência Total de Angola [National Union for the Total Independence of Angola] (UNITA) and the Frente Nacional para a Libertação de Angola [National Front for the Liberation of Angola[(FNLA), were already as much jockeying for position between themselves as seeking to defeat the Portuguese army. That in turn reflected the fact that they all had their external backers with wider objectives than simply Angolan. Agostinho Neto, the MPLA leader, who had spent many years in Portugal as a medical student (and as prison inmate) looked towards the Soviet Union (and Cuba). Liberation and 'modernization' would go hand in hand. Cuba was an attractive model. The other two, Jonas Savimbi and Roberto Holden, were somewhat unpredictable ideologically, but normally 'Western'. Savimbi, who had earlier spent time in Portugal, Switzerland and elsewhere, prided himself on his mastery of languages – European and African. That made him, he thought, a world figure. Ideological positioning ran alongside personal ambition and regional allegiances in the success or failure of their movements. Whatever course they eventually followed, Protestant missions or parentage played a significant part in these men's early development. It left them with little enthusiasm for 'Catholic Portugal'.

At various points in the past, Portugal had dreamt of linking Angola and Mozambique in a single Portuguese Central Africa extending from coast to coast, but its dreams had never become reality. The Portuguese army found itself engaged in two protracted conflicts, not to mention those being fought in Portuguese Guinea. It was neither losing nor winning, but the experience for the troops was dismal. Their discontent, from top to bottom, grew. The government in Lisbon, for its part, was worried that too large share of its budget was being allocated to military spending. Something had to give. An 'Armed Forces Movement' went beyond the complaints of Generals Spinola and Gomes and staged a successful military coup in 1974. It set up a ruling junta, with Spinola as the initial President, but its thrust was clearly to the left. Socialist and Communist exiles came back to the country. The 'New State' of 1928 was clearly dead but in 1975 it was far from clear what was going to replace it. What was true in Portugal was true in its erstwhile 'overseas' world. Old certainties, European and African, were dissolving together. The European uncertainty was further compounded by the return 'home', fleeing or ejected and to no very eager welcome, of many thousands of Portuguese from Africa. Guinea-Bissau, already substantially 'lost', became independent in 1974 and federated immediately with Cape Verde. Angola (with Neto as president) and Mozambique (with Machel as president) both became independent in 1975, but independence was followed, immediately and later, respectively, by 'wars of succession' rather than peaceful evolution.

South Africa: disturbing the peace

South African governments had inevitably watched this evolving African world with alarm. Ever since the Sharpeville massacre of 1960, their internal policies had been under sustained attack. The UN, with its increased African membership, was the forum for regular criticism. Attempts had been made, under Article 39 of the Charter, to identify South Africa as a threat to international peace, but as yet they had not succeeded. The USA and the UK were only prepared to see it as 'disturbing the peace'. The 'world' would not leave South Africa alone. The possibility of 'sanctions' at some stage could not be discounted. The feasibility and utility, and at what cost, of trying to change the South African government by such means was being argued over in private and public. The 'world' as South African governments had perceived it in the first two post-war decades was changing rapidly. As a bulwark against the advance of Communism, its diplomatic leverage was waning. Quite suddenly, the white government in South Africa looked as much 'out of place' in the 'new Africa' as Israel looked 'out of place' in the Middle East: indeed the two countries, in their common pariah status, sought mutual comfort.

The Rhodesian Unilateral Declaration of Independence (UDI), however, came at a time when the South African economy was bouncing back. South African government circles sensed a strengthening of their position. The bans on the African National Congress and the Pan-African Congress remained in place. The prison on Robben Island, off Cape Town, retained its inmates. In a continent of instability, South Africa even seemed a stable place in which to invest. The National Party, under Hendrik Verwoerd, won the 1966 election handsomely. The architect of apartheid was determined to press forward with schemes to develop 'Bantustans'. Some legislation was already in place. In September, however, Verwoerd was assassinated. His successor was Johannes (known as John to English speakers) Vorster, the Minister of Justice (b.1915). A graduate of that nursery of South African prime ministers, the Afrikaner University of Stellenbosch, he was to remain in office for twelve critical years. His past overhung him and complicated the formation of a coherent 'South

African world-view'. His vehement youthful opposition to South African involvement in 'world war' in 1939 and his membership of the Afrikaner *Ossewabrandwag* (the pro-German organization in the Second World War) had dubbed him 'pro-Nazi'. The 'English-Speaking World' held no attraction for him and a republic outside the Commonwealth would suit him well. London was in no sense 'home'. The Afrikaners were not 'Dutch overseas'. They had made their own language and civilization in Africa. All of this was frequently rehearsed. In fact, however, as was seen in the election battles of 1970 and 1974, there was bitter division within the Afrikaner *Volk*. One side, mindful of 'the world', sought some modest changes without endangering 'separate development' as a whole. Their opponents disagreed – in relation to mixed sport, for example. Unlike his predecessor, however, Vorster was not an ideologue. He simply wanted to come out on top. 'Homeland' development had been set on its complex course, and he would not stop it. As time passed, however, implementation proved ever more difficult. He could not altogether disguise from himself that there was something wrong with the plan.

The central external issue was whether South Africa's sphere stopped at its borders or extended beyond. That problem took several forms. The country had administered the former German South-West Africa under a mandate from the League of Nations since 1920. It was a measure of the changed world that its successor, the UN, was under pressure, over a long period, to revoke that trusteeship. In 1966 the South West African People's Organization (SWAPO) began fighting South African units. In 1970 the Security Council declared that South Africa's occupation of what was now referred to as Namibia was illegal. The following year the UN recognized SWAPO as 'the sole authentic representative of the people of Namibia'. Should South Africa simply give up a territory which was not 'integral' or should it fight on, in hot pursuit, if necessary into Angola where SWAPO had bases? And, if in Angola, how deeply to become involved in getting the outcome it wanted? Namibia was a special case, but the issue it raised applied to all South Africa's frontiers. South African forces were well-equipped but even they could be overextended. Rhodesia itself was a case in point. What bearing did its fate have on South Africa's own? Initially, South Africa was not going to let the Smith regime go under, though it did not extend formal diplomatic recognition to it. As time passed, however, Smith was being urged to explore an 'internal solution'. Whether South Africa was weakened or strengthened by maintaining a 'perimeter fence' was a matter of perpetual debate – as was whether it should seek to cajole or coerce its neighbours into some kind of co-operation. Dr Banda in Malawi, for example, received both sticks and carrots. Might the government even succeed in persuading distant African countries, say the Ivory Coast, to adopt a somewhat more sympathetic stance? There was no agreed or simple answer to the definition of a South African world.

Central/East/North-East Africa: disputing neighbourhoods

All the countries to the north and west of Rhodesia/Mozambique – Swaziland, Zambia, Malawi, Tanzania – were independent and all belonged to the Commonwealth of Nations. The neighbouring conflict hung over their politics and drew in their governments. External would-be liberators sought support, sustenance and safe havens ahead of the final overthrow of colonialism. Their commitment to 'liberation' ran alongside refashioning their domestic economies to assert indigenous control. It was essentially the same revolution. National Development Plans were the order of the day. The Zambian government, for example, in stages, steadily extended its control over copper mining. That industry was so central to the economy and the overwhelming source of the country's export earnings. Such dependence, however, as the world crisis of 1973–75 demonstrated, left the country exposed. Copper prices halved. It took Kaunda only a few years after independence to decide that the country needed only one political party, his own. Zambia would be a one-party state, though a 'participatory' one, and only he could guide it effectively. Somehow, Zambia had to set out its stall in the world. It could not be, and should not be, a mere site of transplanted 'Western capitalism' or 'Eastern Communism'. It had to absorb, synthesize and then strike out on its own. Basic African values were communal. Christianity, rightly understood, reinforced rather than countered them. 'Zambian Humanism' emerged with presidential endorsement. Julius Nyerere, to Kaunda's north, although his country's economy was rather different, spoke and wrote on similar lines. A 'Declaration' emerged in the town of Arusha which set out a vision of an 'African Socialism', suffused, he supposed, with traditional values. Both men began life as teachers and their didactic impulses remained powerful. Only King Sobhuza II of Swaziland, independent since 1968, felt able in 1973 to dispense with the 'constitutional' aspect of his monarchy without issuing an explanatory tract for the times. In Malawi, Hastings Banda inexorably concentrated more power in his own hands. So, further north, in Kenya, did Jomo Kenyatta. Successive constitutional changes enhanced his formal powers, and in presidential elections he was unopposed. Entering the 1970s, Kenya became effectively a one-party state, one in which Kenyatta's own Kikuyu people dominated its apparatus. The Treaty of East African Co-operation, which Uganda, Kenya and Tanzania had signed in 1968, never amounted to anything substantial. The 'big men' in Kenya had a greater appetite for a buccaneering capitalism than for expositions of 'African socialism'.

In 'ex-British East Africa', however, unlike in West Africa, the military had not seized power though, shortly after independence, the Kenyan and Tanzanian governments had reluctantly called in British forces to deal with unrest in their armies. Only in Uganda, in 1971, did the army commander, Idi Amin Dada, overthrow the one-party regime which Milton Obote had consolidated since independence. It seemed to be for Islamic reasons that he targeted the Christian majority, both Anglican and Catholic. An Anglican archbishop, a vice-chancellor and judges were amongst the many thousands – somewhere between 100,000 and 300,000 – to be murdered or who fled into exile over the immediately coming years. His fellow general, Joseph Mobutu, since 1965, had been imposing order, with some success, although not gently, over the sprawling territory of neighbouring Congo. The country was being given an explicitly Africanized 'national unity' – symbolized in the adoption of a new name – Zaire – and new first names for its president.

In North-East Africa, Mohamed Siad Barre (b.1919), who had seized power in Somalia in 1969, was likewise preoccupied with identity – creating a new orthography for the language, advancing its use, and reducing that of English or Italian. He tried trying to weld 'clans' into a nation. The future of the Ogaden region, largely inhabited by Somalis, but within Ethiopia, was a running sore. Eritrea remained another problematic issue in the Horn of Africa. Barre concluded an agreement with the Soviet Union in July 1974 which granted Moscow naval facilities at the Gulf of Aden port of Berbera in exchange for a Soviet commitment to train and equip the Somali army. Public banners, picturing Barre alongside Marx and Lenin, unexpected comrades for a man who had been trained by the national military police force of Italy, made a world statement. In September, however, Mengistu Haile Mariam, another colonel, toppled Haile Selassie in Ethiopia and also proceeded to inaugurate an avowedly 'Marxist–Leninist' regime. Moscow was confused. The stage was set for a reversal of alignments.

African Unity: aspiration and reality

Given the immediate local violence, there was some irony in the fact that the headquarters of the Organization of African Unity (OAU) remained in Addis Ababa. The gulf between aspiration and the picture in various locations which has just been sketched could scarcely have been greater. Ethiopia itself was in turmoil. The OAU meeting in May 1973 was the last held when Haile Selassie was still on the throne. The mood in the city, however, was very different from what it had been ten years earlier. Ethiopia was afflicted by drought and famine and perhaps on the point of collapse. Its crisis, however, was but part of a continental crisis in which public debt quadrupled between 1970 and 1976. There was now a hollow ring to the founding rhetoric of a decade earlier. The conference issued a call for a New International Economic Order which would bring about a massive increase in development assistance, and the cancellation of outstanding foreign debts. 'North/South' issues, which will be elaborated in the next part of the book, came to the fore. Global economic resources, it said, should be allocated on the basis of need. The Non-Aligned Conference, referred to in the last chapter, meeting in Algiers, endorsed this proposal, as did the General Assembly of the UN in the following year. These initiatives were framed in the context of the oil crisis – but that very fact also made unlikely the massive reallocation that was looked for. Increased availability of aid, however, might only lead to increased corruption. In country after country, 'civil society' had been marginalized or destroyed by centralized power, normally military power. Assassination had become almost the normal means of transferring power. Individual holders of such power, in many cases, evidently could not distinguish between private and state wealth. A vicious circle had developed, with no clear solution in sight: poverty produced instability; instability sealed poverty. Even those in the world beyond Africa who took a more optimistic view were dispirited by the fact that the next African Unity summit, in the summer of 1975, was to be held in Kampala, Uganda, under the less than genial presidency of Idi Amin. The decade that had passed had indeed brought 'Africa' onto the world stage but the scale of its internal problems seemed to make the possibility of a 'continental voice' a distant one.

Part 4 further reading

Addison, Paul, *No Turning Back: The Peaceful Revolutions of Post-War Britain* (Oxford University Press, Oxford, 2010).

Babb, James, *Tanaka* (Pearson Education, London, 2000).

Balfour-Paul, Glen, *The End of Empire in the Middle East: Britain's Relinquishment of Power in Her Last Three Arab Dependencies* (Cambridge University Press, Cambridge, 1991).

Clogg, Richard, *A Concise History of Greece* (Cambridge University Press, Cambridge, 2002).

Dockrill, Saki, *Britain's Retreat from East of Suez: The Choice between Europe and the World?* (Palgrave Macmillan, Basingstoke, 2002).

Heimann, Mary, *Czechoslovakia: The State that Failed* (Yale University Press, London and New Haven, CT, 2009).

Iriye, A. ed., *The Chinese and the Japanese* (Princeton University Press, Princeton, NJ, 1980).

MacMillan, Margaret, *Seize the Hour: Nixon in China* (John Murray, London, 2006).

Pappe, I., *The Israel–Palestine Question* (Routledge, London, 2006).

Venn, Fiona, *The Oil Crisis* (Pearson Education, London, 2002).

Welsh, David and Spence, J.E., *Ending Apartheid* (Pearson Education, London, 2011).

Wasserstrom, Jeffrey N., *Global Shanghai, 1850–2010* (Routledge, London, 2009).

Zürcher, Erik, *Turkey, A Modern History* (I.B. Tauris, London, 2004).

Part 5
1975–1989/91: COMING TO CONCLUSIONS

This part of the book ends as the world wobbles towards the end of that Cold War/Cold Peace which had been its condition, with fluctuating intensity, since 1945. Its formal conclusion, and the ensuing consequences, are considered in the final part. The world 'wobbles' is not a mistake. The chapters in this part do not describe an easily discerned process over more than a decade leading to an apparently predictable termination. The shift in relationships which culminated in a 'turning point' depended on many interacting factors. And, just as the Cold War had different practical meanings and impacts in different parts of the world, so the pace and nature of change varied. Particular causes of conflict which had been tied in, tightly or loosely, to global confrontation did not lose their independent origin and often continuing vitality. 'Events' changed the politics of individual countries or continents. In 1975, for example, in India, Indira Gandhi arrested opposition leaders, the president of Bangladesh was murdered, King Faisal of Saudi Arabia was assassinated, a brigadier replaced a general in charge of Nigeria, and an attempt was made on the life of Gerald Ford, president of the USA. That list of 'happenings' is by no means complete. No part of the world escaped examples of political violence against individuals, insurgencies against existing governments or continuing or fresh inter- or intra-state violence. Even the UK and Iceland began a modest 'Cod War'.

What was true in 1975 remained true, with a different cast of characters and happenings, over subsequent years covered by this part of the book. There was no ubiquitous global outpouring of benevolence fuelling an ardent desire for peace and reconciliation. Matters that had been contentious did not disappear before an advancing amity, whether between Israel and all its neighbours or between India and Pakistan, to take but two topics which reappear, with their customary regularity, in these chapters. New problems, too, loom large.

Independence from Portugal for Mozambique and Angola provided further confirmation of the 'End of Empire'. End of European Empire, however, did not mean the end of conflict. New rulers of new states put down riots, rebellions and resistance with as much severity as the departed rulers. The virtually completed creation of a world of states, probably nation-states, badged, flagged and labelled as such, likewise did not mean that disputes about territory and

Map 8 Europe's communities, 2012

sovereignty would become a thing of the past. Even as the Cape Verde Islands joined the throng of states, the frailty of this notion was evident. A more cynical analysis suggested that no empire ever quite ended and no 'independence' was ever fully achieved. Continent after continent continued to experience bewildering sequences of integration and disintegration as tensions between communities rose and fell. Political order in post-imperial Africa was still uncertain. No one could predict what would happen in South Africa. At another level, if there were signs of a diminution in the classical routines of confrontation between the Free World and the Communist World, they might be being replaced by another overarching encounter – between 'North' and 'South'. Release from a world in which 'the West' stood over against 'the East' might only usher in a different set of priorities and assumptions. They might prove as difficult for the world to handle.

Different chapters, therefore, will continue to give attention to these locally generated developments. It is only right, however, to begin with the 'heartland' of 'Europe' where fixed worlds, if perhaps sometimes less tense ones, still faced each other and division remained explicit. The Soviet Union and the USA secured the status quo. It was what was happening there on which much world attention came to focus a decade after 1975. The change that was taking place, unpredictable though the outcome might still be, would ripple out elsewhere. As global analysts assembled in 1975, however, the notion would have seemed strange that at the heart of developments in the mid-1980s was a man who was then the Communist Party First Secretary of Stavropol, in the North Caucasus.

18

Europeans: Identifying a Common Home?

Gorbachev: peripheral figure to core player

'Europe is our common home' was Mikhail's Gorbachev's startling assertion in Paris in February 1986. A 'European common home', however, one in which, at its extremities, Dublin and Stavropol all had a place, and knew their place, looked an excessively ambitious notion. If taken seriously, it would be a major shift in perception, both in Europe's capitals and elsewhere. There were, however, not many grounds for taking it too seriously, at least not yet. The self-identification of Europeans with 'Europe' remained uncertain in a continent still teeming with national sensitivities, sometimes trivial, sometimes profound. This chapter brings out the many forms of 'Europe' on display. The 'common home', as it presently existed, still had many diverse rooms. Straying between them for different purposes, whether economic, military, cultural or political, could be hazardous. Shared accommodation sometimes came at an unacceptable price when national preconceptions and interests were at stake. When they looked at 'Europe' on the map, non-Europeans were inclined to give 'Europe' a greater coherence than 'Europeans' themselves did. They might in the future have a 'common home', but in the early 1980s the conflicting ideological standpoints of governments, in London and Paris in particular, made a coherent 'world-view' impossible. Whether, when and how the Soviet Union might 'fit' was another matter.

Stavropol, where Gorbachev was Party Secretary, with its mixed population of Russians (predominant), Armenians, Tatars and other ethnic groups, seemed far away from 'Europe'. His primary task was to bring home the harvest. The Soviet Union was suffering a grain shortage. He was on home ground, having been born into a peasant household in this very region. He knew about milk production. The world war had come to his district. For his generation, as he later put it, that experience marked 'our view of the world'. When Europe's political leaders assembled in Finland in August 1975, Brezhnev apart, few would have known where precisely Stavropol was. South-west Russia was a world away from 'Europeans' assembled in Helsinki, as considered in Part 4, to discuss a possible new relationship between East and West in Europe. The Soviet Union held the key.

It would take time for worlds to come into contact. Gorbachev's vision, however, had not been restricted to life in the North Caucasus. In 1955 he had graduated in law from Moscow State University. He had once caught a glimpse of Stalin – in his coffin. A full member of the Community Party since 1952, he accepted the party's view of the world. Both he and his wife, however, had knowledge of brutality en route to the future. They had grandfathers who had been beaten, tortured and one indeed killed. There were charges against these men, ill founded, of anti-Soviet subversion. They had persuaded themselves, however, that Stalin could surely not know how the NKVD (Secret Police) behaved. Filing past Stalin's coffin in 1953, Gorbachev had some mixed feelings, but none which caused him to doubt Marxism's view of the world. In 1966 his first visit abroad had been to East Berlin to study economic reforms in the GDR, followed, a few years later, by visits to Bulgaria and Czechoslovakia. The post-1968 situation in Prague meant that he did not meet Zdeněk Mlynář, erstwhile Secretary of the Praesidium of the Czechoslovak Communist Party, a friend since their student days together in Moscow.

It was only after his appointment in Stavropol that a visit outside the Soviet bloc became possible. In the mid-1970s he visited Belgium, France and Federal Germany. He was surprised both that Western European Communists could disagree among themselves, relatively equably, and that living standards in these countries were higher than at home. A car trip round France confirmed that latter impression. Schooled in the belief that socialist democracy was superior to bourgeois democracy, his observations raised questions, but mildly. The future of Soviet agriculture was more pressing than a global comparison of politico-philosophical systems. He became a Party Central Committee member in 1978 (which in turn led to full membership of the Politburo in 1980). Such was the background of the man who, in March 1985, led the Soviet Union as the new General Secretary of the Communist Party.

The one incontrovertible and conspicuous aspect of his appointment was his age. Brezhnev, uniform, medals and all, had been placed in his coffin in November 1982. His over-strained body had at length abandoned the struggle. He and other members of the Politburo had not neglected the personal needs of their respective families. Yuri Andropov, long-time head of the KGB, succeeded Brezhnev: party and security police were as one. Much speculation has swirled around Andropov's personal origins, in north-west Russia. He worked for a time in the Karelo-Finnish Soviet Republic before moving to Moscow. In 1954 he became Soviet Ambassador in Budapest and was there during the Hungarian Revolution. Communist regimes, he was convinced, should not flinch from force to sustain their life. Later, the KGB was in the van in crushing the 'Prague Spring' in 1968. After Hungary, he headed liaison between the Soviet Party and Communist Parties in 'Socialist Countries'. The liaison was tight. The supposition is sometimes advanced, though rather flimsily, that Andropov loved speaking English ('secretly'). Even if so, he did not love the English-speaking world.

Andropov had never liked the Helsinki Accords. The language of 'human rights' was not welcome in his 'Soviet world'. Nothing in his surveillance and suppression of dissent since 1967 suggested otherwise. After what had been agreed in 1975, however, there was an international treaty provision, unpalatable though he found it. 'Helsinki Human Rights Watch' groups sprang up to 'monitor' Soviet compliance. Such activists became 'well known to the police': the physicist Yuri Orlov, for example. They were to find, however, that 'Helsinki' gave them no real protection. Their attempts to form a network with like minds elsewhere in the Soviet bloc and even with 'Euro-Communists' in Western Europe faltered. Arrested in February 1977, Orlov was sentenced to seven years in a labour camp, to be followed by five years of internal exile. In September 1982 Elena Bonner revealed that the Helsinki Human Rights Groups were so depleted through arrest or exile that they could no longer function. Her own husband, Academician Sakharov, had been exiled to Gorky in January 1980. It was a city foreigners could not visit. A group of dissenting Orthodox priests, claiming to act in defence of Believers' Rights, received short shrift. Their campaign was identified as 'anti-Soviet'. Brezhnev warned incoming President Reagan in 1980 that mouthing 'pseudo-humanitarian slogans' amounted to interference in the internal affairs of the Soviet Union. Yet the very fact that the Helsinki Accords had made provision for 'follow-up' meetings – Belgrade in 1977–78 and in Madrid in 1980–83 – meant that a certain 'outside interference' had to be accepted. 'In the long term', therefore, the Accords had some destabilizing effect and played some part in the eventual collapse of communism.

Discipline, Andropov believed, would choke off dissent. A laxness, with more than a tinge of corruption, was perceptible in officialdom everywhere. Widespread drunkenness was a public manifestation of malaise. So, to demonstrate the virtues of austere application, Andropov initiated at speed a significant turnover of personnel, at almost all levels. His own health was not good – he was launching an elderly assault on the complacency of the elderly elite. By February 1984 he was dead. 'Discipline' had some impact in terms of increased industrial output and agricultural production, though it did not necessarily make for popularity. Andropov knew that it could not in itself solve pressing economic issues. The relationship between central planning and its local implementation was, as it had been for at least two decades of intermittent debate, crucial. He brought in, and gave some scope to, men and women with reforming ideas, but he did not commit himself. If time had been allowed him, he might have done. Yet his caution had a fundamental explanation. While he guardedly made the admission, a rare one, that the leadership needed to understand the society 'in which we all live', no such understanding could undermine Marxism–Leninism. That could never change.

Konstantin Chernenko, who succeeded Andropov, was the last of the Soviet leaders to have been born before the First World War. He had been Brezhnev's faithful lackey but failed to become his successor. He had latterly, however, in Andropov's absence, been chairing the Politburo. His supporters, not anxious to be disturbed in their own spheres, managed to secure the succession for him. His opponents, not conscious that anything else commended him, took comfort from his physical frailty. There was no applause. Andropov had probably wanted Gorbachev to succeed him but had left it too late to engineer it. Gorbachev had been busy, with Andropov's approval, considering various schemes for economic reform, though Andropov did not necessarily tell him all he wanted to know. He became Chernenko's deputy. Jockeying for position at this juncture was inescapable. Opponents of Gorbachev, not all of them septuagenarians, said he only knew about agrarian affairs. To escape from this image, he began to position himself in the world beyond the Soviet Union. The path led to Rome, with a glance, no more, at the Vatican.

European crossroads: Poland and a Pope in Rome

In June 1984 Gorbachev led the Soviet Party delegation to Italy to attend the funeral of Enrico Berlinguer, Secretary of the Italian Communist Party. No visit to Rome at that time, however, could avoid resonances which extended far beyond Italy. In particular, there was now a Polish Pope in the Vatican, the first non-Italian to hold the office since 1522, and the first to come from a Communist country. 'Rome', therefore, featured in the political world not simply because the Italian state was in crisis, allegedly, but because John Paul II was in the Vatican. His appointment, at different levels, was of global significance. It was in Rome in May 1981 that he was shot in an assassination attempt. It was inevitable that some would see behind the gun of the Turkish would-be assassin, Mehemet Ali Ağca, a sinister Bulgarian hand, and, if so, more remotely, a Kremlin one. Henceforward, the papal messenger toured the world behind bulletproof glass. That Karol Wojtyla was a Pole rubbed home that, whatever some Italians might think, the Vatican was not an Italian job. Catholicism was worldwide and, in theory, any cardinal was eligible to become Pope – though a non-European was not yet likely. His Polishness, however, placed the Pope at the very centre of a post-Helsinki 'East–West Europe' that both affirmed 'agreed borders' and also established 'rights' which transcended them. It meant that the Soviet Union had to reckon with an uncontrollable Pole – at a time when Poland was also in crisis.

Personally, as a European man of the 'East' living in the 'West', John Paul II was a cultural hybrid. As Pope he could not be 'at home' anywhere. He had at least seven languages more or less at his command. He linked Rome with a multiplicity of worlds, many of which were 'foreign' to him and which would remain so, though he had already visited North America, Australasia, much of Latin America and most of Europe. For a Pope, he was young. His resulting vision was unique. Over the course of time, he would further travel the world as no other Pope had ever travelled (and he did not slip into countries unannounced): Ireland, Britain, Italy, France, Spain, Brazil, Mexico, the Philippines and the USA being among the countries visited, perhaps ultimately travelling some 670,000 miles. The full scale of this outreach, however, lay ahead. It was Poland which remained close to his heart and on whose behalf he became, in effect, his own secretary of state. His experiences there, not unexpectedly, informed his whole outlook. He was very firm that the Church was not itself a democracy. He had no mean conception of his own authority – as Jesuits, Latin American 'liberation theologians' and the Church in the Netherlands discovered. When he visited the Netherlands in 1985, the Dutch Prime Minister, a Christian Democrat, warned him that 'Rome' seemed a very long way away and the Dutch people were deeply attached to their democratic traditions. When

Queen Elizabeth II, Supreme Governor of the Church of England, paid the first state visit to the Vatican of a British monarch in October 1980, however, it is unlikely that she ventured deeply into contentious waters.

In June 1979 John Paul paid his first return visit to his homeland, welcomed by millions assembled in Warsaw and Krakow. Even the regime purported to give a welcome. A Pope may only have 'soft' power, but in its deployment John Paul had timing: the timing of an actor. Worker militancy, intellectual criticism and ecclesiastical obduracy worked in substantial unity in confronting a Communist government struggling once again with economic difficulties and resorting to an increase in food prices. In Hungary, Czechoslovakia and elsewhere, intellectuals, taking their cue from the Helsinki Accords, had been talking cogently about human rights. In Prague, more than two hundred added their names to a document 'made famous' as Charter '77. Perhaps, however, it was only the response from the government that gave it any prominence. The population as a whole did not eagerly embrace the philosophical considerations which might underpin a future 'civil society'. Poland, by contrast, had a shipyard electrician, Lech Walesa – who was no reader of such philosophers as Husserl or Heidegger – at the helm. After a tense stand-off in the shipyards, he won fundamental concessions as embodied in the Gdansk Agreement of 31 August 1980. Edward Gierek resigned as First Secretary of the Polish Party in the following month and an ineffective successor appeared, given the mission of renewing the party. In November 1980, Solidarity was officially recognized as a legal free trade union. Many millions rushed to join, uncertain whether Moscow would tolerate it. No other Soviet bloc country had gone that far and got away with it.

In mid-December 1980 the US National Security Advisor, Zbigniew Brzezinski, rang the Pope at midnight: a Soviet invasion of Poland, he said, was imminent. It was a conversation in Polish. Brzezinski had been born in Warsaw. His diplomat father was serving in Canada at the outbreak of war and had stayed there. Zbigniew paid his first post-childhood visit to Poland in 1957, the year before he became a US citizen. In his academic career in the USA he wrote on 'totalitarianism', drawing on his family's experience. He then moved into his key position in the Carter administration. The Pope reacted to the call by sending Brezhnev a message warning against an invasion. Brezhnev also heard from Gierek's successor, Kania, that an invasion would provoke a national uprising. One did not take place. In February 1981, however, Wojciech Jaruzelski, Minister of Defence, took over as prime minister, the first time a military officer had taken on this role in a Communist country. In the same month, Solidarity issued its programme, fusing national traditions, Christian ethical principles, political democracy and socialist social thought. The common economic hardship being experienced throughout the country produced a strong sense of togetherness. In December 1981, having been prompted by Brezhnev for months to take action against 'counter-revolution', the Polish government declared martial law and sent security forces onto the streets. Solidarity was banned and leading activists, and many others, imprisoned. Jaruzelski implied that his action forestalled a Soviet invasion. Other sources, however, now reveal Andropov telling the Politburo that it would be too risky to introduce troops into Poland.

There remains much scope for speculation on Jaruzelski's motives and intentions. The outcome, however, was the replacement of a Soviet-controlled civilian dictatorship by a Soviet-controlled military dictatorship. In June 1983 John Paul and General Jaruzelski confronted each other in Warsaw's Belvedere Palace. The former, dressed in white robes with a gold cross, argued that the agreement with Solidarity should be honoured. The latter, in military uniform with rows of ribbons, argued that martial law saved Poland enormous human suffering. John Paul's message, delivered at a televised service in Warsaw, called for a time when Poland would again take its place in Europe between East and West. The wait might be a long one.

A funeral in Rome: Communism and Catholicism

In coming to Rome in 1984, therefore, Gorbachev was well aware of this recent history. He came to bury Enrico Berlinguer, a Communist, not to meet a Catholic. Soviet President Podgorny had met Pope Paul VI in 1967 but there had been no regular Moscow road to Rome thereafter. Gorbachev came at a time when the Italian state looked shaky. Berlinguer (b.1922), the Italian party boss since 1972, did not share Gorbachev's modest origins. His relationship with Moscow, as the Soviet visitor well knew, had been rocky. Some even said that a car crash Berlinguer had sustained a few years earlier in Bulgaria had been a Kremlin-orchestrated attempt to kill him. 'Communism', supposedly the transnational movement of the working class, was in crisis. Probably a million people came to the funeral – a great Italian occasion – for his appeal extended beyond the Communist Party.

Berlinguer had found fame in the 1970s as a key exponent, alongside French and Spanish colleagues, of 'Euro-Communism'. In June 1976 the conference of European Communist Parties failed to endorse the leading role of the Communist Party of the Soviet Union (CPSU) and reiterated each party's right to find its own way to socialism. The Italian party had openly criticized the Soviet invasion of Czechoslovakia in 1968. The 'dictatorship of the proletariat', Berlinguer declared, should be abandoned and the existing Italian constitution defended (Italy being often supposed to be on the verge of collapse). There were terrorist acts from both Left and Right. He offered a 'historic compromise', a notion later transmuted into a 'democratic alternative', whereby Communists would co-operate with other parties to protect the institutions of the state. A complication was that the guardians of the state were not infrequently enmeshed in deals with business interests or the Mafia. Even 'independent' Berlinguer still received secret Soviet financial support which helped him to accelerating electoral success. In June 1976 the Communists had gained roughly a third of the votes cast. The number of seats gained, though still short of the Christian Democrat total, made them appear a potential alternative government. In March 1978, they gave parliamentary support to the Christian Democrat-led government under Giulio Andreotti. The previous year, Berlinguer had issued a kind of 'Encyclical' in which he stated that the Communist Party respected religion and could give it a positive place in the construction of a Socialist society. The Vatican newspaper, *L'Osservatore*

Romano, sought clarification. Berlinguer's respect entailed escorting his wife to mass, but then waiting outside the church.

Then, also in March 1978, came a great shock. Aldo Moro, Christian Democrat leader and former prime minister, was kidnapped and held hostage by terrorists, the Red Brigade. He would be spared if 'political prisoners' were released. The Prime Minister and Berlinguer, in agreement, resisted the demand. The Pope pleaded 'on his knees' for his friend to be released, but to no avail. Moro's body was found in a car in central Rome two months later. The Pope personally celebrated the state funeral mass that followed. The unity of condemnation at this exalted level, however, did not remove profound suspicions between 'ordinary' Italian Christian Democrats and Italian Communists. The latter, in the eyes of the former, for all their professed independence, were still identified with a Soviet Union which, in 1979, was invading Afghanistan. The Italian Communist Party condemned this action, but some of its members could not accept Berlinguer's opinion that the 1917 'Bolshevik Revolution' had exhausted itself. The Communist vote in Italy failed to continue on an upward curve and, except at regional level, the party had no role in government. Christian Democrat predominance, however, which had existed since the foundation of the Italian Republic, seemed to be ebbing away. In 1981–82, in Giovanni Spadolini, a Republican, post-war Italy had its first non-Christian Democrat prime minister. In 1983 the Christian Democrats lost one in seven of their voters.

In June 1984, when Gorbachev came for Berlinguer's funeral, Italy had its first Socialist prime minister in Bettino Craxi (in a coalition government with the Christian Democrats). In February 1984 a new concordat was concluded with the Vatican removing Catholicism as the state religion and Rome as a designated 'sacred city'. In return, the Vatican no longer needed to inform the government of the appointment of bishops and bishops were no longer required to swear allegiance to the Italian state. Many issues clustered around Italian identity at this juncture. Italy itself was perhaps a fiction, precariously glued together by networks which only masqueraded as political parties. The 'Christian civilization' envisaged by the post-war Christian Democratic Party was in disarray.

When Gorbachev came to Rome, therefore, it was to a capital in which, for the Italian government, for the Italian Communist Party and for the Vatican, there was a pervasive ambiguity and uncertainty. Were all sides on the brink of further 'historic compromise', or further, and perhaps deeper, confrontation? For Gorbachev, here was a Communist Party which supported, or at least accepted, Italy's membership of NATO and hence its place in 'the West'. Here too was a party deeply and publicly unhappy with events in Poland, one perhaps finally distancing itself from the Soviet model. Perhaps, at this juncture, merely by being there, Gorbachev was presenting a fresh Soviet face in Europe. Maybe he was a 'reformer', burying previous Kremlin hostility to the dead man. Berlinguer's popularity did not escape his notice. There were audiences which he too might woo and win. Soviet general secretaries had not been conspicuous for such public communication skills, but those skills should surely not be left to inhabitants of the Vatican. Gorbachev returned to the world of Moscow with his cards close to his chest.

Britain and the Soviet Union: business opportunities?

Six months after his party visit to Rome, Gorbachev headed a parliamentary delegation to London. 'Britain' and 'Russia' both had pasts which rendered wholehearted endorsement of 'the European idea' complicated. Both countries, in a sense, were outriders where its future was concerned. On 18 December 1984 he addressed both Houses of Parliament in London. In both academic and official circles he had already been identified as a coming man. Prime Minister Thatcher, on meeting him for the first time, found herself liking him. He smiled and laughed. 'We can do business together' was her celebrated conclusion. There was plenty of business to be done. The decade since 1975, the year in which she had defeated Edward Heath for the Conservative Party leadership, had not seen steady improvement in that 'detente' between the Great Powers which seemed, a little earlier, to have started.

The British invitation to Gorbachev, and his decision to accept, indicated that, while diminished in power, the UK could still perhaps be an effective go-between. The specific developments of this decade – in the Middle East, Africa, Latin America – contributed, as will be seen, to a climate of renewed global coldness. The arms race overhung everything. In private conversation with Thatcher, Gorbachev pulled out a diagram of the nuclear arsenals of the world. It was divided into a thousand squares, each one signifying an arsenal which would destroy humanity. It might now be time, he told British parliamentarians, to negotiate a way out of East–West confrontation.

Margaret Thatcher had come to power when the Conservatives won the May 1979 general election. The Callaghan government had lost a vote of confidence in the House of Commons in March 1979. In 1979 Thatcher was the same age as Mikhail Gorbachev was in 1985. There was indeed a certain similarity between the situations in which these two figures took office. They both had a sense that 'something had to change'. In neither country did inherited politico-economic structures work effectively. Gorbachev, as the new General Secretary, spoke about 'the transformation of the material technical bases of production'. There had to be a decisive turn in transforming the Soviet economy so that the highest world levels of productivity were achieved. None of this, however, was apparently to involve any change from the 'strategic line' laid down by his predecessors. What all that meant was unclear, but it did reveal a 'man of action'. Margaret Thatcher, undoubtedly a 'woman of action', was impatient for her own kind of change – 'Thatcherism', however, had yet to be invented. Both politicians, therefore, were predisposed to seek new 'business opportunities'. They were also both aware that the expanded and expanding EC came increasingly into the East/West picture.

Northern entrants: Britain, Denmark and Ireland 'join Europe'

Denmark, Ireland and the UK had become EC members in January 1973. Their distinct histories brought another way of looking at 'Europe'. Ireland became the first member state not also to be a member of NATO. Norway had originally applied to join at the same time, but the Norwegian electorate voted against and the application was withdrawn. The process of EC expansion was evidently neither inevitable nor inexorable. Each of the new members had their particular reasons for joining. Their membership had different implications and consequences. Denmark's accession gave 'Scandinavia' its sole 'European' presence – not that it had a mandate from its northern neighbours. Ireland looked to forge a renewed 'European' identity for itself. Its diaspora, however, was global, largely in the English-speaking world beyond Europe. The crisis in Northern Ireland, at this juncture, was exacerbating Dublin–London relations. This fact made it unlikely that Britain and Ireland would take a joint pan-insular stance on European political issues.

It was British membership, however, which inevitably made the most significant impact and perhaps caused the greatest problems. Its economic and industrial difficulties might make it 'the sick man of Europe', but it required a place at the 'top table'. There was still much domestic argument about the terms and conditions of British participation. Public suspicion of, indeed hostility towards, 'Europe' remained conspicuous. A British politician, Roy Jenkins, became President of the EC Commission in January 1977, but the British perspective he offered was scarcely typical. The UK first held the rotating Presidency of the Community in the first six months of 1977 but had little 'vision for Europe' to offer. Its preoccupation was the Common Agricultural Policy (CAP). The British were vigilant for any signs of 'creeping centralization' or incipient supranationalism. Even so, institutions which were in some sense 'European' could not be avoided. The prospect of a currency union held little attraction in London. In 1979 Britain would not join the new European Monetary System (EMS) as a full member. These matters, of course, were not being considered in academic detachment. Britain was in a wide-ranging political and economic crisis. Inflation was rampant, and had peaked at 26 per cent in 1975. Its Labour government in 1976 agreed, with difficulty, to the cuts required by the International Monetary Fund as a condition of its loan. Some believed that joining the Community only added to rather than solved Britain's difficulties. 'Orchestrating Europe', in short, was not an engaging activity.

Margaret Thatcher did not envisage the wholesale 'Europeanizing' of Britain. Her educational background was scientific and legal rather than historical. Skiing in Switzerland, from 1960 onwards, had not given her a cultural crash course. She did not put 'Europe First'. She did not believe that any other European leader really did so either. The essence of the Community was hard bargaining between the members fighting for their national interests. A British prime minister should primarily protect British interests. The British thought that the CAP, shaped before British membership, had to be reformed. The early years of the Thatcher premiership therefore witnessed battles over budgets and rebates. Her stance played well, generally, with the British public but irritated, indeed angered, the French and Federal German governments. Privately, and sometimes publicly, it was asserted that Britain was insufficiently *communitaire*.

Southern entrants: Greece, Portugal and Spain 'join Europe'

The admission of three new members – Greece (1981), Portugal and Spain (both 1986) – added another dimension to the Community. In 1981, following the general election, Andrea Papandreou, son and father of Greek prime ministers, formed the first socialist government in Greek history. The election result was seen elsewhere as a sign that Greeks now fully embraced 'democracy'. Two years earlier, both Papandreou's party and the Communists had boycotted the parliamentary debate on Community membership. In theory, the new government wanted a referendum on the principle – but that never happened. By 1984, having obtained some minor changes from 'renegotiation', Papandreou made it clear that withdrawal was not an option. Greece benefited too much from agricultural subsidies. Yet, under Papandreou, the 'orientation' of Greece was not straightforward. He had spent two periods of exile abroad (in the Second World War and during the rule of the Colonels), and indeed had become a US citizen (later renounced). On his second return to Greece, his rhetorical tone was anti-American, though the country did not withdraw from NATO. He stepped out of line in 1984 by paying an official visit to meet General Jaruzelski in Warsaw, the first 'Westerner' to do so.

It was difficult, therefore, to judge where precisely Greece under Papandreou sought to position itself. Outside observers, whether or not they welcomed his social policies, felt nervous about their budgetary base. There was also alarm in the European West about the state of Greek–Turkish relations. Cyprus remained a flashpoint. In 1982 Papandreou became the first Greek prime minister to visit the island. The Greek government lobbied to ensure that, Turkey itself apart, no state extended recognition to the 'Turkish Republic of Northern Cyprus' declared by Turkish Cypriots in November 1983. Greece's 'NATO ally' was being designated as the main threat to its territorial integrity. It is not surprising, therefore, that Greece occupied a rather singular place in the Community. It was being 'incorporated' into a 'European' structure designed in a very different part of Europe. Its 'incorporation' did not remove Greek suspicions that the country was being bullied into conformity with 'alien norms'. The northern and western 'bullies', for their part, feared that Greece was not being bullied enough. They did accept, though tacitly, that some Greek 'idiosyncrasies' would have to be tolerated. Membership, it was hoped, would strengthen Greek democracy as South-East Europe as a whole became more unstable.

In May 1980, in Slovenia, Marshal Tito, the bemedalled, much-honoured, much-married and many-mansioned President of Yugoslavia, died. His life had always lived at points of intersection. He had navigated between the nationalities of his own 'Yugoslavia', between East and West in Europe, and globally between Washington, Moscow and the fluctuating alignments of the 'Non-aligned World'. There was no comparable figure to replace him. Immediately, his death raised questions about the survival of the Yugoslav state. It was Tito personally who had kept it together – and perhaps no one else could. The Cold War still largely, if diminishingly, defined Balkan alignments. Greece, however, drew on a long past in seeking Balkan support in its Aegean disputes with Turkey. No one could tell in what company Nicolae Ceauşescu of Romania would appear next and what his presence indicated. June 1978, for example, had found him as a guest of Queen Elizabeth II in Buckingham Palace, London. The British government praised his independent-mindedness. Romania revived an old strategy in posing as a 'Western European' country, though unfortunately located in South-East Europe. There was a general international anxiety that Balkan ethnic disputes, which had been frozen for decades, were now coming out of cold storage.

The admission of Greece to the Community constituted a precedent for Portugal and Spain. Both Iberian countries had lodged applications to join in the late 1970s, but it was not until 1986 that they were admitted. A decade earlier, the politics of Portugal had been very confused in the wake of revolution. There were tangled personal and organizational relationships on the Portuguese Left. Mario Soares (b.1924) steered his Socialists ahead of the Communists, but his 1976 government only lasted a couple of years. A series of prime ministers followed in quick succession until Soares returned in 1983, though once again, not for long. He did largely persuade Portuguese opinion that the country should join the Community. He had used his years of exile in France to establish close links with European Socialist leaders such as Mitterrand and Brandt. His success, episodic though it was, projected a Portugal which was conforming, or endeavouring to conform, to a notion of Europe as 'essentially' Social Democratic. Certainly, he projected the image of a country that was neither conservative nor Catholic, though in certain respects it still was.

The 'new politics' in Spain, although less openly bumpy, were, nevertheless, complicated. Franco had died in 1975 but was 'Francoism' also dead? Juan Carlos (b.1938), born in Rome and educated partly in Switzerland and partly in Spain, had immediately assumed the revived Spanish throne. The trick in 'the transition to democracy' was not to frighten conservative elements. Adolfo Suárez (b.1932), with a Francoist past but working with an initial broad-based Cabinet, was the man the king entrusted with this task. The civil war still hung over all Spanish politics but determined efforts were made on all sides not to make 'the transition' simply an opportunity to settle old scores. In Suarez and the Socialist leader, Felipe González (b.1942), the King turned to men of his own generation. In European terms, Spain had a youthful leadership. After full parliamentary elections in 1977 in which the centre-right Democratic Centre Party gained the largest number of seats, Suarez remained in office until 1981. A new constitution in 1978 had established the country as a constitutional monarchy. It also devolved power, in varying degrees, to no less than seventeen autonomous regions. In 1981, after Suarez was succeeded by Calvo Sotelo, an attempted army coup failed. In the following year, after a sweeping electoral victory, Gonzalez formed the Socialist government which was in office when Spain joined the Community: it was time to 'modernize'. Indeed, in a remarkably short time, it seemed that Spain had settled into the 'normal' European pattern of electoral oscillation between parties of the Left and the Right.

The three new member states, however, together with Italy, gave the Community an enhanced Mediterranean aspect. Globally, as will later be seen, the contrast between 'North' and 'South' was increasingly being stressed. In terms of relative economic wealth and 'political capital', 'North' and 'South' also applied within the Community. Greece, Spain and Portugal (with the UK) stayed outside the Exchange Rate Mechanism designed to operate the new EMS. Creating 'cohesion' out of such European diversity, while also celebrating distinctiveness, was either a 'challenge' or 'folly'.

The future of 'Europe' was indeed difficult to predict. What was indisputable, however, was that, with every accession, its image, both internally and externally, shifted. Portugal and Greece joined the ranks of its small states – Ireland, Denmark, the Netherlands, Belgium – but a resurgent Spain was rather different. It was set to 'rejoin' the European 'mainstream' in a significant way. Its membership, and that of Portugal, in turn brought the Community into extended commercial, cultural and linguistic contact with South and Central America (and some South Americans began to come 'home'). In November 1982 Pope John Paul, visiting Santiago de Compostela in Galicia, issued an appeal, in the presence of King Juan Carlos, to 'old Europe', calling on it to be the beacon of civilization for the whole world. It soon became clear, however, that 'Catholic Spain' was itself not as solid as the Pope supposed. The González government proceeded to legalize abortion and to take other 'liberalizing' steps which offended the Church. As regards its international stance, in 1986, after a referendum, Spain, led by González, confirmed its membership of NATO (Portugal had been a member from its formation). His party had in the past opposed membership. Gibraltar's future upset otherwise excellent relations with the UK.

Integrating and devolving? States, nations and regions

'New Spain' launched itself impressively. Internally, however, the balance between its regions, particularly Catalonia, the Basque country and Galicia, and central government in Madrid raised an old question: who speaks for Spain? 'Balance' had many echoes elsewhere in almost all member states, to one degree or another. The alignment of region, nation, state and community was under stress. Some observers talked about 'the rise of regional Europe'. The formation of the Community, at the inter-governmental level between states, ran alongside a widespread though not uniform pressure for internal 'devolution'. It had long been customary, for example, to think of France as a highly centralized state impatient with the country's surviving cultural or linguistic diversities. 'Paris' had decided everything. However, the decentralizing law passed in France in March 1982 gave a fresh impetus to 'regionalism' in the new administrative structures that emerged. France did not become a federal state but it was no longer the polar opposite of Federal Germany. German *Länder* were much admired in centralized countries. Some but by no means all regional 'autonomists' threatened to undermine the very foundations of existing states. How much autonomy Corsica should receive within France, for example, was a topic of recurrent but unresolved debate. 'Devolution' was also much debated in the UK. However, in a 1979 referendum in Scotland and Wales there was insufficient support for new structures, though the issue might return. The UK remained the scene of political violence – in Northern Ireland. There, conflicting regional/national identities were anchored in Catholic/Protestant differences. Their common membership of the Community did not in itself mean that the British and Irish governments could find an acceptable solution. Brussels, the very home of the European Commission, was itself a city teeming with sensitivities on the subject of language: French or Flemish/Dutch. The 'capital' of the EC was the capital of a Belgium which might be dissolving into two as more and more powers accrued to its two constituent parts. Brussels itself was no doubt perfect as the 'capital' of the initial six-member Community, but its location seemed far away from Athens or Lisbon.

In different ways, therefore, many states of the Community now embraced a variety of federal and quasi-federal structures. Enthusiasts greeted further 'democratization', but sceptics doubted the calibre of regional government. Sometimes it seemed that the very existence of the 'nation-state' was at stake. That possibility touched on the very nature of the Community itself. Just as, in a certain sense, the Community was integrating, so also its constituent states were disintegrating. Perhaps a 'Europe' that had inflicted its notions of 'nationalism' on the world was now leaving 'nationalism' behind. For others, however, 'regionalism' was certainly not 'bringing power to the people'. It was weakening the existing states in the interests of a centralizing project in which 'Federal Europe' was at the end of the road, whether 'the people' wanted it or not.

France, Britain and Federal Germany: big players

'Community' notwithstanding, however, nothing altered the fact that 'big players', Britain and France particularly, accustomed by history to global roles, could not bring themselves altogether to abandon them. As will emerge, neither showed any significant disposition to move towards a 'common foreign policy' for the Community, unless it was on their own terms. Federal Germany was a major player within the Community but, unlike its major partners, lacked the continuing linguistic/cultural linkages which still gave governments in London and Paris a kind of global presence, 'decolonization' notwithstanding. Its own past, and indeed its present constitution, ruled out any global role that might require the projection of force. The question of the future of 'Germany', a topic of permanent interest, also made its position different from its partners. Between them, the 'big players' worked out, with much argument, what 'Europe' thought of 'America'. The internal situation in Italy, earlier alluded to, reduced its diplomatic weight. Smaller countries tagged along as best they could. Whether a Community of twelve states could formulate a common view of the world remained problematic. Correspondingly, the outside world could not know who 'spoke for Europe'. There were many telephone numbers to try, though the ones that mattered were known.

It was not until the summit of the European Council of Ministers at Fontainebleau in June 1984 that agreement was reached on reforming the CAP and the budget (including the question of the British contribution) set. In its wake, the Council set in motion two committees to examine the future of the EC. The European Parliament, modestly endowed with power, but now directly elected, was eager to assert itself and disrupt what some saw as an intergovernmental stranglehold on the Community's development. It floated an 'Act of Union'. There was a widespread sense that the Community was a mess. It should either press on to some kind of more formal integration or, in effect, grind to a halt. Very different views were on offer. The British Labour Party, in the 1983 general election, wanted Britain to leave to leave the Community, but it did not win. Not that a re-elected Margaret Thatcher was eager to place Britain in the van of 'Union'. She supported the creation of a real internal market, from which economic benefit would flow all round, but did not want grandiose constitutional projects. The veto which states possessed should be retained. In March 1985, one of the Fontainebleau committees reported. Then a Franco-German paper entitled 'Draft Treaty of European Union' was presented to the Milan Council summit a few months later and a summer of negotiation began, seeking, one more time, to set out Europe's future. Yet the individual perspectives of the 'big players' remained strong.

Where France was concerned, some commentators had initially supposed that Giscard d'Estaing, President of France (1974–81), would be more 'Atlanticist' than Gaullism, refined by Pompidou, had been. That turned out to be only mildly so. In the Middle East, especially, France had its particular interests and in a host of small but important ways saw the world differently from the USA. It was perhaps not too late for France to head up a network of Arab, African and European relationships and 'solve' the Middle East. When the Ayatollah Khomeini returned to Tehran in February 1979 from exile in Paris, it was in an Air France jet. Giscard seemed much more eager to meet Brezhnev – whether in France, Moscow or Warsaw – than he did to meet any American president. Meeting Brezhnev in Warsaw looked like a deliberate attempt to show that France was not greatly bothered by the Soviet invasion of Afghanistan. Giscard and President Carter overlapped in office for four years (1977–81), but only met once on an individual basis, in 1978 in Paris. The two men then visited the Normandy beaches. Carter complained that de Gaulle had been cold towards the USA, France's liberator. Giscard explained that the general had had to restore French self-esteem. To demonstrate that time moved on, however, in Normandy Giscard spoke publicly in English, as he was perfectly capable of doing, but France would not settle for a subordinate role within an 'Anglo-American' world.

François Mitterrand (b.1916) was elected President of France at his third attempt in 1981. He had a helpful suggestion: Britain was being so awkward that it should cease to be a full member of the Community and instead negotiate a 'special status'. Thatcher would have none of it. The confrontation between these two figures was in part the traditional Franco-British jockeying for poll position in any organization in which they played a common part. It was also, however, a matter of personal background and experience. In 1943 when a callow Thatcher began quietly studying chemistry at the University of Oxford, Mitterrand was joining the Resistance having, until then, since his escape from a German prisoner-of-war camp, worked for prisoners of war under the Vichy government. His controversial wartime past was very different from hers, and it was not only European memory, or the lack of memory, which divided them.

Mitterrand operated the constitution of the fifth republic with vigour, untroubled by his previous criticism of it. He dissolved the National Assembly and the election secured an absolute majority for the Socialists and their allies. The government, under Pierre Mauroy, contained four Communist ministers, though that party, fighting separately, had seen its total of seats drop sharply in the second round of voting. Apparently, the new regime was going to make as decisive a 'break with capitalism' as Thatcher was determined to make with socialism. In the event, however, confronted by a balance-of-payments crisis, budgetary deficit and rapid inflation, Mitterrand placed a brake on the break, though not without much inner-party dispute. He was in some quarters accused of Americanizing the Socialist party and diluting its allegiance to Marxism. France, it seemed, partly because of the EMS, could not go it alone. Those in the party who wished to leave the EMS, and who resisted deflation, were defeated. A new generation of French ministers shed some of the slogans which they had themselves youthfully adopted in 1968.

Mitterrand initially took a frosty stance towards the USA. An itinerary which took him to Mexico, Algeria and India in 1981–82 purveyed an impression of non-alignment. A Franco–Mexican declaration expressed solidarity with rebels fighting the US-backed junta in El Salvador. Two years later, however, the head of that very junta was being received in Paris. Mitterrand had no intention of taking France altogether outside NATO or of giving up French nuclear weapons. When he went to Moscow in June 1984 he lectured on human rights. The previous year he had even addressed the Federal German Bundestag, urging it to accept Pershing IIs and Cruise missiles – responses to the Soviet SS20s – on German soil. The Left, in various European countries, had opposed their deployment. No American missiles, however, were going to be located on French soil, and his advocacy of their presence in Germany at least raised the occasional eyebrow in the Bundestag. The official view in Paris was that, as regards the Middle East, France understood and sympathized with the Arab position. Even so, Mitterrand became the first French president to pay a state visit to Israel. So, while 'anti-Americanism' was a constant aspect of French thinking, whether on the Right or the Left, it was only 'anti' up to a certain point. French public opinion actually seemed to like the new US president, Ronald Reagan. It did not like the imposition of martial law in Poland. France, therefore, remained in 'the West', but insisted on its own distinctive perspective. Between 1976 and 1984 it busied itself far beyond Europe in carrying out underground nuclear testing in French Polynesia and brushed aside the opposition of South Pacific states. French security agents even blew up the Greenpeace vessel *Rainbow Warrior* in Auckland harbour, New Zealand, in July 1985. The French defence minister resigned, but by the autumn Mitterrand himself flew to the South Pacific atoll where testing had taken place to give a secular blessing to continued testing.

Britain, too, still had some small outposts in the world beyond Europe. The Falkland Islands crisis of 1982 brought this home to a British public which was largely unaware of their existence. Following the Argentine invasion of that year, the British government sent a task force which recaptured the islands, at a cost. The fate of two thousand faraway 'British' islanders did matter. Britain could not acquiesce in such aggression, however distant. There were not likely, however, to be many other comparable operations. An assault on the remote British island of Tristan de Cunha in the South Atlantic was unlikely. The Prime Minister herself did not feel that enthusiasm for the Commonwealth which its titular head, the Queen, so obviously felt. Community solidarity with the British case on the Falklands was not conspicuous. The Irish Republic was distinctly unhelpful at the UN. The British ambassador there found himself relying on the Commonwealth for diplomatic support rather than from Britain's 'European partners'. There were reasons for their lukewarm support. Argentina had acquired a significant Italian-descended population. The Falklands campaign therefore expressed a British patriotism rather than a general European sentiment. What mattered to the British government at this juncture was the attitude of the US administration and the rapport between Prime Minister and President was fundamental. Although there were occasional wobbles, as when Thatcher was upset when the US invaded the Commonwealth island of Grenada in the Caribbean, the two leaders breathed fresh life into the Anglo-American relationship. To a large degree, they shared a view of the world.

Helmut Schmidt (b.1918), the SPD Federal German chancellor (1974–82), had the basic conviction that Germany could not provide 'world' military or political leadership, though he was intensely interested in the world's dynamics. His mindset was rather 'British'. It was in English rather than in French that he was fluent – having briefly, it seems, been a taxi driver in Boston, Massachusetts. He revelled in Hanseatic practicality – he came from Hamburg – and was quite willing to do deals with East Berlin, making use of Bonn's financial strength to increase the flow of German visitors from the West to the East and thus keep alive the unity of 'the German nation'. But what that unity really was remained uncertain, and whether, indeed, 'the German nation' was now something, in an allegedly 'post-national' Europe, to focus on. Historians in Germany turned to debating these matters with uninhibited vigour. Schmidt's unwillingness to flirt with 'neutralism' brought increasing tension within his own party. His government fell in 1982. It was Helmut Kohl, his Christian Democrat successor, who had to deal, as will be seen, with the most dramatic aspect of 'the German question' in the late 1980s. How European countries reacted, then, to the prospect of German unity would test the extent to which they had indeed buried historic anxieties and accepted that they were living in some kind of common home.

19

The Middle East: Putting it to Rights?

The USA avowedly proclaimed that it made one out of many. If external leaders did not know the telephone number of 'Europe', speaking to 'America' was straightforward. There was only one White House, though it was a residence in a city awash with would-be opinion-formers. Few inhabitants of Plains, Georgia, however, worried about the complexities of the world and America's place in it. In such a community of around 500 people, the 'outside world' rarely impinged directly. Peanut farming, for the Carter family, was a difficult enough business. Plains was remote from Washington. Atlanta, the nearest city, was some 120 miles away. Globally, even Stavropol was better known. The conventional wisdom was that world-views that mattered were those formulated by politicians and officials in capital cities. Even so, men in Washington reached the summit of power with preconceptions or presuppositions formed elsewhere 'in obscurity'. It sometimes turned out that the 'local' and the 'global' were more connected than one might suppose.

Plains speaking

So it was with Jimmy Carter, former Governor of Georgia, elected US President in November 1976. His election, some said, meant that the South had at last joined 'the American Nation'. That meant that the long shadow cast by the Civil War was at last disappearing. Yet 'American unity' was coming under fresh strains. The 'American nation' was still being forged out of ever more diverse populations as the world impacted on the USA, even as the USA impacted on the world. Even Georgia, in the aftermath of the Vietnam debacle, came to acquire a small Vietnamese population. The USA was the repository of global freedom. To emphasize that would heal the nation's wounds. So the incoming president thought.

Carter's father's peanut farm had not hosted gatherings of the global great. Jimmy had not attended an elite university but had enrolled in the US Naval Academy, from which he graduated in 1946. Unlike his immediate predecessors in office, therefore, he had not seen war service. In the navy, over the next seven years, as a submarine officer, he had travelled extensively, though a submariner gains a somewhat restricted view of the world. There were, however, some surface, if superficial, moments – as when he spent a few days at various seaports along the China coast in 1949. The campfires of Communist forces could be seen on the hills behind the Nationalist-held ports. Boyhood pictures of China presented in slideshows by Baptist missionaries on furlough in Georgia came back to Carter's mind. Then he had saved his nickels and dimes to help the missionaries in their work of providing hospitals, schools and a knowledge of Jesus Christ. An uncle sent him postcards of Shanghai and Tsingtao. Even in Plains, therefore, the outside world crept in.

Carter, in the campaign of 1976, conscious of the mood of the country, was able to make being an 'outsider' a virtue. He was not a lawyer. He had not been a member of Congress. He had not served in Washington. There were other Americans 'out there' who wanted to renew their country's standing in the world. In his inaugural address he recalled words of the Old Testament prophet, Micah. The mistakes of the recent past required a reaffirmation of the basic principles of the nation. That meant an absolute commitment to human rights, the limitation of armaments and, as an ultimate goal, the removal of all nuclear weapons. America, he said, was a proudly idealistic nation but perhaps had to recognize its limits. It could neither answer all questions nor solve all problems. In economic terms, he would emphasize fiscal responsibility. The federal government should not be seen as a bottomless cornucopia. Carter's rhetoric jarred with more cynical or sophisticated observers. It would surely come to nothing. His approach differed sharply from the elaborate linkages of Kissinger's *Realpolitik*. When, after a few months, Carter's Director of the Budget had to resign because of irregularities in his previous banking career, this administration looked much like any other. The president's unabashed Christian convictions also caused concern. Presidents were not expected to take them so seriously. Carter customarily referred to 'the Europeans' but soon found, in his dealings with Thatcher, Schmidt, Giscard and Andreotti that there was no standard model of 'the European'. Cultural cleavages in the Euro-American world seemed to be widening, not diminishing. They were even wider, as the President discovered, in the world beyond.

Carter stated that the USA could never be indifferent to the fate of freedom 'elsewhere' – that is to say everywhere – though in reality, it had been indifferent for some time. It had strong ties, military or economic, with countries whose commitment to freedom was modest. Even the establishment of a new Bureau on Human Rights inside the State Department might not bring about a transformation. For thirty years from the signing of the UN Charter, as we have seen, human rights had been given universal endorsement. The Helsinki Accords had just reaffirmed them. Yet there was no enforcement mechanism. Nor was there universal agreement in defining freedom or in prioritizing its desirability. For some countries, social cohesion might be more important. Philosophers could mull over these matters. The White House had to make decisions.

Iran: rights and revolutions

When the Shah of Iran read Carter's inaugural address of January 1977 it was not the first time that 'human rights' had reached his desk. The International

Commission of Jurists and Amnesty International had both produced documents highly critical of the suppression of freedom in Iran and of the use of torture by the internal security service, SAVAK. Carter's emphasis gave encouragement to some Iranian intellectuals to circulate open letters and petitions calling for change. American diplomats might now put pressure on the Shah to improve civil rights. The Universal Declaration of Human Rights was referred to in some of these petitions, though not one relied on by those from the religious opposition. In Washington, in November 1977, US police used tear gas to disperse a mob of Iranian students – there were at this time probably a hundred thousand Iranian students studying in North America and Europe – protesting against the Shah, who was visiting the White House. Carter was the eighth American president he had met. The gas caused the Shah to produce a handkerchief to wipe away his tears. The president did his best not to blink in front of the cameras. This was new. Carter subsequently recorded that he regarded the Shah as a likeable man and a strong ally. They had private discussions in which the American suggested some 'easing off' of strict police policies. The Shah replied that while troublemakers were in a tiny minority, the menace of Communism remained very serious.

From this point on, however, stability increasingly disappeared. Iran became another of those 'troubled areas' which attracted media commentary. There were, however, a collection of oppositions to the Shah rather than a single front. Westernized liberals supposed that the street demonstrations of the summer would cause him to allow free elections – he was making noises to this effect. Elections would pave the way to an Iran which would truly be a constitutional monarchy. Such intellectuals did not anticipate a revolution which would leave them stranded. The Left and the religious opposition (itself diverse) had other objectives. In the face of this increasing dissent, the Shah shuffled his ministers and shut casinos. A massive demonstration in September led to martial law – and to many killings. A military government followed in November in a country tumbling out of control. The White House thought it extraordinary that such an experienced monarch, with his huge army behind him, should be suddenly so vulnerable. In January 1979 the Shah left Iran on an extended 'vacation' to a rather unusual medley of destinations. However, he had not abdicated: hence the widespread suspicion in Iran that '1953' would be repeated: the Americans would engineer his return. That, however, was not the plan in a Washington desperately searching for a 'middle way' in Iran between the monarchy and the Islamic republic.

Khomeini orchestrated the Islamic Revolution from Paris, where he had been living since 1978, having left Iraq. Western-educated men in his entourage expressed 'democratic' aspirations. Khomeini himself, however, thought that democracy was an alien Western notion. Islam alone would suffice. He received a massive welcome at the airport on his return to Tehran in February 1979. Over the next four years he and his followers took over and directed hitherto diverse revolutionary strands. In this new situation, foreigners, not to mention natives, found the relationship between clerical power on the one hand, and an elected parliament and presidency on the other, obscure. It did not produce a country which respected 'human rights' as Carter interpreted them. However, the administration was not going to 'step in' and 'restore' the old regime. Allowing the Shah to enter the USA to receive cancer treatment triggered the occupation, in November 1979, of the US embassy in Tehran. The 'hostage crisis' began and consumed the attention of the president for nearly fourteen months. Staying put in Washington to deal with it became his 'standard policy'. The USA broke off diplomatic relations with Iran in April 1980. Only on his last day in office in January 1981, having lost the 1980 election to Ronald Reagan, was a deal with Tehran concluded and the hostages released. It was all an ignominious commentary on Carter's inaugural address of but four years earlier. Of course, his advocacy of 'human rights' had not 'caused' the Islamic Revolution in a direct sense, but their general advocacy worldwide could evidently trigger unpredictable consequences. Khomeini set the country on a new course which seemed in 'the West' to deny all that the West prized in 'modernity'. The Ayatollah was not perturbed. In the maelstrom of Iranian politics, no one could say how his vision would actually play out. The Shah's long promised 'Great Civilization', however, was never going to arrive. Iran would now attempt to offer a new revolutionary model for the Middle East, and perhaps beyond.

In September 1980 Saddam Hussein's Iraqi forces invaded Iran. The Shatt al-Arab border, theoretically set out in a treaty between Iran and Iraq signed in Algiers in 1975, had in fact remained contentious. Saddam Hussein saw his chance. Iran looked unusually vulnerable and there seemed good reason to suppose that, as things stood, the Western world would regard him as the lesser of two evils. After some initial success, however, Iranian armed forces and volunteers fought back. Invasion consolidated the Iranian regime. Each side bombed the other's oil installations. A military stalemate ensued, but neither side was going to abandon the struggle. Pope John Paul II had been prevailed upon by Carter to write to Khomeini concerning the American hostages, but without effect. It was not for Christians to involve themselves in the Islamic world. Yet what was now happening was a many-sided battle within that world. In the struggle for power, state, nation and religion were once again jumbled up. The Shi'ite majority in Iraq, living in a state ruled by the Sunni minority, might be seduced by a meddling Iran (as might the Kurds in northern Iraq). The Arab minority in oil-rich Khuzistan (in Iran, close to the border) might perhaps be seduced by Arab Iraq. It was not an altogether straightforward battle between states. Clear victory, in any case, looked increasingly remote. Stalemate, however, was not uncongenial both to neighbouring countries and to distant Western ones.

Only a couple of years earlier, none of this had been forecast. At the end of December 1977, Carter had paid a return visit to Iran and praised the country as 'an island of stability' in a troubled Middle East. This comforting assessment seemed to accord, in general, with the information sources which flowed into the State Department. The American community in Iran, largely commercial, did not study Shi'ite theology. Neither did the president. Stopovers, in any case, astutely stewarded by hosts, rarely provide any serious inter-cultural engagement. They did not on this occasion.

Palestine: promising land?

Carter was on a trip which took him to Poland, India, Saudi Arabia, France, Belgium and Egypt. Iran was a key player. The 'Middle East' did indeed remain one of the most 'troubled areas of the world'. The King of Jordan had joined the Shah and Carter in Tehran on New Year's Eve to consider, once again, the options for an acceptable peace in the region. These particular men, all fluent in English, could speak to each other directly. The following morning the Shah and King Hussein agreed that they would each go to Saudi Arabia and Egypt to express support for Sadat. The endgame of the tour, from Carter's perspective, was his own meeting with the Egyptian President, on whom so much now depended. Iran and Egypt, the outlying Powers, could perhaps determine the fate of 'the lands between'.

Here, now, was an American who had earlier seen 'the Holy Land' for himself. Christians in a sense 'owned' it. They knew about the road from Jerusalem to Jericho from reading the Bible. Carter, a Bible-reading Baptist, felt that he knew it intimately, too. Back in 1973, he had accepted an invitation from Prime Minister Golda Meir to visit Israel. Amongst other experiences, he had lunched with the Mayor of Nazareth. He believed that the Jews who had been saved from the Holocaust deserved their own nation, as he later put it. A 'home-land' was compatible with the teachings of the Bible, hence was ordained by God. He admired what the Israelis had done. On coming into office, he still believed that Israel was 'a strategic asset' to the USA.

However, he had no 'strong feelings' about the Arab countries. Indeed, he admitted that he had never been to an Arab country and knew no Arab leader personally. A series of meetings in 1977 in the USA with Sadat of Egypt, Hussein of Jordan and Crown Prince Fahd of Saudi Arabia, and one in Switzerland with Assad of Syria, ended that deficiency. The more Carter dealt with Arab leaders, however, as he later put it, the more he discovered a discon-certing disparity between their private assurances and their public comments. The more he talked with them, the more too he discovered the diversity of the 'Arab world'. When he reached Riyadh in January 1978 he received unexpected lessons in falcon hunting and on the Saudi style of government. The USA had its political dynasties, but Saudi Arabia appeared to be an extended family affair. The world he encountered was strange – a word he used on a subsequent post-presidential visit. Its combination of wealth and 'puritanism', however, was not totally unattractive to a Southern Baptist. Generous entertainment in an opulent palace nevertheless offered a limited perspective on the country. Saudi Arabia, with its very substantial employment of foreign workers, had its own 'world within worlds' which he did not see. King Khalid told Carter that he would settle for nothing less than an independent Palestinian state, though there might be a minor adjustment of Israel's pre-1967 border.

There was, however, a new factor in the Middle East. In June 1977, after a general election following the resignation of Rabin, Menachem Begin (b.1913) at last came to power. His arrival, outside observers supposed, would obstruct a settlement. Labour had dominated Israeli governments since 1948. The Likud party, which Begin cobbled together, symbolized something of a shift away from the ascendancy of 'European' Jews (Ashkenazim). Now they were outnumbered by Jews from North Africa and elsewhere (Sephardim). Begin himself, however, had 'European' origins. His past would determine his present. His parents and brother had been killed in the Holocaust. Born in imperial Russia at Brest-Litovsk, he had later been educated at Warsaw University. He had seen the inside of a Soviet labour camp. He had arrived in British-administered Palestine in 1942, after moving around in the chaotic few years following the outbreak of war in 1939. The British might be trying elsewhere to defeat Nazi Germany, but that did not deter him from terrorist activity against their administration in Palestine. He headed the *Irgun* gang from 1944. Its most notorious terrorist act had been the explosion (and heavy loss of life) at the King David Hotel in Jerusalem in 1946. He would fight anybody who stood in the way of the Israel that he wanted. He talked expansively of a 'Greater Israel' – much as, in neighbouring Damascus, President Assad talked of a 'Greater Syria'.

When Begin came to Washington in the summer of 1977 Carter had found him 'a good man'. British official opinion, with long memories, did not quite concur. However, even if not altogether a good man, Begin might be a good man to deal with. The Americans were told by the Israeli that a Palestinian state was out of the question. It would immediately become a Soviet base and put Israel in 'mortal danger'. Any US 'guarantees' would be worthless. Some kind of Palestinian 'entity', he supposed, might be envisaged, but certainly not a state. Carter reiterated the US view that Israeli settlements established on land occupied by military force a decade earlier were illegal under international law. Begin fell silent. On his return home, the Israeli government recognized some such settlements as permanent.

These meetings, together with much private scrutiny of maps, gave the President glimpses, no more, of different Middle Eastern worlds. He had never before tasted desert truffles or drunk camel's milk. These encounters were, however, more than cultural tutorials. They were preludes to that comprehensive peace settlement which, rejecting the familiar expressions of hopelessness, Carter believed still to be possible. In October 1977 Washington and Moscow had agreed that they would summon a Middle East peace conference at Geneva in December under their joint chairmanship. All relevant states would be invited. The scheme ran into difficulties, however, chiefly because of Israeli objections to the participation of the PLO. But the scene had been transformed by the news that came out of Cairo in November 1977. That was what made it worthwhile for Carter to stop off very briefly in Aswan in January 1978, to see Sadat and, unexpectedly, share a photo opportunity with another visitor, Helmut Schmidt. Egypt might hold the key.

Egypt: Sadat going solo

About-turns were Anwar Sadat's speciality. The expulsion of Soviet advisers in 1972, followed by the unilateral abrogation in 1976 of the Treaty of Friendship with the Soviet Union, set a pattern. He then embarked on the policy of *infitah*, or 'Open Door' to foreign investment. Many domestic door-openers also seized their business opportunities at this time. Public displays of individual wealth were conspicuous. The Nasserite generation of army officers (Sadat himself being one), bureaucrats and technocrats, remained in power but Nasserite Socialism, and the ideology which accompanied it, dropped away. The regime lost interest in global non-alignment and instead concentrated, if that is not too excessive a word, on the paradoxes of Egypt's position. The country's population continued to expand rapidly. The pressure on cultivable land increased. Cairo mushroomed and looked a city out of control. Egypt was, in one sense, the most powerful country in the Arab world but it was also highly vulnerable. Its economy was precariously based. A significant expansion of its productive capacity, anticipated as a result of foreign investment, had yet to work through. The remittances sent home by the more than a million Egyptians working in many capacities in Arab countries were vital (alongside tourism and Suez Canal tolls). Egyptian professionals looked for opportunities even further afield. The 'Open Door' saw a passion for foreign goods amongst the minority that could afford them. A contemporary cartoon had two Egyptians exclaiming, 'Fantastic, it must be imported' – as they gazed at the Great Pyramid. There had been food riots at the beginning of 1977, triggered by proposals to reduce government subsidies. Troops were used to quell disturbances for the first time since the fall of the monarchy. The unrest was a warning to the US and Arab rulers that the masses would not take too much austerity. For several years, gingerly, the regime had permitted the formation of different political 'platforms'. The pro-regime platform was shortly to emerge as the National Democratic Party. It swamped other groupings. This partial liberalization also allowed greater religious activity. Muslim Brotherhood publications, formerly banned, called for Egyptian structures to be more Islamic, and criticized the regime as an agency of 'Westernization'. There were signs of greater tension between some Muslim groups and some Coptic Christians. The old question returned: were Egyptians Arabs, or Egyptians primarily, or indeed solely?

That was the domestic background when, on 9 November 1977, Sadat had risen to address the People's Assembly in Cairo. It was only a few months after Carter's inauguration that Sadat had come to Washington – the first Egyptian president to do so – to find out what 'global human rights' meant in practice. In their talks Carter detected in the Egyptian an intention to make progress without delay. In his November speech, raising himself above procedural wrangles, Sadat declared that he was willing to go to Geneva to attend the proposed multilateral peace conference. At such a conference, he would support the legitimate rights of the Palestinian people, including their establishment of a state. There was little unexpected in these remarks – until the final paragraph, in which he declared a willingness to go to the ends of the earth to avoid future bloodshed. Yasser Arafat, who was listening, joined in the applause but was then appalled to discover that 'the ends of the earth' in fact meant the Israeli parliament, the Knesset. Two days later, on Israeli television, Begin directly addressed the Egyptian people. Attempts to destroy the Jewish state, he said, had been and would be in vain, but there was no reason for hostility. In 'ancient times', Egypt and Israel had been allies against a common enemy – from the north. The implication was obvious. An invitation duly arrived in Cairo. On 20 November, Sadat was in the Knesset delivering a lengthy address to which Begin responded. Both men knew that 'the world' was watching, flabbergasted, as Sadat put it. There were many words and many symbolic gestures. Whether real progress might be made was another matter. Begin's lengthy response made no reference to a people who might be 'Palestinian'. Sadat, however, stated that peace could never be made 'without the Palestinians' and without withdrawal from all land occupied by armed force. The Israeli denied that his people had taken a 'foreign country'. They were returning to their homeland. This was public theatre – with due attention to Abraham/Ibrahim as the forefather of both Arabs and Jews – but it perhaps created a moment of opportunity.

In the months that followed it did not look as though it would be seized. Normally, Arab gatherings expressed solidarity even when there was no solidarity. Not this time. Sadat's pilgrimage was condemned by the state media in Damascus and Riyadh. Only in Rabat and Muscat was there distant – and inconsequential – approval. There were mixed reactions in Cairo itself. The notion that Sadat could speak for 'the Arab nation' was threadbare. He looked in vain for any substantial shift in the Israeli position which would ease his isolation. The direct talks between the Egyptians and Israelis, despite American prodding, were going nowhere. At this point, Carter invited both men to Camp David in Maryland in September 1978 for an intense period of negotiation which he and his colleagues would facilitate. It proved to be an intense experience. The rest of the world allegedly faded from the minds of the participants. Eventually, two 'framework' documents for an Egyptian/Israeli peace and for peace in the Middle East were agreed. There was, naturally, much detail in both. The essence was that Israel would withdraw from Sinai over a period of three years. In return, Egypt recognized Israel as a state and accorded it access to the Suez Canal and the Straits of Tiran. There were then to be further negotiations concerning some form of self-government which Palestinians could possess (under Israeli sovereignty) in the West Bank and the Gaza Strip. Both governments reserved their positions on Jerusalem. A formal treaty was supposed to follow within three months, though it only arrived on 26 March 1979. Carter himself visited both Cairo and Jerusalem to aid the diplomacy. Further negotiations were then supposed to follow, into which Jordan might be drawn, to establish a Palestinian self-governing authority in the West Bank and Gaza which would provide 'full autonomy to the inhabitants'. These words looked rather empty.

Both Camp David and the March 1979 treaty caused furious condemnation of Egypt in other Arab capitals. Sadat was pilloried as a traitor to the cause. President Assad of Syria orchestrated a 'Steadfastness Front' of the faithful. An ostracized Egypt was expelled from the Arab League and that body's headquarters left Cairo. There was even talk of Syrian–Iraqi unity. Most Arab states severed diplomatic relations with Egypt. Such measures were intended to demonstrate that this was a bilateral deal, not a comprehensive Middle East settlement. Too many awkward issues, not least concerning Jerusalem, had been 'parked' or not settled with the necessary clarity – all no doubt as a result of trying to achieve something. Critics said that the Palestinians had been betrayed for American dollars (annexes to the Camp David accord provided for US aid for Egypt amounting annually to $1.5 billion, a figure which grew steadily thereafter). Sadat affected to regard the verbal attacks on him, both inside and outside Egypt, as a temporary spasm. It was one, however, which lasted intensely for a few years, although then, quietly, some contacts began again, initially with Jordan. Some Arab oil money reappeared in Cairo.

It was not with Sadat himself, however, that these tentative steps were taken (and it was not to be until 1989 that Egypt was readmitted to the Arab League). In October 1981, after a summer of mounting inter-communal violence, Islamist assassins killed him. He had in fact been making some concessions to Islamic groups and the constitution had been amended to designate *sharia* as a major source of Egyptian national law. In Sudan, contemporaneously, Nimeiri went further in the same direction and, in doing so, exacerbated the tensions between north and south within his country. Some commentators suggested that by taking such steps Sadat sealed his own fate. They did not, however, say how else Islam should have been 'accommodated'.

There was a major American turnout at the funeral: the three American former Presidents Nixon, Ford and Carter, an unparalleled performance. After the death of the Shah in Egypt in the summer, the kind of Middle East which they thought they understood, and could rely on, might also be dying before them. They found that Sadat's funeral was unlike any funeral to which they were accustomed. It all seemed 'peculiar' to Carter. He had not really understood the milieu of the man he called his friend. If Carter had been re-elected in 1980 Sadat seems to have supposed that the two men could have returned to the Palestine question with fresh vigour and produced that elusive final settlement. Mount Sinai, Sadat had thought, would be an ideal location for a ceremony, and even the Pope could be brought along for good measure. All that, however, was fantasy. Those present at the funeral showed that worlds were not meeting: Begin's attendance ensured that no Arab state except Sudan was represented.

In the short term at least, the new course which Sadat had taken seemed secure. Hosni Mubarak, his Vice-President since 1975, was nominated by the People's Assembly on the day after Sadat's assassination. He immediately made clear that Egypt would continue to adhere to the Camp David Accords and the Peace Treaty. He tried to balance firmness in dealing with militants with the symbolic release of some critics of the Sadat regime. A new government in 1982 had two Copts in prominent positions. Mubarak was ten years younger than his predecessor and was not one of the original group of officers who had set Egypt on its course. In this sense, there was a new beginning, but the regime fundamentally remained a military one. Mubarak became a 'politician' as chairman of the National Democratic Party but his training and career had been in the Egyptian Air Force. In 1983 diplomatic relations with the Soviet Union were restored. There was a certain neatness here. Mubarak had spent several years, some two decades earlier, receiving training as an air-force officer in the Soviet Union, in Moscow and elsewhere. It was the Soviet world which he had known at first hand, not 'the West' to which he was now firmly aligned. Such knowledge was perhaps counterbalanced by the fact that his wife, born in Egypt, had a British mother. Her Egyptian father had studied medicine in Britain. There could scarcely be a better illustration, at this particular juncture, of the fact that Egypt remained at the crossroads where East and West, North and South intersected.

It had not been in the Middle East but on the White House lawn in Washington that the March 1979 Israeli–Egyptian Peace Treaty had been publicly signed: West and East were both 'involved'. Yet was this just a show? The previous year, the American publisher, Random House, brought out a book entitled *Orientalism*. It had little anticipation that it would become a world phenomenon, with translations flowing into many European languages, but also into Persian, Japanese and Chinese. The author, Edward Said, was a Professor of English and Comparative Literature at Columbia University in New York. He had, however, been born in Jerusalem in 1935. His mobile businessman father spent time in the USA and became a US citizen. Later, he became an Anglican Christian and had moved to Cairo. Edward went to school there and, in all probability, English became his first language, though it jostled with Arabic all his life. Edward had proceeded to Princeton and Harvard and then to teach at Columbia. It was in America that he again found his Palestinian self, though, as his later autobiography proclaimed, he was always a man 'out of place'. *Orientalism* was a polemic. From the outset, it had its admirers and detractors. Scholars picked holes or saluted. Said, however, never revised the text. It thus took on a sacred character, though written by a secular intellectual (there is very little in the book on religion). Its theme was that 'Western' writing about 'the Orient', suffused with feelings of racial superiority, denigrated the 'Orient' as a prelude to its colonization. Such a mindset, he thought, still had an enduring legacy. Others argued that Said's 'West' was a selective and implausible construct. What about a millennium in which 'the West' had found itself on the defensive against an Islamic 'East'? So, they said, there was no balance. Its value as a historical account – and Said did not claim to be a historian – might be dubious but to many readers, both in Euro-America and in the Middle East, it seemed to explain how the East–West world of 1978/79 had come about.

Carter lost the election in November 1980. He had little to show, in the end, for his emphasis on 'rights'. The gap between aspiration and achievement was yawning. The USA, under his successor, Ronald Reagan, would strike a different note. The Middle East, however, still remained a contentious region 'between worlds'. Engagement had run into sands.

20
A Question of Latitude: 'North' and 'South'

'West' and 'East' in the Middle East rarely disappeared from the headlines. Yet there was a concurrent attempt, though in equally bold simplicity, to plot the world. 'North/South' terminology became commonplace. In the eyes of many commentators, this, not East/West, was the 'great divide'. Since its formation in 1965, the UN Conference on Trade and Development (UNCTAD), in a sequence of conferences, had regularly been pressing the claims of developing countries for a New International Economic Order. Yet, in the presenting of such a case, neither in South America nor in Africa was there a homogenous 'South' over against an equally homogenous 'North' (North America and Europe). The extent to which the politics and culture of North Africa was 'Middle Eastern' needs no further fresh reminder here. 'South Africa' did not directly meet 'North Africa', rather a series of African North/Souths collided and sometimes conflicted. Any African 'Southern' unity against the Northern hemisphere from which it had been colonized, so briefly as it was now beginning to appear, was fragile. Sections of this chapter explore these ambiguities.

The Brandt Commission

In September 1977, the former Federal German chancellor, Willy Brandt, agreed to head what was formally described as the Independent Commission on International Development. Earlier in the year, the American, Robert Macnamara, then President of the World Bank, urged some such informed enquiry. In Paris, a few months earlier, Giscard d'Estaing hosted a conference to consider the relationship between 'developed/industrialized' and 'developing/primary producing' countries. The time was ripe. Edward Heath, former British Prime Minister, was among the most prominent members of the new Commission. So was Shridath Ramphal (b.1928), who had taken office in 1975 as the second Secretary-General of the Commonwealth of Nations. The Commonwealth had 34 member states in 1975 and by the time Ramphal concluded his third and final term in 1990, membership had risen to 49. An Indo-Guyanese lawyer, educated in London and Harvard, he had previously been Guyana's foreign minister and in a sense spoke for the anglophone

Caribbean. He was therefore uniquely qualified to explore North/South relationships. The Commonwealth itself, with roughly a third of the world's states and a quarter of its population in its ranks, straddled North and South (and East and West) and could help the world to negotiate. A 'Commonwealth view', however, could only come about by sometimes difficult internal negotiation: there was now no 'natural' Commonwealth consensus.

The 'Brandt' Commission held its first meeting in December 1977 and remained in existence until 1983, when it issued its final document entitled *Common Crisis*. It was, however, its 1980 Report which received much global publicity. Its starting point was that the world, as it existed, did not provide social and economic equality for humanity. There was an urgent need to redress the disparity between the Northern and Southern hemispheres. To do so required a large-scale transfer of resources to the South. The international economic system, with its rules and regulations, was dominated by the North. The Commission stated that the needs of the poorest countries had to be given priority. The report then systematically considered those issues – poverty, health, housing, education and the status of women – where the disparity was most pronounced. It teemed with recommendations for reform. Only the acceptance of 'global responsibility' could rescue the world. A summit of world leaders could shift the international perspective on these matters. It was not, it argued, a simple question of scaling back the North in order to enrich the South. There could be mutual benefit even though, for the North, there would be some sacrifices 'in the short run'. The leitmotiv of the document was that national and global progress went hand in hand.

Government after government 'welcomed' the report, but the decade after its publication saw little evidence that 'global responsibility' was in fact being globally accepted. The independent nature of the Commission was both its strength and its weakness. Its members, 'influential' though they might be, were not executives in power. Before long, the report sat on shelves alongside other world audits. 'Political will' was needed to generate change, but how could it be generated? 'Western' governments, for their part, urged 'practical steps' and grew impatient with the sweeping resolutions characteristic of UNCTAD conferences. 'Practical steps' meant the kind of protracted discussions held under the mechanisms of the General Agreement on Trade and Tariffs (GATT). The Uruguay Round discussions began in 1986. An enhanced 'North/South' focus therefore limped along slowly in a Cold War world still accustomed primarily to thinking about itself in terms of 'West' and 'East'. It also became apparent that dividing the world approximately at a latitude of 30 degrees north was a pretty crude step. The Brandt Commission recognized that its hemispheric division designated certain countries inaccurately. Further, the Commission itself was not and could not be globally comprehensive. No Communist country took part in its proceedings. India, Japan, South Korea and Saudi Arabia gave some funding support but the bulk came from Western Europe (from the Netherlands in particular). The Commission's members came from Europe (France, the UK and Sweden), from Asia (India, Indonesia, Japan and Malaysia) from Africa (Algeria, Tanzania and Upper Volta) from North America (Canada and the USA), from South America (Chile, Colombia and Guyana) and from the Middle East (Kuwait) This was indeed diverse, but a different composition could have seen matters differently. Further, a 'country' perspective could be deceptive. 'North/South divides' were common within countries in both hemispheres. Local struggles to control resources, or to assert cultural, religious or ethnic hegemony internally, hindered, or even precluded, a hemispheric 'solidarity' either of 'North' or 'South'. So some unpicking of terms was necessary.

South America: shifting positions

The presence of three South Americans on the Brandt Commission, as also the earlier representation of Argentina, Brazil, Mexico, Peru and Venezuela at the antecedent Paris conference, perhaps at last signalled South America's significant presence on the 'world stage'. The Brandt Commission allocated all Latin America to the under-developed 'South'. However, a South America perceived through Chilean, Colombian and Guyanese eyes – Ramphal was scarcely a 'typical' South American – could not be the complete picture. The Brandt Report appeared at a time when the 'Parisian Five', and some of their neighbours, had been showing significant expansion in manufacturing. Economists talked about export-led dynamism. Argentina, Brazil and Uruguay were being identified as 'newly industrializing countries' which were 'joining the world' more comprehensively than before. At this juncture, this projection of dynamism sat oddly with their inclusion in a South designated as 'stagnant'.

Whether this expansion could be sustained was another matter. Indeed, within a few years, a very different picture was being presented. Dynamic improvement gave way suddenly to financial collapse – as happened in Argentina in 1981/82. A more general crisis then developed when it became clear that country after country, in a global economic recession, could no longer generate sufficient income to service incurred debts. Mexico was a particular case in point. It had also, of course, been true that accelerating growth rates did not in themselves eliminate poverty across the board. Thus the image of 'Latin America' was a puzzling combination of fiction and reality. One year a country could appear intoxicatingly vibrant, the next it was unable to pay foreign creditors. As a whole, Latin America could not be reduced to simple and uniform characteristics. European or American visitors to São Paulo could think that they were at home. If they went to other parts of Brazil, however, their impressions could be very different. They at least saw how vast and diverse the country was. The military government, which had been in power since 1965, believed that it alone could keep the country together. Only in 1985 did it step down. After a new constitution, elections in 1988 saw the return of a civilian government. The country shared with other Latin American countries both 'First World' and 'Third World' facets. In fact, hybridity – ethnically, culturally, linguistically and even religiously – was characteristic of the whole, with predominant elements differing widely: Argentina was not Ecuador, Columbia was not Uruguay, and so on. Latin America was no longer uniformly and completely Catholic and, within Catholicism, advocates of 'liberation theology' and 'tradition' clashed. Stereotypes took a long time to shift.

The feature common to most states, however, was that the underlying basis of government remained problematic and contested. Military men, in apparently time-honoured fashion, took power and amended constitutions to their satisfaction. Pinochet's military regime in Chile, firmly in place, promoted privatization and was seemingly achieving an 'economic miracle'. No miracles, however, brought back those the regime killed. Argentina too had its 'disappeared' at the hands of the military regime which in 1982 had launched the attack on the Falklands. It had received a message of support from Fidel Castro, but his expression of solidarity in the struggle against an obsolete European intrusion was to no avail. In the aftermath of failure, Raúl Alfonsín struggled to maintain civilian government and restore the rule of law. 'Revolutions', in one direction, and then back again, seemed so endemic that they were frequently described as 'typically Latin American'. Cuba remained a source of inspiration for various guerrilla groups. Their operations, however, had only limited success. Civil wars in Central America – Guatemala, Nicaragua and El Salvador – were devastating. The assassination of Archbishop Romero in San Salvador in March 1980 resonated around the Christian world. Three years later, the Pope paid a visit to Central America but found navigation across the political divisions difficult. Nicaragua was not like Poland. The boundaries between state, nation and faith were being stretched, sometimes to breaking point. It was with great difficulty, too, that the President of Costa Rica brought together the five Central American countries in 1987 in a renewed commitment to democratization and demilitarization.

And in the background, and sometimes in the foreground, was the USA. In a speech to a joint session of Congress in 1983, President Reagan revealed that El Salvador was nearer to Texas than Texas was to Massachusetts, with the corollary that guerrilla movements in Central America could threaten the security of the USA. The world beyond the Americas suspected that this overstated the position. The relationship between 'North' and 'South' in 'the Americas' continued to shift. Earlier, Carter had not ignored Latin America since his 'human rights' spotlight shone everywhere, or almost everywhere. He took a bold step in agreeing to a complete withdrawal from the US-controlled Panama Canal Zone by 2000. Hitherto it had been regarded as vital to the security of the USA. The emphasis in Washington moved, though not completely, from 'counterinsurgency' to a Kennedyesque espousal of political liberalization and social reform (in general terms). Regular visits to the White House from South/Central American leaders enabled encouraging political prognoses to be made. In January 1986, the President of Ecuador, filling his cabinet with self-made businessmen like himself, was deemed a philosophical and political soulmate. This 'kinship' was not entirely surprising, since the President had been educated in the USA. It was vital to find South American political groupings that were neither extreme Left nor extreme Right (as Washington interpreted these terms). That was not easy. This particular soulmate, faced with an insurrection, was soon being accused by his opponents of human rights abuses. Nicaragua proved to be the site where policy contradictions were exposed. In February 1979 US support for the dictatorial regime of Anastasio Somoza was abandoned and in July he fled to the USA. The Sandinista rebels formed a government. The incoming Reagan administration, however, formed the impression that the Sandinista were more interested in fostering Communism than in furthering 'human rights'. Washington, therefore, by one means or another, funded the 'Contras' in neighbouring Honduras in an attempt to bring down the Nicaraguan government. It did not, however, intervene directly with that objective. It also supported the government of El Salvador against a left-wing insurrection. It invaded Grenada in 1984 on the pretext that this small Caribbean island was about to become another Cuba.

There was no doubt, therefore, that the shepherd in the White House still envisaged 'the Americas' as a special set of relationships. North and South (and Central) constituted a cultural continuum in which the English- and Spanish-speaking worlds (and Portuguese-speaking Brazil) both clashed and co-operated in a particular way. Even to think in terms of these 'worlds', however, over-looked an increasingly vocal set of cultural and ethnic 'mixtures' being asserted across South America. A limit to US 'superintendence' was being reached. The Organization of American States (OAS), for example, refused to agree to the US suggestion that it should send a peacekeeping force to Nicaragua. Its major members had no wish to become players themselves 'out of area' and rejected Washington's pressure. It was becoming more and more necessary to think of a kaleidoscope of interstate relationship rather than a monochrome encounter between 'North' and 'South' (with a host of volatile 'miniature' states in between). Mexico, of course, was not miniature but, as already hinted, its oil revenues made it particularly susceptible to volatility. It was, of course, the actual neighbour of the USA. Mexico City continued on its headlong rate of expansion and ranked as one of the major cities in the world. It had thus the problems of housing, transport and pollution from which few of them were exempt. It was erratically dynamic. Was this the capital of 'North America's 'south' or of 'South America's 'north'? Put in that form, no simple answer was possible. As immigrants, legal and illegal, came into the USA in growing numbers, the first expressions of northern alarm about 'Hispanicization' emerged. The USA began to climb up the table of countries with Spanish-speaking populations. Baseball players from the Dominican Republic now played in US leagues. California, some said, might at a not-too-distant point be 'lost' to a USA deemed 'essentially' to be English-speaking. If the entire border could not be completely policed then the solidity of the states it enclosed might dissolve over time. A further ambivalent step in this respect might be a free-trade agreement between the two countries.

Such an agreement had been signed between Washington and Ottawa in 1983. It might lead to a comprehensive North American Free Trade Area, a step with considerable political implications. The US–Canadian agreement, however, was itself not simply one between anglophone good neighbours. The 'Canadian crisis' had been running in its existing form for a decade. English-speaking Canada worried, to different degrees, about American penetration of Canada, economically and culturally. French-speaking Canada worried about English-speaking Canada. A referendum in Quebec on sovereignty-association for the province did not carry (60/40 per cent), but the rights of both language groups continued to be contentious and ultimate political questions remained. Indeed, there were federal–central stresses in all three countries of the new 'North America' which might be emerging. In sum, as in Africa, 'North' and 'South' terminology only did duty at a basic level. The boundaries of 'the Americas' were porous. Florida, with its large Cuban population, was just across the water from Cuba – and on that island many different worlds met.

Cuba in Africa: North/South meets East/West

Cuba, however, was certainly more than a Caribbean 'irritant'. It remained a 'global' island rich in the rhetoric of 'global revolution'. A quarter of a century on, Castro had survived, indeed had in certain respects flourished, despite economic boycotts and other pressures from the North. It seemed obvious to the incoming Reagan that he was a surrogate, a man who gave Moscow its toehold in the Americas. Now Castro was going worldwide, or at least acting as Moscow's foot-soldier in Africa. In 1975 some 25,000 Cuban troops had crossed the Atlantic by sea and air to play a vital part in ensuring the success of the MPLA in the struggle for power in Angola. Castro became so caught up in it that one might believe he had lived in Angola all his life. So wrote his friend the celebrated Colombian writer Gabriel García Márquez. This African initiative was in fact probably Castro's own. Soviet assistance came in after the operation had begun. Castro visited Angola in March 1977 and received a triumphant welcome. Cuban assistance continued in technical, medical and educational aspects. At one point it was said that two-thirds of all doctors in Angola were Cubans. The Non-Aligned Summit, meeting in Colombo, Sri Lanka, in 1976 praised his role and awarded its forthcoming 1979 conference to Cuba. Before it was held, however, Cuban troops were also in action in the Horn of Africa. This time, the Soviet Union was involved from the outset, transporting some 16,000 Cubans in early 1978 to drive invading Somali troops out of the Ethiopian but Somali-inhabited province of Ogaden. Their involvement turned the tide against Somalia and buttressed the new Marxist regime of Mengistu in Addis Ababa. Cuban troops remained in Ethiopia for a decade, though they were not directly involved in the Ethiopian/Eritrean war. The latter was a conflict which rumbled on through the 1980s, with the Eritreans gaining the advantage. Soviet advisers moved into Addis Ababa. Castro argued that Cuba was only following the US example in sending troops abroad.

Havana, for a time, therefore, was the place where 'East/West' and 'North/South' met. The Angolan intervention, from one perspective, was an exercise in 'Southern' self-help, mediated, ironically, through Iberian languages. 'Africa' and the 'American Caribbean' was being re-established as an 'axis of progress'. History was being reversed. Castro's heroic status as a (Southern) Third World leader looked assured. However, the tangled and shifting struggles between Ethiopia and Somalia, with Eritrea thrown in, hardly constituted a natural sphere for Cuba or a conspicuous local example of the 'South' in revolt against the 'North'. What was crippling for Castro, in terms of Cuba's global positioning, was the Soviet invasion of Afghanistan, some three months after the 1979 Havana conference ended. In the UN, Cuba voted against the resolution, passed by a large majority, condemning the Soviet invasion. The Afghan regime, he said, should be supported against 'fundamentalists' – then perceived to be 'pro-Western'. However, his standing was damaged, and was only partially recovered by his impassioned campaigning for the cancellation of Third World debt. Speaking to Latin American journalists in 1985, for example, he argued that establishing a New International Economic Order was more important than achieving a few more revolutions. By the late 1980s, Cuba had resumed diplomatic and trading relations with the leading Latin American economic powers, as it did with Spain: another 'world' was reviving. Western Europe, however, was as much a part of 'the West' as the USA in insisting on debt repayment. Castro's new emphasis reflected an awareness that the mood in Moscow was changing. He had always been viewed there as something of a maverick. Now the Soviet Union was primarily going to attend to its own internal problems. Cuba was not going to be abandoned, but neither would it be an obstacle preventing Soviet–American accommodation. Such a Soviet priority, however, only fuelled the 'Southern' contention that, despite all the decades of East–West tension between opposing systems, both the Soviet Union and the USA were basically 'Northern' Superpowers sustaining their own particular brands of 'Northern' values and interests.

African kaleidoscope: no centre of gravity?

There had been a time, immediately post-independence, when Nigeria looked to become the global 'voice' of Africa. Twenty years later, however, with its interstate, inter-ethnic and inter-religious conflict by no means stilled, its external projection could not gain momentum. It was, however, Africa's most populous state, though the exact population and its composition were matters of ritual dispute. Men at the top, civilian or military, came and went. They were not known to be poorer from office-holding. Much oil revenue, which was supposed to provide the country's passport to global eminence, disappeared into private pockets. Corruption was described as endemic. A Nigeria which might 'lead' Africa exhibited in microcosm the problems of the continent as a whole. The OAU wrestled ineffectively with its disunity. There were ample expressions of purpose and intention but no means of implementing a 'continental strategy'. The eager endorsement of pan-African unions between states, characteristic of the OAU's early years, proved empty rhetoric. Such 'unions' between states as were sometimes announced left no discernible trace, particularly those announced in Tripoli. Rulers struggled to maintain the integrity of their states and try, if possible, to create a 'national' unity. Even where the outside world sometimes perceived there to be a common cultural/religious heritage – as in the Maghreb – there was protracted conflict. Mauritania, Morocco and Algeria were locked in dispute over the future of 'Western Sahara'. The common cultural/religious heritage of 'the Maghreb' seemed to count for little. The continuing civil war in Chad was a reminder of historic North–South struggles across the length of the Sahara. Gaddafi of Libya, whose family/clan had stemmed originally from that zone of borderless borders, meddled. 'West Africa' was no nearer an entity, though its francophone and anglophone states sought separately to develop Economic Communities. The languages of Europe continued to be a vital means both of communicating with the 'outside world' and maintaining internal government and administration amidst a plethora of indigenous languages.

The boundaries established by the colonial powers proved unexpectedly durable, though, in West Africa, French forces were often on hand to sustain them. The interethnic and often related inter-religious tensions, alluded to in earlier chapters, remained disruptive. Violence was never far below the surface. Population growth was rapid. While some military dictators were overthrown – Idi Amin of Uganda, for example, made his way (via Libya) to an agreeable retirement in Saudi Arabia in 1980 – others remained firmly in place. A coup by Samuel Doe in Liberia in 1980 seemed to have ended the domination of the country by Americo-Liberians, but a decade later Charles Taylor, an Americo-Liberian, led an invasion force and a civil war began. The most egregious example of military rule, however, was provided by Joseph Mobutu in the Congo. In other states there was the problem of transition when a 'founding father' of the nation died – as happened in Kenya on the death of Kenyatta in 1978. His successor, Daniel Arap Moi (b.1924), was a former schoolteacher. Initially he had gingerly to rely, as a member of a minority tribe, on Kikuyu support. There were delicate, and not so delicate, tribal manoeuvres. The Kenya African National Union (KANU) was declared the only legal political party in 1982 (as Kaunda's party had been declared in Zambia). An ambitious Development Plan suggested a more 'free enterprise' future than the African Socialism which Julius Nyerere struggled to produce in neighbouring Tanzania. Nyerere stood down in 1985. His unusual achievement had been to translate Shakespeare's *Julius Caesar* into Swahili. The possibility of assassination was indeed not far from the minds of most African leaders. It was a dispiriting decade.

There was a paradox in Africa's relations with the world beyond. Independence notwithstanding, 'outside intervention', some examples of which have just been given, appeared to be accelerating into the early 1980s. There was scarcely a country in Africa where the two Superpowers, or their allies or proxies, were not to some degree active, covertly or openly. They backed individuals, factions or parties sympathetic to their interests or ideologies. Sometimes clients switched sides. The White House in September 1985 found President Machel of Mozambique to be quite a guy. It was good to know that he intended to be 'non-aligned' instead of 'a Soviet patsy'. Visiting leaders from Togo or Botswana could be crisply labelled: pro-West, anti-Communist, or 'for free enterprise and democracy'. There was not much else to talk to them about. In the maelstrom of indigenous conflicts, however, the real objectives of clients proved difficult to discern. Labels attached to political parties or development programmes did not seem to mean very much. External involvement was held to exacerbate, if not cause, instability. 'Africa' as a totality, in these circumstances, could rarely make its mark in the world. Rather, a new kind of 'division of spheres' was appearing. The argument was that if the Superpowers had not meddled, Africa would have been more stable.

There was, however, the contrary argument that this rivalry enabled African rulers to prise various kinds of aid out of their patrons (whatever use was made of it). If the overarching 'world struggle' were to diminish, or end, external

Powers might lose interest in Africa. They already displayed little appetite for direct military intervention to 'maintain stability'. The unhappy US experience in aiding Somalia to resist an Ethiopian post-Ogaden invasion counselled against any intervention elsewhere. Even the Cubans probably found themselves staying longer, and more complicatedly, than they had originally anticipated. Lacking anything better, Superpowers found themselves backing regimes lacking ideological purity or democratic legitimacy: Joseph Mobutu hardly furthered American democratic ideals. A lack of interest in African problems, however, might simply produce 'failed states' –with serious consequences for the world.

The image of an 'independent Africa' riddled with intertwining poverty, corruption, tyranny and violence established itself externally to an accelerating degree. In ex-colonial European states such assessments mingled awkwardly with a sense of responsibility, or even guilt, for the picture being disclosed. The European Powers were now witnessing, from a distance, extreme patterns of indigenous domination and exploitation as bad as or worse than any they had themselves imposed, or so they thought. How far could the colonial era be held responsible for the present? Whatever the answer to that question, the 'African world', it increasingly seemed, was never going to follow the prescriptions handed out in the 'decolonization' package. A 'pre-European' past could not return, but neither could or indeed should a fading European superimposition trample over 'tradition'. But what counted as 'tradition' stretched the minds of ethnologists and anthropologists. It was time, perhaps, to redefine *négritude*. How, in religious/political terms, did 'Euro-Africa', 'America–Africa' or 'Africa–Middle East', intersect? The terminology of 'North' and 'South', except as a general indication of 'wealth' and 'poverty', could not do justice to this complexity. Islamic, Christian and 'indigenous' religious worlds continued to overlap. 'Africa' might already be, if enthusiasm, numbers and commitment constituted the yardstick, the dancing if poor heart of the 'Christian world'. If so, it would not be dominated by that European Christian world – with its supposed contemporary aberrations – from which it had sprung. There were, therefore, tender ties that bound continents, but their terms needed renegotiation – and might not succeed. Moreover, given the extent to which, in varying proportions, Christianity and Islam existed throughout the continent, there was often a hard edge to their coexistence which was not so evident, at least as yet, in Europe. That continent seemed bent, predominantly, on achieving a public 'secularism', though one which took many forms. Historic images characterizing continents were in flux.

It was, of course, in southern Africa that the relationship between indigenous whites and blacks remained central. Southern Africa was a world issue. The local and the global again intersected. In 1977 President Carter appointed an Afro-American to be his country's ambassador to the UN (the first). New Orleans-born Andrew Young (b.1932), a Protestant pastor, had been prominent in the Southern Christian Leadership conference. He was in Memphis when Martin Luther King was assassinated. He had subsequently been elected to the US Congress. 'Speaking for America' from such a background in the UN advertised to the world that America had changed. Its ambassador, however, felt it had still not changed sufficiently. 'The world' had a view about southern Africa, though scarcely a uniform one. In Rhodesia, though in no position to exercise it, Britain still had a constitutional responsibility. The past had left a British legacy, a contentious one, in South Africa. However, in 1975, the British government did not attempt to extend its use of the Simonstown naval base in South Africa. The USA, for its part, had an overarching sense of the global significance of southern Africa. It was no surprise that Henry Kissinger, on several visits, sought, though without much success, to find solutions acceptable both to the 'frontline' neighbouring African states and the South African government.

The UN General Assembly heard many denunciations of apartheid. The 'archaic' notion that the internal affairs of a state were its business alone was swept aside. A Special Committee on Apartheid was formed. Afro-Asian states had the votes to pass condemnatory resolutions but had no means of implementing them. Young's appointment to the UN was made in that context. In London and Washington, a settlement in Rhodesia seemed the first priority. Given an African brief, Young and the British foreign secretary, David Owen, toured African capitals. The independence of Mozambique, a weakening of South African support and a waxing guerrilla campaign were combining, by this juncture, to put increased pressure on the Smith regime. Discussions between all the parties began, ended and began again. The term 'majority rule' was being variously interpreted. Smith cobbled together his own alternative settlement but the British government would not accept it, nor, of course, would the Patriotic Front (which ostensibly fused the rival ZANU and ZAPU parties of Mugabe and Nkomo, respectively). In 1979 a new constitutional settlement presented by a new British Conservative government was agreed to. By this juncture, however, Young was no longer in post. He had spoken out too freely, not only on African matters, but had also established a covert contact with the PLO. A new black face could only go so far.

The implementation of the London agreement saw a brief period of British rule, followed in February 1980 by elections on a universal suffrage (though with some seats reserved for whites), and Rhodesia became independent as Zimbabwe in April. Mugabe's ZANU achieved a sweeping victory in an election not devoid of intimidation. It did not take long, however, for the ZANU/ZAPU and, in tandem, Shona/Ndebele relationships to worsen. Seeing a Marxist future in a one-party state under a professed Catholic ahead, a white exodus gathered pace. The White House found Mugabe a very opinionated man. Only a rump remained optimistic about the country's black/white future. Whites, however, remained prominent in business. In 1985 their reserved seats in parliament were abolished. Questions of landownership moved to the fore. There was unfinished business.

All along, however, it was the future of South Africa which was the main issue in southern Africa. The facts, at one level, were still simple, but becoming starker. A white population of 3.7 million out of a total population of 21.7 million in 1970 became 4.9 million out of a total of 33.6 million in 1985. South Africa could claim to be the only fully functioning multi-party parliamentary democracy in Africa – but it was one which only its white population engaged in. The 'world', whether democratic or not, could not countenance this situation. The process of turning South Africa into a pariah state accelerated. Its products could be boycotted. Sanctions and embargoes could be imposed. That was what the outside world could do, and to some extent did do. Not to take such steps could seem to condone an intolerable situation. Yet such pressure might still not produce the desired change, or only too tardily. Further, the South African economy was sophisticated and 'developed'. If it collapsed it would be blacks who suffered first. Banning arms sales to Pretoria might, and did, stimulate domestic arms production. Some states, in addition, did not like the precedent which this example of 'interference' in internal affairs constituted.

Some states thought that 'positive engagement' rather than ostracism could persuade the South African government to change course. Quiet diplomacy, President Reagan told a visiting bishop, Desmond Tutu, was making considerable progress. He thought his visitor naïve, unaware of the extent to which the South African problem was tribal, not racial. Western states hesitated. In 1987 the UN Security Council established a 'contact group' consisting of the USA, Canada, Britain, Federal Germany and France to talk with South Africa about the future of South-West Africa/Namibia. Later, in 1985–86, an 'Eminent Persons Group' drawn from the Commonwealth attempted to broker a deal between the government and the ANC. The total collapse of the South African economy, it was recognized, would destabilize fragile neighbouring states. These states were already 'exporting' labour to South Africa. If there were no pressure from outside, however, a cataclysmic climax looked likely.

Defence Minister P.W. Botha (b.1916) became South African Prime Minister in September 1978. He never forgot that his father had fought against the British in the Anglo-South African war. He had a definite view of the world beyond his country's borders, though he knew little of it at first hand. What he saw, he told an audience a few months after his appointment, was a Third World War already in progress. There was an external attempt to control minds and spirits and soften people up ahead of a military onslaught. Marxism was at work and, by unleashing revolutionary warfare, was trying to force South Africa to change its domestic policy in favour of what he called 'Pan-Africanism'. His government, however, would not wilt. What was so puzzling, he thought, was that the USA could not see South Africa as a firm ally in opposing Communism. It was surely undeniable that there were Communists at the highest level in the ANC? Washington did indeed know that, but considered the government's repressive policies only likely to increase their importance. Afrikaners, Botha implied, knew that the world was always against them, but they would endure. Such language evoked a ready response. It was difficult, however, to keep the National Party together and a conservative faction split off.

Botha did not suddenly become 'liberal'. He did, however, speak of doing 'justice to every population group' and tried to turn the tables of argument. A wise government, he claimed, recognized the diversity of South Africa: Africans, coloured, whites and Indians. It was appropriate, therefore, to make new constitutional provision for this diversity. The result was a constitutional shake-up in 1983/84 which saw Botha becoming an executive State President with a parliament consisting of three chambers for whites, Indians and coloureds, each in theory responsible for its 'own' affairs. The way the system was supposed to work was bizarre. The equally bizarre existing patchwork of African 'homelands' was supposed to become independent – and thus demonstrate that South Africa was undertaking its own 'decolonization'. However, when the Chief Minister of Kwazulu, Mangosuthu Buthelezi, refused to take the offered 'independence', the dream world of the project became apparent. The Zulus were the largest African ethno-linguistic group. Botha also made some changes, including recognizing African trade unions and decriminalizing sexual relations across the colour bar. He nevertheless still saw himself in embattled defence of civilization. This was war. Internally, it necessarily involved using nasty men and taking nasty actions. State security became paramount. Vigorous 'defence', in the process, eroded the values it claimed to defend. Whether, externally, the best form of defence was attack – an incursion into Angola, raids into Zambia, assisting rebels in Mozambique – remained perpetually problematic. The South African defence forces were strong but would be weakened by too wide a deployment. The mounting campaign of sabotage suggested a grim future, but could still probably be contained. The more militant elements within the ANC saw sabotage as but the prelude to an inescapable war. Whether such a war could be won was another matter.

South Africa was the product of multi-layered conquests. Its future could only be a matter for speculation, but no easy solution beckoned. Much centred on whether there was or could be a nation that was a 'South African nation' to which all could belong. The ANC was not the *South* African Congress but neither was it the African *Nationalist* Congress. But the 'African nation' was ambitious. Was there not a Zulu nation, to name only one possibility? The National Party did not add the word Afrikaner to its title, but no one doubted what nation it had in mind. The 'British' in South Africa still did not know quite what to call themselves. Coloureds lent one way, now another. So did Indians.

'Ethnicity' naturally encompassed many variations in social behaviour, none of which, given the country's plurality, could be deemed normative. Its Christianity was dominant but, notwithstanding the role of particular church leaders, such as Desmond Tutu, the churches themselves often reflected rather than transcended ethnicity. The outside world largely communicated with South Africa through the medium of English, notwithstanding that Afrikaans was the Cabinet's first language. Only a minority of South Africans, however, perhaps 10 per cent, habitually spoke English at home. No member of Nelson Mandela's well-connected family had ever been to school before him. There he had been given the name Nelson – he could never understand why – by his English teacher. From his prison on Robben Island, he could not directly participate in the unfolding scene, but Nelson's eye was not blind. Different countries elsewhere also watched and waited, only too aware that the fractious issues of state, nation and faith in South Africa were theirs too. The long road to freedom was universal. The Union of South Africa had been created by the British Act of Parliament in 1910. The Republic alone, of all states in Africa, had 'Africa' in its name. Its future was precarious. It might in the future gain some new name. Its retention thus far was not only because no agreed alternative could be found but also because it constituted a statement that 'Africa' existed.

21
Afghanistan to Sri Lanka: 'South Asia'?

No Asian state had Asia in its title. There was no Union of South Asia. It was a matter of opinion, as has already been seen, where it began and ended. If it extended from Kabul to Colombo that might only be because it had formally and formerly been in a certain sense 'British', though never administered by them as one entity. That imprint, by the mid-1970s, had been removed for a quarter of a century, though still not entirely erased. Nothing had directly replaced it. There was evidently some kind of 'South Asian' space, but who controlled it, and on what terms, was problematic. At the 'extremes', the affairs of Afghanistan and Sri Lanka spilled over their boundaries. Some thought that Afghanistan was part of 'the Middle East' and not 'South Asian' at all. It was all a question of vantage point. There could be no dispute, however, that it now found itself locked into wider worlds beyond either.

Kabul's cabals

Kabul, in the mid-1970s and thereafter, was a city where no one felt very securely 'in place'. President Daoud, having deposed his cousin, the King, and ended the monarchy in 1973, sought help wherever he could get it – from Moscow, Tehran or elsewhere. Before the country could be meaningfully connected to the outside world its internal communications needed to be transformed. Afghanistan, as the British in particular had known in the past, was difficult to hold together. Only despots managed it. In 1978 Daoud was overthrown and killed. The People's Democratic Party of Afghanistan (PDPA), formed in secret in January 1965, took over. It had itself split into two factions, the Khalk and the Parcham. The former had a largely Pashtun composition and the latter drew upon Tajiks, Hazara and other ethnic minorities. Personal quarrels, and worse, seemed endemic within these ethnic groupings. Mohammed Taraki (b.1917), an early graduate of Kabul University, proclaimed a Democratic Republic of Afghanistan and, in theory, united the two factions. The symbolism of replacing a green flag by a red one was not lost. His 'programme' in 1978 was designed to bring Afghanistan into a 'modern world': land reform, basic literacy and 'women's rights'. In December 1978 he signed a Treaty of Friendship with the Soviet Union. By that juncture, however, identified as a Communist, he was already facing open revolt. Miscellaneous insurgents professed an Islamic bond. Fighting between the two PDPA factions further complicated the position. The army could not be relied on. Soviet arms, equipment and advisers were in the country by the spring of 1979. Afghan soldiers, however, had a habit of slipping into the night and taking their arms with them.

Kabul, home to the country's 'educated elite', as identified externally, was full of cabals. Hafizullah Amin, the Prime Minister, disposed of Taraki and took over. No Kabul government, however brutal, could control a country which was still overwhelmingly rural and 'tribal'. Outsiders liberally employed the stereotype that 'Afghans', if they existed, were (genetically?) 'fiercely independent'. Washington, Moscow, Tehran, Islamabad (with a link to Beijing) and Delhi nevertheless all 'had views'. Events in Iran might spill over into Afghanistan in a way uncongenial to either 'East' or 'West' (not that Moscow was east of Kabul).

The Soviet Union decided to act. Brezhnev, though basking in his recent 'unexpected' award of the Lenin Prize for Literature, had not, in his excitement, lost his grip on his 'Doctrine'. The Kabul regime, though arguably dysfunctional, had established a 'Socialist state'. The course of history could not be challenged by a ramshackle collection of 'reactionary' Islamic warriors. Even so, earlier pleas for assistance had been ignored. In late December 1979, however, Soviet forces successfully invaded. The Soviet Union, it might extenuatingly be said, was simply taking the Russian Empire a stage further. Initially, indeed, as a sign of 'brotherhood', some of the Soviet troops deployed deliberately came from the Central Asian republics. It appears, however, that these troops became rather too fraternal and were withdrawn. Hafizullah Amin proved a casualty of the liberating invasion which he had ostensibly invited. Moscow had always suspected that he was putting out feelers to world capitals where feelers should not be put. Amin, like Taraki, had had a spell studying at Said's university, Columbia in New York (of course, before Said was there). His English was excellent, his Russian non-existent. It could not be denied that he was a Marxist, but he was very much an Afghan one, indeed a Pashtun one. So he was disposed of and replaced by the more malleable Babrak Karmal (b.1929), who came in the Soviet baggage. He was a son of one of the monarchy's major-generals and another of that Kabul generation entranced by illicit Marxism. He tried to mend fences with Islamic clerics by indicating respect for the sacred principles of Islam. Some clerics were despatched to see for themselves how Islam flourished in the Soviet Union, a research trip which required careful selection of destinations. The 'Limited Contingent' that was the Soviet troop presence of around 100,000 men had not expected the kind of war it was fighting. Sooner or later, however, Brezhnev, Andropov, Chernenko and, initially, Gorbachev, assumed that the constellation of the *Mujahideen* would be defeated, by one means or another, though the cost was proving excessive. The Afghan army was arrayed, gloomily and uncertainly, in the middle. Official information about Afghanistan was kept to a minimum in the Soviet Union itself, but news filtered through. It was difficult to discern what kind of 'world' would eventually emerge victorious in this confused conflict.

The USA was not displeased that the Soviet Union was bogged down in Afghanistan. It was having its own 'Vietnam'. It has sometimes been supposed that a trap for Moscow had been set. With American help, insurgents could make life so difficult for the Afghan government that the Soviet Union would feel bound to intervene. Then, when the Soviet Union did intervene, it could be pilloried in the West for ignoring state sovereignty. Western European states suggested, 'Helsinki' notwithstanding, that they were still vulnerable to such aggression. Their Communist parties were at least embarrassed by the Soviet action, and sometimes more. The USA, accustomed to hearing from the Middle East, and elsewhere, that the 'Jewish lobby' controlled its foreign policy, was pleased that even the most anti-Sadat of Arab regimes now condemned Soviet violation of a Muslim land. In the UN, after a while, 108 states 'strongly deplored' the Soviet action and only 18 did not (with 18 abstentions). Carter pondered an appropriate punitive response. The grain embargo, which he had always hitherto opposed, was a 'weapon'. Brezhnev knew that no American military action was likely. Carter's Rapid Deployment Force of 100,000 men, announced earlier in 1979, could not be rapidly deployed: it did not yet exist. One obvious option presented itself in these circumstances – to boycott the Olympic Games. Moscow intended them (in June 1980) to be the world's greatest sporting occasion. In the event, 45 states prevailed upon their 'independent' national Olympic Committees to withdraw from the Moscow Games. Needless to say, such a 'world action' did not lead to a Soviet withdrawal from Afghanistan. The war continued.

India: Indira's red carpet

Britain and Russia had played a nineteenth-century 'great game' in Afghanistan. In 1979, however, all this was history. No British government supposed that British forces would ever be fighting in Afghanistan again. But, whereas in the past 'Afghanistan' had been a problem for a single unit, a British-ruled India, now it impacted on its two contending successor states. Moreover, simultaneously, both countries, India and Pakistan, were themselves being wracked internally by comparable issues of identity and allegiance. 'Afghanistan' impacted on them. For India, there was Kashmir in the north-west and Assam in the north-east, together with the 'Tamil question' in the south-east (and in Sri Lanka). 'Overspills' therefore abounded as states, nations and faiths struggled for self-definition and, with it, for supremacy.

Indira Gandhi had made a close relationship with the Soviet Union a cardinal aspect of India's foreign policy. In her 'Disciplined Democracy', the Soviet Union was on hand to help in the 'hard work' of tackling India's poverty. Gandhi declared that she had no intention of enforcing one-party rule, but this pledge might not be honoured. The processes of parliamentary government, as operated since 1947, were more or less in abeyance. The Prime Minister had her own inner circle of advisers, and her younger son Sanjay (b.1947) became very influential. Russians became familiar faces in the capital and in the main Indian cities. A chain of Soviet bookshops sprang up across the country. A predilection for Five-Year Plans was already firmly established in Delhi. More industries were nationalized. India was not 'going Communist', but 'Controlled Capitalism' was being taken further, 'tilting' India away from the USA. Nixon's 'tilt' towards Pakistan, and his behaviour during the Bangladesh crisis, had upset Indian opinion. The arrival of a Democrat president helped to improve relations somewhat, though it was disturbing that Americans seemed more interested in visiting China than India. There was another factor, too. In 1974 India had carried out a successful nuclear explosion in the Rajasthan desert. Literally and metaphorically, it vibrated in Pakistan. There was an Indian denial of any intention to become a 'nuclear weapons country'. Even so, a signal was being sent to China and Pakistan, in particular, and to the world in general. India might be a poor nation but it could also be some kind of Great Power. Over these years, the Delhi government had been busy reorganizing its north-eastern region bordering on China and Burma with security in mind.

Yet, despite its favourable attitude towards the Soviet Union, India remained, at a certain level, a part of that English-speaking world which found its politico/cultural expression in the Commonwealth of Nations. India retained its membership on a pragmatic rather than sentimental basis. The 'Emergency' upset the 'principles' to which the Commonwealth aspired, but there was no rupture. Yet it might be that 'Western civilization', late-British style, as moderated institutionally since 1947, was not in fact embedded for all time as part of 'Indian identity'. Indians, it was said, had been used, for centuries, to being *ruled*. In existing circumstances, that was perhaps the most salient fact. In 1974 Indira Gandhi had publicly accepted that the world found India difficult to understand: it was 'too, deep, contradictory and diverse' to be easily comprehended. Its free expression of opinion, comparatively speaking, meant that its underlying unity was missed. A few years later, however, 'free expression' was not very evident. In prison, J.P. Narayan (b.1902), veteran voice of the rural poor, wrote that he had never believed that Mrs Gandhi was a democrat. By inclination and conviction she was a dictator. The Soviet Union was backing her to the hilt. The time would come, however, when the Russians would dump her 'on the garbage heap of history' and install their own man in her place. What a shame, he said loftily, that India would become another Pakistan or Bangladesh.

It was, however, the Indian electorate in March 1977 rather than the Soviet Union which, as it were, dumped Indira on the 'garbage heap'. In January she had released her leading opponents from prison and suspended the ban on political parties. Her opponents, uniformly elderly, regrouped, cobbled together the Janata – a coalition of four parties – and gained a clear majority over Indira's Congress, thus ending the party's thirty years of uninterrupted power. India made a fresh start under an octogenarian, Moraji Desai, assisted, if that is the word, by Cabinet colleagues from different groups, all of respectable vintage. They were preoccupied with positioning themselves to succeed the Prime Minister. Desai's determination to remain in office, with his son wheeling and dealing in his shadow, was the only clear message. Only one thing looked evident – the waxing strength of Hindu nationalism as represented by the Jana Singh group within the coalition. What was billed as 'the last chance for democracy' did not last long. The Indian President, running out of physically or politically eligible prime ministers, dissolved parliament and ordered fresh elections for January 1980. The contents of Narayan's dustbin were then recycled. Indira Gandhi and her Congress Party emerged triumphant with a two-thirds majority. This time it would be a government that actually functioned as such. It might be, after all, that India 'deep down' did need what Mrs Gandhi would now administer. The election also returned, for the first time, her son Sanjay. A succession seemed assured.

The election had taken place with the Soviet invasion of Afghanistan occupying the headlines. The Janata government had soft-pedalled the Soviet connection somewhat but retained the Friendship Treaty. It had, however, not developed any very distinctive policy concerning Afghanistan. The likelihood that the new Gandhi government would instantly condemn the Soviet action was slight. Taking a call from Carter offering her his congratulations, the US President found her polite but cool. At the UN, it transpired that even Cuba was more reticent than India in its public support for Soviet action in Afghanistan. In private, however, though without effect, Moscow was urged by Delhi to withdraw. Policymakers in India well knew that, over centuries, it had been conquerors from the north-west who had created the multi-layered identity of India. Was Afghanistan the prelude to another conquest?

That might be far-fetched, but not even a sympathetically inclined government could be sure. It might even be conceivable, but surely no more than conceivable, that in these circumstances India, Bangladesh and Pakistan would together defend the enigmatic space that was 'South Asia'. For the moment, however, whatever reservations it might have, Delhi could only see disadvantages in any victory which might ultimately come to the *Mujahideen*. In F.A. Ahmed (1974–77), India had its second Muslim President. His appointment was a further signal that there was a clear place for Muslims in the Indian polity. The world was also not allowed to forget that there were more Muslims in India than there were in Pakistan. The reverberations from a revivified Islamic Afghanistan, however, might well be disturbing, not least within Pakistan.

Pakistan: different directors, different directions

Diplomatic relations between Pakistan and Afghanistan had been broken off in 1973 and were not restored until 1977. Both governments, not without justice, accused the other of sheltering dissidents and fomenting insurrection. Boundary questions between the two countries had been endemic ever since the creation of Pakistan. One particular flashpoint was Baluchistan, in the west, part of which Afghanistan had long claimed. The Pakistani army was deployed to fight a rebellion there in the mid-1970s. Dissent in that culturally diverse province could not easily be reconciled. Making Pakistan a genuinely federal country adequately expressing both its diversity and its unity was only beginning. A new constitution adopted in 1973 pointed the way, but achievement was another matter. The tasks before Bhutto were huge. He failed to carry the popular following which he enjoyed, at least in some parts, into an effective parliamentary system with viable political parties not based on patronage. Some see the 'two faces of Bhutto': the Oxford-educated 'progressive' and the ancestral 'feudal despot'.

These two strands in his make-up were perhaps never reconciled. Such a depiction is tempting, but superficial. Pakistan as a whole had two faces, indeed many faces. The displacements of 1947, now compounded by 'redefinition' with the 'loss' of Bangladesh, left its place in the world enduringly problematic.

Bhutto had little prospect of making new Pakistan a significant voice in South or South-East Asia. His orientation, rather, was westwards, but not to 'the West'. He took Pakistan out of the Commonwealth in 1972 – it was subsequently to be in and out of membership. More specifically 'anti-Western' was his withdrawal of the country from SEATO. Pakistan's future axis, it seemed, was to be an Islamic one. The 1973 constitution affirmed that Islam was the state religion. Only Muslims could be president or prime minister. The state should facilitate the living of Islamic lives. Minorities, chiefly Christian, were accorded their own right to worship but would inevitably be subjected to social pressure within such an enveloping Islamic framework. This burgeoning alignment received confirmation when the Conference of Islamic States held its 1974 conference in Lahore. It had brought, amongst others, Yasser Arafat, King Faisal of Saudi Arabia and Presidents Assad, Sadat and Boumedienne together. Most spectacularly, speaking in the new Gaddafi stadium in the city, the Libyan leader declared that his country's resources were Pakistan's. Even if that proved to be somewhat inaccurate, a Pakistani course had been set. So too had been one which would lead Pakistan to produce a nuclear weapon, the 'Islamic bomb' (it was observed that 'Hindus', 'Christians' and probably 'Jews' had such bombs). The argument specifically was that, post-1971, Pakistan needed a nuclear shield for protection against its larger neighbour. The USA, which felt that its 'tilt' towards Pakistan had received scant reward, tried by sticks and carrots, but unsuccessfully, to thwart the Pakistani nuclear project. Pakistan's burgeoning Middle Eastern/Islamic orientation existed alongside a strengthening of the existing relationship with China. It was not only Islamabad's largest supplier of arms but both countries agreed to construct a highway which directly connected them through the Kunjerab Pass.

By 1978, however, when this Karakoram Highway was completed, Bhutto was no longer in office and the 'experiment with democracy' had come to an end. A year later, he was executed, having been found guilty of being responsible for the death of an opponent. General Zia ul-Haq (b.1922), Chief of Staff of the Pakistan army, carried out a coup against Bhutto in July 1977 under an appealing codename, 'Operation Fairplay'. It soon became clear, however, that this was more than an exercise to 'restore order' (there had latterly been much disorder) and, as initially stated, to prepare for fair elections. It signified, rather, the inauguration of a serious period of military rule. Zia, expressing scepticism about the suitability of 'Western democracy' for Pakistan, retained his military post but combined it after 1978 with the office of President. He lasted far longer than many thought likely. He managed to achieve a massive endorsement of his rule in 1985 and shrewdly combined a lifting of martial law in that year with further enhancement of his own powers.

Zia knew different worlds. Born in East Punjab and educated at St Stephen's College in Delhi (which also, in F.A. Ahmed, produced, as we have noted, a Muslim President of India), he came from a middle-class military background.

His own youthful wartime service had been in the (British) Indian army in Burma, Malaya and Java. In 1947 his family had struggled across the border from Jullundur, his birthplace in India, to Peshawar in Pakistan. Serving in the new Pakistan army, he steadily rose through the ranks. Seconded to Jordan in 1969 to train the Jordanian army, he helped mastermind King Hussein's operations against the PLO. Pakistan's orientation towards the Arab world – many Pakistani workers, particularly from Punjab, were to be found in the Gulf states – seemed to be confirmed.

Internally, Zia was a skilled manipulator whose deployment of military men in some key civilian positions cemented the army's central position in the country. Reagan, noting that Zia was a good man (cavalry), got along fine with him on their first meeting in December 1982. Zia's background predisposed him to push forward further with Islamization. Personal conviction and political strategy conveniently combined to suggest to Zia that it was the key to Pakistan's stability. Islamization, however, was a protracted and contentious process. It could not be instantly implemented. Some 'Western-educated' elements in society remained attached to aspects of the British-inherited legal code. More problematic, however, was agreement on what a truly Islamic system actually was. The process brought out, and indeed exacerbated, conflicting Shi'a (the minority) and Sunni (the majority) interpretations. Differences of religious practice between an austere 'puritanism' on the one hand and the ceremonies associated with *sufi* shrines on the other also came to the fore. At long last, to the satisfaction of the 'orthodox', the campaign to have the Ahmadi sect categorized as non-Muslim was succeeding. Christians, latterly, found themselves in danger of severe punishment if any remarks they might make about Mohammed could be interpreted as derogatory.

By the time Zia was killed in a mysterious plane crash in August 1988 the cumulative effect of the process which he accelerated was substantial. To the outside world, Pakistan was more conspicuously an 'Islamic state' than it had been in 1977, even though what kind of Islamic state was still in doubt. A 'Western world' preoccupied, it seemed, with 'women's rights', found them differently interpreted in Pakistan. Not everybody agreed that presidential government (Zia fashion) was the form 'nearest to Islam' or that political parties were non-Islamic – both rulings in the early 1980s of the advisory Council of Islamic Ideology. So, perhaps the regime's pursuit of elusive unity through Islam was only succeeding in revealing the fissures in Islam itself. The crosscurrents were difficult to determine. 'Fissures in Islam' were part and parcel of ethnic, linguistic and cultural alignments. In that respect, therefore, Islamization could not in itself create a unity that was 'national'. There was a continuing claim that Pakistan was still being subjected to 'Punjabization', but whether that claim was made in Sind (home of the 'martyred' Bhutto'), Baluchistan or elsewhere, critics could not counter it effectively. How many 'nationalities' did the Pakistani 'nation' have? No clear answer could be given. A visitor to Karachi, no longer the capital but still the country's major port and commercial hub, with a population some twenty times greater than its halfmillion of 1947, would have found a city struggling to cope. Different ethnic groups occupied different districts and monopolized particular occupations.

Drug addiction and trafficking were rife. Gangs with guns were on the street. Law and order could break down at any moment.

'Afghanistan' played into this situation in multiple ways. Refugees from the fighting flooded into Pakistan – estimated figures vary, but probably, in time, came to a couple of millions. Pakistan in turn became the base from which certain Afghan groups, by no means of one mind and with different backers, sought to direct operations across the border. What might be called a continuum of conflict emerged in which 'internal' issues became enmeshed in the wider struggle. Carter had authorized arms supplies – of Eastern European origin so as to appear to have come from Afghan army defectors – for the resistance fighters in Afghanistan. Co-operation with the Pakistan Intelligence Service was vital for this conduit to be effective. Carter's successor, from 1981, was less timid and the weapons which reached Afghanistan increased in sophistication. More fundamentally, however, the successive US administrations came round to giving Pakistan continuing financial support. This buttressed the Zia regime, though it did not prevent the country's very high level of military expenditure unbalancing its economy and pushing it into crisis. In relation to Afghanistan, Zia attempted to orchestrate the Islamic world (and Saudi Arabia was a very large financial contributor) to support resistance. He did not live, however, to see the Soviet endgame in that country.

After his death, Zia was replaced by Benazir Bhutto (b.1953). Two broad groupings had fought elections and her Pakistan People's Party (PPP) gained the largest number of seats, but not a majority. From the beginning, however, although the army beat a formal retreat, hostility towards her was scarcely disguised. If her government had shown itself to be competent and incorrupt her position would have been stronger, but it was not. Her 'national' base was weak (only in Sind and the north-west did her party have a majority). In 1989 her future did not look bright, as was shortly to be confirmed. In a wider sense, her personal position illustrated the paradoxes of her country. Her father had been determined to give her a 'Western' education (at Harvard and Oxford for a total of eight years, 1969–77). English had become her first language, with Urdu alongside it. Neither of these universities was especially likely to curb an already powerfully developed arrogance. Where was she 'at home'? She found herself the first woman prime minister in a country which had now, for years, been impelled in an Islamic direction. Only in her ancestral Sind did she have a strong political base, yet it seems that she could scarcely speak Sindhi. She was the first subcontinental politician in office without a personal memory of 'British India'. All these facts held individual significance, but they translated into no clear strategy.

India: mother to son

If Bhutto's grasp on power in 1989 was tenuous, that of Rajiv Gandhi (b.1944), her fellow-dynast, was being swept away in the general election of that year. Five years earlier, however, Congress, under his leadership, had won a massive electoral victory, even coming close to an absolute majority of the popular vote. If it had been fought by his mother, observers suspected, she would not have gained such a victory. His mother, however, was dead, shot by her guards on 31 October 1984. He naturally gained a 'sympathy vote', but his youth appealed, together with the 'modernity' which must accrue to a former airline pilot. He had been sent to his grandfather's university, Cambridge, to study engineering, though he did not do so very assiduously. His wife, whom he had met there, was Italian. This too was 'modern'. Supposing that his brother Sanjay would succeed their mother, Rajiv had kept clear of politics. The inheritance became his when Sanjay was killed in a plane crash. In office, he began unpicking, though gingerly, the regulation-bound Indian economy, apparently sharing the view that it was being stifled by distinctly red tape. It was particularly galling in Delhi that even Pakistan was achieving a higher rate of economic growth at this juncture. Other 'East Asian tigers' began roaring and soaring away. It was time to change and a 'middle class', loosely now amounting to a hundred million (albeit only around an eighth of the population) generally wanted some 'liberalization'. Shady ventures, however, seemed to be its accompaniment. Rajiv's finance minister, V.P. Singh, attacked certain industrial and commercial enterprises for tax evasion. Moved to the defence ministry, he refused to desist from his enquiries. One such enquiry, on 'kickbacks' allegedly paid by the Swedish defence contractor Bofors, came near the Prime Minister himself. Singh resigned and Gandhi's standing was damaged. Losses in state elections confirmed the impression that the government's focus was wrong. It was Singh who was the leading figure in defeating Gandhi in the 1989 elections.

'Planning' as it had been executed in the early post-independence decades had also been intimately related to 'nation-building' and to a politics that rested on the ubiquitous presence of 'Congress'. Notwithstanding the 1984 election victory, however, Congress was not what it had been, either centrally or in many states. All these elements were in simultaneous difficulty. Voices declared, with increasing vehemence and popularity, that India was 'essentially' a Hindu state. Post-independence 'secularism' had allegedly lost the country its soul and rendered it anaemic. Recovery of Ram's Ayodhya birthplace from its Muslim 'occupiers' became the highly symbolic objective of this movement.

Then there was another issue. Indira Gandhi's bodyguards had both been Sikhs. The 'Sikh question', over the previous few years, and particularly in 1984, moved centre stage. Punjab, which had itself been divided between the two countries in 1947, had been further divided in 1966 by the Delhi government into three states: Punjab, Haryana and Himachal Pradesh. This small Punjab (Punjabi-speaking) had a Sikh majority and Haryana (Hindi-speaking) a Hindu. Living standards in the former were far higher than in the latter. They shared a capital in Chandigarh (which was centrally administered). Chandigarh was symbolic. When Lahore was 'lost', India, it seemed, had to create a new city which rivalled it. European architects, the most famous being Le Corbusier, were employed to do the job. Nehru proclaimed in Chandigarh an India looking to the future and unfettered to the past.

The past, however, was not easily unfettered. A Sikh party, the *Akali Dal*, pressed separatist demands, among them that Chandigarh should become the capital of Punjab alone. The party took office in Punjab in 1977. Zail Singh became India's first Sikh President in 1982 but the appointment did little to dampen Sikh disaffection. Jamail Singh Bhindranwale (b.1947), initially backed by Congress centrally as a counter to another Sikh leader, turned extremist. In early 1984 he and his armed followers took control of the sacred precincts of the Golden Temple in Amritsar. They would only leave when Delhi promised autonomy for Punjab. A stalemate ensued but in June, in 'Operation Bluestar', the heavy guns of the Indian army went into action. The seat of Sikh authority was desecrated. Bhindranwale and his followers were dead, as were thousands of others. It was a more brutal demonstration of power even than the British General Dyer, also in Amritsar, had displayed in 1919. Some observers, noting the dismissal of other prominent individuals in Kashmir and Andhra Pradesh, saw the action in Punjab as a sign of Mrs Gandhi's determination to end 'separatism' in India once and for all (she had sent a very clear 'unity' message herself, on her return to the Indian parliament, the Lok Sabha, by taking the seat in South India for which she had been elected rather than one in her family's northern heartland). 'The mother of the nation', as Rajiv described his own mother, had signed her death warrant by ordering 'Bluestar'. Terrible violence against Sikhs in Delhi then followed, as government lost, or would not assert, control. The legacy of these events was long-lasting. Rajiv signed 'The Punjab Accord' in July 1985 which, among other things, promised to transfer Chandigarh to Punjab. However, the Sikh leader with whom it was signed was himself assassinated shortly afterwards. Transfer was 'postponed'. President's Rule was imposed on Punjab in May 1987 and the state was then governed autocratically. Its border location, in the eyes of Delhi, meant that a tight security grip was essential. Indeed, India had mounted a massive military exercise there in 1986 to emphasize its presence 'overlooking' Pakistan. However, unrest and arrests continued – as they did in Kashmir, where disorder was never far below the surface. India and Pakistan were still far apart on this issue.

Gandhi's modest liberalization at home was paralleled by some mending of fences with the USA. His mother had a reputation there for arrogance but Reagan thought that was because she was shy and small. Rajiv seemed a warmer character. He first officially visited in mid-1985. Addressing Congress, he stressed the democracy which bound the USA and India together, but did not elaborate on the implications. A further visit, two years later, also had a positive emphasis. However, some signs of cordiality no more meant that India was reneging on its Treaty of Friendship with the Soviet Union than it indicated that the USA was abandoning Pakistan. It did mean, however, that both countries wanted to ease the friction. However, 1989 saw no Indo-Pakistani 'final settlement'. The election of two young prime ministers without historical baggage, some had thought, might make a breakthrough possible. Benazir and Rajiv did meet cordially enough in Islamabad in December 1988. Noises were made about cultural co-operation and both premiers agreed not to attack each others' nuclear facilities. Given more time, the two young leaders might have gone further, but they did not have more time.

The Islamabad meeting referred to, however, was not a bilateral occasion. It was a gathering of the South Asian Association of Regional Co-operation founded in Dhaka in December 1985. The headquarters of this group of seven states – India, Pakistan, Sri Lanka, Bangladesh, Nepal, Bhutan and the Maldives

– was established in Kathmandu in 1987. It looked a promising assertion of a 'South Asian' identity in the world – with India as its core. All concerned were well aware, however, that beneath such a purported corporate identity there were unresolved bilateral issues. It was not only the India/Pakistan question. Trouble in the Maldives, for example, led India to intervene in 1988. There were problems in the Indian eastern states, in the aftermath of Bangladeshi independence, which continued to involve Delhi and Dhaka. Activists who wanted to carve a Nepali-speaking area of West Bengal into a 'Gurkhaland' strained Nepali–Indian relations.

However, the most troublesome relationship was that between India and Sri Lanka. The Liberation Tigers of Tamil Eelam were the most militant of the Tamil groups on the island. They wanted an ill-defined autonomy in the north-ern and eastern districts for their 'Nation' (*Eelam*). Listening to the President of Sri Lanka in June 1984 the situation, to Ronald Reagan, seemed like Northern Ireland. Tamils saw themselves becoming a marginalized minority in a Sinhalese Sri Lanka. Much sympathy and some support for the Tamil islanders came from Tamil Nadu and, indeed, from Tamils from across the world. Gandhi could not be indifferent, but intervention was perilous. There was fierce fight-ing. After earlier attempts to broker a peace had failed, India and Sri Lanka agreed a deal in Colombo in July 1987. It looked simple. The Sri Lankan army would withdraw south and remain in barracks. An Indian 'Peacekeeping Force' would enter Jaffna and disarm Tamil fighters (who would, it was supposed, comply willingly). What happened instead was that the Indian troops, sent across in increasing numbers, found themselves engaged in a bloody struggle with the Tigers. That battle was still going on when Rajiv resigned office. It was his successor who pulled Indian troops out a few months later. There was, however, one final denouement to this unsuccessful Indian engagement. Gandhi was assassinated in May 1991 by a Tamil suicide bomber (as was the President of Sri Lanka, two years later). The Sri Lankan internal struggle went on.

In sum, therefore, a sense of being an identifiable 'South Asia' in the world, one which stretched from Pakistan's north-west, perhaps even Afghanistan, to the Maldives in the Indian Ocean was at best only embryonic. The prior and dominant question, which preceded any attention to a wider 'region', was whether the existing states could settle 'nationality' and do so 'democratically'. What 'India' itself was would determine its place in the world. There would be a different Kashmiri answer in the city of Srinagar from that given in the city of Jammu, there would be different answers in Amritsar and Bihar, and right across the country, different in states where the literacy rate reached 90 per cent from those where it barely reached 50 per cent. There would be different replies given by India's 'global elite' from those given by the many more million Indians who 'stayed at home'. The mosaic that was India was indeed in itself a world.

22
East Asia/Pacific: Flexing Muscles?

The 'outside world', looking at their physical size, their ever-mounting populations and the challenges facing their governments in alleviating poverty and bringing about social transformation, tended to lump India and China together as 'Asian giants', prickly in their border relationships. They were also odd giants, that is to say they had or could have nuclear weapons, and thus be deemed 'Great Powers', but not possess, or not yet possess, a pervasive overall level of technological sophistication. They stood in 'South Asia' and 'East Asia', respectively, but the contours of the latter were no more self-evident than the former. 'East Asia' rubbed shoulders with 'Asia Pacific', Oceania and that even more tantalizing hybrid, South-East Asia. The future of China was on all minds in the mid-1970s. What did its rulers, and perhaps even its people, now make of 'the world'?

China's 'new era'?

In Beijing in November 1978 a 'Democracy Wall' was allowed to exist, displaying wall posters critical of the government. Some of these explicitly argued that the Chinese people had less freedom and control over their governments than existed elsewhere in the world. Mao was even criticized by name. The 'Wall' was closed down at the end of 1979 because of the critical 'excesses' to which it had led elsewhere. This episode, specifically the comparisons with 'other countries', indicated a growing global consciousness – even if, in reality, there was little or no direct experience of what 'freedom' amounted to elsewhere. There was plenty of scope for debate about the relationship between systems of government and economic growth, between freedom and direction, between 'planning' and 'the market'. In China, the central and now global figure was Deng Xiaoping.

His path to China's present began in the western Chinese province of Sichuan. Han Chinese dominated in the province, but there were also linguistic, ethnic and religious minorities, particularly in the west. There he first encountered different worlds. In 1911, when he was a 7-year-old primary schoolboy, China, and the Qing dynasty in particular, was in crisis. Revolts broke out across the country, including in Sichuan. In Chengdu, the capital, where Deng's father, a modest peasant proprietor, had attended courses on law and politics, there was much uncertainty about 'modernity'. Popular feeling against 'Western influence' had taken a violent turn. It was scandalous to be encouraged to cut one's hair short or to unbind the feet of women. Revolutionaries, however, saw the queue (pigtail) as a symbol of racial subservience. The cost of the new railway in the province was much criticized (along with doubt about its necessity). Christian missionaries from the USA and the UK in Chengdu were busy establishing a hospital and educational institutions. That was the mixed world of Deng's boyhood (completed in 1919 by his schooling in Sichuan's second city, Chongqing). The remoteness – which had enabled Chiang Kai-shek to maintain his wartime capital there – should not be taken, however, to mean that Sichuan was cut off from the cross-currents of ideas sweeping China at this time. It was exactly thirty years after he left school there that Deng returned to Chongqing as its governor and to inaugurate the People's Republic.

Another thirty years later, in 1979, this diminutive chain-smoker – who held no office as head of state, head of government or general secretary of the Communist Party but who nonetheless led China in the 'new era' of this chapter – was discussing the world with the President of the USA in the White House. The two men, according to Carter, agreed that it would be a serious mistake to unite against the Soviet Union, though Deng thought that the USA had not done enough to contain the Soviet Union. The Soviet invasion of Afghanistan reinforced Beijing's perception of Soviet hegemonic ambitions. The USA at last broke off formal diplomatic relations – and was to abrogate its defence treaty – with the Republic of China (Taiwan), though it subsequently became clear that Washington would still maintain close contact with its government, something in which Beijing acquiesced.

Unsurprisingly, the level of cordiality shown in this conversation was not invariably sustained over the next decade. The future of Taiwan remained divisive. US restrictions on trade upset Beijing and had to be argued through. There was a modest improvement in Sino-Soviet relations. Brezhnev made apparently conciliatory speeches in 1982, significantly in Tashkent and Baku, stating that the Soviet Union had no territorial claims on China. China, however, continued to look for the withdrawal of Soviet forces from Afghanistan and from Outer Mongolia. The Soviet support for Vietnamese forces in Kampuchea also rankled. In short, there were phases of coolness and phases of warmth as China weaved its way between the USA and the Soviet Union. The Superpowers in turn moderated, strengthened or deepened their relationship with China in a complex triangular pattern. China's place in the world was gaining stature but it was not a 'Global Power' as they understood the term.

Such eddies were only to be expected, but at the personal level, direct contact made re-entry possible. Worlds which had once met, but had since ruptured, could be brought back into the present. The man from Plains, Georgia, recalled his boyhood support for Christian missions in China. The man from Guang'an, Sichuan, recalled their presence and admitted, reluctantly, that there had been some good missionaries. Deng insisted, however, that many of them had really been engaged in changing the Oriental lifestyle to a Western pattern. Missionaries should not come back and Chinese Christians did not want them back. Critics, however, were to argue that the 'new era' which Deng would preside over made its own dent in Oriental lifestyles. Deng arrived in Washington wearing a short jacket without a tie. When Chinese Communist Party (CCP) General Secretary and Premier Zhao Ziyang visited Washington in 1984 his suit and tie yielded nothing in quality to Ronald Reagan's. On the latter's 1984 visit to China he had reputedly dozed off while listening, in translation, to Deng Xiaoping's exposition. These two men evidently did not discuss the benefits and drawbacks of Christian missions. In odd moments, however, statesmen were wont to range off limits. These two noted that the Chinese and the French each seemed to have the belief that their civilization was superior. Let us put it this way said Deng: in East Asia, Chinese food is best and in Europe, French food is best.

Deng had a distant memory of French *cuisine*, though his experience of it had not been very *haute*. Travelling steerage, he had arrived in Marseilles in 1920. Having learnt some French in Shanghai, he was in France in a scheme which took young Chinese both to study in French schools and to gain 'work experience'. His teachers in Chongqing had told him that he would be able to learn knowledge and truth from the West – in order to save China. Deng picked up useful knowledge as a fitter at the Renault car factory in the Paris suburb of Billancourt. It was in France that he discovered Marxist truth, a discovery deepened by study in Moscow in 1926. His return to China in 1927 meant that his young adulthood had been spent outside his native country. His career thereafter in the Communist Party, both before and after 1949, had been full of ups and downs. He and his family had been targeted during the Cultural Revolution. Purges had come his way. In 1976, following the death of Zhou Enlai, homage was paid to him by a crowd in Tianenmen Square. Deng was identified as responsible for this display and was stripped of his party posts, though not his party membership. It looked as if he was again 'out' and pilloried as 'number two capitalist roader'. He wisely retreated to Guangzhou (Canton). However, after the death of Mao, also in 1976, he outmanoeuvred Mao's appointed successor, Hua Guofeng, and gradually consolidated his leadership position at a time of great confusion and uncertainty. The excesses of the Cultural Revolution could be blamed on the 'Gang of Four' who were placed on trial and given prison sentences. Although eschewing both grand titles and a personality cult, roughly from 1978 through to 1989, Deng became China's paramount leader. A 'New Era' was the Chinese term.

The new era had to come to terms with all that 'Maoism' meant. That in turn entailed grappling with Mao the man. He might be a monster – biographers in different parts of the world were to reach conflicting conclusions – but in post-Mao China there was an indelible sense in which Mao had put China on the 'world map'. He had not done so, however, by projecting himself as an 'international statesman', someone familiar with the capitals of the world and their culture. It was no longer possible, however, for the 'second generation' to keep China cocooned in the peasant world of Mao's romantic imagination. In his own life, Deng had been involved, at close quarters, with so many of the seminal events which had shaped his country in the half-century after his return in 1927. At the age of 74, he pressed ahead with what were called the 'Four Modernizations' which were to transform many aspects of the economy over the coming decade. It was, however, to be 'socialist modernization' – though what that meant was not readily apparent. One of Deng's early overseas missions, in November 1978, was to visit Lee Kwan Yew, like himself a Hakka Han Chinese (a people renowned for moving on in the world). The Singapore Prime Minister suggested that there were better things for China to be exporting than Communist ideology. Capitalism was going to exist in the world for a long time to come.

The details of the structural 'opening' cannot be followed through here but, lurking beneath every aspect of change remained the question of the identity of China itself (and hence its view of the world). Chairman Hu Yaobang remarked in 1984 that what really mattered was the great patriotic unity of China's 1,000 million people. This figure was now being quoted with confidence as a result of the population analysis of the 1982 census made by 29 giant computers. Mao had appeared to believe that there could never be too many Chinese, but within a few years population control – the one-child family – was being envisaged as part of overall development policy. China's population made it different from any other country in the world, even from India. That might explain why it was very different in other ways as well.

The 'opening-up' was not to be one which saw China's true self swamped by 'the West', whether culturally or commercially. The announcement in December 1978 that Coca-Cola was to be bottled in Shanghai was in some quarters only swallowed reluctantly. Commercial contacts with foreign countries were indeed increasing rapidly, though not without complications. In 1979 Den Xiaoping established four 'special zones for export' – Zhuhai, Shenzhen, Shantou and Xiamen – which offered foreigners facilities and various preferences if they set up. In Shenzhen, later, a rare statue to honour Deng was erected. He had created the city virtually out of nothing. The latter two had been 'treaty ports' (and given 'British' names) imposed on the dynasty by the British in the nineteenth century. This time, however, Chinese supervision would ensure that that past was not repeated. The zones were not all equally successful, and only later was Shanghai added, but they sent a signal of intent.

In the course of a few years, therefore, China was ceasing to be a rather impenetrable and exotic country unknown to travellers. Tourism took off (some 200,000 visitors in 1981 and growing thereafter). Social interaction with tourists, however, remained restricted. Where in the 'new era' was a line to be drawn, and who was to draw it? For example, could people wear what they liked? Young people increasingly seemed to think so. Traffic in the other direction was even more significant. China needed knowledge that could only be found in universities in the USA and Europe, therefore students had to be sent there. It was able students from 'key universities' who could benefit themselves (and the country) from studying a wide range of scientific subjects. It could be assumed that they had already acquired a good knowledge of English, or would do so shortly. What could not be guaranteed, however, was that all these students would return home. Chinese academics cautiously made contact with each other academics across the world. Some Chinese scholars, meeting their British counterparts, recollected their time at Oxford before 1939. Was the university still the same? After thirty years it was possible, to a degree at least, to engage in a cultural dialogue with 'Western' writers. Yet no Chinese who engaged in these matters did so in a spirit of obsequious deference to Western wisdom. China had to give, not merely to take. It should 'receive' the foreign but not be absorbed by it. Debates about 'catching up', characteristic of the first quarter of the twentieth century, resumed. There had this time to be a two-way process. The encouragement to learn English in China would have to be matched, at some point, though not yet, by encouraging the learning of Chinese in 'the West'. What kind of Chinese, however, was an issue. Deng's own speech patterns, betraying his Sichuan origins, were not perhaps wholly exemplary. Any analysis constantly ran up against the diversity of a large country. In talking about 'Chinese culture', both the words 'China' and 'Culture' were problematic. There was talk of a 'new Confucianism'. There were reports of a 'Christianity fever' in certain rather remote areas. The wider consequence of these mixings, national and universal, was also unpredictable. These issues skirted around what was sometimes referred to as the 'Fifth Modernization', namely 'democratization'. Deng, admittedly at a science gathering, had spoken in 1978 of 'letting a hundred schools of thought contend', but that would not be 'free speech'. Political pluralism, as spoken of in 'the West', simply did not suit China. It carried the risk, 'as history showed', that the country would fragment. Pragmatically, Deng was inaugurating a kind of 'socialist capitalism', an amalgam 'made in China' which did not fit either American or Soviet preconceptions. In time, the political system might become more 'democratic', but that time had not yet come. One thousand million people could not be effectively governed as though China were an American democracy, supposing, that is, that American democracy did govern itself effectively. Deng explained to Carter, whose enthusiasm for human rights recognized no bounds, that China was struggling to create a uniform system of justice. The country had few lawyers and, looking around the world, he doubted whether more of them would be an advantage. That was one benefit of a global outlook.

China: consolidating our common home

China still needed an emphasis on unity. That meant a major expansion of the rail and even more, the road, network. By 1989 it was claimed that all its villages were linked to a national system. Dredging and wharf construction enabled ships to travel further up the major rivers. These programmes had a double benefit. They both promoted internal cohesion and communication but also made the 'outside world' more accessible commercially. There were other signposts to the future. In December 1978, the Boeing Aircraft Corporation announced in Seattle that China had ordered three 'jumbo' 747 airliners. The drive to 'link up' went on relentlessly. Yet, no matter how much general development there was, 'modernity' and 'backwardness' still coexisted uneasily. The rural/urban divide was acute. The high-rise buildings in Shenzhen were 'a world away' from much of rural China. They smacked of life in neighbouring but still British-controlled Hong Kong. Restoration of China's full unity and assertion of its place in the world were conceived as the same process. There could be no loosening of controls in the Chinese 'autonomous regions' of Tibet and Xinjiang. In both cases, improved communication links with China 'proper', general economic development and an indigenous determination to preserve cultural and religious traditions, Buddhist and Islamic, pulled in contrary directions. The severity of the assault on the latter during the Cultural Revolution was moderated and Beijing placed most hope for tranquillity on the benefits of economic development. The existence of the Dalai Lama and his followers in India nevertheless ensured that Tibet's future continued to receive some international attention, but it did not cause Beijing to modify its stance. It was, however, prudent, as on the occasion of a visit by Hu Yaobang to Tibet in 1980, occasionally to deprecate Han arrogance and condescension. China needed to show that it could manage 'integration'.

The basis on which Hong Kong would 'come home' required much discussion between the British and Chinese governments. Both came to agree that the future of the island colony, ceded to Britain in perpetuity in 1842, and that of the 'New Territories' held on the mainland under a lease due to expire in 1997, should be considered together. Initially, when talks had formally begun in 1982, the British Prime Minister thought that the colony might be retained, but the Chinese were adamant. A Sino-British Joint Declaration on Hong Kong was reached in September 1984 and formally agreed at a signing ceremony in Beijing in December. Sovereignty over Hong Kong would revert to China in July 1997, with Britain continuing to administer in the interim. Only in 1986 did the British introduce elections for membership of the island's Legislative Council. The two governments agreed that for half a century Hong Kong would become a Special Administrative Region (SAR) with a capitalist economy. Stipulated rights and freedoms were to be guaranteed by law. The formula was 'one country, two systems'. Assuming that the settlement would indeed be implemented, the outcome reflected current global realities. Mrs Thatcher, renowned for her toughness in negotiation, recognized that ultimately she had no hand to play. Deng Xiaoping had been polite but obdurate. English was to remain the official language of the SAR and the whole experiment represented a kind of world in miniature. After a fashion, 'East' and 'West' would coexist harmoniously. It remained to be seen whether the formula would work.

Hu Yaobang, in his emphasis in 1984 on the existence of 1,000 million Chinese people, was addressing Chiang Ching-kuo, son of Chiang Kai-shek, who had been re-elected as President of Taiwan in that very year. An estimated 31 million of the 1,000 million were living in Taiwan, Hong Kong and Macao. Deng too addressed an appeal to Taipei in 1984 urging the Nationalists to rejoin the descendants of the Yellow Emperor (a common ancestor who had ascended to heaven in 2697 BC). The irony was that for a short time, sixty years earlier, the two men had been classmates in Moscow. Chiang Ching-kuo had married a Soviet woman and had lived in the Soviet Union for a dozen years before returning to China in 1937. He had eventually followed his father across the Straits. There were thus many twists in the recent Chinese past which belied its simple interpretation.

These appeals to Taiwan in 1984 aimed to coax the government there also to 'come home', but they did not succeed. Political transitions were taking place on the island. Chiang Ching-kuo appointed as his Vice-President in 1984 a Taiwan-born politician, Lee Teng-hui (b.1923) (who succeeded him on his death in 1988). Lee knew different worlds, too. He had grown up on the island when it was under Japanese control. He had a college education in Japan. After the war, however, he had obtained a Ph.D. in the USA. The days of Taiwan as the fiefdom of the mainland Nationalist elite might be drawing to a close. Chian Ching-kuo blossomed as a kind of democrat. He moved towards legalizing political parties and creating a properly functioning parliamentary system. Some newly elected politicians emphasized Taiwan's independence, abandoning any claim to be 'the Republic of China'. Martial law was lifted in July 1987. The island continued to prosper economically. Contrary trends therefore existed. For Deng's Beijing, prosperity was something which China as a whole, in time, could achieve but without 'democracy'. Taiwan, however, was embarking on a more democratic path. Taiwanese, whose ancestral links were with the southern Chinese province of Fujian, welcomed personal, cultural and commercial contacts with the mainland but not absorption into it, at least not yet. Our 'Common Home', for the moment at least, therefore remained incomplete.

Japan: the constraints of success

Japan, too was an 'Asian giant'. It was still the economic core of 'Pacific Asia', one perhaps that extended to Australia and New Zealand. Its place within it, and its political as opposed to economic stature, remained complicated. At this juncture, it was an odd giant, uncertain of its world role. The 'rise' of China and the 'normalization' of Sino-American relations came together to disturb the assumptions which had prevailed since 1945. The 'normalization' of Sino-Japanese relations, a central consideration, was not easily accomplished. What had happened before 1945 still carried too many memories. Beginning shortly after the conclusion of the Treaty of Peace and Friendship with China in 1978, however, there was a considerable flow of Japanese aid to China, either in the form of loans and grants or in technical assistance in big infrastructural projects. Japan did not pay reparations but this development programme functioned in lieu. Such participation was accepted but not greeted with enthusiasm. It was, of course, not without benefit to Japan, too, in providing a booming market for Japanese exports. The economic ties became close but they did not obliterate underlying suspicions and tensions. The conspicuous nature of the Japanese presence led to some accusations that China was being subjected to a second Japanese occupation. China itself – in relation to Hong Kong, Taiwan and Macau – placed increased stress upon common 'Chineseness'. Museums and monuments were built dwelling on the suffering of the Chinese people at the hands of the Japanese invader. One such museum was opened in Nanjing in a determined response to attempts in right-wing quarters in Japan to deny or minimize the massacre there in 1937–38 (some Chinese estimates put the number of deaths then at close to half a million).

In 1982, a dispute flared on the subject of Japanese textbooks and the 'screening' of terminology by the Ministry of Education. Was it banning the word 'aggression'? The Chinese Foreign Ministry protested that the discussion of the Nanjing massacres 'constituted an obvious distortion of the historical facts'. Governments, press and civilian groups in Taiwan, Hong Kong, North and South Korea, Singapore, Malaysia, Thailand, Indonesia, the Philippines and Vietnam joined in the criticism. A full-blown diplomatic row developed from which the Japanese government extricated itself with difficulty. It flared up again a few years later. Critics said that Japanese society had shied away from examining its past in its single-minded concentration on achieving economic success in the present. Some strands of Japanese opinion still saw Japan's campaigns in South-East Asia, if not in China, as an Asian 'liberation' from Western control. That interpretation was not popular in Britain, France or the Netherlands. Officials there could point out, in relation to the textbook controversy, that protests had come from 'liberated' Asian countries. The 'Japanese moment' in South-East Asia could not be other than ambivalently perceived.

There was, therefore, a continuing ambiguity, both in Japan itself and amongst its neighbours, about the country's place, specifically in Pacific–East Asia but also in the world as a whole. Japan operated globally both as an importer of raw materials and as an exporter of finished consumer products. It was often externally perceived as an 'economic animal', devoted, with unusual passion, to work, and able, with extraordinary dexterity, to extricate itself from oil shocks. By the early 1980s, Japan had become the world's largest car manufacturer. It was an 'advanced' country which flooded American and European markets with goods of high quality. It also flooded world historic sites with Japanese tourists clicking Japanese cameras. Its economic power was one thing; however, its political power, another. Japan, for a century, had sought to learn from 'the West'. Now the roles were being reversed. Business leaders abroad were told to learn from Japan. The ethos of its companies, and its interface between government and industry, were both considered exemplary. When imitation was attempted elsewhere, however, it became clear that Japanese 'solutions' could not simply be transplanted. These arrangements were a reflection of Japanese cultural assumptions and its post-1945 social consensus. Japan was indeed a democracy but, like every other democracy, it functioned in its own inimitable way. Factionalism in its politics seemed endemic and the whiff of scandal was never far away. No prime minister lasted long enough in office, had sufficient authority in that office or was adequately incorrupt to reconcile the contradictory elements in Japan's self-image and global position. It was 'rich', taken as a whole, but social consensus, naturally never complete, began to fray as the extent of domestic inequality became conspicuous. Japan's population was ageing. It had hitherto been a country with very few 'ethnic minorities', but now it looked as though it needed more labour – from abroad. Japan was 'joining the world' in a new sense, but could its strong sense of identity become 'multicultural'? There were, therefore, anxieties about the future which increasingly surfaced. The world's second industrial power and its first financial power – as it had become, according to most calculations, by the mid-1980s –

remained a densely populated set of islands substantially devoid of the raw materials and energy resources on which its prosperity depended.

It was 'success', however, which continued to cause problems. Japan's persistent trade surplus, despite a supposed 'deceleration' in response to criticism, brought fresh friction in the international trading arena. The so-called Plaza Accords of 1985 revalued the yen in a further attempt to shrink the surplus. This issue had worldwide trading ramifications, but had wider implications in Japanese–American relations. Was the USA, to which Japan had 'outsourced' security, suffering unduly? Was there something unsustainable in Japan's 'neutered' global political stature? If China was becoming more crucial than Japan to Washington's view of Asia in the world then it might be time to revisit Japan's security. Even to contemplate its not insignificant defence force being allowed to function outside Japan, however, would revive all the old regional fears of Japanese imperialism. So there was an unresolved paradox, but an increasingly prominent one.

Other 'East Asias': making their own mark

A global focus on China and Japan was understandable, but there was another 'East Asia/Pacific' which was not content always to be in the shadow of giants. In comparison, most were small, either in territory or population. Economic success, as some but not all proved, was not just a matter of size. This section moves through a sequence of distinct countries, from South Korea to Australia, all of whom were in some sense neighbours, though what that amounted to in any terms of regional self-perception and alignment remained problematic.

Just as Japan had 'imitated' the West, so some of its smaller neighbours began to 'imitate' Japan. By targeting specific products, they were outstripping their model. South Korea, Taiwan, Hong Kong and Singapore moved in smartly to export cheaper versions of items often first developed in Japan. They fused state management and laissez-faire capitalism – all with 'the world' as a market in mind. Domestically, South Korea saw a dominant position being assumed by family-owned conglomerates. A combination of cultivated technological skill, in some sectors, a sound educational base, and low labour costs, appeared to do the trick. Collectively these countries were for a time referred to as the 'Gang of Four'. Their performance in manufactured exports outshone any other part of the 'developing world'. Western manufactured goods could not compete in East Asian markets. Western governments complained of the devices which restricted their access to those markets and sought, in turn, to invent their own exclusory devices. It was, however, a 'containerized' world that was fast developing, but in this case the enveloping linkages, when Japan is also brought into the picture, transcended any simple continentalism or construction of an 'East Asia' that was 'integrated'.

The 'Four' were themselves not by any means 'the same'. While the peninsular crisis continued, South Korea, whatever its global export performance, daily depended on the USA for its security against the North. Talks between the two Korean states periodically occurred, but made scant progress. Both sides reasonably supposed that unification would mean the triumph of the other. In the North, Kim Il Sung stood guard over the regime as his son, Kim Jong Il, was groomed as the forthcoming 'Beloved Leader'. Three great revolutions – technology, ideology and culture – Pyongyang declared, would confirm that Socialism was Science. The South, however, was both more populous and more prosperous. There had long been a pattern of Korean emigration to other countries, but significantly, in the South, this pattern began to be reversed. After the assassination of Park Chung Hee in 1979, another general, Chun Doo Hwan, soon took over after Park's immediate successor had made some gestures towards civilian government. Demonstrations against military rule were met with force. In these circumstances, the apparently perpetual peninsular confrontation hardly constituted a classic example of a conflict between 'dictatorship' and 'democracy'. Carter 'made representations', and even threatened Seoul with US troop withdrawals, but neither he nor his successor could contemplate South Korea 'going under'. In 1988 South Korea showcased itself to the world when it staged the Olympic Games in Seoul. The other three members of the prospering Gang also, in different ways and to different degrees, were 'authoritarian'. Hong Kong was living under imperial rule, but one on borrowed time. Taiwan appeared to be operating 'offshore', successfully indifferent to the fact that few states were prepared to recognize its existence. Singapore was Singapore. Economic prosperity, achieved without democracy, perhaps, some said, achieved because of its absence, might be what 'the people' in East Asia were really interested in. Whether this was true or not, the prosperity of the 'Gang of Four' was capable of being imitated by other 'neighbours'.

The states of South-East Asia, in forming the Association of Southeast Asian Nations (ASEAN), showed every sign of no longer being content to be suppliers of petroleum, wood and other resources for their northern neighbours. They could continue to export these commodities, with all of their price volatility, but they could themselves industrialize and undercut the 'Gang of Four'. The resulting pattern, operating at different speeds, produced a common set of urban–rural tensions. Capital cities, Bangkok, for example, mushroomed. However, while the economic and social changes had much in common, the cultural and religious contexts remained different. In the small but oil-rich country of Brunei, which became independent from Britain in 1984, the thirtieth Sultan (b.1946) kept all the important offices to himself. Strong personal and political ties were maintained with Britain. In Thailand the actual or symbolic status of 'traditional' rulers and their political role was contentious. Thailand's King, Bhumabol Adulyadej, had come to the throne in 1946 and was bidding to be both the longest-serving monarch in the world and in Thai history. His education had been largely through the medium of French in Switzerland. Some Thai opinion thought his role was too political; others thought the reverse. The King navigated through both military and democratic regimes as the symbol of unity who must never be insulted.

Mohammed Mahattir (b.1925), who became Prime Minister of Malaysia in 1981, was determined to keep the rulers of its states in their place. His background, in Kedah state, was modest. He had, therefore, not taken the Malay aristocratic route to an education in England. He had, however, mastered English as a small boy and eventually graduated in medicine. He successfully practised in his home state before entering politics and rising, not without complications, to the top. The full flourish of his policy, emphasizing Malay social and economic emancipation, had yet to emerge, but its direction was clear. Malaysia should 'look East' and not be beholden to 'the West' – though it was obscure where 'the East' was. A spat with the British government on an issue affecting Malaysian students in Britain resulted in an injunction, later removed, that his people should 'buy British last'. Malaysia, however, remained within the Commonwealth. Relations with Singapore, where, in the British era, Mahattir had graduated, remained prickly. The ethos of Mahattir's Malaysia was to be firmly Islamic, a stance which inevitably caused problems for non-Malay minorities. That of course mainly meant the Chinese, already worried by the economic 'rebalancing' that was taking place. In January 1984, however, President Reagan was pleased to hear from his guest, Mahattir, that Malaysia was well along in developing democracy and attracting foreign capital investment.

In Kampuchea/Cambodia in 1976, Saloth Sar ('Pol Pot'), born in the same year as Mahattir, had another kind of future in mind. He had been in Paris for four years after 1949. The study of radio electronics there had yielded place to spreading Marxism, picked up in France, amongst his fellow Cambodian students. He had charm and ruthlessness. Over the next two decades, 'Brother No. 1' , leading the country's Communist Party after 1963, fought his way to power amidst the criss-crossing currents of 'Indo-China'. The Cambodian 'Year Zero' of 1976 carried more than an echo of revolution in France in 1789, though it drew specific inspiration from Pol Pot's months in China during the Cultural Revolution in 1966. The Khmer 'brave new world' banned all religions and ejected from influence individuals who had been corrupted by a knowledge of French and 'Western' ideas (not an exclusion applied by Pol Pot to himself). Phnom Penh, the capital city, packed with refugees, with its French colonial buildings and boulevards, could find much evidence of both. It was best, therefore, to close it down. Capitalists, deprived of their milieu, were stranded. Without delay, 'agrarian socialism' was inaugurated. Intermediate steps were unnecessary. On the 'killing fields', there was action. Figures remain contentious, but probably between 1.7 and 2.5 million Kampucheans met their deaths, around a fifth of the country's civilian population. The word Kampucheans is used, but the heaviest proportion of deaths was incurred amongst ethnic minorities – amongst them Vietnamese, Thais and Chinese, for issues of ideology and ethnicity were all mixed up. The minority Cham people – in Kampuchea, Muslims; in Vietnam, Hindus – suffered particularly severely. Pol Pot's alignment with China went hand in hand with the elimination of domestic Chinese, not all of whom were 'capitalists'. Chinese support remained because of Beijing's hostility towards Soviet-orientated Vietnam. The fate of the regime was thus bound up with the ongoing struggle for succession in 'Indo-China'. In 1979, it was a Vietnamese invasion, with support from within, that brought the Pol Pot regime to an end. It was, however, difficult to say what 'normality' had returned. Vietnamese troops remained in the country and buttressed the ensuing government. Strangely, that government, regarded as a Vietnamese puppet regime by the USA and the Association of South East Asian

Nations (ASEAN) countries, was not given Kampuchea's seat at the UN. Pol Pot himself retreated into the interior, an ominous if distant presence. The confused political scene remained one in which 'interfering neighbours' and indigenous groupings struggled for position.

Elsewhere, too, as the following examples suggest, the orientation of states often reflected the personal heritages and allegiances of their rulers. There was no simple Pacific or East Asian view of the world. The Ferdinand Marcos who died in exile in Honolulu in 1989 had moved between different heritages. He had been given, as no other Asian leader had, a Christian name which honoured a King of Spain. He had been baptized in the new Philippines Independent Church (in communion with the Anglican Communion worldwide), itself an indication of a distinctive Filipino Christian identity (though most Filipino Christians remained Roman Catholics). Marcos's religious commitment, however, did not prove to be defining in a presidency which came to an end in the 'People's Power Revolution' of 1986 after twenty-one years. He had stayed close to the USA and regularly received prominent Americans in Manila. 'English-speaking Americanness' still flourished in certain sections of Filipino society. Further, a large and steady stream of Filipinos went abroad to work. Their remittances were an important element in the domestic economy. Both of these things continued to make the Philippines oddly, though only partially, 'Western'. Its 'crony capitalism' had initially been justified as a means of releasing Filipinos from a domestic Chinese commercial 'stranglehold'. The increasingly authoritarian character of Marcos's government over his long rule included a phase of formal martial law. The politics of patronage dominated. Showpiece infrastructural development in the 'new Philippines' went hand in hand with corruption. Marcos, aided by his acquisitive wife, advanced to a position where, according to one index, he was the second most corrupt leader in the world.

Suharto continued to preside over the 'New Order' in Indonesia, his position regularly 'legitimized' in unopposed elections held at three-year intervals. His military regime swung away from Sukarno's positioning of Indonesia in the world. Suharto's stance was firmly anti-Communist. In 1986 President Reagan was encouraged to learn that Suharto was anti-Libya and anti-PLO. Suharto further let slip that inflation, which had reached 600 per cent, was now under control and rice production was back up. Without the stability that he imposed, he argued, industrialization and economic growth could not take off. Outside investment was then encouraged. Into the 1980s, strong annual rates of growth were being recorded and claims made for a reduction in poverty. Indonesia, at last, seemed to be punching its populous weight in the world. However, considerable growth rates in Suharto family wealth were also being achieved. It was he who relegated Marcos to second place in that great mystery, the global wealth index. Two political parties were allowed to function but not to a degree that allowed them to be significant. An army-sponsored organization, Golkar, gave the regime its claim to be 'representative'. Suharto's enforced success, however, could not disguise the continued existence of fissiparous tendencies. A rebellion in Aceh (northern Sumatra) was put down by force in 1976, but discontent rumbled on. The conquest of Portuguese Timor in the preceding year did not produce a tranquil 27th province, notwithstanding a giant statue of Christ presented to its Catholic people by their new rulers. The 'Chinese problem' continued to be 'dealt with' – by closing Chinese-language schools and banning Chinese script in public places. Chinese were encouraged to take Indonesian-sounding names. The country had no diplomatic relations with China. None of this, however, prevented Suharto from working closely with certain Indonesian Chinese business cronies.

His 'New Order' was another kind of third way, hostile both to Communism and 'political' Islam. It was the latter which caused Suharto increasing difficulty. Among Muslims, influences coming from outside mixed unpredictably with indigenous emphases. Suharto himself had no wish to project his country as Islamic in the sense increasingly used elsewhere, and sometimes took strong action against 'militants'. Javanese himself, careful image-making could turn him almost into a 'traditional' Javanese king, with an attendant spiritual authority. His wife, helpfully, had modest Javanese royal connections. 'Royal' rituals, most conspicuous at the substantial number of Suharto family weddings, did not please influential imams. A bureaucratic elite, increasingly discovering 'modernity' through the English language, kept the country operating, with the army, wherever deemed appropriate, cracking down on dissent.

General Ne Win (b.1910) resigned the presidency of Burma/Myanmar in 1981, though he retained the chairmanship of the Burmese Socialist Programme Party until 1988. Prominent in earlier decades, he had dominated the country since the coup of 1962. He, too, was not a man to be contradicted. Insights gained from astrology aided the formation of policy. There were many analogies between his country's problems and those of his neighbours. It had been Indians (though also Chinese) from whom commercial control had been wrested (some 200,000 Indians had been sent back 'home' in 1962). The question of citizenship, however, remained unresolved until the military passed an act on the subject in 1982. Full citizens were Burmans or members of other indigenous ethnic/linguistic groups who could prove descent from residents living in the country in 1823 (when the first Anglo-Burmese war began). 'Associate' citizens, however, were those either naturalized or 'native' but born after 1823 – Indians and Chinese in particular. Associates were denied important rights. Such legislation, devised by a Dutch-trained Burman lawyer, ignored the outside world as it sought to fix the country's true identity. There was no foreign investment (until 1988) and no encouragement to tourism. Internationally, Burma became virtually invisible. The regime was already 'tilting' towards its Chinese neighbour and expressed its solidarity with Beijing's condemnation of Soviet action in Afghanistan. That Burma was overwhelmingly Buddhist was evident but, although prudently, he ordered a pagoda to be built, Ne Win did not want Buddhism to be the state religion. The 'amorphous autonomy' possessed by Buddhist monks was curtailed. The role Ne Win played was reminiscent of the power of Burmese kings before the British brought the monarchy to an end. A past had returned.

In Wellington, the thought that New Zealand was part of 'Pacific Asia' had at least to be considered. The government was still smarting after the 'betrayal' represented by the decision of the 'mother country' to join the European

Economic Community (EEC) in 1973. New Zealand had to make urgent economic readjustment. Was there a political realignment to accompany it? Should it, could it, 'join Asia'? The map, however, still suggested that Asia was 'far away'. The culture of its 'neighbours', as outlined in the above paragraphs, remained 'remote' and alien. The pattern of its post-war immigration had still been very substantially from the UK. The Crown still cemented a sense of identity which transcended distance. If there was cultural adjustment to be made, it was within the country itself – in recalibrating the relationship between Maoris and 'Europeans'. New Zealand, in short, briefly looked north in its irritation, but then looked away.

Australia might be a different matter. Its Northern Territory tipped towards Papua New Guinea, given its independence by Canberra in 1975, and also towards the western half of the island of New Guinea, now the Indonesian province of Papua. Papua New Guinea's independence had been what turned out to be the last significant act of the Gough Whitlam Labor Government. The 'democracy' of the new state that Whitlam hailed soon fell below Australian standards. But what were those standards, and what was Australia? Some historians busily worked away to unveil a new identity, one liberated from distant shackles. In politics, however, Whitlam found himself dismissed by the country's governor-general. It resolved the deadlock on supply legislation between the two houses of the Australian parliament. Critics argued that the Queen of Australia, who lived in London, would not have dared to use such a prerogative in her local realm. Therefore, it was argued, the governor-general who did duty for her in Canberra acted improperly. The dispute, whatever its rights and wrongs, fitted into a pattern of Australian self-examination. Whitlam had aspired to a more 'independent' foreign policy but displeased party zealots by continuing to regard the American alliance as fundamental. The pattern of immigration had brought a 'new Australia' in the shape of European immigrants who might, in time, learn to play cricket but were not otherwise emotionally wedded to the UK as the 'home country'. By the 1980s, Melbourne had a Greek community of over 200,000, making it one of the main centres of Greek population in the world. It was an ideal location in which to argue fiercely about what Macedonia was and to whom it belonged. Yugoslavs, too, lost no appetite for disputing, at a distance, that fate of their 'home country', if indeed it was one country. An economic decline in the late 1970s and early 1980s added to a sense that Australia needed a new identity and/or a new direction. Whether that could really be 'Asian', however, was another matter.

The Oxford-educated Rhodes Scholar, Bob Hawke (b.1929), brought Labor back into power in 1983 (and further electoral successes lay ahead for him). He affirmed the US alliance but gave his foreign minister some scope to develop a 'regional role'. Nothing very clear emerged. Canberra stood with the USA after 1984 when a new Labour government in New Zealand would not allow nuclear-armed ships to dock. The USA refused to indicate which of its ships were nuclear-armed. It was an episode which revealed something of a gulf between Australia and New Zealand. From time to time, it had been suggested that the two countries might 'unite'. Now they seemed to be drifting apart. In the further future, however, for both countries, economic and political considerations could not remove the 'Asian option'. Not that South-East Asia would necessarily welcome 'Anglo-Saxon Asian neophytes' into the fold. Neighbouring rulers did not relish democratic admonitions. Mahattir, a civilian and a fellow Commonwealth member, felt obliged to point out that Australia, although a large country, and not a reticent one, had only a small population. It was, in other words, marginal in the space that was Pacific–East Asia. The formation in 1989 of the Council for Asia-Pacific Economic Co-operation which brought together the ASEAN countries – Canada, Australia, New Zealand, Japan and South Korea – gave a further twist to relationships.

23

Gorbachev and Reagan: Turning Point, 1985–89

In March 1985, when Mikhail Gorbachev became General Secretary of the Soviet Communist Party and Ronald Reagan was a few months into his second term as US President, neither could accurately gauge the changes in 'East–West' relationships that lay immediately ahead of them. For four decades, the world had been substantially shaped by the fluctuating relationship between their two blocs. There was scarcely a state which, to one degree or another, had been not been caught up in its ramifications. Generations had grown up knowing no other world. 'Cold War' had both spawned and sucked in antagonisms, from Ecuador to Eritrea or Cambodia to Colombia, which had a life of their own. Even if the principals 'called it off', subordinates, for their own reasons, might continue. So, just as the Cold War had itself 'emerged', ending it had various beginnings. In December 1989, however, on board a Soviet ship off the coast of Malta, new American President George W.H. Bush and Gorbachev announced that the Cold War had indeed ended. It would have been rash to predict such a statement four years earlier. Their declaration was not a 'world' conclusion, reached by comprehensive multilateral conference. It was, in the end, an abrupt and laconic bilateral announcement.

So much had rested on two men in 1985. Many messages were exchanged between Washington and Moscow over the summer as both sides felt their way towards direct engagement. A smiling Shevardnadze replaced grim Gromyko as Soviet Foreign Minister in July. It was finally agreed that the principals would meet on neutral territory. Geneva, location of so many of the twentieth century's attempts to create an enduring world peace, was the choice. The world's cameras clicked in large numbers. In private discussion, Reagan immediately struck a personal note with Gorbachev. Here they were, he said, two men born in obscure rural hamlets, both poor and from humble beginnings. They were probably the only two men who could start a world war and, by the same token, the only two who could ensure world peace. They met in private four times. It was for the Soviet Union and the USA to do business. Allies could express their views, but they decided. The joint communiqué declared that a nuclear war could never be won and therefore one should never be started. Indeed, no war between the two countries should be started and one would not seek a military superiority over the other. The two men broadcast televised messages of goodwill to each other's peoples on New Year's Day 1986. They undertook to meet again.

Gorbachev's journey from rural hamlet to the brink of high office formed the opening section of this chapter. The question asked in Washington was whether the new man meant what he said. Nixon, sent to make a face-to-face assessment in July 1986, thought he glimpsed a 'steel fist' beneath the soft glove of friendship. Soviet goals, he supposed, remained the same. Gorbachev was not a new Soviet breed but simply a smarter (and younger) specimen of the old. It was necessary to be wary. If he was really trying to create a better Soviet Union maybe the USA should help him – but might there not be a better world without any kind of Soviet Union? There should be more to hope for than a new improved Leninism. What Reagan himself thought was opaque: a circumstance which suited him. He was not, however, the dinosaur initially and mistakenly identified by Gorbachev.

The Reagan meeting Gorbachev for the first time in 1985 seemed rather different from the man the Kremlin had watched for four years. Reagan's path to the White House had of course been more open and public than Gorbachev's had been to the Kremlin. The symmetry in their backgrounds, if a little forced for conversational purposes, might indeed give the basis for a new look at the world. There had been nothing grand about the Reagan family as it moved around Illinois in his childhood. There was nothing academically pretentious about the Illinois liberal arts institution, Eureka College, he attended. He shared with his mother an undogmatic Christian faith. He had gone into radio and then, as 'everybody knew', to a film contract in 1937 with Warner Brothers. His near-sightedness had barred him from military service overseas. He was not a great traveller. During his years as a film actor he had only travelled abroad once, and that was to Britain – and for filming purposes. Both before his election as Governor of California in 1966, and during his subsequent pursuit of the presidency, he did not become a regular globetrotter, though he did accept some foreign missions on behalf of Nixon. After 1981, as President, he did indeed go on his travels, though claiming to look back fondly on an era when presidents stayed at home. Visits had their part to play in cementing understanding. In China he accepted Nixon's advice to consume whatever appeared on the table and not ask questions. Reagan proved good with chopsticks. His overseas visits were selective, and for big occasions. The rest of the world made a point of showing up in Washington for a kind of regular inspection: kings, queens, presidents, prime ministers, all carefully calibrated. No one dropped by more frequently and agreeably, if ultimately pointlessly, than the King of Jordan. It was no doubt helpful to know that the President of Togo was 'pro-West' and 'anti-Communist' or that the President of Botswana adamantly stood for free enterprise and democracy – but not much more needed to be known about them or their countries. They did not feature prominently on the White House's real map of the world. What Reagan did not do during his first term, however, was to visit or receive his Soviet counterparts. A joke was that they were not living long enough to make forward planning for a meeting a useful exercise, but that was not the full story. Reagan, as President, was a man in his seventies, content with the American world he knew. He would choose the moment. His view of the world, and America's place in that world, had not been greatly troubled by personal exposure to its distant complexities. The patient before him, which was going to benefit from the optimism which he could bring, was the USA itself. The evangelist Billy Graham dubbed him 'a Pastor to the Nation'.

The American people had to recover their self-confidence, end the 'Vietnam syndrome', end the 'drift', and end that apparent erosion of US power and influence in the world. Their present troubles would be overcome by the restoration of a dynamic economy (tax cuts would do the business). 'Reaganomics' was being born. The first foreign guest to appear in the White House, perhaps a sign that the 'human rights' agenda of his predecessor would be soft-pedalled, was Chun, President of South Korea. He was told that US troops would stay in his country. Four years later, a million Koreans lined the streets waving Korean and American flags to welcome the Reagans. The reinvigoration of American patriotism to meet the Communist threat was vital. The 'ugly reality' of that threat he believed he had seen at work, on the direct orders of the Kremlin, in Hollywood in the 1950s. It had not gone away. Reagan's focus remained on the Soviet Union. He did not believe that the division of the world reflected some eternal geopolitical reality. There could be a better and non-Communist world. His ancestral heritage was Irish–British. Reagan was politically comfortable coming to London (with one family visit to Co. Tipperary in Ireland). The Brits, from his point of view, got up to fewer diplomatic antics than the French. Few other visiting Heads of State in London, he was pleased to note, got to go riding with Queen Elizabeth. He understood Margaret Thatcher readily, and she made sure he did.

In June 1982, speaking to a joint session of the British parliament– the first American president ever to do so – the Soviet Union was identified as the focus of evil in the modern world. Speaking to the National Association of Evangelicals in Orlando, Florida, in March 1983 he branded the Soviet Union as an 'evil empire', a term that stuck. Such terminology, even though softened within a year, deliberately struck a combative note. The forward march of freedom and democracy, as he understood the terms, would leave Marxism–Leninism 'on the ash-heap of history' (a popular location, one identified, on other lips, as a suitable place for capitalism). It was necessary, however, to push this march forward by rebuilding American military power. Some thought that the Soviet Union would not be able to keep pace, or, in the act of trying to do so, would implode. The Soviet Empire had latterly had it too easy. That did not necessarily mean that American military power would actually be deployed. Using the Central Intelligence Agency (CIA) might be sufficient to expose Soviet weakness beyond its heartland. A 'Reagan Doctrine' placed the emphasis on American 'support' for freedom fighters everywhere, so long as it did not entail direct major US military involvement. The power was there, in reserve, and its existence would encourage Moscow to negotiate – about nuclear weapons in particular. There was a reawakened fear in the USA of a sudden and total annihilation of the human species. Reagan privately watched the bleak television depiction of *The Last Day* (November 1983). He shared this public mood and regarded the orthodoxies of M(utually) A(ssured) D(estruction) as mad.

Hence his enthusiasm for a space-mounted defence shield (the Strategic Defense Initiative, or SDI), announced earlier that year, which would stop nuclear missiles from reaching the USA, rendering them useless and obsolete. By March 1985, therefore, external impressions of 'the Reagan Years' were confused. Reagan himself saw in his re-election the return of a 'glad confident morning' in America.

Gorbachev's morning was not so confident. In the Soviet Union there were internal questions at every turn: his own role, the bureaucracy, the military, technical backwardness, Afghanistan. They were all linked and there was so much to be done. The Soviet state required nothing less than a comprehensive reconstruction (perestroika). Quite what that entailed was difficult to tell as one 'Mark' of it after another was rolled out in the years ahead. The acceleration of change, however, did not signify that the Socialist system was doomed. His March 1985 message had been that the impending 'change' that lay ahead required no deviation from authentic and correct Leninism. It was to be assumed, incorrectly as it turned out, that his inchoate enthusiasms would spread to stiff-necked Communist leaders in Eastern Europe. What did spread, however, in April 1986, though not to all their countries, were radioactive particles from the nuclear power station explosion at Chernobyl in Ukraine. A picture of incompetence was revealed. It was time for there to be more openness (glasnost) about what was going on in the Soviet Union. The twists and turns of policy in these years cannot be detailed here, but what became evident, even to Gorbachev himself as time passed, was an entire system in crisis. The destination of the Soviet Union was no longer clear. A new significance had to be given to 'peaceful coexistence'. Moscow simply could not sustain the burden of military expenditure. It is not surprising, therefore, that talks about arms, conventional and nuclear, were central in these years.

It was not until October 1986 that Gorbachev and Reagan met again – in Reykjavik, Iceland. The former had suggested a 'preliminary' summit to consider medium-range missiles. A formal meeting would subsequently be arranged to ratify whatever might be agreed. The mood music had changed somewhat. There had been a spying incident and the US had bombed Libya (the death of an American serviceman in Berlin was held to be Libyan-inspired). Moscow felt obliged to indicate displeasure at this retaliation. Further, Reagan hinted that at the end of the year the USA might not keep to the SALT II limits on the number of intercontinental missiles. The Reykjavik meeting was extraordinary. Gorbachev stated that within ten years the Soviet Union would abolish all its nuclear weapons if, over the same period, Reagan froze all development work on the SDI. Declining to do so, the President simply walked out. Gorbachev told the Politburo in the aftermath that the Americans, 'true bandits', would increase pressure. The Western Europeans, fellow members of the 'common home' or not, could not be tempted to diverge from the Americans. Pressure did increase. The USA carried out two nuclear tests in early February 1987 and the Soviet Union responded with one later in the month. In August, visiting Berlin, Reagan issued a challenge at the Brandenburg Gate: Mr Gorbachev, tear down this wall. But such public rhetoric did not stop the talks that had been going on at the official level on the vexed issues of missiles, both intermediate and long-range. In

September, substantial progress made at talks in Geneva was followed by the third summit meeting held in Washington in December 1987 (it was Gorbachev's first time in America). An agreement was reached to eliminate all intermediate-range nuclear weapons from Europe by 1991 – the Soviet Union would have to destroy twice as many as the USA. An inspection mechanism was put in place. There was no American pledge to abandon the SDI.

Reagan visited Moscow six months later formally to ratify the Washington agreement and to set in train further negotiations aimed at reducing the principal nuclear weapons held by both powers. The two men strolled through Red Square. 'Gorbymania' had broken out in the USA. In February 1988 Gorbachev announced that Soviet forces would withdraw from Afghanistan. An agreement to this effect was signed in April in Geneva. The USA began removing the trade embargoes imposed because of the invasion. In December, at the UN, Gorbachev announced that the Soviet Union would unilaterally reduce its armed forces by 500,000 within two years. These specific decisions were accompanied by ringing declarations that universal human values were to be the basis of Soviet foreign policy. Taken together with other changes, it did appear that a new world was arriving fast. George W.H. Bush, Reagan's successor from January 1989, was not to be hurried. Reagan, some said, had been too trusting. Bush did not have, or yet have, Reagan's particular bond with the American people. Gorbachev was facing similar criticism and perhaps increasing vulnerability. His 'peace strategy' might be driven by a desire to give him time to tackle the economic problems which were crowding in. He was more popular abroad than at home. After his pause for thought, however, Bush maintained the momentum and made his way to meet Gorbachev off Malta. We encounter them shortly at the beginning of the final part of the book. The interaction between Reagan and Gorbachev, in 'ending the Cold War' had been personal. Sealing the outcome by Reagan's successor made it fully 'national'.

It had apparently only taken two to tango. The rest of the world watched, not knowing quite what to make of it. Historians worked hard to keep up with events, and fell behind them. Paul Kennedy, an English historian writing in the USA, concluded his analysis of the Soviet Union's problems in 1986 by rejecting the notion that the USSR was close to collapse, though neither should it be regarded as a country 'of almost supernatural strength'. His analysis of the USA suggested that it still constituted 'Number One in Relative Decline''. It was not given to any society to remain *permanently* ahead of all the others. Its share of the world's wealth and power since 1945 , which might be taken to be 40 per cent, was way above the 16 or 18 per cent which might be thought 'natural' given its size, population and natural resources. Even if, at some stage, the USA did come down to its 'natural' position – and American vitality suggested a capacity to 'manage' decline intelligently – it would even so remain a major Power in the world. For the present, what the USA did or did not do was much more important than what any other Power decided to do. The controversy reflected the fluidity of the time and the extreme difficulty of unpicking terms like 'rise' and 'fall'. 'Power' comes in many different forms. The ending of the Cold War might look like a victory for the USA and 'the West'. If so, it was one which left many questions unanswered.

What was unquestionable, though, was a sense that the world as a whole was moving away from the moorings of the previous decades. Some slippages stemmed directly from the withdrawal of distant backing. Through 1989 the 'established order' in Central and Eastern Europe was crumbling at an accelerating rate, the most symbolic evidence being the opening, on 22 December, of the Brandenburg Gate before which Reagan had spoken just over two years earlier. The destruction of sections of the Berlin Wall had begun on 10 November. More detail on what it entailed for 'Europe' and its place in the world will be tackled in the final part. It is sufficient to note here that nothing now seemed quite what it had been since 1945. Western European leaders were astonished to learn of the deal that might have emerged from the Reykjavik summit. They urged a nervous Bush, when he visited them in the summer of 1989, to meet Gorbachev face to face. The door could not be closed. Eastern European leaders were facing the end of the world they had known. The Soviet Union itself might be in jeopardy.

Further afield, Vietnamese troops were withdrawn from Kampuchea, which resumed life in the world, though not yet a peaceful life, as Cambodia. Cuban troops were withdrawn from Angola, though its fourteen-year civil war might not be over. Gorbachev had visited Cuba in April 1989 and, unsurprisingly, Castro was not impressed by Soviet 'new international thinking'. A Soviet withdrawal might quickly undermine Cuba's security and economic viability and damage its 'Third World' role. What was true in Cuba also applied in Ethiopia and elsewhere. Less directly, but still significantly, the end of the Cold War impacted on the politics of South Africa. It gave room for a new attempt to work out a deal between the country's communities. F.W. de Klerk became State President in September 1989. It was no longer credible to portray the ANC as a Trojan horse for that 'total onslaught' by the Soviet Union, something long conjured up by his predecessors. A new turn in world history had been reached: it was, he said, as if God had taken a hand. Other 'new turns' happened, however accounted for. Some great figures simply died. In June Ayatollah Khomeini died in Iran, but not before issuing a *fatwa* in February calling for the death of the Indian-born British-resident Salman Rushdie, whose novel *Satanic Verses* was held to be blasphemous. Here was global reach indeed. The previous month in Bradford, England, British Muslims had publicly burned the novel and the author had gone into hiding. The Emperor of Japan died in January, ending a 62-year reign. In doing so, he missed accepting, over the months that followed, the resignation of successive prime ministers – arising out of bribery and sex scandals, respectively. There was a military coup in Paraguay which ended the 35-year regime of Alfredo Stroessner. And so on. 'Events' still happened and, as will be seen, 'the new world order' had some flimsy and rather precarious foundations.

Part 5 further reading

Bradnock, Robert, *India's Foreign Policy since 1971* (Routledge, London, 1990).

Brown, Archie, *The Gorbachev Factor* (Oxford University Press, Oxford, 1996).

Carter, Jimmy, *Keeping Faith: Memoirs of a President* (University of Arkansas Press, Fayetteville, 1995).

Cohen, Warren, *America's Response to China: A History of Sino-American Relations* (Columbia University Press, New York, 2010, 2012).

Hirst, David and Beeson, Irene, *Sadat* (Faber & Faber, London, 1981).

Keddie, Nikki R., *Modern Iran: Roots and Results of Revolution* (Yale University Press, London, 2006).

Kingston, Jeff, *Contemporary Japan: History, Politics and Social Change since the 1980s* (Wiley-Blackwell, Oxford, 2010).

McDermott, Anthony, *Egypt from Nasser to Mubarak: A Flawed Revolution* (Croom Helm, London, 1988).

Morley, Morris H., *Imperial States and Revolution: The United States and Cuba, 1952–1986* (Cambridge University Press, Cambridge, 1987).

Okey, Robin, *The Demise of Communist Eastern Europe: 1989 in Context* (Arnold, London, 2004).

Preston, Paul, *The Triumph of Democracy in Spain* (Methuen, London, 1986).

Schoenbaum, David, *The United States and the State of Israel* (Oxford University Press, Oxford, 1999).

Waswo, A., *Modern Japanese Society 1968–1994* (Oxford University Press, Oxford, 1996)

Part 6
1991–2011:
NEW WORLD ORDERS?

A final part can have no finality. Any account which terminates in 'the present' will always be overtaken by events. A 'conclusion' being written in 2012 is no exception, and emphatically so. Global 'uncertainty' is pervasive. The present part begins around 1991, with what then seemed a fundamental point of transition: the end of the Cold War. The air was full of talk of a 'new world order'. Its actual contours, as time passed, however, were difficult to establish. The first chapter, in particular, considers the impact of these developments on the two Superpowers dominant since 1945. It was tempting, in simplistic terms, to see 'the Free World' triumphant. A decade later came '9/11', 2001, the aerial attack on New York and Washington, an event, it was then claimed, which 'changed everything'. Not one but two 'turning points', therefore, feature in this part. Yet, to suppose that 'everything' did change, whether in 1991 or 2001, reveals a narrow perspective. Though the tremors of these years were indeed far-reaching, they did not impact everywhere equally. Some things did not change and some things changed for different reasons. So great has been the diversity of experience that it remains difficult, if not impossible, to make any assessment that is truly universal. The 'aftershocks' of '9/11' continue, and no fresh turning point has arrived to give this part a self-evident termination. Everything, in short, remains provisional and impermanent.

The present, however – taken to be 2011 and the immediately antecedent years – presents difficulties beyond the absence of a conspicuous 'points of transition'. Politicians and commentators in all continents express a sense that the world has 'lost its bearings'. There is a 'world crisis'. Doubt is frequently expressed about 'the world's capacity to function'. Assumptions, spoken or unspoken, about world order which have been dominant for decades are called into question. Media commentators are not slow to extrapolate from the present. They produce headline-grabbing assessments: 'decline of the USA', the 'failure of Europe', the 'rise of China', the 'resurgence of Russia', the 'debut of Brazil', or whatever. There is general agreement, however, that the world is currently 'out of balance' and in danger of 'seizing up'. How equilibrium between states and systems can be created, and over what timescale, cannot be identified in this book.

Map 9 The
world in 2012

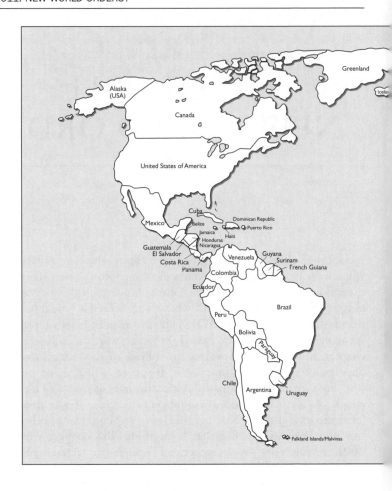

'Global history' has to site itself within this web of interconnectedness. Only a very few countries, and no major ones, can even aspire to 'non-participation' in a networked world. Individual and collective decisions at state level can only go so far before they are constrained by factors and forces 'beyond our control'. Governments, agencies and corporations, at the interface between 'public' and 'private' sectors of varying size and scope, can no more clearly, easily and swiftly manage interconnectedness than historians can pinpoint its essence or its 'centre'. Contemporary historians, in these circumstances, not infrequently both say that it would be foolish to make predictions but then go on to either make them or expire in breathtaking banality. At 1991, 'we' have reached 'a point of historic crisis', concluded the British historian Eric Hobsbawm. He accompanied it by an instruction that 'Our world' (of 1991) must 'change', and in a later book explained how that might be done. A description of a 'historic crisis', however, loses its impact as it lingers on and becomes 'how things are'. The world has of course 'changed' in many particulars since 1991 but 'it' can neither change itself nor simply respond to the injunction of an historian, however eminent. The world, it seems, has only a

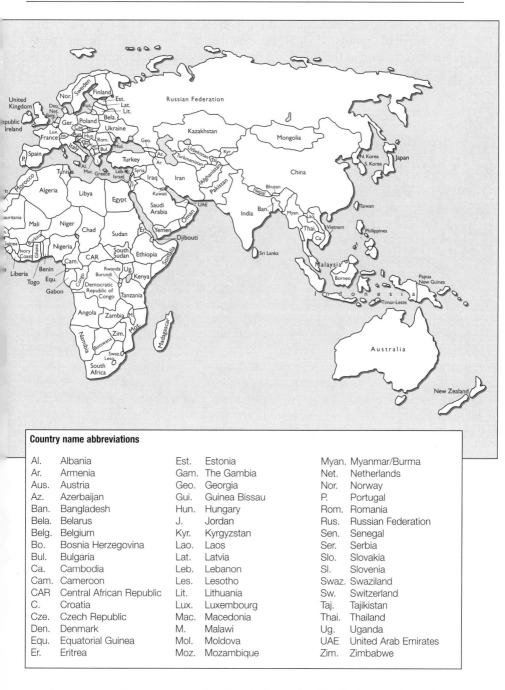

Country name abbreviations

Al.	Albania	Est.	Estonia	Myan.	Myanmar/Burma
Ar.	Armenia	Gam.	The Gambia	Net.	Netherlands
Aus.	Austria	Geo.	Georgia	Nor.	Norway
Az.	Azerbaijan	Gui.	Guinea Bissau	P.	Portugal
Ban.	Bangladesh	Hun.	Hungary	Rom.	Romania
Bela.	Belarus	J.	Jordan	Rus.	Russian Federation
Belg.	Belgium	Kyr.	Kyrgyzstan	Sen.	Senegal
Bo.	Bosnia Herzegovina	Lao.	Laos	Ser.	Serbia
Bul.	Bulgaria	Lat.	Latvia	Slo.	Slovakia
Ca.	Cambodia	Leb.	Lebanon	Sl.	Slovenia
Cam.	Cameroon	Les.	Lesotho	Swaz.	Swaziland
CAR	Central African Republic	Lit.	Lithuania	Sw.	Switzerland
C.	Croatia	Lux.	Luxembourg	Taj.	Tajikistan
Cze.	Czech Republic	Mac.	Macedonia	Thai.	Thailand
Den.	Denmark	M.	Malawi	Ug.	Uganda
Equ.	Equatorial Guinea	Mol.	Moldova	UAE	United Arab Emirates
Er.	Eritrea	Moz.	Mozambique	Zim.	Zimbabwe

ponderous capacity to respond collectively and effectively to those issues which, by common consent, threaten global life: population, climate change, the environment, natural resources among them. While these matters have been and remain 'global', the subject of innumerable international conferences at every conceivable level, such gatherings reveal that 'the world', as such, cannot take a view. Consensus in these matters, where it is possible, only arises when different 'points of view' are explored and reconciled. So, the 'parts' remain prominent, as the following chapters explore, with their particular fears, aspirations and inequities.

24
Superpowers: Rethinking Required

New epoch? Bush and Gorbachev in Malta

Two men initially set the tone. The language used by Mikhail Gorbachev and George Bush on board a ship anchored in a Maltese harbour in December 1989 was ambitious. The former declared that the world was leaving one epoch and entering another. The latter spoke of transforming the East–West relationship into one of 'enduring co-operation'. George W.H. Bush (b.1924) knew much more about the world on the ground than most US presidents. His initial caution had been welcomed by his fellow-Republicans but others, including some in his own party, felt that the time had come for eloquence. The USA could not give the appearance of being in second place behind a Soviet Union now apparently eager to make the world safe for democracy. Ironically, therefore, 'enduring co-operation' initially manifested itself in verbal competition to own this 'new world'.

The inhabitants of go-between Malta in 1989, though not specifically asked, were well placed to remind their powerful visitors of complications ahead. Their own insular history, over centuries, 'between worlds', did not illustrate 'enduring co-operation' between East and West. The 'transformation' that Bush spoke about understandably had 'Moscow' and 'Washington' primarily in mind. However, even a temporary co-operation between 'East' and 'West', conceived more broadly, might be difficult to achieve. Even in harbour, Maltese waters in December 1989 were choppy. There was to be no smooth passage to a new epoch. 'Old worlds' did not vanish overnight. Some state structures, seemingly secure in 1991, subsequently collapsed. Old animosities, which had appeared buried, revived. Notwithstanding such developments, however, 'new world order' discourse, while often vacuous, did somehow express a collective sense that the world, as it had largely been portrayed post-1945, had moved on. An old framework was being replaced by one in which the very concept of order looked problematic. 'Free Worlds', 'Communist Worlds' and 'Non-aligned Worlds', which had at least given interpretative bearings, gave way to fluidity and uncertainty.

The UN: fit for purpose?

By 1989, Gorbachev had been in full flow for some time in presenting 'new thinking for our country and the world'. In December 1988 he spoke in these terms before the UN General Assembly. It was time, he said, for the Organization's centrality to be emphasized. The Cold War had prevented the Security Council from carrying out the role for which, he claimed, it had been designed, but now things would be different. A new 'atmosphere' amongst its permanent members was indeed discernible. The British representative, for example, noted the emergence of new combinations of states. On some issues he found himself closer to former adversaries than to old friends. The non-aligned Group of 77 was fragmenting as all states, in a sense, were non-aligned. For the moment, at least, there was fluidity. And there were new issues. In 1987 the report of the Brundtland Commission on Environment and Development triggered enduring debate on matters which transcended state boundaries.

But there could surely be no simple going back to what might have been in the minds of the Great Powers in 1945. The UN, multidimensional though it had become, was a product of an earlier epoch. A contemporary world might need a revitalized UN, but who could revitalize it? Questions of finance, organization, competence, disinterestedness, function and composition clustered together around the UN itself. In what sense could a Secretary-General embody *the* aspirations of the world? Since 1982 the Peruvian diplomat Perez de Cuéllar (b.1920) had held that post. His predecessor had been the Austrian Kurt Waldheim, now his country's President, a man whose stature had diminished as controversy over his wartime career had mounted. A South American in post was itself a modest sign of 'global emergence', but his term was drawing to a close. There would be the inevitable lobbying to find an 'acceptable' successor. It turned out to be Boutros Boutros-Ghali (b.1922), an Egyptian Coptic Christian, a man with strong intellectual and personal links with Paris and, later, with the francophone world. One of his first actions, in 1992, was to issue what he called an 'Agenda for Peace'. A Secretary-General, however, might set an agenda but might not do much else, or be allowed to do much else. It was in New York, therefore, that the singularity of the world came face to face with its strident pluralities. No amount of talk about the centrality of the UN in the 'new world' could disguise the extent to which its operational capacity, even at the most basic level of finance, depended upon the engagement of a world of states, all with their particular interests. The proliferation of international organizations, and the remits which they itched to expand, rubbed up against not only legal notions of sovereignty in the abstract but concretely against the spheres that national leaders, sometimes responsible in a general sense to electorates, wished to keep for themselves.

In speeches to Congress in September 1990 and elsewhere, Bush nevertheless sketched out a partnership which would enable the goals expressed in the UN at last to come to fruition. The detail, however, still remained opaque and, in so far as the new order rested upon a personal relationship between two men, Gorbachev turned out to have but two more years in power. There was also to be no second term for Bush. He was defeated in the US presidential election in

November 1992. The new 'epoch' being identified in Malta was in this respect short-lived. A new Soviet–American 'partnership in co-operation', even as it was apparently being minted, was being replaced by a more complicated pattern of world relationships. Gorbachev, in talking up the UN, did indeed at the same time see a world evolving in which he identified the USA, the Soviet Union, Europe, India, China, Japan and Brazil as the major powers. It is these entities, together with 'the Middle East' and an 'absent' Africa on which the remaining chapters largely focus.

The world had still to reckon with major powers. It was just that there were more of them and, within a few years, one of the seven 'major powers', the Soviet Union, had disappeared. Another, 'Europe', had to be defined afresh. It was also unlikely that these 'major powers' all thought of themselves as 'major' in the same way, though that might change. As things stood, there was little likelihood of a common desire on their part to underpin the world through the UN. Besides, there was a certain arbitrariness in this selection of 'majors' and other candidates (Iran or Indonesia) might have qualified. There were also 'minor' powers, particularly in the Middle East, whose control of crucial world resources made them, in this respect, 'major' players. Gorbachev's list, of course, carried a message about continents. The most obvious one was that Africa was without a major power. The Middle East continued to be volatile and indeed was soon to pose major and divisive issues for the 'international community'.

Civilizations: clashing?

Other ways of looking at the world soon emerged in the 1990s. The Harvard political scientist Samuel P. Huntington (b.1927) published *The Clash of Civilizations and the Remaking of World Order* in 1996, elaborating views earlier expressed in the journal *Foreign Affairs*. In all his writing, Huntington specialized in clashes. His title in itself ensured worldwide attention. A global map portrayed in terms of Free World/Communist World/unaligned nations obviously had to be scrapped. In its place, he thought, should come a map encapsulating 'civilizations'. 'Western' meant North America and a Europe which extended east, but not too far east, that is to say one which left space for an 'Orthodox world'. 'Latin America' and 'Japan' were worlds on their own. There were also 'Buddhist', 'Hindu', 'Sinic' and 'Islamic' worlds. The last-named constituted a fairly obvious bloc (a generous North African and East African littoral came within it), but delineation raised at least the possibility that there was also an 'African world', a non-Islamic one. To picture a world of civilizations was hardly a breakthrough. The global fame of the British historian, Arnold Toynbee, who had unstintingly pursued their challenges and responses, had passed, but civilizations had not. What Huntington injected was the belief, increasingly, that 'people' defined themselves on the basis of ancestry, language, religion and customs. The distinctions that mattered were not based on ideology or economic status but were cultural. Conflicts that were emerging, or had for a long time been unresolved, could be found where world civilizations met: most conspicuously Bosnia, Chechnya, the Caucasus, Central Asia, Kashmir, 'the Middle East', Tibet, Sri Lanka and Sudan. His conclusion was stark. 'Clashes of civilizations', rather than of states or nations, would be the defining characteristic of the emerging era. On this reading, the world focus should no longer be upon states and nations.

The world's nature, as at once a singular and plural place, impressed itself afresh on commentators worldwide in the wake of the controversy sparked by the book. The 'constituents' of civilizations continued to resist assimilation, absorption or incorporation into coherent global wholes. They have sensed that an institutionalized globalism, floating free, threatened their cherished identities, beliefs and heritages. Such fundamental tension became more acute in the late twentieth century as 'cultures' accelerated away from the territorial anchorages which history had formerly given them. Technological developments were creating situations in which communities, though resident in one country, could now continue to see and participate in the life of their 'home' country. Cultures might no longer need 'territories'.

Though he claimed no 'universal solution', Gorbachev had been busy detecting new worlds everywhere. He thought that in a multidimensional (though possibly contradictory) way, there was a universal longing for independence, democracy and social justice. There were so many problems – food, energy, the environment – which required global solution. The transport and communications revolution sweeping through the world made its oneness visible, tangible and perhaps organizable as never before. Yet such general characterizations had different local implications. The TV Tower in Vilnius, capital of the Lithuanian Soviet Republic, was at once a part of that universal 'communications revolution' to which Gorbachev referred, but, as he found, it also had its own disturbing local significance

Baltic trigger

A new world in which the Soviet Union ceased to exist, however, was not something Gorbachev had wanted in 1989. Neither, indeed, had it been a specific 'Western' objective. Even so, its existing structure was under pressure. In the spring of 1990, the city of Vilnius was in ferment. Lithuanian parliamentarians, hitherto figures of little consequence, voted to secede from the Soviet Union. In the preceding August, some two million people, drawn from the three Baltic Soviet republics, had formed a human chain of protest. The goal of a resumed 'independence' looked, to them, more and more appealing and possible. Gorbachev tried an economic blockade of Lithuania but it did not change minds. On 13 January 1991, however, Soviet Interior Ministry troops stormed the Vilnius TV tower. Hardliners in Moscow wanted to control this particular communications site. It was hardly the action to be expected from a state whose President (as Gorbachev had recently become) had been awarded the Nobel Peace Prize in the preceding October. When the troops advanced on the Lithuanian parliament in that month thousands of people linked hands to stop them. Fourteen were killed. The military advance, however, was not pressed home. Gorbachev took a different tack, proposing an amendment to the Soviet Constitution so that it emphasized its character as a Union of *Sovereign* Socialist

States. There was indeed no more slippery word, at this juncture, than the word sovereignty. In February 1991 over 90 per cent of Lithuanian voters favoured independence (as did those in Latvia and Estonia in March, though with smaller majorities). Gorbachev persisted in thinking a new and 'voluntary' Union Treaty could still succeed, somehow, in keeping the whole together. He had one such ready for signature in August 1991. It was then that a coup against him was attempted. The conspirators claimed they could and would stop the Soviet Union unravelling. It was in Moscow that the drama was played out. Gorbachev was in the Crimea (and would not give in). The coup failed. In the aftermath, 'Moscow Centre' could not hold the Union together. By September, the USSR State Council had formally recognized the independence of the three Baltic republics and supported their application for membership of the UN.

Not that, on their part, there could be any simple return to a 'Baltic past'. There was nothing simple, for example, about Vilnius, a city of multiple names, to return to. In the inter-war period it was in Poland, and some two-thirds of its inhabitants then regarded themselves as Polish and one-third as Jews. 'Lithuanians' were scarcely to be seen. In 2001, only a bare majority regarded themselves as Lithuanians. The complex story of Vilnius serves as but one example of the widespread definition and redefinition which was going on in the 'Baltic world'. Different from each other though they were in particulars, not least in their much larger Russian populations, Estonia and Latvia joined Lithuania in facing the same major problems of economic adjustment. Once the heady atmosphere of regained independence was over, developing effectively functioning democracies was no easy matter. Their pasts gave no very helpful guide in this respect. Political parties mushroomed in more than ample numbers, with coalition governments their inevitable and sometimes unstable consequence. The 'Baltic world' was being reconfigured in a context where present ethnic balances and 'indigenous' versions of national pasts could easily clash. Lithuania, Latvia, Estonia, Poland, Belorussia/Belarus, Sweden and Finland, and of course Russia itself, had to forge new relationships. Metaphorically, however, the three reconstituted Baltic states took the 'path to the West' (and for some citizens the path was not only a metaphor), however complicated the journey might be. Applications for membership of NATO and the European Union were successful in 2004. They came to play an important though minor part in the politics of the European Union thereafter.

Remaking Russia

Russia, that is to say the Russian Federation, stretched from Kaliningrad on the Baltic to Vladivostok on the Pacific Ocean, neighbouring, as the latter did, China and North Korea. It remained vast in extent and complexity. Another question, an old but still central question, followed. What was this Russia and to what world did it now belong? The 'Russian question' had come into sharp relief in the conflicts of 1990–91. It had been Boris Yeltsin (b.1931), at logger-heads with Gorbachev, who had, in steady stages, pressed home the Russian as opposed to the Soviet case. His role in the coup crisis in Moscow in August 1991 had been critical. The previous month he had been sworn in as President of the Russian Federation, receiving, in the process, the blessing of the Russian Orthodox Church. Here, perhaps, was a first sign of the renewal of Russian wholeness. It was time for Russian men to receive the baptism which their families had unaccountably neglected. This new vision perhaps came in a nationalist package. Kiril I was installed as Patriarch of Moscow in February 2009 at a service attended by President Medvedev and Prime Minister Putin. In the past he had had extensive external contacts, through the World Council of Churches. That did not mean, however, that he had become some kind of 'Western liberal'. Indeed he rejected the false materialism alleged to be inherent in Europe's Renaissance, Reformation and Enlightenment (conceived by him to be a continuum). He had a fresh but ancient spiritual *symphonia* to offer. But if this vision was really the 'Orthodox way' to the future, how many Russian citizens shared it?

Vladimir Putin (b.1952), plucked by Yeltsin in August 1989 to be another of his prime ministers, was born in Leningrad. His age meant that he had no personal memory of the Great Patriotic War. The death of Stalin in 1953 had not impinged on a baby. Leningrad's wartime experience, however, lingered long and deeply in its contemporary life. A boy growing up there and studying in its state university would not escape that ambient legacy of its historic wartime siege. Leningrad, poised between East and West, expressed both Russia's glory and vulnerability. This particular law graduate entered the KGB (National Security Agency). In 1985 he was stationed in Dresden, another city whose wartime trauma lingered. Putin had not come there, however, to explore the city's European cultural heritage or hanker after 'a common European home'. His spying concentrated on other matters in a country, a 'Soviet bulwark', which in one sense kept 'the West' at bay. The GDR, however, dissolved around him. Taken up by its then mayor, his next sphere of activity was back in his native city as it returned to being St Petersburg. Such a civic 'restoration' erased one kind of past but did not indicate a clear future.

It was difficult to say quite what political and economic system was evolving in the helter-skelter of Russian change in the 1990s. It was a time for big deals, with attendant corruption. The external world made the acquaintance of 'oligarchs' of sudden great wealth who had sprung apparently from nowhere as state assets were sold off. There was democracy of a kind, even if it was not quite what Western eyes thought democracy was. Yeltsin's hand was not steady, for various reasons, but he survived. Outside commentators, however, seeing policy lurches in one direction or another, thought that transformation in Russia would require a decade, maybe two. Insiders, experiencing it, thought six months should suffice. One fundamental problem, common elsewhere in similar circumstances, was discovering what a political party actually was. Political groups formed and dissolved with considerable rapidity. Russia had to make do and mend.

In 1999 Putin was initially an unknown Prime Minister. It looked as though he was being 'anointed' as Yeltsin's successor. In 2000 he was elected as President in a national election. Four years later he gained 71 per cent of the vote. He proved as adept as any Western leader in establishing a 'brand' for himself. The 'personal rule' that evolved was not dictatorial, but neither was it

'Western'. He both created and benefited from a sense that Russia was 'coming through' – but on its own terms. Yeltsin had wanted to see Russia inheriting the Soviet Union's world position, but in the domestic circumstances of the 1990s that had scarcely been possible. Putin's 'restoration' of Russia changed the situation. Outside observers, whether in the USA or Western Europe, could not quite make up their minds whether to be relieved to see stability (and a polarized domestic prosperity) or alarmed by the strength of a Putin hybrid regime, democratic by Russian standards but 'peculiar'. His election to serve another term as President in 2012, transferring from the prime-ministership, meant that this uncertainty continued. There were accusations about the fairness of elections and some public evidence of discontent. Witnessing developments, some came to believe, after all, that there was such a thing as Russian national character. There was the further paradox that in the 'new Russia' not only was the Russian population ageing, it was also diminishing.

'The former Soviet Union': restructuring

A 'Slavdom' might have some surviving substance. Within its surrounding world, Russia might still exercise some kind of hegemony since so many roads still led to Moscow. 'Near neighbours' could scarcely avoid some kind of 'special relationship' with it. There were, after all, still Russians everywhere in the ex-Soviet world and by no means all would want to come 'home' (or even knew where 'home' was). In Moldova, though uniquely there, sufficient numbers of Russians resented 'Romanianization' to be able to set up their own republic in the east of the country. Russian protection enabled this regime to survive and, over time, the two governments in Moldova evolved a curious working relationship. There was every reason for Moscow to press for the continued use of Russian as the lingua franca which still linked the ex-Soviet world. The Commonwealth of Independent States (CIS) emerged in 1991 and, with the exception of the departing Baltic States, all the successor states initially signed up to it. Its headquarters were in Minsk in Belarus rather than in Russia, though Russian personnel dominated. From the outset, the CIS had to square a circle. The questions to be discussed were predictable: common currency, common economic area, common military forces, or at least military strategy. No agreement proved possible across the board and in practice over the next two decades, operationally, the CIS meant as little or as much as each member wanted. There was no single approved menu. Individual states signed up to bits and pieces. They all stressed their independence but nevertheless continued to meet as though they were not in fact quite independent. An aura of the old therefore lingered on, whatever it signified, and only Georgia, in the wake of its much later military conflict with Russia, actually withdrew from membership.

The 'Slavic core' of the old Soviet Union now consisted of three states: Belarus, Ukraine and the Russian Federation. Whether, and in what respects, they were at all 'fundamentally' different from each other was a question which rumbled on, defying, two decades later, any definitive resolution. Since inter-state differences also reflected the shifting cultural, economic and demographic balances within these states, any clear-cut or early outcome would have been surprising. A lot of time could be spent, by some, praising or decrying alleged 'family ties'. History, whether of the Grand Duchy of Lithuania or of 'Kyivan Rus', was sometimes invoked to buttress or undermine the new status quo. It offered plenty of scope for both strategies. Byelorussia, now renamed Belarus, which had never been an independent state, had most difficulty with its identity. How to define the Byelorussian language offered much scope for reflection. Many more people in Belarus spoke Russian than spoke Byelorussian. Alexander Lukashenko, who came to power in a presidential election in 1994, and whose occupancy seemed permanent thereafter, looked to very close ties with the Russian Federation, particularly if he could be at the helm in both. Yet the relationship between Minsk and Moscow was not invariably brotherly. In dealings between the two governments, as elsewhere within the Slavic ex-Soviet world, the commercial 'terms of trade' were contentious. Lukashenko's direction of travel, however, was emphatically not 'westwards'. His method of securing and maintaining power did not commend itself to the European Union (EU).

Ukraine's future constituted both a more complex and more important question. After a referendum, Ukraine formally withdrew from the USSR at the beginning of December 1991. It was a country, however, which had its own internal East–West fissures - linguistic, cultural and religious. It is no surprise that here too, two decades later, where Ukraine positioned itself remained 'open'. Some individuals, with substantial sections of the population behind them, pushed to join 'the West' (that is to say membership of the EU and NATO) as the 'direction of travel'. Their opponents, on the contrary, stressed the importance of a close relationship with the Russian Federation. Then again, was Russia using economic power to control Ukraine or was it simply ceasing to 'privilege' Ukraine in the prices it charged the new state? Significant individuals, conscious of the complex strands in their inheritance, vacillated between these two courses. Bifurcation was also apparent in another way. Ukrainian workers, in large numbers, were to be found in Russia and Central Europe. The country's first President, Leonid Kravchuk (b.1934) had been born in what was then part of Poland. His own path to the 'independence option' had not been straightforward. And after it had been taken, the 'Soviet past' was still present – not least in the shape of the Russian Black Sea Fleet, the subject of protracted negotiation before agreement was reached in 1997. Crimea itself was a flashpoint. After a turbulent period, it became an autonomous republic within Ukraine but from time to time, when relations between Moscow and Kiev were tense, Ukraine alleged that Russia was meddling in the Crimea. Russian opinion, in general, found it difficult to believe that the Crimea was really part of 'Ukraine'. Chekov's Yalta villa was surely not in a 'foreign' country? Identity issues therefore played a prominent part in the stormy course of Ukrainian internal politics after 2004. The 'Russian question' was always present. Elections became very frequent but effective government much less frequent. 'People power' appeared and disappeared. Population declined. All of this suggested that, two decades on, 'transformation' had only begun.

To refer to 'the break-up of the Soviet Union', however, misleads if it conveys the impression that rupture was absolute or implies that the succession states swiftly obliterated all elements of shared pasts, perhaps unwillingly shared pasts. The USSR had not been a Raj from which the erstwhile ruler retreated to some remote insular homeland. Russia would be always 'next door'. The web of links constructed in the 'Union era', personal and otherwise, might shift in their weight and significance, but it was unlikely that they would be obliterated. What the totality would thereafter amount to, however, was unclear. 'National liberation' posed questions about the identity of 'the nation' everywhere. In the past, 'Moscow', for various reasons, had altered the boundaries of republics, and those existing in 1989 could be challenged again. There were enclaves of one nationality within the territory of another. The future could, and did, prove explosive. The 1988 war between Armenia and Azerbaijan generated substantial transfers of ethnic Armenians and Azeris between the two states. Some countries, such as Armenia, could look to a global diaspora for support. There were almost as many Armenians scattered across the globe, including in Russia (not least in 'remote' Vladivostok), as lived in Armenia itself. External remittances were significant. Linkages with worlds beyond, in this and other instances, played importantly into local bargaining. Some half a million Germans living in Kazakhstan departed for 'home' in the 1990s.

So, whether immediately or on a longer time scale, 'imperial dissolution' was likely to be accompanied by further attempted dissolutions, reconstructions and departures. Population balances, not only between town and country but also between ethnic communities, shifted significantly over the ensuing two decades. New leaders emerged, their career patterns and ages reflecting the reorientations that were taking place. Mikheil Saakashvili (b.1967), who succeeded Eduard Shevardnadze as President of Georgia, belonged to a different world from his predecessor. Graduating from Kiev State University, he had then taken degrees in New York and studied in France. Not that these exposures, and a perfect command of English, guaranteed him wisdom. The secessionist conflicts in South Ossetia and Abkhazia which had followed swiftly on Georgian independence had only been partially stilled thereafter. In 2008 Georgia came off worst in its military encounter with its big neighbour, their protector. Russia proceeded to recognize the independence of these territories. In the wake of its defeat, the Georgian government's aspiration to join NATO and the European Union stalled. No matter what new mental alignments were made, there were geopolitical realities which could not be ignored.

Separating these non-Slavic states from Slavic states was one obvious, if crude, way of considering the unfolding situation. 'Slavdom' might be problematic, but the 'non-Slavic' states presented no alternative quasi-homogeneity – ethnically, culturally or religiously: Turkmenistan was not Armenia, Georgia was not Kazakhstan. The succession states offered no common 'world-view'. Muslim-majority states, however, stressed, though cautiously, their links with their Muslim brothers beyond their borders. Powerful presidents, like Nursultan Nazarbayev (b.1940) in Kazakhstan, erstwhile proponents of Soviet-style atheism, were seen to be restoring mosques and even themselves undertaking a *hajj* pilgrimage. Nazarbayev had not been an enthusiast for the dissolution of the Soviet world. Twenty years later, however, once it had happened, he was still in control. Elsewhere, too, it would still be some time before a new 'non-Soviet' generation came to power. This 'Central Asia' came to have increasing world significance as its states sought to 'relocate' themselves, some with oil resources, others whose great significance derived from conflicts beyond their borders (in Afghanistan in particular). The Caspian Sea lapped many competing identities.

The outside world was made aware of these issues most specifically, though not uniquely, in the case of the Chechens, a small people with a bitter experience of displacement in the Stalinist past. The complexities thrown up in this dissolving world can be seen in the career of Dzhokov Dudayev (b.1944), Chechen Soviet Air Force General, whose varied career had latterly found him in Estonia as the Baltic crisis unfolded. He had married a Russian woman. In December 1991, however, he was back in the Chechen capital of Grozny proclaiming an independent Chechen republic. Boris Yeltsin insisted, however, that Chechnya belonged within the Russian Federation. A bitter and bloody struggle for power ensued. Dudayev himself was killed in 1996, but resistance continued and led to a further war within a few years. A settlement never seemed to last for long. Grozny was at one point razed to the ground. Whatever degree of 'autonomy' might or might not be forthcoming, it was clear that the Russian military presence would remain and, with it, the possibility of Chechen terrorism in Moscow and elsewhere. Putin, however, was adamant that he too would pursue a 'War on Terror' without reservation.

On 25 December 1991, therefore, when the flag of the Russian Federation flew over the Kremlin for the first time, many other flags came to flutter uncertainly throughout the 'ex-Soviet world'. In distant ex-Soviet places, the tone that emerged from Moscow expressed a Russian determination to 'inherit' what 'Union' assets it could. It was a criticism which brought out a fundamental, and enduring, difference of perception. Russians, particularly outside Russia – engineers and other technical experts, for example – saw their role very positively. A 'Kazakhstanization', they thought, which encouraged the departure of Russians, would be bad for Kazakhstan. Non-Russians, portraying themselves as exploited, thought Russians were domineering 'colonists'. They should go home.

It is not surprising, in all these circumstances, that the 'essence of Russia' continued to be contested, both internally and externally. 'Europe' loomed large and gained fresh significance, but Moscow still had to look in many other directions. It could not be other than a world power even if, initially, its chaotic transition masked its continuing global importance. It was not until 1997 that Russia joined that group of countries (the G7) whose meetings had come to assume such importance in tackling 'informally' global economic and environmental issues. The rationale for such meetings was that the members were responsible for roughly half global output and broadly shared the same political and economic systems. It was at such gatherings, invariably described as successful, that leading countries could, as it were, bypass 'the world' as embodied in the formal diplomatic procedures of the UN. The Russian President now belonged in that club. There was irony, however, in that it was in the following year that the rouble collapsed and Russia announced a simultaneous devaluation and debt default. While this was humiliating, and foreign investors were not amused – it marked a turning point. The Russian economy became more competitive and growth resumed. The worst was perhaps over.

The USA: lonely eminence?

Out of Control and *Pandemonium* were the titles of books published in the USA in 1993 by Zbigniew Brzezinski and Daniel Patrick Moynihan, respectively, both men given to reflecting on the USA and its place in the world. The titles pointed to a paradox. Both at the time and subsequently there seemed much substance in the notion that the Free World, headed by the USA, had 'won' the Cold War. Nearly two decades later, when a statue of Ronald Reagan was unveiled in front of the US embassy in London, this conclusion was again publicly proclaimed by British politicians. In the USA itself, however, for more than a decade, scholars had sought to discredit the 'Reagan victory' school. Some noted that the build-up of American military capacity had begun under Carter. Some argued that a new generation of Soviet leaders did not need the advent of Reagan to persuade them that the policies of their predecessors had to be abandoned. Yet, despite scholarly critiques, a public perception remained that the 'North Atlantic world' had won the Cold War. At the very least, it remained generally accepted that 'containment' had worked. Given what had happened in Eastern Europe and to the Soviet Union itself, this assessment looked irrefutable.

At another level, however, and for the USA in particular, 'victory' brought ambiguity. Confronted by a wayward world supposedly lurching towards disaster, the above titles convey anxiety and alarm. However, in other US quarters there was a sense of 'job done'. There was nothing 'natural' or 'inevitable' about the shape of the American global involvement which had evolved since 1945. A 'balanced' role between isolationism and interventionism was required. The USA had ample domestic issues to engage policymakers without the 'distraction' presented by apparently perpetual deployment overseas. Such views seemed both attractive and plausible to many. The outreach of the USA had become excessive and distorting. It was time for the American people to 'come home' to themselves. Just as the Soviet world was 're-placing' itself, so the USA should be 're-setting' itself. Europe, the Middle East, Africa and Asia, released from the overarching constraints of the Cold War, should find their own place in the world. If the resulting process of adaptation looked like pandemonium, so be it. It was a necessary process.

Thinking on these lines fused two rather different approaches. On the one hand, it reflected self-centredness. Even at the height of America's global projection, a not insubstantial section of domestic opinion still seemed resolutely detached from the outside world. American TV networks closed foreign bureaux and dramatically reduced the foreign content of news programmes in the decade after 1989. People, it seemed, were not interested. Paradoxically, perhaps, the USA was both parochial and globally pervasive. Domestic ignorance of 'the outside world' was of course not uniquely an American accomplishment but, from external vantage points, it was an odd aspect of such an 'advanced' country. It was perhaps explained by the very size of the USA. It was true, on the other hand, that 55.5 million Americans took international flights from US airports in 2000, a figure which had been constantly growing over the previous decade. These pieces of information suggest ambiguity. More Americans travelled overseas to a variety of destinations than any other people at this time (though it is not clear how many of them were duplicate travellers). Many such travellers were notoriously inquisitive, yet many more stayed at home and did not want to know. The 'American public', therefore, was not a simple entity. It accommodated both the sentiments of 'America First' and those of 'global idealism'.

'Disengagement', however, also appealed to those Americans hostile to global military and political projection. They argued that fear of Communism's advance had led successive administrations, fearing Communism, to support 'inappropriate' regimes across the world. There had been too many murky episodes which sullied the name of America. Now, they thought, this kind of interfering involvement was no longer justified. Their opponents, however, believed that this stance misunderstood the relationship between the domestic and the foreign. The web of the world was such that almost all governments had to operate in both domestic and foreign spheres. It was facile to suppose that a clear 'withdrawal' was possible. There might be room for some subtle redirection of policy, but the notion that 'the domestic' could replace 'the foreign', in one fell swoop, was absurd. Further, while the world had changed, it had not changed utterly. The 'pandemonium' of the present was real. Over time, the USA might draw down forces long stationed beyond its borders, but to do so precipitately would be folly. The country did still underpin particular regional orders (in Korea, for example) and could not simply 'go home' without serious consequences. It might be that 'world Communism' was now a thing of the past but other dangers, from an American perspective, remained. It was not illegitimate to have 'national interests' and not improper for the USA to retain the capacity to deploy its military capacity overseas if those interests (for example, access to oil) were threatened.

The scale of its military resources, however, placed the USA in a unique global position. Circumstances had combined to make it the sole Superpower with the capacity and experience to operate globally, if deemed necessary. Such power, even so, remained relative. The USA could not take on 'the world'. The existence of nuclear weapons, and their possible further proliferation, restricted its capacity to intervene everywhere on the ground (supposing it ever wanted to do so). There was, however, nothing which was necessarily permanent about the military advantage which the USA possessed. Critics of 'over-extension', as earlier, believed that there were unacceptable costs, indeed unsustainable costs, in seeking to maintain its world position. And, even supposing that the costs could be afforded – naturally not a topic on which economists spoke with one voice – did they generate proportionate benefits?

Argument about what constituted the national self-interest of the USA at this juncture was only to be expected. It took place, however, alongside a renewed sense that the country had a mission beyond the pursuit of self-interest. There was a new world struggling to be born, George W.H. Bush had told Congress in September 1990. It would be quite different from any previously known. The rule of law would supplant the rule of the jungle and the strong would respect the rights of the weak. Such rhetoric, and other examples from other American lips, struck a deep chord. It presaged not eager detachment but fresh involvement. The world could not be left to its own devices. The USA was a kind of universal laboratory for humankind. Such reiterated convictions, however, were sometimes perceived, particularly externally, as dangerous evidence of self-deception. The USA had a habit of defining 'the rule of law' in ways which suited it. It did not pass serenely and dispassionately through the jungle. The outside world continued to perceive a puzzling combination of perceived bullying and benevolence in its global stance. Critics spoke of the USA confronting or even waging war on 'the world'. Supporters, on the contrary, saw it as the world's anchor, preventing it from slipping into dangerous regional conflicts. Such contrasting verdicts expressed the prevailing uncertainties. What could not be done, almost anywhere, was to ignore the presence of 'the American brand' – whether packaged as food, film, fashion or music. Was 'the American Century' drawing to a close, or was it, with the collapse of Soviet Communism, on the brink of its fullest global impact?

Familiar issues, in this respect, received never-ending rehearsal over the next two decades. Diagnoses of the economy produced contrasting verdicts (not that, over the ensuing decades there was ever a steady-state condition to analyse). Notions that industrial arteries were perilously hardening were countered by the evidence of dynamism as the information technology revolution accelerated. It was a picture which again disclosed the diversity of the USA. It also brought home the implications of the 'global economy', now more than ever the topic of attention, in which the USA was enmeshed. The relative advantages and disadvantages of 'globalization' were scrutinized afresh. 'Globalization', seen specifically in its economic aspects, was frequently seen outside the USA as 'Americanization' but, if so, it was an 'Americanization' which hit home. Successive administrations had little option, in the face of American domestic pressure, to identify ways in which they thought Americans could succeed in a global economy that was slipping, or had slipped, beyond their power to direct. Debates on these matters revealed sharp divisions, by no means all on party lines. 'New eras', as proclaimed by presidents, seemed doubtful. States had ceased, or were ceasing, to be the only international actors as multinational business corporations flitted from country to country.

The scale of the US defence budget, and the size and technical sophistication of its armed forces, gave continuing substance to its position as 'the world's only superpower'. No other country could deploy such power across the world. With this pre-eminence, however, came a nagging question. In the 'new world', in what circumstances would it effectively be used? It was difficult to define an 'enemy' in a world of assorted rivalries and political systems. There was perhaps a mismatch between an awesome possession of power and a capacity to exercise it effectively. Circumstances on the ground, as past events had demonstrated, might again expose the limitations of 'hard' power. These were matters for particular debate in the USA. Few discerned the precise manner in which they would be put to the test.

External projection and internal self-perception naturally went hand in hand. It is not surprising, therefore, that the same puzzling mixture of confidence and doubt was evident internally. The USA was not about to fragment, as the Soviet Union fragmented. Yet the basis of its own identity was under pressure. The 'nation of immigrants' might have come to the limit of its capacity to absorb substantial numbers of immigrants. Pressure grew for legislation designed to restrict the flow. More immigrants, some nine million, arrived legally in the 1990s than had arrived in the first decade of the century. The number of illegal arrivals, by definition, could not be counted precisely but around the turn of the century may have stood at seven million. Both categories came substantially from Latin America – but also significant numbers from the Philippines and Vietnam. Indeed, in whatever proportions of the whole, the 'world' continued to make its way to the USA and, to varying extents, immigrants retained a connection with the life of their homelands.

It was the continuing Spanish-speaking influx which gave fresh rise to most cultural anxiety. The American melting pot, it was argued, had been stirred with a spoon labelled in English. What was now happening was threatening 'one nation'. The debates that followed and the attempts, at some state levels, to reinforce the position of the English language, revived old controversies. The 'new wave' played complicatedly into an American story presented in 'traditional' white/black terms. There was a sense in which 'old whites' and 'old blacks' had a common fear of being unsettled by the rebalancing of the American population. 'Multiculturalism' both dented white superiority and encouraged white solidarity. It gave further status to black aspirations but perhaps also saw 'new Americans' – Iranians, Vietnamese and others – occupying the economic and cultural spaces sought by blacks. The advantages and drawbacks of immigration found their respective spokespersons. Whether, how and when 'illegals' should be made legal was highly divisive. It was alleged that foreigners were disproportionately involved in smuggling drugs into the country. Prisoners from 'the world' were incarcerated in American prisons in ample numbers, awaiting deportation at the end of their terms. This varied picture could result in the paradoxical position in which the 'world's Superpower' simultaneously felt itself to be 'under siege'.

The identity of America at this juncture, therefore, was also in a peculiar and complex sense locked into the future of the world. How it evolved and how Americans interpreted that evolution mattered. One such interpreter was Francis Fukuyama (b.1952), whose 1989 article 'The End of History' attracted worldwide attention when it appeared in book form a few years later. It was not the prophecy of doom which the title might suggest. The American people, he believed, taken in the round, had achieved a particular level of material prosperity and understanding of their rights. This achievement, however, was not something peculiarly and 'essentially' American. Rather, it constituted a paradigm of what the whole world could achieve without extinguishing distinctiveness. Although taught by Huntington, Fukuyama did not foresee 'Western civilization' inexorably locked in conflict with other civilizations. He did not ignore the tragedies which had disfigured the twentieth-century world before he had been born, but he did not believe their repetition inevitable. Contact between civilizations could be creative. Wars would die out as states realized that was no sensible alternative to liberal–democratic–capitalist organization. What his thesis precisely entailed could be variously interpreted, and was sometimes taken up to buttress agendas which he did not support, but it expressed a sense that America and the world were at a turning point. His perspective gained resonance from the way in which it chimed with his family's history. The Russo-Japanese war (1904–05) had brought his Japanese grandfather to the USA and, much later, he had experienced internment there in the Second World War. His father became a Christian (Congregational) minister and sociologist. His mother was the daughter of a Japanese academic. Fukuyama himself was raised in Manhattan. He did not learn Japanese but admired what Japan had achieved since 1945. His was not a 'typically American story', for there was no such thing, but in America different global histories were always coming together and were forging a new history. It was an ongoing process.

25

The Middle East: Still at the Centre

George W.H. Bush and Fukuyama belonged to different generations, but their message was not radically different. In his State of the Nation address in 1990, Bush argued that the USA was not just a place, it was an idea. That idea, however, could be the world's. The world needed an idea. In other places, however, there were other ideas, also ones which transcended place. The Middle East, with its particular sites of violence, once again moved to the fore as the place where, in new circumstances, 'East' and 'West' again met. What was not anticipated in 1991 occurred in 2001, namely 'its' violence came to the USA. A new kind of world war seemed to be taking place with at least the semblance of a war of 'civilizations'. As the world was in the Middle East so the Middle East had entered the world.

Kuwait: a test case

In August 1990, the Iraqi army invaded the neighbouring hereditary emirate of Kuwait, thereby doubling Saddam Hussein's control over the world's oil reserves. He might move on Saudi Arabia and the Gulf Emirates. 'New world order' rhetoric was therefore put to the test. What was at stake, Bush argued in January 1991, was more than the fate of one small country. It was whether nations would stand together in a common cause 'to achieve the universal aspirations of mankind'. They just might. The Security Council passed a resolution condemning the invasion and calling for the withdrawal of Iraqi forces. It was extended in late November by a demand that all Iraqi forces be withdrawn by 15 January 1991. Failing that, all necessary means would used to ensure this outcome. The Soviet Union did not exercise a veto, although it tried to be a go-between. Iraqi forces were not withdrawn and the liberation of Kuwait began. The actual land fighting in 'Operation Desert Storm' was very concentrated and effective. A ceasefire came into effect on 28 February. The invaders, suffering heavy casualties, retreated back across the border in disarray.

Saddam Hussein proclaimed that the USA was fighting Iraq. George Bush proclaimed that Iraq was fighting 'the world'. Neither claim was strictly correct. The USA, with just over half a million men deployed, was clearly in command, but other countries combined to supply approximately half that figure. The UN did endorse the action and in that sense 'the world' approved. The coalition of some European and Arab states, together with financial support from others, held together. Even so, it was far from being 'the world' in action. The intervention involved only some one in eight of the total membership of the UN. The absence of the major states of Asia, in particular, gave the 'international community' a lopsided character and left obscure what kind of 'global precedent', if any, it in fact created. Its 'United Nations' aspect had only been possible because, with some wobbling, the Soviet Union did not oppose intervention, though it did not itself participate. The USA itself, however, could draw the conclusion that the 'Vietnam syndrome' had been overcome. From a position of distance, by virtue of its technological superiority, it could achieve a victory with minimum loss of life. Yet, as events were soon to demonstrate, 'victory' was an ambitious word.

The restoration of Kuwaiti independence signified that a sufficient number of states stood behind the defence of statehood. Aggression would not pay. A specific 'principle' had been endorsed. However, it did not signify any profound reshaping of the landscape of the 'Middle East'. It did not mean that the 'Middle East' had become, or was becoming, a coherent component bloc in the post-Cold War world. This was in part simply the continuance of the divisions within the 'Arab' world or the 'Islamic' world, as amply illustrated in earlier parts of this book, but it also illustrated that the 'outside world' dictated outcomes. The boundaries of the 'Middle East' did not become less opaque, riddled as they still were with internal patterns of exclusion and inclusion.

The situation was further complicated by the notion that the old confrontational West and East of the Cold War – with 'clients' of one side or other clearly marked – had been superseded by a 'West–East' which appeared to be jointly committed to 'democracy', albeit broadly conceived. 'The world', therefore, in theory should only be moving in one direction. If so, this message fell on stony ground in 'the Middle East'. Perhaps, some said, the Western powers had only themselves to blame. *Realpolitik* had required them, it was claimed, to maintain intimate relations with regimes that were far from 'democratic' in the way 'the Atlantic world' used the term. In the new circumstances, the carpet of long-established support given to particular governments – political, economic and military – was not going to be removed immediately, but in time its significance might change.

Iraq: what mission accomplished?

In January 2002, in his State of the Union address, George W. Bush had spoken of an 'axis of evil' and specifically identified North Korea, Iran and Iraq as 'rogue states'. Through their agency terrorists might get access to weapons of mass destruction. Over the year that followed, policy rhetoric began to shift. To rely on 'containment' was too great a risk. The USA might take action against emerging threats 'before they were fully formed'. The focus shifted back to Iraq. It was more than hinted that Saddam Hussein protected al-Qaeda and might help it acquire the kind of weaponry which he himself was believed to be developing. The notion that it was time to 'take out' Saddam Hussein gained ground. 'Neoconservatives' were confident that the USA was in a unique position to advance, and if necessary impose, its views. It would make the world a better place. Benevolent hegemony, however, was often perceived elsewhere as ignorant arrogance.

The Middle East was to be its test case. The coalition forces assembled to liberate Kuwait, back in 1991, the forces so hated by Osama bin Laden (to be discussed below), had not continued to Baghdad in order to 'finish the business' and topple Saddam Hussein. A coalition could not have been assembled for such an objective. The supposition that Saddam would be toppled internally proved a mistake, underestimating his strength and resilience. Trouble from the Kurds in the North and the Shi'a Arab population in the South was dealt with harshly but effectively. The rebels received no direct outside support, though Western-maintained 'no-fly' zones later offered some protection. The resilience of the regime could not be denied. Was it enhancing its weapons capability, something prohibited under the terms which ended the 1991 war? If so, both scale and nature were contentious. A UN monitoring team was required by Saddam Hussein to withdraw. Accusations and denials concerning weapons of mass destruction flourished. Steadily, the crisis moved to its climax. Success in Iraq, Bush declared on 23 February 2003, could bring a new stage for Middle Eastern peace and celebrate progress towards a truly democratic Palestinian state.

On 19 March 2003 the USA launched its war to bring down the Saddam Hussein regime. Its firepower swiftly achieved its objective. Bush in person arrived to announce mission accomplished. The 'ageless appeal of human freedom' had apparently triumphed again. The invaders, however, soon found themselves faced with a violent internal conflict which their existing resources did not enable them to control. Simple victory, and a touch of Texas would solve the problems which had plagued the country throughout its entire short existence, notably the Kurdish question and Sunni–Shiite relations. The failure to find weapons of mass destruction made the advertised reason for intervention appear a pretext. Yet to withdraw 'precipitately' seemed out of the question. Despite the continuing level of casualties, the USA would do whatever it could to sustain a frail and fledgling democracy struggling to be born. But, as Iraqi killed Iraqi in an apparently unending sequence, and as foreign forces both inflicted and sustained losses, the mission was far from being accomplished.

The entire 'Iraq' enterprise was frequently portrayed in the invading countries themselves as a disaster, probably 'illegal' and 'immoral' to boot. Iraq was not going to be transformed overnight into a beacon of democracy, and the cost of intervention had been too high. The invasion, and what followed, tarnished political reputations. It led, in the British case, eventually to a full-scale inquiry into how intervention had come about. For their part, Muslims around the world, not least in the invading countries, reiterated their contention that foreigners – 'crusaders' – had no business at all in 'Muslim lands'. Non-Muslim foreigners, sardonically noting the zeal Muslims displayed in killing Muslims in such lands, were not impressed by the notion that 'Muslim lands' constituted a world exclusion zone. It was later commonplace amongst the invaders that many 'mistakes' had been made as 'West' and 'East' met in Iraq, but it did not necessarily follow that no intervention should ever be contemplated. The issue of Iraq, in short, sprawled into many domains. The USA had gone to war without a specific UN endorsement. The best that it could extract from diplomacy at the UN had been a resolution which called upon Saddam Hussein to give up all his weapons of mass destruction. It did not authorize war if he did not comply. Whether this made going to war illegal depended upon what one understood international law to be. 'Realists', who were not greatly bothered with such 'legalism', nevertheless argued that the invasion was folly: it simply could not deliver. The USA could 'defeat' but it could not 'win'. Its blinkered notion of 'power' had prevailed. Defenders of the American action argued that while UN authorization might have been welcome, the reality was that the UN could not in practice galvanize the world. Its own organizational failings were referred to in Chapter 1. No one could surely doubt that Saddam Hussein had been a brutal ruler. Only the USA could remove him. But where might intervention on such grounds end? A doctrine of 'pre-emptive strike' might apply, in theory at least, in many other troubled areas of the world. But there were also those who suspected that the war had no high-minded objective at all. It had 'really' been all about oil. Around the world variations on these arguments could be heard. Debate was perhaps most intense within countries previously most closely associated with the USA, particularly in Europe, as will subsequently be seen.

Egypt and Syria: awaiting freedom?

The gap between the 'Western' message and Western relationships with Middle Eastern countries remained wide. Thus, President Mubarak of Egypt continued to be seen as a staunch ally on whom the USA could rely. The language of diplomacy avoided the word 'dictatorship' to describe his regime. Pressure to 'reform' was muted and a premium was placed on the country's 'stability'. For two decades, this pattern survived largely intact. Egypt had a regime which had its origins in a military coup and had then acquired a constitutional scaffolding. That was better than nothing. Egyptian dissenters, it was said, if they gained power, might be even more oppressive. The spectre of power in the hands of the banned Muslim Brotherhood caused a shudder. The same arguments were deployed, with local variation, across all the regimes of the 'Arab world', whether 'traditional' or 'revolutionary'. The outside world thought it saw an 'Arab model' where rule remained strongly personal and where political control was exercised by an 'inner circle' resting on family or on loyalties frequently described as 'tribal' or 'sectarian'. The extent to which such authority rested upon power was never constant but never absent.

Such a picture evoked different and fluctuating responses. In some quarters, the prevalence of broadly 'authoritarian' regimes throughout the Arab world suggested that it 'suited' the circumstances of that world. Social, economic and religious factors came together in a specific fashion, and were likely to continue to see 'dictators' at the helm. Sometimes, as in the case of the Assads of Syria, they became dynasts. In 2000, Bashar (b.1965) succeeded his father Hafez on the latter's death. 'Dictators' in any case were not all of a piece either in style or substance. Those in sober suits saw no need to echo the exotic flamboyance of Colonel Gaddafi. Bashar, fluent in English, initially destined to be an ophthalmologist, had trained in a London eye hospital in the early 1990s. He married a Syrian girl, brought up in London, whom he had met at this time. He knew 'the West' at first hand. A straightforward implant of its current domestic political systems, however, was not something he thought either desirable or possible. The faultlines in Syrian politics still rested on group identities and their regional concentrations. The Assad dynasty's ascendancy admittedly rested on the Alawite minority, but that minority might be more protective of other minorities, Christians for example, than a Sunni majority regime would be. In short, where issues of identity and allegiance were not simply 'national', that is to say frequently, some observers thought 'strong men' inevitable, and perhaps essential. Their countries needed them, particularly since individuals, families and 'tribes' had often welded them together in the first place. If that was true, then the 'Arab world' would not be likely to change rapidly, if at all. In this light, the restoration of Kuwaiti independence in 1991 heralded nothing. Not only Kuwait, but all Arab states were fictions whose scripts were being rewritten by rulers whose ambitions were as much personal as 'national'. Syria undoubtedly 'interfered' in Lebanon at various levels, and its subsequent formal withdrawal by no means ended its involvement. But what was Lebanon? It was a question which its internal divisions still required to be asked. Likewise, it might be said that the tension, for a long time, between Damascus and Baghdad was not between 'Syria' and 'Iraq', but between the Assad nexus and the Saddam Hussein nexus.

Israel/Palestine: no lasting accords

Israel/Palestine as the 'core conflict' of the Middle East remained unresolved in 2011. In November 1988 the PLO had been prodded into recognizing the state of Israel and in return had direct access to Washington. In October 1991, James Baker, the US Secretary of State, managed to get Israelis, Palestinians and other Arab leaders to meet round a table in Madrid. Only after 1992, however, with the election victory of Labor under the soldier-politician Yitzhak Rabin, was anything taken forward. Secret contacts between the two sides in Norway produced the 'Oslo Accords'. The White House lawn was again brought into service in September 1993. President Clinton, Rabin and Arafat came for the formal signing ceremony and a reluctant appearance before the TV cameras.

The theory behind the Accords was that the really difficult issues – Jerusalem, Jewish settlement and Palestinian 'return' – could be put on one side. There could be progress on Palestinian autonomy in Gaza and the West Bank and, as trust emerged, so it was argued, intractable matters could then be dealt with. Jordan and Israel signed a formal peace agreement in October 1994. A few months earlier Arafat was allowed to return to Israeli-occupied Gaza and set up there the new Palestinian National Authority. It took a further round of negotiations in 1995 before the complex relationships between Israeli control and Palestinian autonomy in the West Bank were in theory agreed. May 1999 was supposed to be the date by which formal agreement on the status of the occupied territories, including Jerusalem, was to be reached. It was not. In November 1995 Rabin was shot dead by an Israeli student in Tel Aviv. Both amongst Israelis and Palestinians there were vocal elements, from opposite points of view, who regarded the 'Accords' as a betrayal and dismissed the premise underlying them. It was absurd to believe that a settlement of Jerusalem, for example, was 'round the corner'. Benyamin Netanyahu (b.1949), the new Likud leader and Prime Minister 1996–99, took the view that the future of the city was 'non-negotiable'. Probably most Israelis agreed. Jewish settlements in occupied territory proceeded. Palestinian terror, however, might make Israelis 'see sense': Palestinian terror made Israelis decline to see sense. In the summer of 2000 further abortive talks took place at Camp David. September saw the start of a second Palestinian uprising. Under another military/political figure, Ariel Sharon, in 2001 Israel started to build a 'Security fence'. Its line and symbolic significance were inescapably contentious. In January 2003, following another election, Sharon proceeded to withdraw Israeli settlers from Gaza, something opposed by the foreign minister, Netanyahu, who resigned. One had to be an optimist, however, to believe that success in Iraq would in fact 'set in motion progress towards a democratic Palestinian state'. Over the subsequent years talks between the two sides began and petered out. Palestinians, as between Gaza and the West Bank, in turn differed amongst themselves. They came together, to an extent, in pursuing in 2011 at the UN international recognition of a Palestinian state. It was a step strongly opposed by Israel and regarded as inopportune by the USA. There had to be negotiations ... .

The uncertainty highlighted the extraordinary character of the US/Israel relationship. Israel's survival in its existing form was 'non-negotiable' in the eyes of most American Jews (though not only of Jews) and no lobbying effort was spared to ensure that no American administration wavered in its support. Paul Wolfowitz (b.1943), Deputy Secretary for Defense in the Bush administration, grew up in a Polish Jewish household in New York haunted by the European Holocaust. There was no firmer advocate of a short, swift and apparently cheap war in Iraq. Yet 'success' in Iraq did not inject significant 'motion' into solving the 'Palestine question'. Sharon had a stroke that removed him from the political scene. By 2009, Netanyahu had returned as prime minister. The first holder of the office to be born in Israel, he would do nothing which he believed would jeopardize Israel's security. For periods both in the 1950s and 1960s his family had lived in the USA where he had gone to school. He polished links with the USA. When he spoke before the Congress in 2011 some said he had the Philadelphian accent he had taken on in his youth. The Congress gave him a standing ovation. The President in the White House, however, frustrated by continuing Jewish settlement in the occupied territories, gave him a cold stare. It was not an expression of brotherly love.

Another round of warfare, with unpredictable consequences was very often being predicted. The clients of Iran were implacable opponents of Israel. The great difficulties experienced by Israeli forces in battles in southern Lebanon during its incursion in 1982 suggested that the assumptions about Israeli military superiority, long held, might be overstated. The 'Arab spring', shortly to be discussed, once consolidated, might facilitate a settlement which Israel could accept or, on the contrary, if joined, as looked to be the case, by Turkey, might further increase Israel's isolation and challenge its existence. The Middle East sprang surprises.

This kind of picture often prevailed in the 'outside world'. It counselled inaction, even indifference. That was the way things were. In a world of sovereign states, there was nothing that external powers could or should do to produce more 'enlightened' regimes. Yet, for other elements in the 'outside world' non-interfering aloofness smacked of the notion that 'oriental despotism' was an inherited and intrinsic aspect of 'the Arab world'. Such was surely not the case. No country or society, it was argued, had 'essential' national characteristics. The pursuit of 'freedom', therefore, should know no boundaries. In principle, it justified 'interference', though what kind of interference, and to what end, was another matter. Yet no state which relied upon oil supply from one or other Middle Eastern producer could in fact be indifferent to its internal development.

A world utterly changed? 9/11/2001

On 9 September 2001, '9/11', terrorist attacks on the World Trade Center in New York (and on the Pentagon in Washington) resulted in 3000 deaths. In the USA, it created a 'new era', one with greater emotional charge than the supposed 'epoch-making' turn inaugurated a decade earlier. The attack, however, also struck at 'the world' in so far as nationals of some 90 countries lost their lives. The large number of casualties in a single incident was trauma enough, but the incident destroyed the general assumption that the USA was invulnerable. Pearl Harbor 1941, in a sense, had returned. This, however, was not some formal military invasion by an identified state. The commercial airliners used in the attack had been hijacked from US airports by individuals. The world suddenly lacked its customary mental securities: legal boundaries, formal states, the military and 'world statesmen' were absent. The men involved were all associated with al Qaeda, 'the base', inspired by Osama bin Laden.

The base was everywhere and nowhere. It was a world of its own, mysterious but much speculated upon. Bin Laden (b.1957) was not an outcast at the margins of Saudi society. He graduated in public administration from King Abdul Aziz University in Riyadh in 1981. His well-connected family owned one of the largest construction companies in the Middle East. The construction in which the young man was interested, however, was not a matter of bricks and mortar. It was a matter of rebuilding the world of Islam – from Bokhara to southern Spain, with many places in between. The American-led coalition 'liberating' Kuwait was in reality, from his perspective, an occupation of Islamic holy land. He had already been channelling fighters and funds to the Afghan fighters against the Soviet occupation. In 1994 his Saudi citizenship was revoked and his assets frozen, citing his support for militant 'fundamentalist' movements – though the 'puritanical' Wahhabi brand of Islam strongly present in the country's religious environment was itself sometimes described beyond its borders as 'fundamentalist'. His movements thereafter are not known precisely but a few years later he was operating from Afghanistan. With him there were other figures from other parts of the Arab world, particularly from Egypt, who sharpened their thinking together. The World Islamic Front for the Jihad against Jews and Crusaders was formed in 2000 declaring that all Muslims had a duty to kill Americans and their Allies. The destruction of the Twin Towers came one year later.

Official expressions of sympathy flooded into Washington, even from countries not notably sympathetic to the USA. The 'vitriolic hatred for America in some Islamic countries' was beyond the understanding of the White House, and probably of most Americans. President Bush declared a 'War on Terror' but translating global sympathy into global action proved as elusive as bin Laden himself, now swiftly identified as the prime target. 'The world' could or would not move in harmony from the general to specifics. In the USA itself, and to some of its allies, however, the only way to secure 'homeland security' was to plunge more deeply into the Middle East, an expanding region. Eventually, an extended Middle East at ease with itself would arise, one with which the USA might be comfortable, but its accomplishment might entail a painful path all round. The power of freedom would transform the region. Policymakers in Washington now felt justified and emboldened in seeking to bring this about. That bold action would benefit Israel did not escape the attention of Israelis and members of the administration, Jewish and non-Jewish, committed to its cause.

Enduring freedom's ambiguities: Kabul to Cairo, Tripoli to Damascus, Algiers to Tehran

'Operation Enduring Freedom' was the specific US response to 9/11. It took the US and some of its allies to Afghanistan in October 2001 to remove the Taliban regime there. It had sheltered bin Laden and had its own brand of 'fundamentalism'. In association with a loose Afghan Northern Alliance, a kind of victory looked to be immediately achieved. A decade later, however, US, British and various forces from other NATO countries, operating under different rules of engagement, were still deployed. A question mark hung over the future once foreign forces returned home or ended a combat role. A Taliban government could be removed, but an effectively and approvingly functioning Afghan government in Kabul took time: how much time was constantly adjusted. It became orthodoxy that foreign troops would not remain indefinitely in the numbers judged to be required to blunt (though not defeat) the Taliban opposition forces. An Afghan National Army would give the country as a whole the security it required if its government was to flourish. There was a certain circularity in these assertions. As time passed, the scale of the different worlds in conflict and in partnership became more evident. The continued presence of foreign forces, some said, was counter-productive. As the scale of casualties they sustained continued to grow, so did domestic pressure for a return home. Their governments endeavoured to make the 'exit strategies' they put forward sound convincing. It was not evident that freedom, as the occupying or assisting forces thought of it, would endure. There was also the blight on the reputation of the USA itself arising out of the detainees, arising out of the

Afghan campaign, kept at the Guantánamo Bay prison within the US facility on Cuba. The volume of external criticism mounted, focussing on their original capture, their 'rendition', their treatment and their status. It was the latter which proved intractable in complex legal arguments in the USA which frustrated the intention of the incoming US administration in 2009 to close the prison. Its continued existence kept alive the charge that in defence of freedom the USA resorted to means unacceptable to 'civilized states'.

There could be no certainty that a 'secure' Afghanistan, even if obtainable, would neutralize the prospects for terrorism elsewhere, 'home-grown' (at work in London or Madrid) or orchestrated from outside. The 'base' that was al-Qaeda was mobile. When bin Laden was eventually located and killed by American special forces in 2011 he was living, as he had been for years, safely in Pakistan. How that had come to be the case and what it signified, remained shrouded in mystery. Wherever the truth lay in this instance, it highlighted the extent to which conflicts overlapped and borders were porous. The futures of 'Afghanistan' and the futures of 'Pakistan' were linked in complex alignments. Government to government relations often bore little relationship to realities at different levels. All the old issues which bedevilled Pakistan from its creation – civil–military relations, corruption, violence, natural disaster, ethnic violence (whether in Karachi or the North-West) religious freedom, Kashmir – had certainly not been 'solved'. In Somalia, Yemen, Nigeria, the Maghreb and elsewhere, there were worlds within Islamic worlds not easily accommodated within the categories of belief and behaviour applied by outsiders.

What 'the Middle East' should be, therefore, remained an issue which went wider than the Middle East. That fact in itself was galling within the region. It remained a patchwork of competing regimes. Authoritarian rule, so widespread in various guises, might be generally oppressive but was not without benefit to individuals or groups in 'family' regimes. Faced with 'strong men', both fear of and admiration for their rule mingled, whether in Libya or Yemen or many other places. In such circumstances, to be urged, whether implicitly or explicitly, to 'come into line' with a western-endorsed prescription for government and society would be, once more, humiliating. Yet it was also humiliating to live perpetually with the notion that 'the Arab world' was indeed chained to various kinds of despotism and the curtailment or elimination of 'freedom'. Various reactions were therefore observable. There was renewed rejection, in some quarters, of the 'democratic agenda'. To accept it as a total package would be an un-Islamic capitulation, for democratic theory and its implicit compromises, suborned how Islam envisaged the ordering of society. But was that in fact the case? Muslims in the 'Christian' or 'Secular' West added their own sometimes discordant voices – 'fundamentalist' or 'modern' – to the debate.

On the other hand, there were also 'non-religious' pathways to a Middle Eastern future. Democracy should come, some said, but not too quickly and in the process should have clear indigenous characteristics. Others, sceptical about such an orderly transition, thought that a complete revolution would be necessary. This would entail far more than the all-too familiar coup in which one individual replaced another at the head of an unchanged apparatus. It might be bloody. Such a revolution, however, given the military power and coercive measures at the disposal of existing regimes, might never happen. Even if it did, given the rifts that were likely to emerge, it was difficult to see how 'democracy' could easily and enduringly take root. It was easier to talk about 'parties' than to know what they aspired to achieve. Islam, it was clear, could simultaneously unite and divide. The paradoxical possibility existed that the ballot box, used too generously, might produce the triumph of a party or coalition indifferent or hostile to 'democracy'.

What had occurred in Algeria in 1992 illustrated these complications. Three years earlier, the president, Chadli Benjedid (b.1929), himself a military man, indeed one who had once served in the French army in Indo-China, took a democratic turn. He brought in a new constitution which legalized other parties besides the Front de Libération Nationale [National Liberation Front] (FLN – which had dominated since independence). This enabled the Front Islamique du Salut [Islamic Salvation Front] (FIS) to make major progress in local government. It then won an overwhelming number of seats in the first round of elections to the Algerian parliament. At that point, the military leadership stepped in. The election was cancelled, parliament suspended and Benjedid ousted. The armed wing of the FIS in turn then launched attacks against military and other targets. A bitter civil war ensued with heavy loss of life, perhaps around 100,000 people. It took time for a truce agreed in 1997 to be really effective in ending violence. A 'National Reconciliation' involving Islamic and 'secular' elements of various hues, proved arduous. The civilian-military relationship remained problematic. 'Ownership' of the 'true' Algerian Revolution was disputed. 1999 Abdelaziz Bouteflika (b.1937) became the country first civilian president. A decade later he was still in office, having removed the two-term limit on presidential office and having been returned with apparently 90 per cent of the vote. A post-independence political generation had yet to make its mark at the top. There were naturally aspects of the Algerian experience which were specific, but the issues that were being fought over in more than words, resonated across the wider Arab world. No single or simple balance looked likely.

In Iraq, and by extension in a wider 'Middle East', therefore, it often seemed only sensible, to some observers to conclude that 'the Islamic masses' were not waiting to be liberated. They were not like Eastern Europeans before the fall of communism, waiting to be liberated. The election, the previous year, of Mahmoud Ahmedinejad, as President of Iran, appeared to show that 'the masses' could be enrolled behind a 'populism' which was vehemently 'anti-Western', capitalizing on an enduring sense that Iran had been bullied in the past. Iran, the regime proclaimed, would never be bullied again. It did not hesitate to crush internal opposition. Its nuclear policy, whether or not its objective was the production of nuclear weapons, was an expression of this sentiment. Yet the internal politics of the country remained complex in terms of the interplay between 'religious' and 'secular' leaderships. Khomeini had died in 1989 and no clerical figure had quite succeeded to his role. Ahmedinejad's world stance seemed to preclude accommodation with 'the West', though sometimes there did appear to be some slight possibility of reaching a deal on the nuclear issue. His hostility to Israel was relentless, expressed in support for Hizbollah, the radical Shiite organization in Lebanon pledged to overthrow 'Zionist imperialism'. Israel's failure to defeat Hizbollah in southern Lebanon was the first dent in the notion that Israel would always win in any military encounter. That heightened its sense of insecurity and led it to see the hand of Iran everywhere. Faced with the thought that Iran would have nuclear weapons there was some hope that the USA would 'take out' that possibility. In Washington, however, there was some anxiety that the Israelis would do it themselves, regardless of what 'the world' thought. The consequences, for either course, would be likely to be unpredictable.

The 'success' of Iraq had in fact made it even more important for US administrations to improve its relations with 'the Arab world'. 'Traditional' Arab rulers, suspicious of Shi'ite minorities and Iran, were not unresponsive. Yet they could not waver in a public commitment to the Palestinian cause (and were active in concerting various possible 'solutions'). The USA needed to show that it understood their importance. The Bush administration made gestures, tried some cajoling and criticism of Israel, but would not push beyond buffers it encountered or its own domestic constituency would contemplate. Setting the 'peace process' in motion was no easier in 2010–11, however, than it had been at any earlier juncture. It might even be, this time, that it was not so much a lack of will as, in the end, a lack of American capacity which prevented the 'transformation' of that 'vital region' on which successive American presidents had spent so much time, seemingly to no avail. Entering 2011, therefore, little appeared to have changed in the landscape of the Middle East. As they had been in 2001, and indeed in 1991, Mubarak ruled in Egypt, Ben Ali in Tunisia, Gaddafi in Libya, Saleh in Yemen and an Assad in Syria.

Suddenly, in the early months, it began to look different. First, popular protest in Tunisia led Ben Ali and his family, accused of corruption, to flee the country. Second, after a more protracted struggle in the heart of Cairo, Mubarak stood down and was then brought to trial. In Libya a rising in Benghazi began a long struggle against Gaddafi through the summer. It saw victory for the groups who formed a Transition Council and whose victory had been assisted by the use of air power, with UN approval, by some NATO countries, chiefly Britain and France. Gaddafi met an ugly death. A power struggle was also taking place in Yemen. In Syria, Bashar Assad did not hesitate to use force against protestors in a protracted struggle to maintain power. It intensified as the months passed and drew in both 'the Arab world' and the wider' international community'. While the Great Powers could deplore the loss of life they could not agree that any solution to the internal conflict would have to require that Assad should depart. At the time of writing, the regime was still in place and the future opaque. Journalistic parlance had invented an 'Arab spring'. Perhaps, after all 'the masses' did want freedom. There was a sudden memory that in 2009 'the people' had been robbed of their victory in the Iranian general election. Young people certainly told the television world that they wanted freedom, saying that they had never known it. So was this a new generation devising a new future or was it an evanescent bubble? The Gaddafi regime was deplorable but it was not clear what kind of government could follow and whether 'Libya', as such, would survive. The overthrow of the regime was also likely to have destabilizing consequences further south – in Mali, for example. In Egypt, too, establishing a viable and generally acceptable system of government was not likely to happen overnight. It left 'the West' in a condition of embarrassment: wary of 'intervention' but, in general terms, approving. Diplomatic pressure had been applied, for example on Mubarak. With the exception of Libya, however, and perhaps, at some stage in the future, in Syria, it was for the Middle East to sort itself out. No observer could tell what all this would mean. It might, or might not, be the case that 'everything' was now changing in the Middle East.

26
Identifying Multipolar Complexity

World in one: Barack Obama

Barack Hussein Obama (b.1961) was elected President of the USA in November 2008. It was a success which carried complex and perhaps fortuitous messages both about and for the USA and also 'the world'. On the one hand, as a Democrat, it was a success which signified a turning away from a Republican ascendancy that had also been a Bush family ascendancy. It might be a soft-pedalling of the assertive external policies discussed in earlier chapters. The oscillation between parties, however, was not in itself surprising. A surprise might have been that the successful candidate was a woman. However, Hillary, wife of former President Clinton, lost out in the contest for her party's nomination. So there was no surprise in the election of a man. What was surprising was the man. By the time he became of age, the world landscapes which had moulded his seniors had changed. While much comment in the USA and abroad focussed on Obama as 'the first black African-American' president, such a categorization underplayed the complexities of his world inheritance. To be born in Hawaii was not in itself especially exotic, but his white mother (British/Irish by descent) had met and then married his Kenyan father, a Luo, when at university in Honolulu. The couple had been studying Russian. Obama senior was on the kind of scholarship which brought potential 'leaders' of 'the new Africa' to the USA at this time.

Obama's 'blackness' therefore, was not that of a man who had emerged from generations of 'black America'. He had, as it were, to meet it himself when he worked as a community organizer on the south side of Chicago. His African past was a new American present. It was a connection which took him to East Africa and the tribal complexities of an emerging country. Not that his father had remained a figure of influence in his young life – his parents split up and his father went home and died when he was twenty - but visiting Kenya later was a visit to a homeland. His mother subsequently married an Indonesian student, called back home when Suharto became President in 1967. They all went to live in Indonesia where Barack went to school for some four years. No American president had ever before come to office with such a background, certainly not one who also was a product of Harvard. It is not surprising, on his own account, that his own identity had early troubled him. His first book (1995) had as its subtitle *A Story of Race and Inheritance*. He declared himself a Christian but he had spent four childhood years in a largely Muslim country and knew about Islam in other ways. No other world figure at this juncture, knew so much about countries outside his own: Africa and South/South-East Asia in particular (he had paid a short visit to college friends in India and Pakistan). It was also evident, too, not only that his connections were extraordinary but also that he had an uncommon gift for writing about them and in projecting his vision in his oratory.

All this, to an unusual degree, made him 'a man of the world'. The medley he represented was his own but it placed him at a point where worlds met and at least mingled. His own family past, however, told him that, on a personal level, mixtures did not always succeed. He also well knew that words in themselves did not resolve intractable situations. The American people had not elected a new kind of 'world President'. They had elected him to represent themselves and American interests as they perceived them. On the supposition that he would want a second term, he had to satisfy the electorate that he was an effective president and could succeed in dealing with the economic problems that burst upon him even as he was being elected. A decade earlier, the Clinton White House had not hesitated to paint a picture of a world that was 'coming together'. The USA could shape a more peaceful, prosperous and democratic world. Obama's second book *The Audacity of Hope* (2006), published when he was a neophyte senator for Illinois had continued in this vein. Yet the economic scene at home swiftly darkened in the wake of a financial crisis. The years that followed saw a protracted wrestling with a worsening situation in a rapidly polarizing country. Its mood changed and, as indicated in Chapter 3, witnessed a renewed questioning of what America stood for and whether talk of 'shaping the world' amounted merely to grandiloquence. Moreover, as has also just been discussed in the previous chapter, issues in the Middle East and its penumbra remained intractable. An American president might not wish to be where he was, but he could not easily escape: Israel, Iraq, Afghanistan, Egypt, Pakistan, as noted, remained centre stage. Obama could deliver a message to an Egyptian audience in Cairo in unique tones and make an impression. There was a certain 'coming together' as Islam and Christianity and East/West again met through an African-American, but it was only another beginning. It might soon be another end. Sensitive antennae were all very well but Obama's feelings, critics said, could not solve problems. A carefully-chiselled message sent to the Islamic Republic of Iran fell on stony ground. In short, Barack signalled change, but change could not simply be whistled up. And, as the American appetite for global tutelage was souring, 'the rest of the world' was bent on going its own way. Continents and countries seemed to be ceasing to suppose that 'new world orders' could be ushered in, on demand, from Washington, Moscow or anywhere else. 'Worlds' now emerged, more confidently, from many directions.

Africa: seeing hope, experiencing tragedy

Gorbachev, it will be recalled from Chapter 1, had not mentioned 'Africa' among the 'major powers' of the world he had seen emerging. There was indeed no single country which constituted its voice. Yet there was one major change. In 1981 the 20-year-old Obama made his first serious political speech at a Democratic Youth Convention calling for a US company to cease operating in South Africa. Ten years later, after several false starts, in South Africa serious negotiations began to find a solution, basically but not simply between the African National Congress and the National Party. It has been cogently argued that an 'overlapping interest' had sufficiently arrived for Mandela and de Klerk, and their lieutenants, to edge towards an acceptable compromise. Neither 'black' nor 'white' could win in the existing circumstances or at least only at a price which would so ruin the country as to render a victor's life miserable. Yet that only puts it in simple terms. Violence rumbled on, particularly in Natal between ANC supporters and Buthelezi's Inkatha Freedom Party (IFP). Agreement had been reached on an interim constitution in November 1993. The issues to be resolved, or at least parked for further scrutiny, during these negotiations were manifold: languages, central-provincial relations, trade union rights, property rights, the election of the judiciary and its impartiality and security of tenure amongst them. Did groups have rights or only individuals? The first General Election was held in April 1994. Leaving aside irregularities in voting, partly stemming from the difficulty in establishing a proper roll, the outcome was heralded as a formidable achievement. The main parties – the ANC, National Party (NP) and IFP – gained 62, 20 and 10 per cent of the votes cast, respectively. Mandela became State President, agreeing to accept appointment for five years (for one term only). Given the apocalyptic outcome sometimes previously forecast for South Africa the transition was a triumph. Not that everything was then smooth or straightforward. A Truth and Reconciliation Commission endeavoured to make individuals, from all sides, confront the truth of what they had done or authorized in the past. In the process some, though not all worlds, came together. Such 'healing' operations had their place and made their impact in ushering in new relationships. There was much to celebrate and South Africa's functioning democracy was held up as an example in a continent where it had proved so frail. Yet there were questions. The electoral success of the ANC was formidable and sustained over subsequent elections. South Africa was not a one-party state in the sense of banning opposition parties, but the majority was so large that there appeared to be no prospect of an 'Opposition' forming a government. Indeed, to be in opposition was to be an enemy. Argument, debate and division took place within the ANC and threatened, for good or ill, to fracture it.

The transitional beneficence of a Mandela could not be repeated (though he himself remained a background guarantor). His successor, Thabo Mbeki, feeling himself to be surrounded by inferior plotters, retreated into an arrogant aloofness. When in England, he had graduated from an English university. He was toppled in 2007 and replaced by Jacob Zuma. Zuma had not graduated from anywhere but he brought a powerful presence. He cultivated an African style that was 'authentic', not least in his personal life. A Zulu like himself apparently had no need to conform to alien impositions. His style embodied the dilemma of South Africa writ large. The Mandela presidency had given South Africa substantial moral capital in the world. The difficulty was to decide what to do with it – and this pointed back to its own continuing internal ambiguity. Its assets in comparison with many African countries were clear: a historical commitment to parliamentary government, though admittedly only for whites, a strong sense of the rule of law and a vigorous civil society. The year 2010 witnessed a century of statehood – but of course 'ownership' could not be equally felt. Alongside a tradition of 'the rule of law' went a pervasive underlying lawlessness, crime and violence. That in turn related to the mixed 'delivery' of social goods and services to the black majority in the new order: the gap between euphoric expectation and reality. It began to thrust back into the centre of politics issues of ownership, whether of land or capital, which had perhaps been skirted during transition. It called into question where South Africa positioned itself in the world. Its 'African role' as perceived by Mandela had not been altogether welcomed in other African states, notably, Nigeria, when he sought to intervene in internal matters elsewhere. Its assets and resources certainly gave it global standing as a 'middle power' distinctive in its apparent stability from so many other African contexts. But was this image an illusion or even a betrayal of what it should be as an African state? Did its elites, of whatever colour, still cling to a heritage that was formed in a European world? It was a question which could be asked of such a 'world figure' as Desmond Tutu had become. It was a question too he could ask of himself. There might be a point at which questions which had once been asked of a white-dominated government concerning freedom and probity might properly be asked about the conduct of an ANC dominated government.

The politics of Zimbabwe provided a kind of test case. The country's economy in the period 1999-2006 looked in a precarious state as agricultural output dropped sharply and inflation raged. The position of Robert Mugabe as President was entrenched, although he faced disparate opposition from a newly-formed Movement for Democratic Change (MDC). Politically, it was questionable whether any election could take place without intimidation. Even so, in 2008 the MDC claimed a narrow victory over ZANU/PF in the parliamentary elections. Its leader, however, refused to take part in the second round of the presidential election on the grounds that the result would be rigged. The land issue hung over everything, that is to say the continued existence of large landholdings of good arable land in white hands. The government condoned if it did not encourage the violent seizure of white-owned land by 'veterans' of the war. Relations between the British and Zimbabwean governments plummeted as argument raged about process and compensation. Spasmodically, developments in the country still attracted attention in Britain. Mugabe used intimidation but equally could draw support internally from the sense in which he was rolling back the colonial past. The circumstances therefore played out differently internationally. In 2009 a compromise agreement between the two men and the two parties was in theory worked out, under international pressure. Thirty years on, therefore, Mugabe remained in power, both ostracized by Western powers and still widely admired in Africa, though not uncritically, as an anti-colonial hero devoted to the advancement of his people. Mbeki found himself in an uncomfortable position. Effective mediation would enhance South Africa's status and therefore simply to parrot condemnation of Mugabe as an echo of criticism emanating from Britain in particular would nullify such a role. There was still a land issue in South Africa itself. If, however, the South African government turned a blind eye to Mugabe's methods, that could send a signal with repercussions inside South Africa itself. South Africa/Zimbabwe therefore presented an ambivalent image to the world beyond the continent.

Elsewhere, in African countries which had been ruled but not colonized from Europe the image largely remained of a continent plagued by poverty, corruption, 'excess' population and bad government. Outside aid agencies, in their appeals for funds to help mitigate drought and famine in Ethiopia, Somalia and elsewhere, though not by design, reinforced a global perception of a continent perpetually unable to make an impact beyond itself. The opposite perception was that African countries continued to be pillaged for resources and were a prey for external predators, amongst whom might now be numbered Chinese. A certain external consensus that 'aid' without 'good government' only fuelled corruption but how the latter could 'emerge' was not evident. Not that the picture was ever uniform or constant. The fundamental 'national' issue remained unresolved, liable to break out in violence, particularly in the aftermath of elections when rivals claimed victory. The country most afflicted was Rwanda, independent since 1962, plagued by violent conflict between Hutus and Tutsis over a long period, climaxing in 1994 in genocidal massacre resulting in some 800,000 deaths.. Elsewhere, rivals, too, harvested the support of particular ethnic/cultural/religious groups rather than campaigning above them on the basis of a particular programme. The result could be a breakdown of law and order, with considerable loss of life, even in those countries which at various post-independence stages had been judged to be both relatively stable and prosperous. In the Francophone world that was true of Ivory Coast, and in the Anglophone, of Kenya. Few states had an absolute control of military power within their borders but where it was true it was not an unambiguous indication of good order. A French military presence 'on standby' ready to be 'called upon' remained a factor in 'French West Africa'. British forces returned to a riven Sierra Leone to restore order. Some states 'failed' more conspicuously than others. Somalia's plight was most frequently alluded to. The Horn of Africa saw the return of piracy as a real threat to the ships of many nations. It also saw endemic famine/drought. While as in Nigeria, there were cases of a return to civilian rule internal divisions were rarely resolved. In 2011 one of the continent's most protracted conflicts at last reached a kind of conclusion with the independence of South Sudan but it was rash to assume that the border region between it and its northern neighbour would be peaceful. Such an outcome could be taken to be a sign of increased stability, but it would be even more rash, to identify clear 'trends' firmly established anywhere. African Unity, in terms of an old rhetoric, had failed. It might be restarted on some more pragmatic basis growing out of specific economic arrangements between countries on a regional basis. Until that did happen, with the ambivalent exception provided by South Africa, the external perception remained that 'Africa' did not provide a 'major global player'.

Europe: only so far, and no further?

The Europe identified by Gorbachev as a major player in the world no more existed on a map in 2011 than it did when he spoke. Speculation on its basis and energetic activity designed to articulate its essential 'coming togetherness' had been endemic throughout the period. It was incontrovertible that the events of 1989-91 reopened a 'Europe' that previous Parts have shown to be seemingly ever more divided. The wall was down. The iron curtain had gone. The very speed of the transition and its unpredicted timing ruled out solemn assemblies reflecting soberly on what the glories and calamities of the European past might suggest for the future. West and East might in one sense be obliterated but nearly half a century of separation still left firm institutional and cultural footprints. And if it was indeed predominantly true that in the East 'the events' had been perceived as 'liberation' that did not necessarily mean that everything in the West was perfect. A Western tutelage, when tinged with arrogance, could be counter-productive yet 'Westernization' in a broad sense is what was desired. Nowhere was this more apparent than in Poland, a country which by virtue of its size, population and evident skill in its 'transition' came to occupy a major European space, the sole East/Central European state even to approach the political weight of a Britain, France or Germany. Not only that. Poles were everywhere. Nowhere, however, was more delicate treading needed, and not invariably found, than in the forging of 'new Germany'. All this was a matter of bridge-building and sometimes bridge builders fell off.

There were fundamental questions which lay behind diplomacy and mutual interaction. 'Coming togetherness' had been presented to the public in terms of specific structures and mechanisms whose purpose was to ensure that Europe's states would never again indulge in interstate wars, or perhaps one might speak of European civil wars. In 2007, fifty years on from the signature of the Treaty of Rome it could be said that its founding signatories did not remotely look as though they contemplated war with each other. If it was this evolving 'Europe' under different names and with changing institutions that had brought about this desirable conclusion it could be accounted a success: the more of it the better. Yet it might alternatively be argued that the European states did not need institutional scaffolding to hold them back from fighting each other. The horror of the world wars was lesson enough. They were too mature and too wise to do it again, even though new generations would inevitably appear for whom these were distant events, though with afterlife. Nothing could in fact be conclusively proved either way.

The question was whether 'integration' was an event or a process, as innumerable seminars considered the matter. An event signified that there should be a defined and fixed 'Europe' - constitutionally, economically, culturally. A plateau would be reached which set out firmly and 'for all time' the balance of powers between 'Europe' at the centre and 'Europe' as perceived at its nation-state base. Where that balance should be struck was problematic, given the wide diversity of points of view, but it could and should be done. It gave comfort at all levels to know how the layers of decision-making intersected and operated. A process, however, expressed scepticism about the feasibility or desirability of attempting to freeze relationships at a particular juncture. Coming togetherness should be flexible and fluid, adjusting to changing circumstances in Europe and in the world as a whole. Uncertainty was no doubt creative, but was there not a vision, an ultimate goal, a Europe which would be 'a major power', not a set of small powers and states, that had not yet quite forgotten that they had once been major powers? In one form or another, debates in all 'eligible' countries polarized around this point. A minority, waxing or waning in all countries, wanted 'Europe' as neither event nor process. It was reminded that a multipolar world was emerging in which size mattered. Only 'Europe' could effectively talk to China or India. Europe's integration, on this reading, was an astute reaction to the way the world was.

There were, however, 'difficulties': the nation, the state, ideology, faith, democracy and 'the other'. The European 'project', as it advanced, subordinated 'nation' and sometimes expressed scepticism about its very existence. No nation existed 'essentially'. Nations were always being made and unmade. The difficulty was that it was evident that large segments of populations while not perhaps 'nationalists' certainly still saw themselves as 'nationals'. Alongside that went attachment to particular institutions which had a particular historical grounding. That citizens, at least sophisticated citizens, could glide easily between the levels of their political existence was true but they would be bereft if all decision-making shifted inexorably in a central direction far away. That was a fundamental question of democracy. It was also a fundamental question of democracy that the process, whatever it was, should be both scrutinized and indeed approved democratically. Countries might differ in how that was done and how regularly it was done (parliamentary votes, referendums or whatever) but unless it was done democracies were de-democratizing themselves without realizing it – until it was too late. Each successive treaty raised these issues. While particular countries, Britain, for example were identified as at root 'Eurosceptic' and others at root 'federalist', the picture was never static. Opinion in the Netherlands, for example, is generally believed to have moved more in a sceptical direction over the period.

And 'nationalism' of a virulent sort, of a kind which most though not all Western Europeans thought they had put behind them, erupted in south-eastern Europe. Or at least that was what many Western European commentators thought they saw when they talked of 'ancient hatreds' again coming to the surface as Yugoslavia imploded. It was particularly upsetting that wars had again come to a European continent which had supposed that it had dispensed with them. The complexities of loyalties – ethnic, religious, economic, linguistic – are too detailed to be examined further here. New states emerged in batches but still replete with unresolved tensions. New names, or old ones revived, now reappeared on the map of Europe – Serbia, Croatia, Slovenia, Montenegro, the Former Yugoslav Republic of Macedonia and most contentiously of all came Kosovo. What happened through all this period, as seen through Western European camera lenses, gave rise to the notion that although this was Europe, it was 'another world'. It was one, however, into which NATO was drawn when it launched a bombing campaign on Serbia in response to its campaign against Kosovars. The term 'ethnic cleansing' was rarely out of the headlines. This outside NATO intervention was contentious. It seemed to some, a curious interpretation of what the organization had been formed to do. But it was also vigorously defended as a humanitarian action. Whatever else the battles and massacres demonstrated, and wherever blame is placed, the crises showed that there could be no natural assumption that nations would spontaneously 'come together'. There was a paradox. The collapse of 'Federal Yugoslavia' reminded observers that 'federalism' was not a perfect arrangement of relationships (though a different Yugoslav federation might have lasted longer). Yet it was the quasi- federalism of the European Union which provided the mechanism which enabled Bosnia to function, albeit precariously, with a central government, a rotating three-member presidency and a two-chamber parliament whose responsibility was for foreign affairs and monetary policy with virtually every-thing else being devolved to the two 'entities' which made up the state. An EU peacekeeping force was present, under an outside High Representative, and it was supposed to keep everything in check.

In a wider pan-European context too, the existence or otherwise of a suffi-cient sense of a 'moral community', was near to the heart of the matter. Any attempt to define 'European values', as part of any constitutional process, was fraught with difficulty, touching as it did on the contested boundary between the secular and the sacred. The possible admission of Turkey to the European Union – an application had been 'on the table' without decision – was a further case in point. Turkey's growing significance, both economically and politically could scarcely be contested. Both secularists and Christians, at loggerheads though they were, tended to share doubts (though to what degree varied in different countries) but if indeed Turkey was not admitted it would be a cultural exclusion of a 'Moslem country'. In reality, however, Turkey remained a 'secular' country with a 'Moslem population', though under its latter-day Prime Minister Erdogan, it might even be showing European countries a plausible way in which democracy, secularism and religion could all be accom-modated.

The reality or unreality of community was naturally pertinent in matters of defence (and a military foreign policy) and monetary union (sharing, to a substantial degree, a sense of common responsibility). It was very evident at the time of the American-led invasion of Iraq that the European Union did not have a common view. Britain, Italy and Spain (for a time) sent fighting troops. France and Germany would not and French criticism of the USA was vocal. The USA, in turn, welcoming Polish troops to the coalition, talked of Europe in terms of 'old' and 'new'. The level of contribution and the rules of engagement set down by European states in Afghanistan reflected differences of perception. President Sarkozy of France moved away from the 'traditional' French distant presence within NATO. It was NATO in 2011 that led the aerial campaign in Libya in defence of civilians but which also sustained the insurgents in the process. It was not an enterprise shared by all its European members. It was Britain and France, in tandem, who took the lead. This, and much else, pointed to strongly held and differing opinions on what 'the European sphere' actually was. Talk of a common foreign policy was never far away but, despite the institutionalization of a 'European Foreign Minister', presumably the recipient of eager messages from across the globe, a common foreign policy never arrived. That is not to say that it could not arrive.

But in 2011 what placed the reality, or otherwise, of Europe's 'moral community' to the fore was the ongoing financial/ banking crisis. The adoption of the Euro in 1995 and its introduction in January 1999 was a major step and saw the currency on its way to becoming the world's second highest reserve currency and its second most traded currency after the dollar. It was used by 332 million 'Europeans'. A 'Eurozone' expressed the belief that there was a suffi-cient sense of commonality to make it work. In turn, its very existence was a further integrative milestone. To this end, a 'Growth and Stability Pact' suppos-edly committed members to certain financial disciplines and penalties for infringement. All applicants were supposedly 'checked' for their suitability and all applicants supposedly supplied unimpeachable data. However, not all European Union members, most notably Britain, adopted the Euro as their currency (a total of 17 out of 27 did). Then what had apparently been a success hit troubled waters. The 'sovereign debt' crisis of 2009–11 threatened its very basis as the laxity in debt management of particular countries (Ireland, Portugal and most acutely Greece) forced member countries to assess the extent to which the problems of some members, however caused, became the problems of all. At the time of writing, solutions, if there are solutions, could go in different directions. Some experts concluded that the project of the euro, misconceived at the outset, was doomed. Others believed that it would survive and that it was essential for Europe that it should do so. The crisis rumbled on without clear resolution. The election of François Hollande, a Socialist, as French President in 2012, added an ideological tension as member states wrestled with a crisis which centred on the fate of Greece but whose ramifications extended far wider. Whatever the ultimate outcome, however, what had again been exposed was the problematic 'in between' nature of contemporary 'Europe'. Only time would tell whether that tension would be resolved by yet further degrees of common policy, at least for a particular group of members, or would move 'back' (as some would say) by 'repatriating' certain capacities to member states. It was claimed by others that Europe would be more harmonious if it were less ambi-tious. How events in fact unfolded would determine whether 'Europe' was indeed a 'major player' in the world.

India: now punching its weight?

If 'Europe' meant 27 'sovereign' states, with still more probably to come, wrestling with the degree to which and the manner in which they could act as one quasi-federal state, India presented the spectacle of one state which contained 28 non-sovereign states (plus some 'Union Territories). In its initial decades, as has been noted, the integrity of the union faced considerable chal-lenges but, while these had not completely disappeared, after half a century, 'India' was firmly in place. Members of the European Union had been having to come to terms with the fact that while continuing provision for linguistic plurality was both necessary and desirable English had become in many respects, commercially and at governmental and bureaucratic levels, its working language. The language in which the Constitution of India had formal written status remained English (though a Hindi translation accompanied it). The impetus to phase out English, so strong in the early decades, waned though it did not disappear. Hindi missionary work was still in place. More modest pedalling, however, reflected awareness that pushing language issues only raised temperatures to little benefit. Language provision in the subcontinent was therefore settled at central and state level by a variety of detailed legislation.

There was a further reason. The year 1991 marked the most significant transition since independence. It signified a new relationship between India and the world beyond. It was a transition brought on by economic crisis. India's English facilitated new connections. The cumbersome intricate attempt to run India as a state-controlled economy substantially sealed off from the world by means of the so-called Licence Raj was more or less abandoned, largely on the injunction of the International Monetary Fund to which India had had to turn. A man was to hand to pilot the process, Manmohan Singh (b.1932), minister of finance 1991–96. In 2011, he was prime minister of India, as he had been since 2004 (being reappointed in 2009 in what had been the largest democratic election ever held in the world). Singh in his person symbolized a new multilateralism. A Sikh, he was the first non-Hindu to be prime minister. Elements in the Amritsar crisis, discussed earlier, remained but a Sikh from Amritsar now represented the world face of India. He had studied in the Punjab University in 'global' Chandigarh and had then distinguished himself in England as a student of economics as an undergraduate at Cambridge and a postgraduate at Oxford. His thesis had been a study of India's external trade. Further international experience came from a period working for UNCTAD (1966–69). He was not a 'typical Indian politician' and some of the more unseemly aspects of Indian political power-broking went on elsewhere within Congress domain still under the sway of Rajiv Gandhi's widow. But, as time went on, he was more than a 'technocrat'. The Indian economy took off and achieved rates of growth not before accomplished. The world's second most populous country – 1,210 million in 2011 – at last took off, though smaller South-East Asian states could still do better. It could show the world pockets of technological excellence. India as a whole, however, might be thought a series of pockets presenting very different pictures. 'Third world poverty' co-existed alongside 'first world' sophistication. By 2011 an overall literacy rate of some 75 per cent had been achieved but that hid very significant differences between states (Kerala at the top and Bihar at the bottom). The 'soul' of India remained elusive. A 'Gandhian inheritance' coexisted with one of the largest standing armies in the world whose equipment needs constituted a significant part of Indian imports (whether from Russia or Israel in particular). Indian industrial conglomerates made European acquisitions, particularly in Britain, and their wealthy owners flitted between continents. Aiding Indian 'development' in these circumstances seemed, to some external minds, an odd commitment. But there were so many Indias in the mirror.

Alongside this 'new India' went a relaxation of the frigidities and ingrained stances of an inherited 'non-alignment'. That world was passing, or had passed. India could maintain or develop relationships across the globe on a bi-lateral basis with other 'major powers' – Russia, the USA, China as appropriate – without much ideological baggage. One tangible sign was the visit of George W. Bush to India in March 2006 and a new accommodation on nuclear matters which had then been reached. Another was the visit of Manmohan Singh to China in 2008 (returning a visit by Hu Jin Tao to Delhi two years earlier, an occasion coinciding with the re-opening of an important pass between the two countries which had been closed for four decades). Trade between the two 'giants' was of great importance to both, to China particularly. This 'Asian partnership' however had still not entirely settled border issues in the Himalayas nor had it the 'sore' that the presence of the Dalai Lama in India constituted. In South Asia India remained prominent in regional associations. It did not intervene, however, in the military struggle in Sri Lanka as it moved to its gruesome climax in the defeat of Tamil separatism. Nor was the focus exclusively Asian. Delhi hosted an Indian-African summit (attended by 15 African countries) in April 2006. 'India' in East Africa had come to an end and a sensitive new relationship was needed. 'India' in South Africa had not come to an end. South Africa as a whole might be a suitable 'partner', and vice versa. In 2011 a British government was busy seeking a 'new relationship' with vibrant India. By the time the Indian prime minister paid his first official visit to Washington to meet a new US president in November 2009 the accumulated wisdom of Asian age could be passed on to a youthful president whose heritage was partially Afro-American.

Not that everything in India was set fair. There was terror in India too. The hotel attack in Mumbai in 2008 received worldwide publicity, but it was only one of a number of incidents. There was Naxalite violence in east and central India. The Kashmir issue was still there. Manmohan Singh had in fact been born in what became Pakistan, and his family had moved eastwards at the partition. The size of India's army could only be explained by the possibility of another round of conflict with Pakistan. There were some signs that the complicated rituals which were required in order to lessen Indo-Pakistani tension might eventually pay off, but eventually was a long time. 'Kashmir' teetered perpetually on the brink of some kind of conflict. The complex and fluctuating relationship between Afghanistan and Pakistan (or perhaps both countries should be put in the plural) required that India itself gave aid, not totally disinterestedly. The multilingual Hamid Karzai (b.1957) President of Afghanistan, had begun his intricate and multi-faceted career as an MA student at an Indian university (Shimla). In October 2011 he was signing an agreement with Manmohan Singh. Like all the agreements Karzai signed with neighbouring or distant countries, this one was not directed against anyone, as he said. India, with the third largest Muslim population in the world, altogether escaped unrest in the 'Islamic world'. It shared with the USA and European countries the possibility that it would become a 'police state' in its surveillance of its citizens to protect their security. Even so, in 2011, with the massive election behind him, Manmohan Singh, approaching eighty, could look out on an India considerably more confident of its place in the world than when he had entered the finance ministry twenty years earlier.

'New' India's progress contrasted with Bangladesh. The most gloomy prognostications of its future were perhaps not realized as both agricultural and industrial output increased. Its vulnerability to natural disaster, however, was inescapable. Nor, since 1991, had it been able to achieve a political system which escaped oscillation between civilian and military rule. India's South Asian pre-eminence was indisputable but there was no hegemony over 'South-east Asia'. There, Indonesia was asserting a claim to be itself a 'major power'. It was still troubled by inter-insular questions and episodes of indigenous terrorism linked to wider Islamic currents. The democracy that it had now developed was not 'perfect' but it reflected a country more free, open and economically successful than when the President of the USA had received schooling there in the late 1960s. Given its population, it had a weight globally which the other states of South-East Asia, who had also embarked on a successful economic path could not match. It was a period which saw the re-emergence of Vietnam and the gradual slipping away of its own domestic and regional preoccupations stemming from that period when it seemed to have been the centre of the world's conflicts. 'Success', however, could easily and rapidly turn to 'failure', in economic terms. There was, said a World Bank study in 1993, an *East Asian Miracle*. By 2011 Singapore, Malaysia, Australia, Thailand, India and Indonesia were to be found amongst the twenty-one largest exporting nations in the world. Even so, among them, it was only India, from a variety of points of view, which could be adjudged to be a 'world power'.

Brazil: breaking out?

Brasilia had 'sprung from nothing' when it replaced Rio de Janeiro as Brazil's capital in 1960. It was designed as the country's administrative centre with the aim of stimulating the North-East and, to some degree, redressing the imbalance of the population distribution. Its own population (in 2010) presented the face of Brazil to the world - half 'white', 45 per cent 'brown' (mixed), 5 per cent 'black' (all approximately). Neither the Asian nor the Amerindian population reached half a percent. Catholics outnumbered Protestants by three to one. The city, however, had rapidly burst beyond its original conception but it still symbolized novelty. It was appropriate that in the decade behind 2011 it hosted a number of gatherings designed to create new alignments and usher in new worlds. Declaration followed declaration. The initiative in entering the world stage for a purpose other than football was Brazilian. In taking the lead Brazil saw itself as giving Latin America its global platform.

In June 2003 the foreign ministers of Brazil, India and South Africa held what they described as a 'pioneer meeting' of three countries from the developing world who were 'active on a global scale'. They also described themselves as 'vibrant democracies'. In the case of Brazil itself such vibrancy was a novelty. It had only been fifteen years earlier that it had equipped itself with a new constitution which provided for a directly elected presidency. Behind, as has been noted, lay periods of authoritarian/military government. The conservative first elected President on this basis resigned in 1992, having been impeached for corruption. A new currency adopted in 1994, pegged to the US dollar, appeared to give the country a way out of the serious inflation to which it, like other Latin American countries, had been prone. The architect of this plan,

Fernando Cardoso, served two terms on its success. By the 2002 elections, however, the currency was again under pressure (the year before, Argentina had defaulted on its debts). Latin America, speaking generally, seemed again to be undergoing another period of economic and financial turbulence of the kind that seemed perpetually to check the much-harbingered period of 'sustained growth'. Cardoso's own chosen successor was defeated in the 2002 elections by the leader of the Workers' Party, a trade unionist and 'man of the people'. 'Lula' (b.1945) as he was known served two terms until December when continuity with his programme was assured when Rousseff, his lieutenant (a woman), won the succeeding election. Both of them, and others in their circle were 'left-wing', Marxists of one description or another but post-1991 there was no 'Communist world' to subscribe to or take distance from. Rhetorical gestures and 'the common touch' apart, what emerged was another variant of 'partnership'. Welcomed measures of social reform were complemented by economic growth which changed Brazil from a debtor to a creditor nation. The richness and variety of the country's resources could keep it on track. The ideological element in Lula's democratic mixture mellowed and his own and his country's success removed any disposition to ape the old regime in Cuba or the more recent, vocal and oil-rich 'global alternative' orchestrated against a 'capitalist North' by Hugo Chavez, former military officer, failed coup organizer and presidential election winner in 1998, in which office he contrived to remain, though with no small element of popular support.

India, South Africa and Brazil had in common the fact that they were large in size. Brazil, as a federal country, had only one fewer 'states' than India. Sustaining unity was something they all faced. Their common declaration expressed aspirations which could only be expected. However, though widely separated geographically ('South to South') the weight of their collective world was more substantial than larger but insubstantial gatherings in the past. The 2003 meeting was only the first in an ongoing sequence across the countries involving heads of government (a fourth 'summit' was held in April 2010). Their meetings addressed current 'world issues' and pronounced on developments which they took in some sense to be in their 'zone', such as Madagascar, Guinea or Haiti. Globally, however, what irked all three was the extent to which the UN, as 'the world body' still so much reflected, in the Security Council, a world which they believed to have passed. Its 'reform' appeared to have got stuck. All three, however, participated in what had become the G20, Their status was apparent from the fact that European governments, such as the incoming coalition government in Britain in 2010 quickly booked flights to these locations.

Brazil's outward orientation had other elements. Another Declaration came out of Brasilia in May 2005 at the conclusion of a meeting between Arab and South American states. Bi-regional areas of co-operation and collaboration were identified and follow-up promises made. World statements were made which satisfied both participants (on the integrity of Sudan and the ownership of the Malvinas (Falkland Islands). In April 2010 Brazil hosted a first summit with leaders from the Caribbean Community (CARICOM) which concluded with a host of plans for increased collaboration across tourism, trade, climate issues, education and culture – all with the objective of bring the largely Anglophone islands closer to 'Latin' America. Indeed, in these years regional organizations proliferated with different inclusions and exclusions reflecting continuing personal and ideological discord. There was even a permanent Ibero-American secretariat in Madrid which serviced 'family reunions'. The notion, more or less explicit, was that collectively Latin America could stand up for itself and distinguish itself from North America. The prestige of the Organization of American States had been dwindling (and, it was argued from the South, it remained too much guided by the USA (and by a Canada which had 'continentalized' itself by joining in 1990). The OAS tried to revive itself by adopting an Inter-American Democratic Charter in 2001 which set out the kind of democracy which it would monitor, indeed enforce. The difficulty was that few members still actually displayed the exemplary categories which were identified. There might even be an uncomfortable paradox. In the USA's neighbour Mexico, the party that had governed the country continuously since 1929 lost the presidential election in 2000. Relaxation of its authority promoted democratic pluralism but also increased the entry possibilities of drug barons – cartels threatened the very heart of civic life. A presidential election in 2006 showed a country almost evenly divided on how whether left or in the event the right would offer a better prospect of tackling its growing problems.

There were, therefore, new senses in which Latin America 'entered' the world but it did so neither uniformly nor to any clear collective agenda, such was the extent of its continuing diversity, still possible economic volatility and still precarious versions of 'vibrant democracy'.

China: east wind blowing a gale

In May 1990 the Chinese President, Yang Shangkun paid the first ever visit by a Chinese president to Brazil (on a tour which took him to Mexico, Uruguay, Argentina and Chile. Over the next two decades there were many 'firsts' either on the part of foreign leaders visiting China or of Chinese leaders visiting parts of the world where they had never gone before. Such high-profile occasions of course were complemented by the day to day conduct of diplomacy through embassies – and in some cases that meant establishing diplomatic relations for the first time. Also in 1990, for example, in August Premier Li Peng became the first Chinese leader to visit Indonesia for 25 years. A return visit from Suharto in November was made after the same interval of years. Li Peng went on to Singapore and he and Prime Minister Lee Kuan Yew agreed to establish diplomatic relations between their two countries. Later in the year he visited Malaysia, the Philippines, Laos and Sri Lanka. Earlier in the year , he had visited Moscow, another first visit for 26 years of a senior leader. In 1991 Li Peng's visit to India was the first by a Chinese premier since 1960. The list in these years could be extended and it accelerated thereafter. Kings, presidents, prime ministers, foreign ministers, trade ministers queued up for a place and were busy with reciprocal invitations. The Asian Games, held in Beijing in 1990, offered Chinese neighbours an opportunity to see China's progress for themselves. China won by far the largest number of medals.

China needed to win medals internationally for, immediately behind this burst of activity, lay the events of June 1989 in Beijing. Immediately the USA suspended all visits between senior American and Chinese military officials, amongst other measures. The World Bank deferred consideration of new development loans to China. In July the G7 leaders in Paris condemned suppression of the pro-democracy movement. The Dalai Lama was awarded the Nobel Peace Prize in 1989. Other strong condemnatory foreign statements could be made. In China itself the party leadership made it clear that 'counter-revolutionary' movements had to be suppressed. Fifty years after the revolution, Jiang Zemin (b.1926) declared that 'hostile international forces' were attempting to undermine the Socialist system in China. In 1993 he became the country's President.

It was only a few years before such 'punitive' outside responses to June 1989 as were made, and they were not much more than gestures, to fade away and contacts to resume multilaterally across the globe, but particularly with China's 'neighbours'. A 'normality' was patched up with Vietnam, though there could still be disputes over the ownership of islands. A trade mission in Seoul could enable contact to be made with South Korea (both Koreas had been invited to the Asian Games). And so on. Scarcely a week went by without reports emerging of great infrastructural projects taking place in one part of the country or another. Scientists from the Chinese Academy of Sciences announced that, using clone technology, they had developed an embryo of a giant panda. An endangered species could be saved. Here was a metaphor. China itself was no longer an endangered species. The Chinese Academy of Science had many other announcements to make. In 1999, a *Complete History of China* edited by the Hui historian Bai Shouyi, was published in 22 volumes. No one should doubt, through all its ups and downs, the greatness and the continuity of the Chinese past. In 1998 Puccini's opera *Turandot* was given numerous performances in Beijing's imperial palace. The director was Chinese, the conductor was Indian, the soprano was American. The message was clear. China could stage such a performance of a Western art form but it was not going to be swamped, this time, by the West. Chinese opera and theatre would travel the world, on equal terms.

The pace of change was breathtaking. The emphasis on education was pervasive. Economic growth accelerated. The per capita GDP of China expanded from $524 in 1980 to $6200 in 2009. It became, after the EU, the world's largest exporter. It became the third largest importer (but, whilst China exported heavily to the USA, that country did not rank among China's leading suppliers – Japan, the EU, Korea and Taiwan). Chinese goods containerized themselves around the world. They filled shops in Europe, North America and elsewhere so that the Chinese 'presence' was part of everyday experience. It was 'the world's discount factory' but was rapidly seeking to move up the supply chain. Foreign investors had to bring technology as well as capital. The Chinese surplus grew. A figure of $2.5 trillion in foreign currency reserves was being quoted. This accumulation perhaps could only continue if 'the West', in particular, continued to purchase. It seemed, however, that a pattern was firmly establishing itself. But was it 'fair'? In 2010 three Chinese state enterprises ranked in the world's top ten corporations. A standard foreign criticism was that Chinese enterprises, supported by the Party and the State had expanded beyond China. It had been able to do so using profits generated in a protected home market. Chinese corporations were active purchasing iron in Australia and Brazil, oil in Africa, Canada and the Middle East. They paid premium prices. Another criticism centred on the working conditions and hours men and women put in to make this 'miracle' a success. Prosperous Chinese were very evident but was too much inequality developing? Continuing disparities between and within provinces could not be denied, though attempts to correct imbalances by building whole cities where none had previously existed before might not in fact work. Economists and business experts devoted themselves to these and kindred questions in analysing the model of 'state capitalism'.

In the global crisis of 2008–11, therefore, much attention was devoted to 'balance'. China's achievement, over two decades, could not be denied. Its success was clearly better than failure but had that very success, over a period, distorted the global economy. Europe and the USA might be particularly suffering but China itself might also do so unless it took what was called 'corrective action' in 'rebalancing' its own domestic economy and making it easier for foreign business to operate. It was an ongoing argument. What was very evident, however, was that whatever steps the Chinese government might actually take, it was a 'major player'.

But it was not solely a matter of economics. Domestic politics, foreign policy and issues of cultural identity overlapped in China's encounter with the world (as vice versa). China still had to complete itself that is to say clarify its boundaries, ensure their security and satisfy its minorities. That entailed discussions at intervals with Vietnam, Kazakhstan, Russia, amongst other neighbours. On the whole, these proceeded to China's satisfaction. Such talks with neighbours, however, did not solve the issue of Tibet or remove the attacks carried out by Uighur nationalists. In 1997, the handover of Hong Kong took place with all ceremony and apparent satisfaction on both sides. After more than a decade, the unique basis on which Hong Kong operated seemed, on the whole, to be working. Portuguese Macau would 'come home' a little later. That left the vexed question of Taiwan to be settled but, despite spasmodic discussions and an improved atmosphere, no 'endgame' was reached. Taiwanese internal politics did not exactly follow what was expected when Chen Shui-ban of the 'Democratic Progressive Party' won the election of 2000 on an 'independence' ticket. By the end of the decade control reverted to the Kuomintang. So there could be acknowledgement of 'one China' but no agreement on what it meant and how it might be brought about.

Symbolically and practically, these were important matters to 'tidy up' but what fundamentally mattered was how China, as a major player, sat alongside the other major players. France, Britain and Germany, it was said, would all have their national commercial and other objectives but only the European Union could partner China. There were indeed forums where this relationship was explored and developed, at a variety of levels. Russia and China could put aside ideological issues and bargain hard about resources. Above all, however, what mattered was the relationship with the USA. In May 1999, during the NATO bombing campaign in Serbia, its missiles struck the Chinese embassy in

Belgrade, setting it alight and causing deaths and casualties. The Chinese Ambassador at the UN described the attack as barbarism. The USA apologized and denied that the attack had been deliberate. It was an episode which reawakened Chinese anxieties and triggered street protests. The particular incident stemmed from an attack on a sovereign country for which there had been no UN mandate. To distant eyes, the pretext that Kosovars had to be protected was no more convincing than that the Embassy attack had been a mistake. It could look as though China was being brought down to earth. Yet only the previous month, President Clinton had made a speech in which he argued strongly against allowing any cold war with China to develop. Global forces were empowering the Chinese people to change their society and build a better future. Four years later, his successor, speaking in China, commented that the country was on a 'rising path'. The USA welcomed a strong, peaceful and prosperous China. Yet, back home, the fact that that could equate to a powerful China caused alarm. In China, the arrival of US and other Western forces in Afghanistan (and their supply bases in Central Asia) equally caused alarm. US troops remained in Japan and South Korea. If North Korea collapsed, they might again appear on the River Yalu. China was being surrounded and hemmed in. Perceptions, on both sides, were just that. They could not be removed. Neither, however, should they obscure so much that was positive, for China and the world, in what had happened over two decades.

The duality found a location in the continued arguments that centred on 'human rights' regularly raised, though not too loudly, by European and American leaders. China was repeatedly told that 'freedom' would undergird not ruin the progress that China had made. China might do better, it was sometimes conceded in reply, but inappropriate cultural transfers should not be made. It was not sensible to be thinking of multi-party democracy and better to think about the Olympics China staged with such aplomb in 2008.This strong sense of nationalism sharply resented any patronizing observations from outside. Every country had to go its own way. It was a message even being delivered by some wayward Chinese Catholic bishops to the Vatican.

Japan: buffeted and bewildered?

The Japanese imperial couple paid the first ever such visit to China in October 1992. Emperor Akihito, at their welcoming banquet, acknowledged the great suffering that his people had inflicted on the Chinese people. He deeply deplored it. That, however, was now some half a century ago. The visit came twenty years after the 'normalization' of relations. Time was still needed. The relationship was equivocal.

It was painful, in political circles and beyond, to see how much attention was now focussed on China by the outside world. The Japanese economy was stagnant. What had but recently seemed to be so admired in the government-directed system now appeared to have led to weakness. In the wake of the oil shocks of the 1970s governments had shielded industries from market forces, stifled initiative and prevented productivity gains. By the 1990s that now came with a price. Economists, looking to talk about 'stagflation', illustrated what they had to say by talking about Japan. The analysis was sometimes widened to reflect on the general condition of Japanese society. The population was ageing. A generation that had propelled the country to its global position was now exhausted. It was no longer clear what 'Japanese values' were. On the margins, some sought to revive old myths, but they led nowhere. Yet there was no past that could be made handy. Pride could be taken in what Japan had achieved since 1945 but it was difficult to enthuse too much about parliamentary democracy. The Liberal Democratic Party (LDP) had been in power continuously since its formation in 1955. The political class was inbred. There was much talk of parliamentary or electoral reform, but little happened. Individual politicians stacked up credit and (not infrequently) profit for themselves in construction projects in their constituencies whose real general benefit was obscure. It was not a pattern unknown elsewhere in the world but it seemed to reflect an overall weakness in government, sometimes referred to as an inner world of revolving doors; ministers came and went and came again. Again this was not unique but the cumulative picture was of a country in the doldrums. It was to be shaken when the charismatic figure of Junichiro Koizumi jolted the LDP in the direction of privatization and labour market deregulation. The whole sclerotic system had to be shaken up. The problem was that while some dynamism returned its costs were high in the sense that it shattered all the certainty of tenure and company solidarity which had come to be seen as core 'Japanese values'. In 2009 the LDP lost the election. That might mean a new set of sweeping changes b y new men, but in the event clear-cut direction was lacking. And then, in 2011, came disaster in the shape of the inrush of the tsunami and then in the catastrophe at the Fukushima nuclear plant. The political and cultural fall-out was enormous. Individual responses to the crisis were magnificent but there was a sense that the 'governing class' as a whole failed to grasp the needs of the moment, a failure which compounded other worries about Japan's condition which have just been alluded to.

This anxiety ran alongside and was related to continuing debate about Japan's place in the world as a major player. Japan's normality was abnormal. Its relationship with the USA was fundamental but as it had been for decades peppered with problems. Reliance upon the USA for defence could not but entail some subordination. Voices repeatedly suggested that Japan should be treated more as an equal. But if the USA did make itself more accommodating to Japanese views it would surely not do so without in some way requiring Japan to contribute more. In turn, however, was not overseas deployment a contradiction for a Self-Defence Force. Once let the military off the leash, some said, and one step would lead to another. However, in 1992–93 Japanese troops were despatched overseas under UN auspices (to Cambodia) as they were later elsewhere. A further break came in 2004 when Japan, under pressure from the USA did send troops to Iraq as a modest part of the 'coalition of the willing'. It was a controversial move domestically but seemed necessary in return for US protection amidst all the uncertainties of North Korean behaviour. The 'security debate', in short, ran on.

Amidst all the talk of UN reform, Japan aspired to a permanent seat on the Security Council. It has not happened. Sino-Japanese relations deteriorated during the Koizumi years. The opposition which the idea aroused in China was yet one further illustration that nothing really was yet 'normal'. In 2011, a combination of domestic and security issues combined to make Japan, of all the 'major players', most uncertain about the world as it has come to exist since its defeat in 1945. And its uncertainty made its neighbours, big and small, uncertain too.

Coda

The world of 2011 was scarcely the 'one world' that Wendell Willkie wanted to envisage during the Second World War. Yet, amidst continuing wars, here and there, as they have appeared in these Parts, and the unending conflicts within and between states, nations and faiths which have been captured to some degree, there is perhaps a sense in which the complexities of the world are now more recognized in all its continents and countries than was ever the case when Willkie wrote. That may make vast global problems no more easy to solve but, perhaps, they are all now accepted as 'ours', wherever 'we' may find ourselves.

Part 6 further reading

Buruma, Ian and Martgalit, Avishai, *Occidentalism: A Short History of Anti-Westernism* (Atlantic Books, London, 2004).

Crystal, David, *English as a Global Language* (Cambridge University Press, Cambridge, 1997).

Fox, J., and Sandler, S., *Bringing Religion into International Relations* (Palgrave Macmillan, Basingstoke, 2004).

Harrison, Henrietta, *China* (Arnold, London, 2001)

Heale, M.J., *Contemporary America: Power, Dependency and Globalization since 1980* (Wiley-Blackwell, Oxford, 2011).

Holden, Robert H. and Villars, Rina, *Contemporary Latin America: 1970 to the Present* (Wiley-Blackwell, Oxford, 2012).

Judt, Tony, *Postwar: A History of Europe since 1945* (William Heinemann, London, 2005).

Kettenacker, Lothar, *Germany 1989: In the Aftermath of the Cold War* (Pearson Education, London, 2009).

Macfie, A.L., *Orientalism: A Reader* (Edinburgh University Press, Edinburgh, 2000).

Miller, Richard W., *Globalizing Justice: The Ethics of Poverty and Power* (Oxford University Press, Oxford, 2010).

Obama, Barack, *Dreams from My Father* (Crown Publishing, New York, 2004).

Pagden, Anthony, *Worlds at War: The 2,500-Year Struggle between East and West* (Oxford University Press, Oxford, 2008).

Wasserstein, Bernard, *Barbarism and Civilization: A History of Europe in Our Time* (Oxford University Press, Oxford, 2007).

Wasserstrom, Jeffrey N., *China in the 21st Century: What Everyone Needs to Know* (Oxford University Press, Oxford, 2010).

Index